SUOMALAISEN TIEDEAKATEMIAN TOIMITUKSIA
ANNALES ACADEMIÆ SCIENTIARUM FENNICÆ

SARJA—SER. B NIDE—TOM. 195

51-19

THE BALTIC QUESTION
1903—1908

BY

PERTTI LUNTINEN

HELSINKI 1975
SUOMALAINEN TIEDEAKATEMIA

Received Oct. 30th, 1974

ISSN 0066-2011
ISBN 951-41-0250-9

Suomalaisen Kirjallisuuden Kirjapaino Oy Helsinki 1975

119/78 Stechrt

CONTENTS

Acknowledgements

Having carried the hobby of studying history this far it is pleasant to remember all who have helped in the task. It is, indeed, surprising how many interested and sympathetic people there are and how very few malicious or bureaucratic. First of all, it is a cause of pride to have been a pupil of the late Arvi Korhonen. It is a pleasant duty to thank Eino Jutikkala, Erkki Kuujo and Jaakko Suolahti, who taught me the joy of studying history, and Tuomo Polvinen, Pekka Suvanto and Olli-Pekka Vehviläinen who have manfully faced the task of reading through these concoctions and expediting them through the academic bureaucracy. The personnel in the Institutes of history in Helsinki and Tampere, and the archive officials in Portugal Street, Bolshaja Serpuhovskaja Ulitsa, Adenauer Allee and Rauhankatu have been kind and helpful beyond any call of duty, as well as the staffs of University Libraries in Helsinki and Tampere. Even a historian needs a belief in the importance of his work, which I. I. Astafjev from Moscow University has given me with his interest and advice. George Maude from London University has read through the manuscript and has offered countless and invaluable advice. Heikki Eskelinen, Markku Järvinen and Veikko and Aulikki Litzen never lost their faith in the ultimate completion of the work and thereby compelled me to go on to this conclusion. Kerttu Seppälä, the headmistress of Kalevan Yhteiskoulu, unhesitatingly let me abandon my pupils in order to indulge in research.

Mere grateful words cannot make good the privations of a historian's family.

The gathering of materials in the archives of Moscow, London and Bonn was made possible by grants given by the Soviet Government and the Finnish Baltic Project. Emil Aaltonen Foundation financed the writing of the work and Suomen Tiedeakatemia the printing of it, for which I am duly grateful.

Pertti Luntinen

THE TASK

On April 23rd 1908 Denmark, Germany, Russia and Sweden signed an agreement in which they pledged themselves to maintain the territorial status quo in the Baltic. Stimultaneously Denmark, France, Great Britain, Germany, the Netherlands, and Sweden concluded a similar agreement in regard to the North Sea. The treaty by which France and Great Britain had in 1855 guaranteed Sweden—Norway was abrogated on the same day.

The unofficial discussions, the official negotiations, the quarrels and the agreements leading to these declarations, and the cluster of problems covered by them, was at the time called the Baltic or, synonymously, the Northern question. My task has been to investigate what in fact was covered by these terms, what the different participating powers tried to achieve, how their aims interacted and what was the net result.

This is a study in the "old diplomacy". The professional diplomats were able to take care of the Baltic question fairly free from the *forces profondes* [1], with which the modern historian ought to be occupied, having been "exhausted by archives and intoxicated by political science".[2] I have enjoyed myself in the archives and I give political science the value which is due to it. — In fact every student must limit the scope of his study. When discussing three great and three small powers and the interaction of their politics it has not been sensible to dig too deep into the domestic background, except in those cases where the "profound forces" immediately influenced the course of events. Neither is this a systematic study of public opinion. The press has been treated as a factor in the diplomatic game.

The most important source materials are the documents of the Foreign Office in the Public Record Office in London, Politisches Archiv des Auswärtigen Amtes in Bonn, and Arhiv Vnešnej Politiki Rossii in Moscow. The great publications "British Documents on the Origin of the War", "Documents diplomatiques français" and "Die Grosse Politik der Europäischen Kabinette" have been most useful. Omang's, Fink's and Pohlebkin's small collections of printed documents give glimpses of Norwegian, Danish and Russian politics. I have assumed that the Swedish scholars (Hildebrand, Lindberg) have presented the view of their government correctly. It would have been interesting to see the archives in Copenhagen, Oslo, Paris, Potsdam, and Stockholm, even if they are of secondary importance, but it has been beyond my means. — In the notes the documents and books have been referred to with the author's name and the usual abbreviations, which are explained in the bibliography. Cyrillic characters have been transliterated according to ISO recommendation R 9, except, of course, in case of a few names like Nicholas II or Isvolsky.

The Northern question was in being in the period between the crises in the Far East and in the Balkans, in the years approximately between 1903 and 1908. It was of minor importance in the flow of events leading up to the First

[1] Renouvin: *Introduction . . .*
[2] Robbins p. 231

World War. British, German and Russian scholars have not written much about these chilly regions. The Danes, the Norwegians and the Swedes have naturally been more interested in their own past and have published some outstanding works. To name only a few, the studies of Troels Fink, Hildebrand, Lindberg, Omang, and, in addition, Jungar from Finland, are deserving of particular attention. The progress of events has been described thoroughly enough, every author telling the story from his own standpoint, Christiania, Copenhagen, or Stockholm, as the case may be. In addition to the nationality factor there is a technical reason why the study of the various aspects of the Baltic question has been treated in a piecemeal fashion. The diplomats and the archivists have kept the documents, for instance of the Baltic and North Sea negotiations, in different dossiers. Of course this is no valid reason for the historian to keep matters so separate, if the separation does not correspond to the living reality of the past.

For this reason I believe that still another narrative is called for to deal with the Baltic question as a whole. I was advised to adopt a general, broad point of view when I started my study of this theme. I have tried to follow this advice notwithstanding some other, even authoritative, recommendations to concentrate on some special aspect of the problem. The essential character of the Baltic question can be seen only when looked at as a whole, and keeping in mind all the aspects of the problem. What has been treated as only an incidental point by my predecessors, most eminent in their respective domains, emerges as the underlaying and dominant theme recurring everywhere when the whole field is observed. — The reader may excuse me if I do not wish to reveal the result of the investigation at this point. — I have tried to study how the different chancelleries saw the problem, what they knew of the intentions of the other powers, and how this knowledge influenced their own actions. But history must also be a story. Therefore my work is burdened with sections which relate well-known facts. Strict chronology is disturbed by the need to tell the same story from different points of view, just as the presentation of the views of each actor is disturbed by the claims of chronology. The desire to draw the whole picture has overcome my fear of criticism in this regard.

The Baltic problem was complicated by a juridical terminology, the political and practical implications of which were far from clear. The term *Mare clausum*, closed sea, refers to something like the Caspian, where the coastal powers have an undisputable monopoly of navigation. In the course of centuries various powers have tried to close seas united with the ocean, for instance Turkey deemed the Black Sea a virgin whose integrity it would jealously guard. In the Baltic Denmark had taken advantage of her privileged position as the guardian of the Straits. Sweden after conquering the coasts around the sea tried to maintain a *dominium maris Baltici*. In the 18th century the Baltic powers Russia, Sweden and Denmark tried to keep the belligerent naval powers out of the Baltic by means of the doctrine of Armed Neutrality. The British and the Dutch supported the opposite idea of the freedom of the seas, a doctrine which seems to have been generally accepted in the 19th century. Both principles were often differently applied to men-of-war and to merchantmen, and it is not always clear which were referred to in the negotiations concerning the Baltic question. Even more vague was the conception of neutrality. In the strictest sense the word meant that the powers had imposed on the country in question an obligation to keep out of all international policy, and often they had simultaneously guaranteed the integrity of the neutral state, as, for instance, was the case with Belgium. On the other hand, a country declaring neutrality during a war indicated thereby that she was not going to join either of the belligerents. In this narrative we shall meet with the idea of a recognized but not guaranteed neutrality, self-declared permanent neutrality, neutrality with reservations, and some contradictory terms like benevolent neutrality. The notion seems most elastic and the different implications caused many misunderstandings. — "Demilitarization" of the Black Sea signified that Russia had no right to keep a navy there, "demilitarization" of the Åland Islands signified that the islands were not allowed to be fortfied. Even independence and integrity could be variously interpreted: if a big country promised to respect the integrity of a small one, had she the right to occupy the small country provided she harboured the intention of restoring its independence after the war?

So the reader is warned against seeking for the "real" significance of any term. These terms had different meanings and emotional values in different contexts, and most often the implications are left obscure.

Geographical terms may also cause difficulties, and even political complications. This was the case, for instance, with the problem of whether the Danish Straits were included in the Baltic Sea or not. — I have myself meant by the term Danish Straits the sea-passages of the Skagerrak, Kattegat, the Sound and the Great and Little Belts. I have used "Scandinàvia" meaning only Sweden and Norway, but many diplomats also implied Denmark in this term. This was sometimes indicated with the adjective "Pan-Scandinavian", but most often one must deduce from the context whether two or three kingdoms are referred to. These states are also called "the Northern Countries", but sometimes even Russia and Germany were "Northern Powers". I have avoided this obsolete term.

THE BACKGROUND

The fate of the Baltic and Northern Europe depended mainly on the relations between Germany, Russia and Great Britain, nor must France be forgotten, although she was not so immediately interested as the other powers were. The Scandinavian countries had been left to live in peace since the Crimean War until the dissolution of their union in 1905, but Denmark was closer to European and world politics. She had to govern the Straits, which tended to draw her into the conflicts of the great powers. In addition she had the heritage of 1864 to disturb her relations with Germany.

Russian foreign policy was led by the colourless but conscientious bureaucrat Lamsdorff, but Nicholas II let irresponsible favourites and adventurers influence his country's Far Eastern policy. At the beginning of the 20th century Russia was moving towards a conflict with Japan, who had beaten China in 1894—95, which in turn made the European powers interested in obtaining spheres of influence in China. Russia coveted so large areas in Manchuria that Japan saw her own interests endangered, and Nicholas II would not listen to the warnings of his diplomatists. The Japanese attempt in 1901 to improve relations was coldly received. But at the same time the British showed interest in an understanding with Japan.

In Great Britain Lansdowne, and after him Grey, led the foreign policy with their advisers in the Foreign Office. King Edward has long ago lost the image of the demonic architect of the *Einkreisung,* which William II loved to imagine; he was an impetuous dabbler in politics. The Cabinet had the decisive influence in questions of foreign policy, but quite often it was apt to accept the view of Landsdowne and Grey. The Secretary of State had to take the opinion of the Parliament and Press into account, too.

Great Britain was reaching the culmination of her imperialistic expansion. It was thought that the time had come to give up splendid isolation, the Royal Navy and the chalk cliffs not being regarded any longer as sufficient to secure British interests all over the world. During the South African War Great Britain had experienced the negative side of isolation as she had had to concentrate her limited forces on the theatre of war, and her Asian possessions were left exposed to the continental might of Russia. The threatened areas were in the Far East and on the Indian borders in Tibet, Afghanistan and Persia. Discussions with Germany did not lead to anything but mutual distrust, and Great Britain sought for other friends. The rival of the enemy was the "natural" ally, and the treaty with Japan was concluded in 1902. The allies promised to observe neutrality if either of them were involved in a war against one adversary, and to help each other if there were more enemies.

The Dual Alliance of Russia and France had become to some extent strained. In 1900 the anti-British feelings due to the Boer War had united Russia and France. But the French did not like the disappearance of Russian troops from the German border to the Far East. They recalled that the obligations of the Alliance did not hold good in so distant a conflict and began preparing an entente with Russia's arch-enemy, Britain. The British on their part had taken fright when they realized that their new liaison with Japan might lead them to a war against the Dual Alliance. In May 1903 Edward VII made his famous visit to Paris to charm French public opinion, while Delcassé worked as the architect of the entente. All points of colonial friction were adjusted, the most important being the understanding by which Great Britain left Morocco to the French, who in turn gave up their claims in Egypt. France did not help Russia in the Far Eastern war.

So the limits of British expansion were drawn. This made it possible, and at the same time necessary, to bring British naval forces home from distant stations. This was necessary because the entente implied an option against the Germans, who saw it as the first step of the *Einkreisung*. The Conservative Government, which concluded the entente, was "naval and imperial, not military and continental"[1] in its outlook, but younger men saw Germany as the Enemy. Admiral Fisher concentrated British naval power in the home waters, denuding the Empire, in order to be prepared against German attack.

In Germany the reins were in the hands of the Emperor William II, his Chancellor Bülow, and the "grey eminence" Holstein. The army and navy, men like Moltke and Tirpitz, had a great influence in questions of foreign policy, too, often in rivalry with the Auswärtiges Amt and its Secretary of State, Tschirschky and, after him, Schoen. Germany's relations with France were irremediably hostile because of Alsace and Lorraine, but it was evident that the neighbour had no intention of attacking alone, and Russia had no wish to attack just to please France. Relations with Russia had suffered when Bismarck had opted for Austria and when the *Rückversicherung* had been given up in 1890, but they were tolerable as long as Austria refrained from advancing in the Balkans. During the Far Eastern conflict Russia and Germany were the best of friends. When Great Britain started to seek an escape from her isolation, the Germans estimated mere friendship cheap and preferred to wait until they were paid something concrete. They were sure that the colonial conflicts were irreconcilable, and that a war between England and Russia was inevitable. Germany needed only to wait for Great Britain to be compelled to pay anything Germany might demand for her support. *Die Zeit läuft für uns* thought Holstein.[2] The Entente of 1904 was a dismal disappointment. A not very well considered counter-move was the challenge for France to let the possession of Morocco be decided in an international conference. France yielded, and Delcassé, who had wished to resist, relying on British support, had to resign. The Germans exulted, and the Emperor made Bülow a prince. But in the Conference of Algeciras in 1906 the powers supported France, the Entente withstood its first ordeal and Germany's isolation began to be seen.

[1] Monger I p. 194
[2] AA Deutschland 131 geheim Bd 9 p. 100— Holstein to Bülow 16. IV 1903

Unsere Zukunft liegt auf dem Wasser proved true in a different way from what the Emperor thought. Admiral Tirpitz reckoned that a powerful German navy would make the risk of offensive action too great for the British, because even in case of a victory their fleet would be too much weakened to defend the Empire against other enemies. On the other hand naval power would make Germany a desirable ally. But when the Emperor declared that the trident belonged to the German hand and promised to speak in a "different tone" as soon as the navy was ready, so that no matter in the world could be discussed without German participation, the British could not afford to believe that the German fleet was simply for defensive purposes. From the British viewpoint it began to loom as the one lethal danger. The irreconcilable quarrels on distant boundaries seemed after all of secondary importance. It was possible to solve disputes about certain patches of colonies with France and even with Russia in 1907 because the very existence of the British Empire was felt to be threatened in the home waters. Bülow began to think that instead of giving Germany the splendid position of *arbiter mundi* between England and the Dual Alliance her naval might was the very cause of the *Einkreisung*. But Bülow was not the man to make the Emperor or Tirpitz turn from their chosen course.

William, bursting with ideas which were often quite brilliant, often also childishly erratic, did not always have the patience to sit and wait until the course of time improved Germany's position. When the Far Eastern conflict was developing he dreamed of correcting the mistake of 1890 and of repairing Bismarck's line to St. Petersburg. He saw in his mind a horrible vision — ridiculed at the time — of the Yeollow Peril, about which he held the notorius "Hun" and "mailed-fist" speeches during the Boxer Rebellion. Japan and England, and possibly also the USA, began to loom in his eyes as a hostile naval alliance. By the Treaty of Shimonoseki in 1895 France, Germany and Russia had compelled Japan to abandon a great part of her conquests. William planned to make this temporary grouping of powers a permanent "continental alliance", which would have been a "natural" counterbalance to the maritime alliance. Austro-Russian rivalry in the Balkans was no hindrance as long as Russia remained engaged in the Far East. France would not dare to remain outside if her ally joined, and would be compelled to give up all dreams of revanche, the Emperor hoped.

William's advisers had difficulties in following these ideas. When the Russian Minister for Foreign Affairs, Count Lamsdorff, showed signs of seeking German support on the eve of the war, he was put off because Holstein was afraid that Russia was trying to estrange Germany from Great Britain in order to be the *tertium gaudens,* which role Germany sought to keep for herself. But William was not to be restrained, and he took the matter up Emperor to Emperor when he met Nicholas just before the war. Germany secured Russia's back when the latter denuded her western border of troops and sent them to the Far East, and German ships supplied the Russian Baltic fleet with coal on its tragic voyage halfway around the world. When Bülow warned that England ought not to be provoked, William answered that it was his Christian duty to aid the Russian navy in its fight for the cross.[1]

During the war in the Far East the Emperors corresponded again about the continental alliance. The Kaiser poured out sympathy and good advice to his unhappy colleague. The Dogger-Bank incident made the Czar so angry with the British that William very nearly succeeded in getting his signature to a treaty of defensive alliance, the need of which he explained with reference to the danger of British revenge on Germany because of the latter's help for the Russian fleet. In fact, the British were afraid of a war against Russia and Germany and possibly even France.[2] William rejoiced at this "historical turning point" and at the mortification of the British and the French. But Lamsdorff made his sovereign realize that the new treaty would be incompatible with the French alliance. Lamsdorff probably apprehended the danger of Russia falling under German domination in the continental combination. Nicholas sent a message to William saying "before signing the last draft of Treaty I think it advisable to let the French see it . . ." [3] It was clear that the French would not voluntarily have consented to any continental treaty with the Germans. His dreams shattered, William wrote angrily *Der hohe Herr fängt an, 'kalte Füsse' zu kriegen in bezug auf die Gallier, und ist so schlapp, dass er nicht einmal diesen Vertrag mit uns ohne ihre Erlaubnis machen will . . .*[4] Lamsdorff he called unprintable names. In the summer of 1905 William tried to take Nicholas by surprise, in the absence of Lamsdorff, at the famous meeting of Björkö (Koivisto) in Finland. He managed to make Nicholas sign, but again Lamsdorff succeeded in persuading Nicholas to withdraw his signature. Even Witte, who favoured William's idea as a preventive against the whole world being Anglo-Saxonized [5], supported the Minister for Foreign Affairs. France could not be expected to submit to German hegemony, and French help was the only means of saving Czarism, because shortage of capital prevented Germany from giving Russia the money to crush the revolutionary movement. And France's price was the unequivocal Russian support against Germany at the Conference of Algeciras. The Germans were disappointed and angry: "Lamsdorff is always mouthing sonorous words about beautiful traditions, about the intimate relations of the courts, about monarchical solidarity, and about disciplining the republics, but he unhesitatingly spurns Germans friendship for French gold".[6] The Russians were "unable to show gratitude for German help during the Japanese war,

[1] Bülow p. 132—133
[2] Marder I p. 111
[3] GP 19 I n. 6126 Anlage Nicholas II to William II 23. XI 1904
[4] GP 19 I n. 6126 William to Bülow
[5] AA Deutschland 131 geheim Bd 10 p. 43— Bülow to William II 25. IX 1905
[6] AA Deutschland 131 geheim Bd 10 p. 49— Schoen to Bülow 4. III 1906

because the loyal and noble German attitude was an uncomprehensible notion
for a people of such a low cultural level".[1] The Asian agreement between Great
Britain and Russia in 1907, and King Edward's visit to Reval in 1908 confirmed the German belief in Russia's participation in the *Einkreisung*. When
the Russians professed their sincere wish to keep up traditional relations of trust
between Berlin and St. Petersburg, William commented *Lüge!*. The Emperor's
"personal government" had not succeeded in changing the course of history.

But on the other hand Bülow and his aides also waited in vain for the great
political upheaval which should have accorded Germany the splendid position
of arbiter mundi. Germany's might did not make her desirable but frightening.
And this fright caused the anti-German alliances, which in turn made the
Germans believe that they were not going to be allowed the place in the sun
they felt they were entitled to, and that without a war of conquest and the
hegemony of Central Europe Germany simply could not live in the increasingly
hostile world.

THE DANISH STRAITS

The Northern question under discussion

The Emperor William's idea of a continental coalition brought the Baltic, alias Northern, question into political prominence. In his plan for a continental defence against the naval powers he took up an aspect of the Northern question which had been discussed academically earlier: neutralizing the North of Europe.

In 1902 the Norwegian poet Björnstjerne Björnson accused the former Danish minister Estrup of having ignored an offer from Russia to recognize Denmark's neutrality in 1889. In fact there had been no such offer. Professor Martens, who served as jurisconsult in the Russian Ministry for Foreign Affairs, had composed a plan for neutralizing Denmark and her Straits, and eventually the whole of Scandinavia, on the model of Belgium or Switzerland. He believed that the Czar Alexander III had accepted the idea and proposed it to King Christian. It seems that Alexander's minister Giers had praised the draft only to satisfy the professor's vanity, and had deposited the proposal in the archives. During the First Hague Peace Conference Martens had again discussed his pet plan with other participants, but these discussions had no official character, either, in spite of Martens's official position.[1]

Björnson himself propagated the idea of a Northern Neutrality, which would eventually lead to some kind of Scandinavian co-operation with Germany, England and even the USA on the basis of Pan-Germanism.[2] The Norwegian Storthing passed a resolution asking the Union government to try to broach the question of the permanent neutrality.[3] These dreams of poets and idealists had no political consequences, the Swedish Minister for Foreign Affairs Wachtmeister declared that neutrality was to be observed to the utmost in practice, but formal and binding international acts were of no use.[4] But the Emperor William II took up the idea of Northern Neutrality as a means of furthering his own intentions.

In March 1903 the Emperor discussed the political situation with the Russian ambassador Osten-Sacken. The latter remembered the outbreak of the Crimean War and the possibility of the renewal of the Crimean combination of powers was mentioned. *Nous nous trouvons à un point où l'histoire fait un grand tournant.* Russia's ally France was not wholly dependable: *ce Delcassé . . a une arrière-pensée. Il veut s'arranger avec l'Angleterre à nos dépens derrière nos dos!* And England, together with Japan, was courting America to throw other powers out of the Yangtse and Amur regions. *Mais alors que deviendra la*

---

[1] AA Schweden 56 Bd 1 Alvensleben to Bülow 13. VI 1902
[2] AA Schweden 56 Bd 1 Leyden to Bülow 27. VIII 1902
[3] AA Schweden 56 Bd 1 Hintze to Bülow 28. V. 1902
[4] AA Schweden 56 Bd 1 Leyden to Bülow 12. IX 1902

2

Baltique?. William answered: "If we (Russia and Germany) don't have Copenhagen as a base for its defence, it is bad. Perhaps it might be possible to unite the northern states, Denmark, Sweden, Russia and Germany to defend the Baltic". The ambassador concurred with a reservation: *Une bonne idée mais difficile à arranger.*[1] William's reports of the views of other persons are not always reliable as he was inclined to attribute his own ideas to them, but here it is his own ideas that are of interest. The defence of the Baltic was an integral part of his continental conception.

The Emperor was starting out to visit Copenhagen on the occasion of the 85th birthday of King Christian IX, but the discussion with the Russian ambassador did not lead to any consequences. Bülow warned hid sovereign that he ought not to give the Russians occasion to make England, nor the British to make Russia, suspicious of Germany. Germany ought to make the alliance to defend the Baltic appear a Russian initiative lest the bitterness and countermoves of the British be directed against Germany, as was to be expected.[2] Evidently the warning had its effect, as the Emperor did not touch on the question in Copenhagen. But he did try to charm the Danes as a preparation for the new relationship between Germany and Denmark.

In the autumn of 1903 Martens took up the matter in an article in the *Revue des Deux Mondes*. He stated that Denmark might declare herself neutral and that such a declaration would have the validity and international security equal to a guarantee and recognition by the great powers.[3] It is possible that Martens's article had some influence on the way in which the Emperor continued the discussion of the Baltic question. Schoen, the German envoy in Copenhagen, reported on the article in question and said "it has undoubtedly not been published without the placet of the Russian government".[4] The menacing conflict with Japan and possibly even with England made it natural to suppose that Russia was anxious to secure the Baltic against aggression. It was easy to suppose that the discussions in Denmark were inspired by the Russians with a view to establishing some kind of protectorate over the country under the cover of neutrality. The Emperor strongly marked the margins of Schoen's report, and when the envoy mentioned the Danish determination to remain outside the combinations of great power politics, William noted "impossible without a fleet".[5]

Denmark was not able to keep either the British or the Russians out of the Straits. On the other hand, Russia and Germany seemed to have parallel interests in the question. It was possible to "help" the Russians and in that way

---

[1] AA Dänemark 37 Bd 2 William II to Bülow 29. III 1903
[2] AA Dänemark 37 Bd 2 Bülow to William II 31. III 1903
[3] Martens p. 314—
[4] AA Dänemark 37 Bd 3 p. 62 Schoen to Bülow 29. XI 1903
[5] AA Dänemark 37 Bd 3 p. 62 margin by William

keep a hand in the game. William met the Russian Czar and proposed that they took care of Denmark together.

The Emperors and the Straits

The Emperors met in Darmstadt in November 1903 and in their discussion reviewed the scope of world politics. In regard to the Baltic William said to his colleague: "If a great power, which has a dispute with Russia somewhere in the world, wants to invade the Baltic, little Denmark cannot close the entrances to the Baltic, and, ignoring her neutrality, the invader can force the Sound and the Belts and threaten Kronstadt, Libau etc." Nicholas replied: "That Nelson has done already once 100 years ago, and the British will, or the Americans, surely do the same again. If the Danes — as is the case — cannot uphold the intangibility of their waters, they must allow us two, who are endangered by this state of affairs, to do it for them, so that we may stop any enemy from coming into the Belts and the Sound in resting ourselves on the Danish forts and Copenhagen as base of operation, instead of having to wait till the invader has reached the open Baltic Sea and has taken possession of Copenhagen and all the outlets".[1]

This is the defensive aspect of the Baltic question in a nutshell. It has not been possible to find sources disclosing the views, fears and hopes of the Russian naval circles on these questions. It is not clear whether the Czar had discussed the matter with his navy at all, or whether he was only echoing the views put forth by the Emperor William. Clearly, William was leading the discussion and Nicholas was following as was usual when the Emperors conversed. Later we shall see that Martens's article was not officially inspired and that the Russian diplomatic service was reluctant to contemplate the closing of the Danish Straits. It is probable that the Nicholas's concurrence was at most a temporary enthusiasm and that he was not representing any broad or permanent opinion in Russia.

The Czar said, according to William's relation, "that the idea had to be discussed at the first opportunity with the King of Denmark personally, without the participation of the ministers, because it was best to keep out Deuntzer (the Danish Prime Minister) who is half a socialist".[2] King Christian visited Berlin soon after and, again according to William, was relieved to hear of the Emperor's plan. The Kaiser's ability to present facts as they suited him makes one doubt if the old king was really happy to hear that his country was to be "defended" by Germany and Russia. But William reported to Nicholas: "He thinks the solution proposed most acceptable, and said that a load was off his heart. . It was to be an agreement secretly made between the 3 Sovereigns. .

[1] GP 18 I n. 5422 *Aufzeichnung* by Bülow 7. XI 1903
[2] GP 18 I n. 5422 *Aufzeichnung* by Bülow 7. XI 1903

that in case of war Denmark was to immediately declare its neutrality, and that we two declare our firm intention to guarantee it, and if necessary to help defend it by force . ." [1] The Czar was "higly delighted" with the result and said that neither he nor Lamsdorff had expected Christian to consent so easily. Nicholas asked William to make Bülow draft the treaty and submit it to Russia and Denmark for further negotiation.[2]

So, for the Emperor William, neutrality was only a pretext by which he was going to ensure the subjugation of Denmark.

The men behind the Kaiser

It has been said of the Emperor William "In the group of colourless monarchs of the type of Nicholas II at the beginning of the century, it is undoubted that William II was distinguished by natural talents, chained by narrow monarchistic ideas, and with his dangerous imagination he provided a good cover for the development of the not at all imaginary arrogant plans of German imperialism." [3] Investigating the background of Kaiser William's plans would lead into the vast tangle of the discussion about Germany's *Griff nach der Weltmacht,* which of course is impossible here. The Emperor thought that in case of a war with Great Britain Germany ought to secure her flanks by letting all delicacy drop in the relations with her neighbours, asking them to answer unambiguously the question "Friend or Foe". The question was to be asked in Paris, Brussels, the Hague and Copenhagen. A negative or an unclear answer would lead to an immediate occupation of the country in question. Independence after the war would be guaranteed to those who would be on Germany's side[4] — although there may have been some dreams of annexing Denmark and Holland with her rich colonies.

In January 1904 William frightened the Belgian King Leopold with these ideas. He said that he would demand a categorical answer to the question of whether the King would be on Germany's side and allow her to use the Belgian railways and forts. If not, William would not guarantee his country and dynasty: "We shall invade immediately and the King will have to bear the consequences". But if Leopold would consent, William would not only guarantee his possessions but also help him restore ancient Burgundy. A guarantee of this kind he could hardly hope for from republican France![5] The hint at the Schlief-

---

[1] GP 19 I n. 5965 William II to Nicholas II 17. XII 1903
AVPR fond sekretnyj arhiv, delo 395/405, n. 25 William II to Nicholas II 5/18 XII 1903
[2] GP 19. I n. 5967 note by Holstein 23. XII 1903
[3] A. A. Ignat'ev I p. 580
[4] Bülow p. 67—68, 75
[5] Holstein IV n. 904 *Anlage* I note by Hans Adolf von Bülow 30. XII 1904

fen plan is evident, and it is clear that the Emperor's *forsches Auftreten* was not due only to his personal whims, although it may be doubted whether the General Staff liked its plans being talked about with foreigners.

The leaders of German foreign policy were not eager to support the All-Highest in his politics. Bülow understood that Russia would have liked to close the Baltic when a war against the maritime powers was becoming apparent and her capital and naval bases were exposed. But he saw no dangers threatening Germany, who was living in peace. If she were to send troops into Denmark to close the Baltic for Russia, she would make Russia's enemies her own. And Japan, England and the USA would be able to cause untold damage to Germany's commerce and colonies, and Russia could not help her in any way nor was it probable that she would guarantee Alsace-Lorraine for Germany against France.[1] Bülow guessed also that in case of defeat the Russians would blame the Germans if they had too eagerly supported the Far Eastern adventure.[2]

Holstein feared that if Germany joined Russia, the maritime powers might drop the war in the Far East altogether in order to defeat the more dangerous Germany first. Then France could be trusted to participate in the war against Germany to get her revanche. "The German people and the German Princes would be unable to comprehend" why it should be necessary thus to provoke the war.[3] The whole conception of the continental coalition was contrary to Holstein's ideas. When he had been dismissed after the Algeciras failure, Holstein wrote: "Phili (Philipp Eulenburg) with his ideas of a continental alliance against England will now become the chief adviser of His Majesty and will bring no advantage to the German Empire. Because according to my view . . . we must get closer to England. ." [4] — This statement also gives a glimpse of the irresponsible advisers around William, who were competing with the constitutional leaders, and whose unrecorded influence may be suspected in several Wilhelminian escapades.

The imminent danger of William's plans for Denmark provoking the Western Powers had to be averted somehow, but it was difficult because the Emperor had promised the Czar to see the matter through and it was not sensible to estrange Russia by disappointing Nicholas's expectations. Holstein proposed to lie to the Czar that King Christian had refused to discuss the matter, because the guarantee by the great powers would imply a confession on the latter's part of Danish inability to defend the country. The King was afraid of losing his laboriously regained popularity; since 1864 the Danish people had had regrettable democratic tendencies, and the King had deemed it right to take them, as well as his English relatives, into account. The best way to overcome

[1] GP 19 I n. 5966 Bülow to Metternich 21. XII 1903
[2] GP 19 I n. 5972 Bülow to William II 4. I 1904
[3] GP 19 I n. 5967 note by Holstein 23. XII 1903
[4] Holstein IV n. 966 p. 374— Holstein to Radolin 23. IV 1906

the King's apprehensions was to let him prepare the draft, and the Czar, who stood nearer to the King, ought to ask him to do it. — This would have made the Western Powers see the initiative as Russian, and the danger for Germany would have been eliminated. — Holstein supposed that these apprehensions did really exist in Denmark, and that protection by Germany and Russia would be *perhorresziert* as a kind of suzerainty, the neutrality the Emperors aimed at being totally different from that intended by the Danes. Therefore the project would miscarry in any case, but the odium for it in English eyes would fall on Germany if she had proposed it. "Perhaps Count Lamsdorff has just this effect in mind."[1] — The Emperor had let himself be the dupe of the Russians, who were trying to entangle Japan's ally (England) with Germany, Holstein seems to have throught.

Bülow asked the German representatives in London and Washington for support. He explained Martens's ideas and stated that England and USA had indeed nothing to do in the Baltic ("right", remarked the Emperor), and the closing of the Baltic would serve the defence of German coasts and commerce. But Germany was far from the areas of conflict, and there was the possibility that the closure might be understood as a service to Russia and not as a defence of Germany's own interests. Therefore the ambassadors were asked to state the eventual reaction of England and the USA to a closing of the Baltic by means of neutralizing Denmark including her Straits.[2] Bülow's explanations indicate that he expected support for his negative attitude, and he was not disappointed.

Metternich, the ambassador in London, warned: Germany had no reason to join Russia. In a war against Russia England would respect German neutrality in order not to add to the number of her enemies, but if Germany were to close the Baltic together with Russia, England's first attack would be directed against Germany. Let Denmark and Russia make propaganda in England, and if the unbelievable should happen and she accepted the closing, then Germany might join the scheme.[3] The ambassador in Washington also warned that Germany's participation in the neutralization of the Baltic would estrange the Americans.[4]

Bülow pressed William to withdraw from the affair and sent him a draft for a letter to the Czar, on the lines proposed by Holstein: "I (William) think it would be well if you (Nicholas) were to write to your grandfather (Christian) that the proposals, if they are to be acceptable to us, must in the first place suit him, and that we therefore ask him to let us have his own ideas regarding neutrality. ."[5] William answered that the Czar had asked "Your Excellency" to

---

[1] GP 19 I n. 5967 note by Holstein 23. XII 1903
[2] AA Dänemark 37 Bd 3 Bülow to ambassadors in London and Washington 21. XII 1903
[3] GP 19 I n. 5968 Metternich to Bülow 23. XII 1903
[4] GP 19 I n. 5969 Speck v. Sternberg to Ausw. Amt 26. XII 1903
[5] GP 19 I n. 5970 Bülow to William II 27. XII 1903 appendix

draft something, "which your concoction simply ignores. ." "This Danish neu-trality question must be carried on with all force, as if in being mainly in the Russian interest while we play the honest broker out of benevolence. But in reality it is from the military point of view a question of life to us!" England worked to isolate Germany, which was easy without Denmark, but with Den-mark Germany's forces would be doubled. And Germany had pledged to secure Russia's rear; William had promised it in Danzig in 1901 and in Reval in 1902.[1]

But in fact the military, or naval, point of view was not so clear as the Emperor had thought. Admiral Tirpitz thought that in the "European war of liberation against the hegemony of the Anglo-Saxons" Denmark would be more important to Germany than even Austria, but he did not like the idea of forcing the small neighbour to co-operate with Germany. He would have preferred to induce Denmark to join Germany voluntarily, if necessary by ceding parts of Sleswig to her.[2] Like the politicians, he was also apprehensive of provoking Great Britain lest she destroy the young German fleet, stop Germany's com-merce and conquer her colonies.[3]

The Chief of Naval Staff v. Büchsel drafted a memorandum in which he explained that in a war where Germany must fight against a more powerful fleet, is was sensible to let the enemy try to blockade both the North Sea and the Baltic coasts of Germany, because the Germans were able to concentrate their forces, thanks to the Kaiser-Wilhelm-Canal, on either sea. "We have there-fore every reason, not only to avoid carefully anything which might prevent the enemy from such an action, but also to do everything to provoke him to such operation". The German torpedo-boats and obsolete battleships could be used in the Baltic and the Danish seapassages under more favourable conditions than in the North Sea. Therefore it was self-evident that an internationally recog-nized neutrality of Denmark and her sea-passages would eliminate these advan-tages, whether neutrality implied closing the Baltic to all warships of non-coast-al states (mare clausum) or whether it only meant a prohibition of operations in the sea-passages. In this light the apparent benefit for Germany's Baltic coastal defence and Baltic commerce, which neutralization might provide, were of no weight. The war, in regard to which Germany must plan a strategic defence on the sea, would put her in so grave a situation that all secondary interests must give way to the prime object of causing the greatest possible losses to the hostile fleets. Danish neutrality might make more difficult a large-scale landing by the enemy, but the latter possibility was so improbable that it did not need to be taken into account. On the other hand, in a war where Germany remained neutral she had no reason to guarantee Denmark's neutral-

---

[1] GP 19 I n. 5971 William II's marginalia to Bülow's letter 27. XII 1903
[2] Bülow p. 80, Tirpitz p. 155—158
[3] Tirpitz p. 143

ity, because her own interests would not be involved, but as the closest neighbour she would be the first guarantor called forth to defend Denmark if her neutrality were violated.[1] From the naval point of view the Emperor's idea was thus quite senseless. In fact, however, the idea of a landing in Denmark was not always regarded as quite so improbable, and Admiral Fisher in England really thought of such an operation. But of course it did not change the German view on Denmark's neutrality. Büchsel further explained to the Emperor that the Royal Navy could indeed be allowed into the Baltic, but only in a situation in which Germany had, while mobilizing, occupied the shores of the Danish seapassages and could fight the British from there. Consequently neutralization was neither needed nor wished for.

Of course, the Emperor had no intention of leaving Denmark out of the action. He had planned to use Danish neutrality as a pretext to "help" the Danes against the violators of their neutrality. But in Büchsel's view it was important for Germany to occupy Denmark first without having to wait for the chance to utilize a pretext to do so.

The attitude of his navy seems to have been decisive; William desisted from his initiative. He wrote to Bülow that the matter was to be left to the Russians and the Danes. The Danes could, if they were so inclined, ask the opinions of the different countries, but Germany would consent only on condition that she were allowed to occupy the coasts of the Belts if the need arose. This letter he signed *Wilhelm I R. qui laudabiliter se subjecit.*[2] To King Christian he wrote "I have narrated the contents of our discussion to the Czar. He was delighted at your response. He would now highly appreciate learning your views, from the Danish standpoint, and I believe that he will contact you personally".[3]

But the Czar never returned to the matter, nor did he take up the question with the Germans. This fact supports the hypothesis that the initiative in Darmstadt had been not Nicholas's but William's. It was not until the meeting at Björkö in 1905 that the Emperors discussed Danish neutrality again.

Although he broke the edge of the Emperor's dangerous plans Bülow was no more anti-Russian than he was anti-British. He hoped that the development of Germany's relations with Russia would continue towards a closer unity of the Empires, which would weaken the Dual Alliance, strengthen Germany's position in relation to England and would be a wholesome means of compulsion to the partners in the Triple Alliance.[4]

---

[1] AA Dänemark 37 Bd 3 p. 100— Memorandum by Büchsel, without date
[2] AA Dänemark 37 Bd 4 p. 7 William II to Bülow 29. XII 1903
[3] GP 19 I n. 5973 William II to Christian IX 6. I 1904
[4] AA Dänemark 37 geheim Bd 4 note by Bülow 29. XII 1903

Germany does not consent to Danish neutrality

For a long time the Danes had worried about their geopolitical situation. The year 1864 had left a heritage of animosity against Germany, which was danger-ous because of the growing might of the southern neighbour. Deuntzer, the Prime Minister of the first Venstre Government, now tried to find a solution which would guarantee the integrity and safety of Denmark without unbearable military expenses. He thought[1] that German friendship would have been the best solution, but it was impossible because of the old animosity. To side with Great Britain or to form an alliance with Sweden and Norway would have been more popular, but these powers had no inclination to unite their fate with Denmark's. Absolute and permanent neutrality seemed to Deuntzer the best realizable possibility. If Germany and the other great powers could be persuad-ed to respect Denmark's neutrality, which was to be openly proclaimed, she would be safe.[2]

King Christian had been ill on his voyage in Germany, which delayed his report and blurred his memory of the discussion with the Emperor William. The mentioning of German "help" to Denmark was shocking, but otherwise the matter seemed to indicate that even Germany might be disposed to consider recognizing Denmark's neutrality. Deuntzer could not know that the Emperor had changed his mind, and in vain he waited for the sequel. At last he sent a letter to Bülow asking for information about the discussion of the Emperor and Bülow with the Danish King.[3]

This was not at all convenient for the Germans, but "because an answer can hardly be avoided" the envoy in Copenhagen was instructed to explain that whereas the matter had been discussed only by the sovereigns without participa-tion by the officials, the German government had had no occasion to deal with the question.[4] It was only at the beginning of February 1904 that Schoen was able to explain the matter to Deuntzer. The latter concluded from Martens's article, from the interest shown by the Russian envoy, and from the information concerning the meeting of William and Christian that Germany and Russia had exchanged opinions about Danish neutrality, and that William had suggested to Christian a stronger protection for Danish neutrality, in case of a war between the great powers, than she herself was able to achieve. He hinted at the ru-

---

[1] or said to the Russian envoy. Fink when explaining Deuntzer's views seems to be citing Isvolsky's report cf. the following note
[2] Fink: *Ustabil balance* p. 152—
AVPR fond sekretnyj arhiv, delo 395/405
n. 2 Isvolsky to Lamsdorff 4. XII 1903
n. 7 Isvolsky to Lamsdorff 18. XII 1903
n. 19 Isvolsky to Lamsdorff 30. XII 1903
[3] AA Dänemark 37 geheim Bd 4 Deuntzer to Bülow 15. I 1904
[4] AA Dänemark 37 geheim Bd 4 note by Holstein 18. I 1904

mours about closing the Baltic, appraising them as absurd but evidently doing this with the hope of trying to detect whether such schemes had been touched upon. Schoen answered according to his instructions and explained that the schemes attributed to Germany were absolutely contradictory to Germany's neutral and loyal attitude.[1]

In April Deuntzer spoke to Schoen anew and explained that he had tried to sound the reaction of the powers to Danish neutrality, not only because of the international situation but also for internal reasons: the defence committee could not proceed in their task if they did not know whether neutrality was to be recognized by the powers, and so the defence problem, the key question of Danish internal policy, remained unsolved. He did not get much comfort from the envoy, who explained that the Chancellor and the Secretary of State had been occupied with parliamentary questions, the Emperor was travelling, and nobody had the opportunity to give speedy attention to Deuntzer's question.[2]

Deuntzer never got anything more out of Germany. The situation was all the more hopeless as his conception of neutrality was totally at variance with German views, as we shall see later. The antipathy of the German navy towards Danish neutrality came up again when the small countries proclaimed uniform rules of neutrality to be observed during the Far Eastern war. Büchsel hurried to ask the Auswärtiges Amt whether this was a manifestation of neutrality only as non-participation in the conflict or whether the proclamation had further significance.[3] He was comforted to hear that the united declaration of neutrality rules by the small countries was no act of international law but only a declaration of the concerted application of practical rules.[4] To the end the neutrality was anathema to the Germans. When in 1911 the Swedish minister Ehrensvärd said that Sweden was striving for good relations with all powers and observing strict neutrality, William's comment was: *Esel.*[5]

William's political nurses had tried to keep a watchful eye on him, but their lively charge had been able to commit a small act of provocation, and Holstein saw his fears coming true: "One can admire the valour and other distinguished characteristics of the Russian army and navy. But the whole world commerce of Germany is exposed as soon as she takes part ... Whether, and how far, the Herero Rebellion (in South-West Africa in the beginning of 1904) is due to the 'Baltic key' may be cleared up by time, but the second strike can fall a little harder, perhaps too hard. Are we at all able to engage the English and the Americans?"[6]

---

[1] AA Dänemark 37 geheim Bd 4 Schoen to Bülow. 2. II 1904
[2] AA Dänemark 37 geheim Bd 5 p. 54 Schoen to Bülow 18. IV 1904
[3] AA Schweden 56 Bd 1 Büchsel to Ausw. Amt 25. II 1904
[4] AA Schweden 56 Bd 1 Heinrich XXXI Reuss to Bülow 27. IV 04
[5] AA Schweden 56 Bd 2 Verdy to Bethmann-Hollweg 10. X 1911
[6] Holstein IV n. 832 note by Holstein 22. II 1904

Denmark's neutrality in the Russian View

The Russian envoy in Copenhagen Isvolsky reported on the Danish reactions to Martens's article. The Left saw it as an encouragement for their policy of disarmament while the Right remarked that neutrality needed weapons to be realistic — both parties saw the question fron the "frog perspective" of the Danish home policy. — The Prime Minister Deuntzer asked Isvolsky whether the article was a *ballon d'essai* by the Russian government, since Martens was a high official of the Russian Foreign Office. Deuntzer said that he himself could not but support the idea, but remarked that there were many practical difficulties: a declaration of neutrality motu proprio would place Denmark in a somewhat ridiculous position, only a guarantee or at least a recognition by the great powers would have any significance. It would be even better if more countries were neutralized together, for instance the three Scandinavian countries.[1]

In December Deuntzer again twice discussed the theme with Isvolsky "earnestly". He explained that Denmark's geographical situation was especially dangerous and that there was no other security but a neutrality formally recognized, if not guaranteed, by the great powers. A Scandinavian union was out of the question: a suggested treaty of arbitration had failed because in her relations with Denmark Sweden wanted to play the role of a great power; a customs union had been impossible because of Denmark's liberal and Sweden's protectionist commercial policy; a neutrality union would fail, too. Economic factors tended to favour a rapprochement with Germany, which was not otherwise popular, as an orientation towards England would have been. Deuntzer himself said he preferred neutrality. It would have helped him to solve also the cardinal issue of internal policy, the question of defence, which was being discussed in a committee but without any progress being made. Deuntzer said that a recognized neutrality would be justified also as a factor of general interest : it would guarantee the liberty of passage to the Baltic, in practice the liberty of the Great Belt, an absolute liberty of passage in peace and war for all ships of war or commerce of all nations, neutral or belligerent. He believed that England might be favourably disposed but was afraid that Germany would object. First of all he wanted to know whether Russia would support him if he asked the great powers for recognition of neutrality. He would at once desist from his initiative if Lamsdorff answered negatively.[2]

To Lamsdorff Isvolsky spoke favourable of Deuntzer's earnest exertions to please Russia. Now the Prime Minister seemed earnestly to wish for Russia's support in his sincere intentions. If Russia failed him, he might turn to a

[1] AVPR fond sekretnyj arhiv, delo 395/405 n. 2 Isvolsky to Lamsdorff 17/30 XI 1903
[2] AVPR fond sekretnyj arhiv, delo 395/405 n. 7 & 19 Isvolsky to Lamsdorff 4/17 and 5/18 XII 1903

Scandinavian solution. Russia had therefore opportunity and reason to influence the policy of this minister.[1]

Martens's article expressed in reality only his personal and academic opinion, as Isvolsky had said to Deuntzer, and the professor had to explain his views to Lamsdorff. Martens wrote that a declared neutrality was by no means ridiculous, it was as good as a recognized neutrality. When declared, no power would probably protest, because it would indicate an intention of attacking; while silence would mean consent. And if Russia recognized Danish neutrality, the other Powers would be sure to follow, even Germany if Denmark promised to put an end to the Sleswig question. Russia ought to be greatly interested in the freedom of the Straits on account of both commerce and naval war. If Chamberlain's imperialist views got the upper hand in England, Copenhagen might be taken and made a mighty Gibraltar as in 1807; or Germany might spread from Sleswig to the Sound. Russia had better act to make even the thought of Denmark's involvement in political combinations impossible. The thought of neutrality might spread to Scandinavia and prevent Sweden realizing her dreams of being a great power, dreams which would certainly work against Russia because of Finland, as had very nearly happened in 1854. A recognition of neutrality by Russia would eliminate all cause to fear the "Russian danger" in Scandinavia.[2]

Martens's favourable view of Pan-Scandinavian neutrality differed from the opinion of other Russians. But Deuntzer, Martens and Isvolsky were unanimous in their view that Denmark's neutrality was a means of ensuring the liberty of the Straits against German or British schemes for closing them and using them as a base against Russia. On the other hand the Emperors had discussed declaring Denmark neutral as a means for Russia herself with Germany to close the Straits against the attack of the imagined naval alliance. Isvolsky had warned Lamsdorff that Deuntzer was perhaps not in the confidence of King Christian[3], and he himself was evidently not informed of the imperial discussions. Therefore Lamsdorff answered Isvolsky cautiously that Deuntzer's initiative might be useful for Russia, but the King's opinion was of more importance, and *sous ce rapport j'ai lieu de supposer que cette question délicate sera très prochainement éclaircie et Vous en serez informé en temps et lieu.*[4] As the German statesmen made their Emperor desist from the plan, the temps et lieu never came.

Lamsdorff's own attitude to the question is not very clear. Later the officials of the Russian Foreign Office stated that "Count Lamsdorff seemed to wish to

---

[1] AVPR fond sekretnyj arhiv, delo 395/405, delo 7 & 19 Isvolsky to Lamsdorff 4/17 & 5/18 XII 1903
[2] AVPR fond sekretnyj arhiv, delo 395/405, delo 29 & 34 Martens to Lamsdorff 6/19 & 7/20 XII 1903
[3] AVPR fond sekretnyj arhiv, delo 395/405, n. 7 Isvolsky to Lamsdorff 4/17 XII 1903
[4] AVPR fond sekretnyj arhiv, delo 395/405, n. 38 Lamsdorff to Isvolsky 9/22 XII 1903

remain on the defensive avoiding pronouncing any opinion as long as the direct pourparlers of the Sovereigns continued".[1] In the light of subsequent information it seems probable that he shared the views expressed by Isvolsky on the Danish Straits question and that he did not like too close a liaison with the German Emperor, which was detrimental to the French alliance and helped to push Russia into the adventure in the Far East which Lamsdorff opposed but was unable to prevent.

Private schemes by two envoys?

On January 15th 1904 Isvolsky reported to Lamsdorff that Schoen had come to discuss Danish neutrality with him, professing a personal interest in the question and denying having any instructions from Berlin. Schoen had said that it was wrong to think that Germany would oppose Danish neutrality which would guarantee the status quo in Sleswig-Holstein. Opposition would come from England, but if an entente were established on this question between Russia and Germany, these difficulties could without doubt be overcome.[2] Fink, who has not apparently seen Isvolsky's report, believes the statement Schoen made to Berlin, according to which Isvolsky had initiated the discussion by declaring that "making Denmark's neutrality part of European international law would be a strong guarantee of peace".[3] One (or both) of the envoys must have lied to his government. Isvolsky did not believe that Schoen spoke without instructions, but we know that the German government had given up the plan of neutralizing Denmark, nor have I found any instructions to this effect to Schoen. On the other hand we saw how eager Isvolsky was to support Deuntzer in his endeavours. It is just possible that the two envoys had discussed this highly dangerous problem of *Grosse Politik* more freely than they dared tell their superiors, and blamed each other for the initiative. Their later behaviour makes this explanation plausible, and it is their later activity that gives significance to this discussion of two envoys in a small capital, in itself of course an insignificant occurrence. The reports do not mention at all the kind of status for the Straits which the entente of Russia and Germany would have established. Of course Germany wanted to dominate the Straits and it is difficult to believe that Schoen would have aimed at anything else. Isvolsky's views haven been explained above. But it will be seen how he came to second Schoen's intentions in this question. — Lamsdorff answered emphasizing once more the need of extreme reserve in regard to this delicate question.[4]

[1] AVPR fond sekretnyj arhiv, delo 395/405, n. 89
   Rapport succinct sur la neutralisation du Danemark 22. II 1909
[2] AVPR fond sekretnyj arhiv, delo 395/405, n. 42 Isvolsky to Lamsdorff 2/15 I 1904
[2] Fink: *Ustabil balance,*. p.158
[4] AVPR fond sekretnyj arhiv, delo 395/405, n. 45 Lamsdorff to Isvolsky 13/26 I 1904

The Danes encouraged

Martens, more of an uncurbed academician than a disciplined official, could not leave his pet idea alone. In March 1904 he granted an interview to the Danish newspaper *Nationaltidende* explaining the views mentioned above and prompting Denmark to act while the conditions were favourable. Deuntzer wished to know whether the situation was really so propitious, remembering his unanswered question in December.[1] The Danish envoy in St. Petersburg was sent to see Lamsdorff, and the Russian minister said that his *Auguste Souverain* was sure to make the decision in harmony with the views of King Christian. Deuntzer understood that Lamsdorff had asked him to confirm his initiative with the explicit consent of the King. Deuntzer obtained the Royal sanction and then remained waiting for Russian recognition of Denmark's neutrality.[2] It was all due to a misunderstanding, but the Dane could not be left completely disappointed, and had to receive some kind of answer. Nicholas sanctioned an answer declaring that Russia had nothing against the projected neutralization in principle, although of course this would refer only to Denmark, not to Norway and Sweden as well. But the practical conditions under which this project might be realized were submitted to further diskussion.[3]

Deuntzer considered that the Russian consent "marked a great step towards the realization of his plan, and it encouraged him to persist on that road."[4] In fact it was, however, a hopeless road. The Russian consent was only in principle, and further negotiations were needed on the details after the other powers had agreed on the principle. But German and British consent never came, and thus Russia had in practice consented very little.

Russia had refused to contemplate a joint declaration of neutrality by the Scandinavian countries. These had together declared the rules of neutrality which they were going to observe during the war in the Far East, and the Russians were afraid that something unpleasant for them might be in the offing. The Norwegian minister Hagerup had said that these rules might serve as a basis for a joint declaration of permanent neutrality by the three northern countries. Deuntzer had denied having anything to do with such schemes, but Isvolsky was inclined to suspect that Deuntzer had harboured some pan-Scandinavian inclinations which he denied later.[5] Martens reported rumours which he had heard in Denmark concerning King Edward's visit to Denmark (when

[1] AVPR fond sekretnyj arhiv, delo 395/405, n. 47
   Isvolsky to Lamsdorff 12/25 I 1904, *"Nationaltidende"* annexed
[2] AVPR fond sekretnyj arhiv, delo 395/405, n. 58 Lamsdorff to Nicholas II 27. III/9 IV 1904
[3] AVPR fond sekretnyj arhiv, delo 395/405, n. 62 Lamsdorff to Isvolsky 1/14 IV 1904
[4] AVPR fond sekretnyj arhiv, delo 395/405, n. 65 Isvolsky to Lamsdorff 6/19 IV 1904
[5] AVPR fond sekretnyj arhiv. delo 395/405 n. 70 Isvolsky to Lamsdorff 15/28 IV 1904

the King discussed with Isvolsky the possibility of an Asian agreement).[1] According to these rumours, said Martens, "it is laboured to create a Scandinavian neutrality under the auspices of England to march in harmony with the Franco-English entente. In this way Denmark could be drawn away from the influence of Russia . . ."[2] — Evidently this neutrality, inspired by Great Britain, was not the kind of Scandinavian neutrality which Martens had thought of.

Of course these were only rumours, but the reports help to make clear why Russia was opposed to a Scandinavian union of neutrality. Sweden was notoriously anti-Russian, and her influence would put the larger union under the permanent domination of Great Britain, who was still Russia's potential enemy and the ally of her actual enemy. It was a long way yet to the entente of 1907.

The British attitude

As regards Great Britain, the matter was taken up by Deuntzer in February 1904, when he spoke to the British envoy Sir E. Goschen about Martens's article and conception of the validity of a neutrality proclaimed by the neutral country alone. Deuntzer wanted to know what the British thought about such a form of neutrality. In his view neutrality implied that "the channels through the Great Belt would, in time of war, be open to ships of war of all nations, including the belligerent powers; that mines and torpedoes could be laid down and that, where there was space to manoeuvre, even hostile encounters could take place so long as territorial waters were not entered".[3]

A couple of months later Deuntzer returned to the question and Goschen repeated to him the message he had sent to London concerning their former meeting. Deuntzer clarified his earlier utterance with the explanation that a guaranteed neutrality was out of the question, a recognition was all that was asked. If he had a reply from Great Britain in his hand he could better press for an answer from Germany and Russia. He anticipated no difficulty with the Russian Government, only some delay owing to the need to reflect. About Germany he was much less hopeful — Germany might evade the question with a pretext "until the agitation in Sleswig-Holstein is stopped there can be no question of Germany recognizing Danish neutrality."[4]

The British War Office and the Admiralty studied the Danish problem and left their statements to the Cabinet. Arguing from historical precedents the War Office showed that the neutrality of any country had been respected only if it had had respectable military might or powerful guarantors. "It is therefore submitted that the proposal of Professor Martens is altogether quixotic". It was

---

[1] AVPR fond skretnyj arhiv, delo 395/405 n. 74 Isvolsky to Lamsdorff 16/29 IV 1904
[2] AVPR fond sekretnyj arhiv, delo 395/405 n. 64. Martens to Lamsdorff 5/18 IV 1904
[3] PRO/CAB 4/1 n. 54 Goschen to Landsdowne 6. II 1904
[4] PRO/CAB 4/1 n. 62 Goschen to Landsdowne 12. IV 1904

inferred that Deuntzer's inquiry proved that he himself was not sure of the soundness of his proposition, it seemed to be a feeler as to whether the active support of Great Britain would be forthcoming if Denmark's neutrality were at any time menaced.

The War Office thought that in a war of Great Britain against Germany or Russia, the occupation of Denmark would not make any difference, if the enemy closed the straits. If he could not close them, there would be no difference, either, because it would be senseless for Great Britain to attack the Baltic coast while Germany could without hindrance move her navy through the Kiel Canal. In a war against Russia the navy had no need to penetrate to the Baltic Sea if it ruled the oceans. It was concluded that the neutralization of Denmark would not be material to British interests in a war in which Great Britain was a belligerent. If not belligerent, it was hardly sensible to wage war against France, Russia or Germany to protect the neutrality of Denmark when there were no British interests involved in the maintenance of that neutrality. Great Britain could promise to respect Denmark's neutrality as far as the other powers did so.[1]

The Admiralty laid down the naval view on the question in a memorandum on the 5th of March 1904. They said that the naval policy had always been to get into touch with hostile fleets with the least possible delay, and there should be no obstacle in the way of pursuing this policy. Unless the Belts were free, the Baltic would be as inaccessible as the Black Sea, and Russian territory in Europe would become unapproachable, if Great Britain did not break the treaty which closed the Straits. The Admiralty were of the opinion that the Danish attempt to obtain neutrality could be supported only on condition that the impossibility of avoiding neuralized territorial waters should not be made a bar to the free passage of belligerents. The stipulations regarding the free passage might eventually apply only to the Great Belt since the closing of all other exits to belligerents would facilitate arrangements for preventing the escape of hostile vessels to open water. Denmark ought to have military power enough to make others respect her neutrality.[2] Later the Admiralty declared the identical opinion that "any restriction of waters which the navy can use without question in war seems opposed to our interests".[3]

There was a marked difference between the views of army and navy. The military men had no intention of invading the Baltic Sea, and so they were rather indifferent as to the status of the Danish Straits and the neutrality of Denmark. They thought that the main battle would be fought somewhere together with the French; this attitude of course anticipated the reality of 1914—1918. Admiral Fisher did not approve of sending the British Expedi-

---

[1] PRO/CAB 4/1 n. 16B Intelligence dept. War Office to Foreign Office 2. III 1904
[2] PRO/CAP 4/1 n. 16B Admiralty to Foreign Office 5. III 1904
[3] PRO/CAB 4/1 n. 66 notes by Secretary of CID November 1905

tionary Force to join the French on the Western Front, he preferred a landing somewhere in Sleswig or on the Baltic coast.[1] "Fisher's favourite spot was fourteen miles of sandy beach on the Pomeranian coast, ninety miles from Berlin, 'impossible of defence' against the devastating fire-power of the British Fleet".[2] The Admiralty made plans and preparations for this end up to 1915, when they decided to abandon the Baltic and to try to penetrate through the Turkish Straits.[3]

Deuntzer never received any answer from London, nor is there any record showing how the Committee of Imperial Defence or the Cabinet judged the situation. Its discussion was contemplated by the CID, but the Foreign Office was not aware whether such discussion ever took place.[4] — In spite of their differences, as the army was indifferent to and the navy reluctant to contemplate Danish neutrality, the summary of these naval-military views is that Great Britain had no reason to encourage Deuntzer in his endeavours.

Half a year later the course of events again brought up the question of the Danish Straits.

The status of the Straits tested in practice

The importance of the Danish Straits was demonstrated in practice when the war in the Far East went wrong for the Russians and they sent their Baltic fleet on its futile and tragic voyage half-way round the world. So the situation was diametrically opposite to what the Emperors had feared a year earlier; there was no attack into the Baltic but a sortie out of it. Denmark observed neutrality according to the principles which Deuntzer had explained to Isvolsky, Danish pilots boarded the ships in Libau and steered them through the Straits without mishaps. The Russians were allowed to stay in the Danish waters to take on coal for 48 hours, the 24 hour limit applying only to a visit in port.[5]

Lamsdorff wrote "If the question of piloting our ships by the Danish pilots and the permission for the squadron of Admiral Rožestvenskij to stay in the Straits taking coal was settled favourably to Russia, it was only due to energetic diplomatic activity".[6] I have not had the opportunity to see the documents produced by this activity. However, the loss is not lethal, notwithstanding the importance of interesting details, because the principal aspects of the question are quite clear. The Russian Foreign Office must have been happy that their August Sovereign had not succeeded in closing the Straits as a result of his discussions with the German Emperor.

[1] Marder I p. 119
[2] Marder I p. 385
[3] Marder II p. 96, 191, Parkes p. 618
[4] PRO/FO 371/57/40566 minute by EAC (rowe) 3. XII 1906
[5] AA Dänemark 37 geheim Bd 5 Schoen to Bülow 25. X 1904
[6] Pohlebkin: *Priznanie.* . n. 58 Instructions for the envoy in Christiania, draft 4/17 XI 1905

The Japanese protested, but the Danes answered that their ships, too, would be piloted through the Straits if asked! It was important for Denmark to get rid of the uninvited guests as soon as possible, and the pilots were given in order to avoid shipwrecks and other mishaps that might lead to endless unpleasantness.[1]

The German reaction

The Danish Prime Minister Deuntzer explained the Danish views to Schoen. International law had never defined clearly whether the Straits were part of the open sea and therefore always open passages, or closed territorial waters, but the treaty ending the Sound duty (1857) indicated the principle of free passage. Denmark was obliged to keep passages navigable and pilot all ships through, as she had done in 1854 and 1870, without Russian or German protest. (The Emperor's marginal note: "We shall not accept this a second time"). Therefore Denmark was entitled to conclude that it was a principle of international law to pilot all ships through difficult waters. (The Emperor: "No, we do not recognize this"). Deuntzer hoped that these questions could be internationally solved, eventually in the peace conference on the basis of the rules followed by Denmark during the war, and in this way Denmark would be brought from a situation of difficult and dangerous uncertainty to a clear, internationally-recognized position. (The Emperor: "No! Denmark is the porter at the German door to the Baltic, that shall *we* regulate with her").[2]

The Emperor's remarks demonstrate with all clarity how different Deuntzer's view of neutrality was from that planned by William in 1903. The Emperor ordered the Chief of the Naval Staff to elucidate the problem.

Admiral Büchsel explained that there was a juridical difference when the straits in question led directly to the scene of battle or to the territorial waters of a belligerent as would be the case with Germany at war, and when the war took place in other parts of the world. Germany could not allow the Danes to pilot her enemies direct to Kiel. Nevertheless the Japanese protest was groundless, even in view of German interests elsewhere in the world. Similarly, Denmark did not break the rules of neutrality in letting the Russians coal their ships, but it would be a breach if the right were given to Germany's enemies. Whether these principles ought to be confirmed in some international agreement was a political question; the admiral only wanted to warn against encouraging Denmark in her undesirable attempts to gain a neutralized status and the Powers in their inclination to recognize such a status.[3]

---

[1] Fink: *Ustabil balance.*. p. 197—

[2] AA Dänemark 37 geheim Bd 5 p. 8 Schoen to Bülow 6. XII 1904

[3] AA Dänemark 37 geheim Bd 5 p. 108 Büchsel's "immediate address" 12. XII 1904
   Fink: *Ustabil balance.*. p. 201

We may leave Admiral Büchsel's juridical competence out of the discussion. Militarily it was clear that Germany had no reason to prevent the disappearance of the Russian fleet from the Baltic — and the results were far beyond expectations: "The new Trafalgar at Tsushima gave the Germans the *dominium maris Baltici* for some years to come". Nor was there any sense in creating precedents which might hamper the movements of German fleets elsewhere in the world. But of course even more important was not to let the passage of the Russian fleet be a precedent for Germany's enemies. The question of the Straits might come up at any moment. Somehow the key of the Baltic had to be got securely into German hands.

The neutralization of Denmark had not been the good idea that the Emperor thought it was, and he remodelled his schemes. He wished to win Denmark over to accepting the friendship and at the same time the tutorship of Germany. In February 1905 he expressed the "ardent hope of an understanding" with Denmark in order to prevent thereby a British attack on Kiel and the Baltic ports. "If Schoen is to earn the praise poured out by me, may he realize such an alliance!" [1]

Again his political guardians tried to cool His Majesty down. Holstein wrote: "A proposal to make an alliance between big Germany and tiny Denmark would inevitably be understood as an attempt to subjugate Denmark . . England would welcome the opportunity to 'defend Danish independence against a forced German alliance' . . Delcassé would be only too happy to prove to the British and the Russians that they had no conflict of interests . . which prevented them from joining together to defend Denmark. Drawing Denmark into the periphery of the German Federation is a great dream of the future, which presupposes that the British fleet is engaged elsewhere or inferior to our own. To-day any step in that direction would only be welcome to the promoters of a Franco-Russo-English triple alliance".[2] Schoen concurred in Holstein's views: the Danes would not voluntarily consent to the alliance, and an attempt to force them would cause a great hue and cry.[3]

The Emperor then desisted, but could not be checked permanently.

Deuntzer's last attempt fails on British reluctance

In the autumn of 1904 Deuntzer once more took up his plan for Danish neutrality in a discussion with the British envoy concerning the passage of the Russian Baltic fleet to the Far East. Goschen said that the British government could not give an opinion on the question without having before them a clear statement of the principles upon which the declaration of Permanent Neutrality

[1] AA Dänemark 27 geheim p. 77 note by Bülow 6. II 1905

[2] Holstein IV n. 876 note by Holstein 6. II 1905

[3] Holstein IV n. 877 Schoen to Holstein 11. II 1905

should be based. Deuntzer replied that Denmark's recent policy towards belligerent vessels could be supposed to be the basis of this declaration, but it seems that he did not wish to bind himself: "it was impossible for him to formulate a basis in writing". The various powers might attach to their regocnition of the neutrality some conditions, which could not be foreseen. It would have been best that the three powers had consented to enter upon negotiations on the subject simultaneously. Lamsdorff had already promised, and Deuntzer hoped that Lansdowne might be inclined to give him similar assurance. It would strengthen his hands in an approach to Germany on the subject.[1]

Thus both parties tried, without binding themselves, to press each other to promise something definite. It is understandable that Deuntzer did not wish to say anything conclusive about the status of the Straits because, according to his utterance, he had realized that "some Power" might demand the closing of them. To Deuntzer neutrality was, after all, not an aim in itself but only an attempt to find an alternative to the traditional enmity towards Germany, which had been found to be too dangerous. Thus it would have been senseless to design the stipulations of the proposed neutrality against Germany's wishes.

But it is easy to understand that Great Britain was not interested in negotiations or promises which might have meant the beginning of the closing of the Straits. In spite of Deuntzer's assurances to the contrary it would have been difficult to withdraw from the negotiations once they had been entered into. On the other hand it would have been unwise to estrange Denmark with a definite negative answer. Great Britain did not answer anything.

But this did not mean that Great Britain was indifferent to Deuntzer's policy and the question of the status of the Straits. The British observed with interest the passage of the Russian fleet. When Deuntzer declared "that exactly the same facilities would be afforded to the Japanese fleet should it ever pass through Danish waters on its way to Kronstadt" (A very safe conception, remarked Eyre Crowe)[2], the British at once took advantage of this utterance. Goschen went to see Deuntzer, who answered "that certainly the same facilities as those which had just been granted to the Russian fleet would be granted to His Majesty's ships should occasion arise". Goschen "presumed that that means that pilots would be supplied when and where they were required, and that vessels of war could remain in Danish territorial waters and take coal without any interference as long as they did not lie in a Danish harbour or roadstead. Mr. Deuntzer replied that that was his meaning."[3]

But after thinking it over Deuntzer seems to have felt that he had said too much. In a note to Goschen he said that the facilities accorded to the Russians

---

[1] PRO/FO 22/578 Goschen to Lansdowne 16. XII 1904
[2] PRO/FO 22/578 Goschen to Lansdowne 21. X 1904, minute EAC
[3] PRO/FO 22/584 Goschen to Lansdowne 2. I 1905, annexed Deuntzer to Goschen 30. XII 1904

would be accorded to other belligerents only during the actual war, and that the pilots had been allowed to proceed to Libau "for special reasons", and in other circumstances they would not necessarily be allowed to do so. The neutrality of Denmark was not invariably fixed by general prescriptions regulating it for indefinite times; on the contrary, the rules of Danish neutrality were not established but for the duration of the war, although it was probable that essentially the same rules would be applied in a future war. Goschen, somewhat annoyed, wrote to London that "this note differs both in tone and the substance from the verbal answer given to me by Mr Deuntzer".[1]

The self-evident explanation for Deuntzer's reluctance is that the Russians had received every possible help from the Danes, and Germany was most unlikely to consent to such a precedent in case of a war between herself and Great Britain. And in his note there is a reproving undertone: Danish neutrality was not regulated permanently by the Powers. In the last sentence he again mentioned his hopes of attaining the recognition of the powers to Denmark's permanent neutrality. Goschen thought that the whole tone of Deuntzer's note "would seem to indicate that, in drafting it, this subject was uppermost in his mind". Lansdowne was given to understand that a general settlement of the question would settle once for all those problems of Danish neutrality which were troubling Great Britain.[2]

In February the Secretary of the Committee of Imperial Defence, Sir George Clarke, wrote a memorandum in which he stated that there was no objection to the recognition of the Danish neutrality by Great Britain, provided that Denmark was not thereby relieved of the duty of providing the means to defend her neutrality. In a letter to the Foreign Office on 26th April 1905 the Admiralty laid a great stress of securing for Great Britain all the rights and favourable treatment accorded to the Russian fleet during its passage through the Great Belt in October 1904. But "Lord Lansdowne expressed the opinion that the question of Danish neutrality could not then be conveniently dealt with".[3]

It was indeed a moment that was anything but convenient for taking up new and complicated problems. The situation in the Far East remained unclear until the Battle of Tsushima on 27—28th May, and there was serious mischief brewing in Morocco where the Emperor William had landed in 31st March. It may be supposed that Lansdowne regarded it as wiser and safer not to encourage the Danes in an undertaking the result of which was not to be foreseen and which might possibly harm British interests.

[1] PRO/FO 22/584 Goschen to Lansdowne 2. I 1905, annexed Deuntzer to Goschen 30. XII 1904
[2] PRO/FO 22/548 Goschen to Lansdowne 2. I 1905
[3] PRO/FO 371/57/40566 minutes by EAC 29. XI 1906

Should Russia close the Straits?

Deuntzer's endeavours to secure Denmark's position by a treaty establishing the freedom of the Straits had miscarried, but the thought did not die. "The study of the Straits question had become a perennial duty of the Russian envoy in Copenhagen."[1] Isvolsky sent a report in March 1905 to Lamsdorff relating some rumours concerning Germany's dissatisfaction with Denmark because of her principle of the freedom of the Straits, which she had applied during the passage of the Russian fleet. The German envoy had naturally denied the existence of such a dissatisfaction, but Isvolsky deemed that it would be advisable for Russia to try to safeguard the liberty of the Straits by an international treaty guaranteeing the neutrality of the Straits, following the pattern of the Suez treaty of 1888.[2]

In the archives of the Russian Foreign Office there is an anonymous memorandum of 12th April on the question of the Straits, which seems to have been drafted in the light of Isvolsky's initiative. It says that Russia was interested in preserving the status quo of the Straits, that is, the free navigation by all kinds of ships of all nations at all times. Because the freedom of any straits uniting open seas had for a long time been part of the international law recognized by all civilized nations, there was no need for a special treaty to confirm the principle, which moreover had been tested in practice when the Russian fleet had passed the Danish Straits. But of course there might be some special reason for making an international treaty about the Danish Straits. It might be in the Russian interest to guarantee herself against unfavourable changes in Danish policy, for example, the formation of a Pan-Scandinavian Union against Russia, which might close the Straits. Or Denmark might wish to safeguard herself against the possibility of an attack in the straits, and Russia had no reason to oppose her. Thus it might be reasonable to support endeavours to create a collective guarantee for the Straits by the European Concert. It would be a natural sequel to the proclamation of 1857 which abolished the Sound dues and definitively opened the Straits to all. Self-evidently the initiative must not emanate from Russia.[3]

The memorandum expressed the main features of the policy which Russia seems to have practised throughout the period of the Baltic question, apart from the Emperor Nicholas's temporary accommodation to the designs of the Emperor William, and certain deviations to be discussed later. From the Russian point

[1] A. A. Ignat'ev I p. 437, 450
[2] AVPR fond kanceljarija 1905 g., delo 35, n. 9 Isvolsky to Lamsdorff 22. II/7. III 1905
  Fink: *Ustabil.* . p. 221 mentions a letter 9. III which might be this one
[3] AVPR fond sekretnyj arhiv, delo 395/405 n. 66
  "*On the Question of the Danish Straits*" 12. IV 1905

of view the memorandum was in accordance with basic interests and hardly needs comment. The memorandum did contain one reservation, however: when and if the Russian government were to participate in such a treaty guaranteeing her interests in the near future, it might be well, said the author of the memorandum, to sign the treaty only for a certain span of time, in order not to deny Russia the possibility in future, in the event of the Scandinavian countries adopting a more favourable attitude towards her, of making a new treaty, similar to the Russo-Swedo-Danish agreement of 1759, that would close the Baltic for all warships trying to intrude that sea.[1]

The anonymous memorandum seems to have been written by the often-mentioned Professor Martens: another memorandum in 1909 recapitulates the identical opinions and names the said professor as the source.[2] His dream of closing the Baltic together with Sweden-Norway and Denmark for all foreign warships would have been the ideal solution for Russia, the Baltic becoming a Russian sea and the defences of St. Petersburg being in Copenhagen. It was very nearly identical with Russian aims for the Black Sea, where Russia fancied opening the Turkish straits for the coastal powers and closing them for all outsiders. But of course it was not realistic to dream of reaching an agreement with the Northern countries only and ignoring Germany and Great Britain, who had much more to say in the matter than the small kingdoms. The author of the 1909 memorandum says "a negotiation of this kind seems, in my humble view, and in the actual conditions, not only dangerous to pursue but also impossible to succeed in."[3]

It is, of course, interesting to see what Russia would have liked to do had the possibility existed. The deepest or most extravagant wishes are seldom recorded in official documents. Such dreams can, however, be actualized if some turn of fate makes them seem realistic.

From the foregoing we can see, then, that preserving the status quo in the Danish Straits was the aim that was accepted as the most practical under the circumstances then prevailing. Evidently Martens's opinion that it was not for Russia to take the initiative was accepted since nothing happened.

It was Isvolsky who again took up the question of the Danish Straits after the Russian fleet had been destroyed at Tsushima. He proposed that the Danish Straits be closed, explaining that "I am carried forward by the logic of events to adopt a new point of view, diametrically opposed to that which I supported. ." He defended his reversal with Bismarck's words *Die internationale Politik ist ein flüssiges Element* — "the destruction of our squadrons and the situation

---

[1] AVPR fond sekretnyj arhiv delo 395/405 n. 66
"*On the Question of the Danish Straits*" 12. IV 1905
[2] AVPR fond sekretnyj arhiv, delo 395/405 n. 89
"*Rapport succint sur la neutralisation du Danemark*" 22. II 1909
[3] AVPR fond sekretnyj arhiv, delo 395/405 n. 89
"*Rapport succint sur la neutralisation du Danemark*" 22. II 1909

due to that fact oblige us, in my opinion, to renounce, for the moment, the neutralization of the Sound and the Belts. We must take precautions against the most pressing dangers, i.e. those threatening our Baltic coasts". It is difficult to say whether Isvolsky really saw some dangers in the Baltic from the British or the Japanese, or whether he only presented an argument he knew to be acceptable: he had discussed the situation and his plan with his sovereign in Tsarskoe Selo and "if I have correctly understood what our August Master deigned to confide to me, it coincided essentially with the plan drawn up by the Emperor William". We have seen how William drew Nicholas to the idea of a continental alliance with his pictures of terror of an attack through the Baltic, and he was soon to renew his efforts at Björkö. "This will facilitate our action and liberate us from all need to take the initiative, we need only to consent to a desire already formulated by the German Emperor". Germany would do the dirty work, Russia needed only to follow, and she had reason to do so, according to Isvolsky "the need for Germany to defend Kiel against an eventual English attack is so pressing that if we do not decide to second this desire, it may be accomplished without us".[1] Isvolsky seems to have thought that a weakened Russia had better howl with the German wolf, who was the real danger in the Baltic. Without a fleet Russia could not prevent Germany from doing anything, but by consenting she might at least have a say in the matter. It was supposed that the Danes were resigned to the thought of surrendering without resistance to the dominance of Germany.[2] And it was only natural that the rupture of the Baltic balance of power caused anxiety in Denmark, where the relative growth of the German might due to the defeat of the Russian navy and the revolutionary disorder of the Russian army observed with worry.[3] "Everything contributes to German domination of Denmark: economic penetration, the personal efforts of the Emperor William, the visits of the German fleet. In case of a European alarm Denmark may be forced to throw herself in the arms of Germany, whose military and naval forces are at hand, and the result would be a permanent upset of the balance in the Baltic. A preceding entente between us and Germany might perhaps prevent this danger".[4] Of course France would not like Russia's entente with Germany, but Isvolsky was not sorry for her: "because it is France who has inaugurated the era of arrangements with third powers (England), why should not we on our part make what Prince Bülow had so spiritedly called *un tour de valse extra*. And for us it is a question of vital interest, not merely a simple transient adventure in Morocco".[5] Isvolsky was prepared to contemplate closing the Baltic, not as an aim desirable

[1] AVPR fond kanceljarija 1905 g., delo 35, n. 20 Isvolsky to Lamsdorff 29. VI 1905
[2] Isvolsky: *Mémoires* p. 84
[3] Fink: *Ustabil balance* p. 243
[4] AVPR fond kanceljarija 1905 g. delo 35 n. 20 Isvolsky to Lamsdorff 29. VI 1905
[5] AVPR found kanceljarija 1905 g. delo 35 n. 20 Isvolsky to Lamsdorff 29. IV 1905

in itself for Russia, but in order to prevent Germany closing it permanently and against Russia.

It is a pity that Isvolsky's message containing the proposition, which he tried to justify in his letter, is not in its place in the binder of documents, nor is there any answer by Lamsdorff. Four years later the British envoy in Stockholm wrote: "When M. Isvolsky was Minister at Copenhagen he submitted to Count Lamsdorff, the Russian Minister for Foreign Affairs, a plan which he appears to have discussed with German statesmen. Germany and Russia, as the two great Baltic powers, were to agree to joint action in the Baltic for mutual defence, Russia was to be freed from the servitude imposed upon her by the Treaty of 1856, by which she was precluded from fortifying the Åland Islands, and she was also, in time of war, to have the free use of the Kiel Canal. Germany was, in return, to receive Russian support in such action with regard to the entrance of the Baltic as she might think necessary for her own defence. Count Lamsdorff in his report to the Emperor pointed out that the proposed arrangement amounted, in point of fact, to an offensive and defensive alliance with Germany, which was incompatible with existing treaties, and also that it was not to Russia's interest in closing the Baltic. The Emperor approved of Count Lamsdorff's arguments, and the matter was allowed to drop."[1] Spring-Rice does not mention any source for his knowledge. A couple of years earlier the French Ambassador in London, Cambon, referred to identical rumours about Isvolsky and Schoen having together in Copenhagen made a study for an arrangement for the Baltic; there had been no follow-up in St. Petersburg, but the project had not been treated as any great secret in the Russian Foreign Office.[2] It has not been possible to check these accounts or ascertain what was proposed in 1905 and what later, for instance, with reference to the Åland Islands. There is nothing impossible in these accounts, however, and Lamsdorff's alleged reaction is in accordance with what is known of his policy.

We have already suspected Isvolsky and Schoen of collaboration behind the backs of their governments, and now these rumours strengthen earlier suspicions. The evidence is circumstantial but consistent; it may be assumed that there is some truth in the story. The whole issue was to become important when Isvolsky was made Minister for Foreign Affairs of Russia, and Schoen Ambassador in St. Petersburg and then State Secretary of Auswärtiges Amt.

But in 1905 it was only scheming by two envoys. Russian policy was still in Lamsdorff's hands. In the autumn of 1905 he said, very nearly in the words of the memorandum of Martens, "for Russia, not only as a European but as a World Power, it is always of first importance that the exit of our fleet out of the Baltic or its entering into the Baltic shall always be free; but the guaranteeing

[1] PRO/FO 371/745 Annual Report for Sweden 1908, by Cecil Spring-Rice
[2] DDF 11 n. 196 Paul Cambon to Pichon 8. XI 1907

of such a freedom with an international recognition of Danish neutrality is not for the present time in the plans of the Imperial Government".[1] No Emperors, Envoys or Professors could turn Lamsdorff away from this line.

---

[1] Pohlebkin: *Priznanie.*. n. 58 Instructions for the Envoy in Christiania, draft 4/17 XI 1905

COMPLICATIONS IN SCANDINAVIA

Scandinavia in the pattern of European politics

In 1814 Norway had been united to Sweden by the decision of the great powers, as a kind of reward for Karl Johan's pro-Russian policy from 1812 onwards. During the rivalry of the Russian and British empires this pro-Russian tendency caused concern to the British. In the 1830s the British consul in Norway John R. Crowe had directed Lord Palmerston's attention to the danger of Russia's expansion westwards through Lapland and Finmark. The consul accused the Russians of keeping alive the problem of the migratory Lapps and their rights on the Norwegian coast in order to gain an outlet on the Varanger Fjord and eventually other harbours in Norway. "In control of the splendid ice-free ports of this region, the great eastern rival might . . threaten the British supremacy on the sea." [1]

But it was the Crimean War that brought this question to the fore. In 1854 the Western Powers tried to make the Swedes interested in joining the alliance against Russia, and offered the Åland Islands as a reward. King Oscar would have preferred the whole of Finland, which seemed too much to the British; and, on the other hand, the King realized that accepting the islands would have resulted in Russia's permanent enmity, without any guarantee of help from the West, and with the outcome of the war still unknown.[2] In the following year, however, on 21st November 1855, Palmerston succeeded in concluding with Sweden-Norway a treaty in which Great Britain and France promised to defend the Union with armed force against an attack by Russia. Sweden-Norway was not obliged to join the war, the kingdoms had only to pledge not to cede to or exchange with Russia their territory nor give Russian subjects any rights of pasturage or fishing.[3] Great Britain was secured against the danger that the Swedes might let the Russians have a strip on the Varanger Fjord in exchange for Åland.[4]

Scandinavia had cast in her lot with Russia's enemies, but had not participated in the war nor, consequently, in the Paris Conference. King Oscar had hoped that the Åland Islands would have been given to Sweden, the Finnish coast demilitarized and the Russian fleet reduced. But the Allies had no reason to demand more from Russia than the convention annexed to the peace treaty, which stipulated that Russia was not to fortify the Åland Islands nor keep there any military or naval establishments.[5]

[1] Knaplund p. 478—
[2] Tingsten p. 38—
   Maude *Finland* p. 30—
[3] Knaplund p. 478—
[4] Maude *Finland* . . pp. 30—47
[5] Tingsten p. 41—
   Söderhjelm: *Demilitarisation* . . .
   Barros p. 3—12

Norway was attached to a western policy, which was only natural on account of the interests of her commercial fleet, but Sweden drifted during the Oscarian years into a more pro-German course in her need of protection against the Russian danger. The Norwegians thought that Sweden was rather too much afraid of Russia and leaned too heavily on Germany; they for their part hoped that Russia might even help them, because the independence of Norway would weaken Sweden, who was hostile to Russia. On the other hand the estrangement of Norway, who drew nearer to Great Britain, caused anxiety in Sweden so that Germany seemed all the better a protector against Russia. The internal causes of friction between the parties to the Scandinavian Union grew as the nineteenth century wore on. In 1814 the Norwegians would have preferred independence, and the vigorous economic, social and cultural growth in Norway nourished separatism. "How can you think that an energetic and alert nation, the nation of Ibsen and Björnson, could live united with a nation of drunken barons?" [1] By the beginning of 1905 the particular quarrel concerned autonomous consular representation, which the Norwegians demanded, while the Swedes kept to the principle of a united diplomatic and consular service. The rupture of the Union seemed imminent.

The Russian danger in the British view

The British were not delighted when then Scandinavian Union began to break up. Together Norway and Sweden had been quite strong for a small power and the joint-state had seemed likely to prevent any foreign power from settling on the coast opposite Great Britain, and the Treaty of 1855 stipulated for her the right to intervene if the situation threatened to get out of hand. Plans to safeguard British interests in the North were sketched even before the actual dissolution of the Union, although of course they could not take any definite form before it was seen how the situation would turn out.

The "rebellious" Norwegians could not enter into official relations with foreign powers, but in Frithjof Nansen and Baron Fritz Wedel Jarlsberg they had two men who had status enough as private persons to be able to discuss with foreign governments.

In March 1905 Nansen discussed the Northern question with Lord Lansdowne and complained bitterly of the Swedish Government. Lansdowne expressed his "deep concern": the disruption of the Scandinavian countries might be the cause of serious international complications, and perhaps lead to undesirable interference on the part of other powers.[2] This seems to have been the gist of the problem. The situation had been advantageous for Great Britain;

---

[1] Danielsen p. 23—27
[2] PRO/FO 73/857 Lansdowne to Rennell Rodd 29. III 1905

any change might be unfavourable. But however she might try to preserve the status quo, her influence was not great enough to prevent the Scandinavians from quarrelling. Nansen observed that "Sweden and Norway, in their present condition, were not likely to present a solid obstacle to such designs. The antipathy between the two had become inveterate. The question might not improbaly have to come before the other Powers whenever Norway had to ask them for the recognition of Norwegian consuls". And Lansdowne added as if a little surprised: "Nansen greatly apprehended interference on the part of Germany, and seemed to be more afraid of this than of what Russia might do." [1]

Russia was and remained the chief rival of Great Britain, at least in the view of the Conservative Government, until the day of Tsushima. Germany was a growing menace, especially in the opinion of the Admiralty,[2] but it took some time before she became The Enemy.[3]

From Stockholm the British envoy Sir James Rennell Rodd reported on a couple of articles published by Novoe Vremja in March 1905. One article insisted on the "duty of Russian diplomacy to follow the crisis on the Scandinavian Peninsula with special care" and went on to say "there is no doubt that another neighbour of ours is watching the movement with keen attention and carefully studying all possibilities which arise under the new régime . . we need but add that Russia would also be seriously interested in Norway's future, were it not that at the present time it had been clearly demonstrated to us that we were unprepared for any active participation in political issues". The other article had reference to a possible neutralisation of the Belts, asserting that "in Sweden and Norway it was already discussed what icefree ports in the North Sea Russia would desire to acquire on the eventuality of the Black Sea regime being also applied to the Baltic". Rennell Rodd reported that articles like these made the Swedes inclined to believe that Russia had inspired Norwegian separatism to further her own ends.[4]

In May 1905 Rennell Rodd sent two messages more about the same "Russian danger", "the supposed ambition of Russia to secure an ice-free port in Finmark".[5] It was impossible for Russia to use the Murman coast in the absence of railways. "The most northerly port that would be of real value to Russia as a naval station was Narvik, which could easily be connected with Uleaborg."[6]

It is remarkable that the reports concerning the articles of Novoe Vremja come from Stockholm and not from St. Petersburg. The British ambassadors in

---

[1] PRO/FO 73/857 Lansdowne to Rennell Rodd 29. III 1905

[2] Sweet p. 455—456

[3] Monger p. 99, 194

[4] PRO/FO 73/650 Rennell Rodd to Lansdowne 16. III 1905

[5] PRO/FO 73/650 Rennell Rodd to Lansdowne 12. V 1905

[6] PRO/FO 73/650 Rennell Rodd to Lansdowne 15. V 1905

Russia, Hardinge and after him Nicolson, were laboriously building an agreement between Britain and Russia, and it is natural that they did not wish to
keep alive the old animosity. Rennell Rodd, on the other hand, "readily accepted what the court and military party in Sweden told him":[1] "In Sweden no one
in those days doubted that Russia aimed at obtaining a road to the open sea
across Norwegian territory, though her recent disasters in the Japanese war
seemed likely to postpone any new adventures for a certain period. Should such
an ambition eventually take shape, there was good reason to believe that Germany would not be content without some territorial compensation, and a Polish
partition of Norway might be contemplated. ."[2] Sometimes one is tempted to
suppose that part of the British concern about the Russian schemes was provoked by the Swedes in order to keep the British interested in preserving the
Union, which the nationalist-minded anti-Russian activists wished.

But of course the fear of Russia in Sweden was genuine; nor does this signify
that the apprehensions felt in London were inspired solely by the Swedes.
Russia was the traditional enemy, and her supposed schemes had already made
the British worry in the 1830s, when the Swedes were Russia's friends. And
since then the British had had experience enough of Russian expansion to feel
concern for the whole of Northern Europe, where the status quo was breaking
up.

In Rodd's report there is one more point of great importance: the Scandinavian question and the status of the Danish Straits were seen as parts of the
same problem. If the rumours of the closing of the Straits by Germany were to
prove true, it was feared that the Russian reaction might be directed towards
the Norwegian coast.

The Russian danger also loomed up behind the Northern question in the
document in which the Admiralty recorded the naval aspects of the disruption
of Scandinavian Union at the beginning of June 1905: ".. the joint guarantee
by Great Britain and France will necessarily lapse.. both countries will be in
continual jeopardy.. if the matters take their natural course, Europe may find
herself confronted by an accomplished fact of far-reaching importance namely,
that Russia had obtained without any serious effort an outlet at Tromsö front-
ing upon the Atlantic... Once in possession of Sweden and Norway, Russia
would be in position to seal hermetically the Baltic entrances, and, in alliance
with Germany, might be expected to make short work of Denmark, even if
Denmark was not flung to Germany as a sop to insure her acquiescence in the
Russian expansion".

At this point the author himself seems to have found the vision he had
painted somewhat apocalyptic, so he continues: "The idea of a Russian absorp-

---

[1] Remark by George Maude, 1974
[2] Rennell Rodd p. 54

tion of Scandinavia may appear visionary and for the moment outside the range of practical politics. But if .. the slow glacial drift of Russian intrigue and Russian territorial expansion was even in 1855 regarded as a real menace by the Scandinavian peoples, the course of Russian policy during the succeeding half-century amply justifies the belief that such a danger is even more existent at the present day."

"In the opinion of the Admiralty, the best safeguard would consist in a general pledge of the integrity of Scandinavia, given in a form of a guarantee by the all the Great Powers, including Russia .. which in her case would clearly be .. a self-denying ordinance .." [1]

The text, of which the most essential points only have been cited, paints the devil on the wall in dark colours and with heavy strokes. But it cannot be taken at its face value. "The soldier must see the possible dangers as if they were menacing. But the duty of the statesman is to prevent them becoming acute!" It would hardly be right to contend that the Admiralty panicked hysterically because of the disruption of the Scandinavian Union. Perhaps one might say that they were anxious on account of the situation and tried to egg the Cabinet and the Foreign Office to act energetically to safeguard the British interests. The Admiralty do not seem to have had any designs of their own on Scandinavia, they only wished to deny it to the Russians. The recent "German danger" seems to be all but forgotten in the revival of the ancient "Russian danger". Again the strategy implied was to fight Russia in the Baltic Sea if the war broke out; the situation in Norway, in the Danish Straits and in the Baltic was regarded as one indivisible whole. The means of preventing Scandinavia from falling under the enemy's sway was to persuade her to sign a "self-denying ordinance"; the Foreign Office had already invented this expedient earlier.

Should the Treaty of 1855 be renewed?

Internationally the matter was taken up by the Swedish Crown Prince (later King Gustaf V) in a discussion with Rennell Rodd. The Crown Prince was worried because Sweden's international position was deteriorating. With the dissolution of the Union she was losing the support which the Treaty of 1855 had given against the Russian menace.[2] Now, in the middle of May 1905, he was anxious to know whether the Treaty of 1855 might still be valid as regards Sweden and Norway separately. Rennell rodd said, as "his personal opinion", that the Treaty of 1855 presumed the mutual support of the two kingdoms implied in the common crown, which would no longer exist. "The two Scan-

---

[1] PRO/CAB 4/1/59B "The threatened dissolution of the Union between Norway and Sweden — Naval aspects of the question". 5. VI 1905
[2] Hildebrand p. 306—307

dinavian states should undertake the same engagements to one another which they desired the guaranteeing Powers to undertake in their behalf."[1]

Rennell Rodd remarked to the Foreign Office that the Swedes were apt to think that "Norway may safely be left to suffer the consequences of her own temerity", but he thought that it was in the British interest "that Sweden should be kept up to a proper sense of her own duties and obligations".[3] As a rule the British tried to refrain from showing their own eagerness to renew the treaty — it was of course wiser to keep the Scandinavians thinking that it was they who were asking. And all the time the British, thinking of the defence Scandinavia, tried to keep the Norwegians and the Swedes as close to each other as possible.

Perhaps the Crown Prince tried to keep up the British interest when he mentioned his forthcoming visit to Berlin and his wish to discuss the future of the Treaty with the Germans. He did not believe in German plans of expansion in Norway, except as a compensation for eventual cession of Norwegian territory to Russia. "Under these circumstances, he thought that the Emperor might receive with favour an assurance that the former guaranteeing Powers were prepared to maintain their guarantee, even under altered conditions."[3]

Lord Lansdowne discussed the threatening dissolution of the Union with the French Ambassador, too. They agreed that both France and England were interested in the Northern question, at least juridically, being signatories of the November Treaty of 1855. But the ancient treaty had been directed against Russia, who was now France's ally. Any new arrangement should be one that Russia could be included in.[4]

Rennell Rodd's report gave Lansdowne occasion to record his views:

"1) We earnestly desire that the integrity of the dual kingdom should in no circumstances be impaired"

"2) British interests would be seriously affected if any other power were to occupy a port on the Norwegian coast, and we should do all in our power to avoid such an eventuality"

"3) We doubt extremely whether the Treaty of 1855 could be regarded as surviving should the kingdoms separate. We shall have to consider with the utmost care the situation which will arise, and the question of replacing the Treaty by some other international arrangement. Our attitude would largely depend on that of the two kingdoms towards one another and towards us"

"4) Any new arrangement for securing the integrity of Norway and Sweden should not be aimed at Russia alone. An agreement to which the other

[1] PRO/FO 371/98/3637 Rennell Rodd to Lansdowne 18. V 1905
[2] PRO/FO 371/98/3637 Rennell Rodd to Lansdowne 18. V 1905
[3] PRO/FO 371/98/3637 Rennell Rodd to Lansdowne 17. V 1905
[4] DDF 6 n. 461 Cambon to Delcassé 28. V 1905

Powers including Russia herself were parties would be preferable"
"5) I propose to consult the French Government confidentially upon these points"[1]

To the Swedish Crown Prince, who on the 15th June 1905 was visiting England, Lansdowne answered on these lines, emphasizing that "we should propose to do nothing behind the back" of Russia, and "we should certainly regard with satisfaction" Germany's adhesion.[2]

Lord Lansdowne's tone was much more unperturbed, but the point of view was identical with that of the Admiralty's. Great Britain had to do something to prevent her rivals from gaining a foothold in the North, especially on the coast opposite Britain. Inviting both Russia and Germany to participate in the guarantee was thought to be the best way of securing the British interests without unnecessarily provoking the two Eastern Empires.

The Crown Prince Gustaf had visited Berlin early in June. There he said to the German Chancellor Bülow that France and England would probably regard themselves as freed from the obligations of the Treaty of 1855, but might be induced to sign a modified one. Bülow seems to have been slightly on his guard and suspicious because of the Western origins of the proposition. He suspected of its being directed against Germany and thought that it was of little use to Sweden because France would never stop her ally, if Russia tried to invade the North. And Germany had no reason to prevent her.[3] But the next day he declared that in fact Germany would not oppose consolidating the situation with a treaty, but naturally, after eliminating Russia as the object of the treaty, it must not be concluded with the Western powers only, as it would then be directed against Germany. Sweden must conclude the agreement with Germany, too. The British could be told that instead of angering Germany, Sweden wished to bind her with the guarantee treaty. — Bülow's cunning advice was unnecessary as Germany's participation was highly desirable to the British. — The Emperor William agreed to this and said that if Norway did split off, a similar treaty might be concluded with her, too; Germany had no reason to estrange Norway, having gained so much good-will there.[4] — It was reasonable to participate in the discussions instead of leaving them to the Western powers although, or because, these were suspected of anti-German schemes.

But the actual separation of Norway and Sweden on the 7th June 1905 caused this question to be put off a for a while while the more immediate complications of the dissolution of the Union were dealt with.

---

[1] PRO/FO 73/653 Lansdowne to Rennell Rodd 23. V 1905
[2] PRO/FO 371/98/3637 Lansdowne to Crown Prince of Norway and Sweden 15. VI 1905
[3] Hildebrand p. 308—309
[4] GP 23 II n. 8024 note by Bülow 6. VI 1905

4

Great Britain and the election of the Norwegian King

In the spring of 1905 the Norwegians used the consular dispute as a sufficiently controversial issue enabling them to break off the Union, which occurred on the 7th of June. King Oscar II was declared to have abdicated in Norway because he did not accept the Norwegian consular law nor the resignation, as a protest, of the Norwegian government. Feelings were running high on both sides, the Norwegians were unanimous in their demand for independence, and the Swedes were hurt and some of them even bellicose because of the "rebellion". As the weaker litigant Norway was in need of foreign help. It was in this connection that the question of the Norwegian constitution was made an international problem.

Many Norwegians were republicans, but they thought that monarchistic Europe would be more helpful if they chose a king for head of state. At first the crown was offered to the Bernadotte family, perhaps as a conciliatory gesture, perhaps only as a feint to provoke refusal and so to make the Swedes recognize the independence of Norway de facto. But King Oscar did not accept nor did he refuse, and the Swedish Diet decided on the 27th July that the Norwegians should hold a plebiscite to confirm the decision of the 7th of June, and that some practical stipulations should be negotiated by delegates from both sides. After that the throne might be declared vacant and Norway free to elect a new king. In fact, Sweden demanded that Norway ask for the independence she had already proclaimed.

The Norwegians tried to play the vacant throne as an ace with which to avoid the humiliation of submission. It seems to have been Baron Fritz Wedel Jarlsberg who suggested that the crown should be given to the Danish Prince Charles (later King Haakon VII), who was King Edward's son-in-law. In this way it was hoped to ensure both Danish and British recognition of Norwegian independence, and Sweden would find herself faced by an accomplished fact and would have to treat Norway as an equal and independet state.[1]

The Danes were favourably inclined. The Foreign Minister Raben seems to have been really enthusiastic, nor was the new Prime Minister Christensen ill-disposed. The thought of becoming a king attracted the prince himself.[2]

The British envoy in Copenhagen Sir Alan Johnstone adopted the cause of Prince Charles, and adopted it much more eagerly than Downing Street did. Once he wrote of Raben that his "idea was to make a name for himself in Denmark by getting Prince Charles on the Norwegian throne even at a certain risk and he may also have been influenced by Wedel perpetually shaking the stick of a Norwegian Republic at him".[3] Substituting King Edward's court for

---

[1] Worms-Müller: *Haakon 7*, p. 80—
[2] Wedel p. 44—, 69—, 142
[3] PRO/FO 22/584 Johnstone to Lansdowne 15. VII 1905

Denmark, one cannot but feel that this reflects the envoy's own attitude.

From Copenhagen Wedel proceeded to London and was allowed to explain his proposition to Lord Lansdowne. "He wished to impress upon His Majesty's Government as strongly as he could that their recognition should not be needlessly delayed". The answer cannot have been quite what Wedel wished: "It would clearly have been impossible for us (the British) to recognize the provisional government immediately, and the time had scarcely come for considering what might happen in the event of recognition being withheld by any of the Powers." [1] One is inclined to think that Wedel was rather foolish to expect Great Britain to throw all her good-will and influence on the side of the Norwegians and against the Swedes.

Wedel was a professional diplomat but he was not very diplomatic, according to his own memoirs. He explained to Lansdowne that if Great Britain would not help Norway through the crisis, she would be compelled to seek support wherever it was to be obtained; it would be in Norway's interest to prevent Russia or Germany from interfering in the Scandinavian question but without help Norway could not pull through.[2] — Of course blackmail was not the way to persuade Lansdowne. And Sir Edward Grey, who was to become Foreign Secretary in December, exhorted the Norwegian to seek an arrangement with Sweden, and sighed that the Union would, after all, have been the best solution for Norway.[3]

Later we shall see that the British Government was not quite insensible as to the German danger in Norway — not to speak about Russia — and that they worked for Norway and for Prince Charles; but certainly not at the dictation of Wedel. For the British it was no national calamity if the Norwegians had to wait a little and even to swallow their national pride. But the British did let the Swedes understand that it would be most sensible and dignified not to postpone the inevitable — otherwise Russia might be the first to recognize the independence of Norway and so reap the harvest of gratitude. There is not much of this unofficial pressure in the diplomatic records, but it is known that Rennell Rodd hinted in Stockholm that Great Britain might really recognize Norway if Sweden temporized too much.[4] The pressure took no official, heavy forms but was implied in polite discussions.[5] Great Britain had no reason to estrange either of the conflicting parties.

In Copenhagen Wedel tried with remarkable energy and deplorable tact to persuade the Danes and especially Prince Charles to adopt his plan. When it

[1] PRO/FO 73/649 Lansdowne to Grant Duff 20. VI 1905
[2] Wedel p. 52—59, Lövland p. 144
[3] Wedel p. 52—
[4] Hildebrand p. 311
Lindberg: *Scandinavia.* . p. 20
[5] PRO/FO 73/650 Rennel Rodd to Lansdowne 26. VII 1905

became apparent to him that the Danish government wanted to wait for the decision of the Swedish Riksdag before letting Prince Charles accept the Norwegian crown, Wedel modified his plan: after the Swedish decision Charles should proceed to Norway and with Danish and British recognition help to get Norway a position of equality with Sweden in the negotiations. Sometimes he was carried away by his own eagerness and the sluggishness of others, so that Johnstone had to remonstrate "with due courtesy" that Denmark could not be forced to tie her hands before the pronouncement of the Riksdag was known.[1] Wedel saw the crown as the means by which Norway could be saved from humiliation, and perhaps he wished to appear the saviour of the nation himself. For Johnstone the main point was to secure the election of the son-in-law of his king. Of course, in practice there was only a slight difference.

King Edward VII had first thought that a Bernadotte king would be best for Norway, but he was delighted and eager when he heard that his son-in-law might obtain the throne. According to Wedel he was ready to egg on Charles to proceed to Norway at once — whatever the consequences for the relations between Great Britain and Sweden, and between Norway and Sweden. — He promised Great Britain's recognition of Norway's king and independence, and in a subsequent letter he promised to try and obtain such a recognition from his government,[2] which shows that there were some difficulties between the King and "his" government. The King's letters are not in the diplomatic archives, but his biographer confirms the story and gives the obvious explanation that Edward was afraid of the ambitions of the Emperor William II; he had heard rumours that William wished to have one of his sons on the Norwegian throne.[3]

The Emperor was indeed dissatisfied with the candidature of Prince Charles of Denmark, as was the Czar, too. This fact had some importance at the meeting of Björkö, which will be discussed a little later.

Of course the King was not the maker of British policy. From the very beginning the Foreign Office eschewed the risky policies of Wedel, mindful of Sweden's reaction.[4] The Danes were advised to wait for the decision of the Swedish Diet, and no recognition was promised for either Norway or Charles in case they hurried to fill the throne before it was declared vacant by the Swedes.[5]

The decision of the Swedish Diet on the 27th July seemed to confirm the fears of the Norwegians that they were to be humiliated. At the beginning of August Wedel tried again to adjust his plan in order to avoid still the national shame of having to submit to asking Sweden for independence. The Swedish

---

[1] PRO/FO 22/584 Johnstone to Lansdowne 23. VII 1905
[2] Wedel p. 162, 172, 177
[3] Lee p. 321
[4] PRO/FO 22/584 Foreign Office to Johnstone 17. VII 1905
[5] PRO/FO 22/584 Johnstone to Lansdowne 20. VII 1905

envoy in Copenhagen Trolle discussed with him a possible solution: when communicating the result of the plebiscite, Norway was to notify Sweden that she was ready to negotiate on the basis of Sweden's conditions when a definite Norwegian Government had been appointed; the Riksdag was to be requested to permit the King to renounce the Norwegian throne.[1] Thus Prince Charles could have occupied the vacant throne, and, with a king, Norway would have been formally equal to Sweden in the negotiations.

With his old methods Wedel tried to get the support of Denmark and Great Britain for his newly modified plan: he let it be known that the offer to Prince Charles was only made under the express understanding that he assumed the conduct of the negotiations.[2] — This may have been an answer to the idea, not very earnestly intended, of the British Foreign Office that Prince Charles should accept the throne but not assume the government of Norway until the acceptance by Sweden.[3] Johnstone, too, tried to persuade his superiors to put pressure on the Swedes; otherwise the Norwegians might proclaim a republic [4], or, if the negotiations between Norway and Sweden were concluded before King Oscar had renounced the Norwegian throne, a Bernadotte prince might be forced upon Norway in answer to her invitation.[5] King Edward tried once more to act on his own. He asked Rennell Rodd for help, because "owing to the punctiliousness of Sweden, Prince Charles ran the risk of losing the Norwegian throne and of appearing ridiculous, which His Majesty would feel deeply".[6] But Rennell Rodd, who regarded the Norwegians as a lot of uncouth fisher-folk, was of no help; to the contrary, he proposed a joint representation of Germany and Great Britain to the Norwegians "as to the importance of coming to terms on the reasonable line proposed by Sweden".[7]

Lansdowne asked "privately" whether the Swedes might consent to an understanding on the lines suggested by Wedel[8] but to Johnstone he answered that there was a better chance of attaining satisfactory solution "if we abstain from pressing our views too strongly".[9] And Lansdowne was beginning to get tired of Wedel: "I would not give any encouragement to Wedel's tactics".[10] — For Lansdowne the main goal was not to secure the Norwegian throne for the Danish Prince. The conflict in the North had shaken a status quo advantageous to Great Britain, and the vital thing was to get the conflict settled with as little

---

[1] PRO/FO 22/584 Johnstone to Lansdowne 18. VIII 1905
[2] PRO/FO 22/584 Johnstone to Lansdowne 5. VIII 1905
[3] PRO/FO 22/585 Rennell Rodd to Lansdowne 29. VII 1905
[4] PRO/FO 22/584 Johnstone to Lansdowne 5. VIII 1905
[5] PRO/FO 22/584 Johnstone to Lansdowne 8. VIII 1905
[6] PRO/FO 73/652 Rennell Rodd to Lansdowne 8. VIII 1905
[7] PRO/FO 73/652 Rennell Rodd to Lansdowne 5. VIII 1905
[8] PRO/FO 73/649 Lansdowne to Rennell Rodd 2. VIII 1905
[9] PRO/FO 22/585 Lansdowne to Johnstone 7. VIII 1905
[10] PRO/FO 22/585 Lansdowne to Johnstone 19. VIII 1905

damage as possible so that relations between Great Britain, Sweden and Norway should remain as unaltered as possible.

Nor was Wedel's plan supported by the Danes. However favourable their attitude towards Norway might have been, they were not willing to upset their relations with the powerful Sweden. There seemed to be no hope of British support in spite of the efforts made by Johnstone and King Edward himself. King Christian did not wish to hurt King Oscar, and his decision was binding for Prince Charles. The Danish King and Government decided that Charles must not go to Norway before King Oscar had abdicated and the throne was legally vacant.[1] And Sweden stood fast on the ground of the decision of the Diet, disowning even the compromise promised by Trolle.[2]

Thus, in the end, the Norwegians had to submit to negotiate on terms dictated by the Swedes. Of course it was a bitter disappointment for the Norwegians, but in fact they did not lose anything essential. The decision of the Swedish Riksdag was actually a recognition that Norway was a separate state, with whom it was possible to negotiate. Sweden did not resort to force.

The plebiscite was held and all Norwegians wanted independence (yea 368 208, nay 194). The Storthing asked for negotiations on the dissolution of the Union, and the delegations met on the 31st of August in Karlstad on Lake Vänern.[3]

But Wedel could not accept his defeat in the star role of kingmaker and saviour of Norwegian sovereignty, and he always had the support of Johnstone. After a discussion with Wedel Johnstone proposed that Great Britain should warn Sweden not to force a Bernadotte prince upon Norway.[4] But Wedel's fears or allegations were not believed in London: "The attempt to create a scare by the prospect of a Republic having failed he is falling back on the Bernadotte candidature."[5] Rennell Rodd warned: "I am inclined to receive any views expressed in Copenhagen by Baron Wedel, whose forecasts have not hitherto been altogether justified by results, with a certain amount of caution."[6] And Lansdowne concluded: "I am not at all inclined to be driven out of our course by Baron Wedel's persistence. . . The Swedish Government are well aware that we should disapprove such a candidature. . If they are more inclined to put forward Prince Charles of Sweden than they were, I doubt whether advice from us would prevent them from doing so". And because the Danish Government had decided not to allow Prince Charles to accept the Norwegian throne without Sweden's consent, Lansdowne thought that "we ought surely not to be more

---

[1] Worms-Müller: *Haakon 7*, p. 91—
[2] PRO/FO 22/584 Johnstone to Lansdowne 18. VIII 1905
[3] Worms-Müller: *Haakon 7*, P. 91—
[4] PRO/FO 22/584 Johnstone to Lansdowne 1. IX 1905
[5] PRO/FO 22/584 Johnstone to Lansdowne 1. IX 1905 minute EAC
[6] PRO/FO 73/651 Rennell Rodd to Lansdowne 4. IX 1905

Danish than the Danes". Wedel was, in Lansdowne's opinion, "a very unsafe guide".

Lansdowne concluded that Great Britain should "leave the negotiations which are now in progress to follow their course without obtruding our own views upon the negotiators".[1]

William compelled to accept Charles

There was a duality in the German attitude to the Northern question throughout: an active and amateurish, nearly irresponsible Emperor, and a markedly careful and restrained political lead.

The plans of the Norwegian kingmakers did not imply German participation and therefore its active expression of opinion was not immediately called forth. But the Emperor was used to expressing his opinions without being asked for them, and he is said to have exclaimed, prompted by the Norwegian "rebellion", that if Bavaria tried to get away from the Reich, he would decidedly know what to do![2]

The Norwegian idea of getting Prince Charles of Denmark on the Norwegian throne and thereby securing British support gave no satisfaction to the Emperor. When meeting the Swedish royalty in Gävle in July 1905 he egged them on to accept the Norwegian offer and to put a Bernadotte Prince on the neighbour's throne, but "unfortunately without any success".[3] Some years later it was said that Sweden ought to have waged war in 1905, but the unwillingess of King Oscar II had made it impossible. To this the Emperor remarked: "Gäfle!"[4] When somebody said that the saddest consequence of the dissolution of the Union was that Sweden had lost Germany's respect when she decided to comply with Norway's wishes without war, the Emperor commented: "Right!" And to the remark that surely in Germany the wisdom of King Oscar was admired when he understood the need to avoid military conflict, the Emperor wrote: "Nein!"[5] William's remarks may not always be reliable evidence, but it seems that the Emperor would really have liked to see a war in the North in order to prevent the British candidate from attaining the Norwegian throne.

William's counter-plans were aimed at the most dangerous direction: "In this situation it seems to me that getting into closer relations with Denmark is the sole possibility."[6] Bülow hurriedly asked his foreign office for arguments against the Emperor's intention to meddle in the affair. The officials explained

---

[1] PRO/FO 22/584 Lansdowne to Villiers 5. IX 1905
[2] Hildebrand p. 345
[3] AA Dänemark 27 Bd 13 Bülow to Ausw. Amt 14. VII 1905
[4] AA Norwegen 4 geheim Henckel to Bülow 19. III 1908
[5] AA Norwegen 4 geheim Treutler to Bülow 5. V 1908
[6] AA Dänemark 27 Bd 13 p. 112 Bülow to Ausw. Amt 14. VII 1905

that Charles would listen to London, not to Copenhagen; and that there was no sense in arousing Danish suspicions, as even preparatory steps might harm, which was seen clearly enough when King Christian had been asked about Danish neutrality the preceding year.[1]

William is said to have preferred Prince Ernst Günther of Augustenborg or Friedrich Ferdinand of Glücksburg for the Norwegian throne. Charles of Denmark was not an agreeable choice for the Kaiser,[2] but still more disagreeable were the threats of a republican form of government which the Norwegians threatened to resort to without taking the German candidates into account at all. The German statesmen saw that it was useless and even dangerous to press the claims of their candidates and advised the Emperor to desist from his attempts.[3] Schoen said to Wedel that if Sweden did not consent to the candidature of the Bernadotte Prince, Norway could take the Danish Prince Charles as far as Germany was concerned if only she would give up the idea of a republic.[4] In the end William with his customary impulsiveness dropped all protests against Charles and played on the floor with his son Alexander, "the Crown Prince of Norway"[5] (who in fact did become Crown Prince and then King Olav V).

In the light of his earlier and also later attempts in regard to Denmark it is possible that William meant more by "getting into closer relations with Denmark" than just trying to work in Copenhagen against Charles's English tendencies. It is also possible that Wedel's threat with the "stick of the fepublic" was more efficient in his memory than in reality. The crisis in Morocco surely explains part of the reluctance of German statesmen to create unnecessary complications in the Scandinavian conflict. In September Germany also refrained from intervening in the quarrel during the Swedo-Norwegian conference in Karlstad, when there was no question of the form of government at stake.

That the Emperor William saw the Norwegian question in the larger context of the Baltic question was already seen at the end of June 1905 in Berlin, where he met Crown Prince Gustav and discussed the renewal of the guarantee treaty. Now from Gävle William proceded to the Gulf of Finland to meet the Czar at Björkö, a meeting which caused much concern to European statesmen.

Björkö

After the failure in previous winter of the proposed continental coalition William seemed to be about to succeed in realizing his pet plan by a dramatic

---

[1] AA Dänemark 27 Bd 13 p. 113 Mühlberg to Bülow 15. VII 1905
[2] Worms-Müller *Haakon 7*, p. 101
[3] AA Deutschland 131 n:o 4 Bd 4 note by Holstein 20. VII 1905
[4] Wedel p. 100—
[5] Wedel p. 138

coup in the summer of 1905. He was not able to make his usual trip to the Norwegian fjords because of the Norwegian "rebellion" and therefore he cruised in the Baltic. After meeting the Swedish King and Crown Prince at Gävle he sailed to the east to an unknown destination. Then he said to his suite: "Now, children, put your dress uniform out, in a couple of hours you will be in front of the Russian Emperor.' — No man said a word, we were thunderstruck, the room was deathly still. None of us guessed the motive of this sudden and secret visit, we all felt the immense political weight of the approaching hours, the consequences of which no one could foresee .." [1] The Czar was waiting at Björkö (now generally known by its Finnish name *Koivisto)* on board his yacht and the meeting took place on the 24th July. "The discussion concerned at first the Norwegian question in which the Czar was lively interested. His Majesty informed the Emperor Nicholas on the situation .. and found full understanding by the Czar in the matter, which he touched incidentally, of the growing British influence in case of the election of the Danish Prince, or of a republic". The Kaiser frightened the Czar with a story which he had probably made up himself: King Oscar had said in Gävle that Germany was free to occupy Bergen, and if England protested, let her take Christiansand as a compensation. The Emperor Nicholas was evidently alarmed over this idea of a partition of Norway and of the British eventually settling down there.[2] "In the end they will shut the Skagerrack and thereby we all are shut up in the Baltic through the occupation of Christiansand".[3] And then also his ports on the Murmansk coast would lose all value.[4]

Nor did Nicholas like the candidature of Charles: "And that, too, that was exactly what we wanted, as if we had not already enough of republics and republic-like monarchies in the world; what shall become of the monarchical principle!" Valdemar of Denmark, the brother of Russia's dowager Empress seemed preferable. "He has some experience of life, an elegant nice wife, and beautiful, staunch children . . . Charles is completely unfit, has been nowhere, no experience of life, insignificant and indolent .." With Charles England will "by fair means or foul" lay her hands on Norway and win influence.

Against the British bugbear the Kaiser had his old patent medicine: the continental alliance, and "by chance" he had the treaty ready in his pocket. Overwhelmed by William's review of the situation Nicholas signed. William informed Bülow that *Friedrich Wilhelm III, Königin Louise, Grosspapa und Nicolai I .. sind in dem Augenblicke wohl nahe gewesen? herausgeschaut haben sie jedenfalls.*[5]

---

[1] Moltke p. 325
[2] GP 19 II n. 6218 Tschirschky to Bülow 24. VII 1905
[3] GP 19 II n. 6220 William II to Bülow 25. VIII 1905
[4] =[2]
[5] GP 19 II n. 6220 William II to Bülow 25. VIII 1905

William saw his dreams coming true, as he afterwards wrote: "the Triple alliance and the Double alliance will form a Quintuple alliance, which will attract Holland, Belgium, Sweden, Norway and Denmark to the orbit of this new centre of gravity and which will be well able to hold all unruly neighbours in order and to impose peace even with force. . " And most important was that France would have to give up the revanche and the entente: "Marianne must remember that she is wedded to you (Nicholas) and so is obliged to lie in bed with you and eventually to give a passing hug or kiss to me, but not sneak into the bedroom of the ever intriguing *touche à tout* on the Islands."[1] Here one can see William's idea of the continental coalition mixed with the dream of a "Greater Central Europe", of which Fritz Fischer has written his outstanding controversial books. The first practical step was again to secure the Danish straits.

In the discussion the "Czar had expressed the wish that a means might be found for Russia and Germany to guarantee Danish territory in order to be able to defend the Baltic north of the Belts." A declaration of neutrality did not seem to be sufficient to close the Baltic. If the enemy did not respect the neutrality she could occupy Denmark without serious resistance and thus had an excellent base against the German and Russian coasts. "His Majesty declared that he was prepared to sound what the Danes thought about neutrality, as he was going to visit Copenhagen presently."[2] The reports from Björkö do not mention this question at all, the sentence above was written twelve years after the Björkö meeting, but evidently something like that was discussed by the Emperors as William telegraphed to Bülow "In Copenhagen I shall question Schoen and hear what is thought there about neutrality".[3]

The Emperor's return to this delicate point frightened his counsellors again. Holstein wrote: "The Norwegian candidatur of Prince Charles cannot be avoided . . it is too late. His Majesty ought to express himself sympathetically about it in Copenhagen. Most decidedly His Majesty is to be advised to avoid any expression which could be understood as an attempt to draw Denmark closer to Germany. The earlier cautious feelers about neutrality and eventual occupation have led only to the result that the Danes have inquired in England how long it takes the British fleet to arrive in Copenhagen. Now the result would be just the same, it cannot be foreseen what the British would do as they are so excited now. . . therefore no excuses and no threats and no persuasion must be used with the Danes. . ."[4]

By energetic exertions through Schoen and Tschirschky Bülow succeeded in preventing his master from touching on the inflammatory matter in Copen-

---

[1] AA Deutschland 131 n:o 4 Bd 4 William II to Nicholas II draft 27. VII 1905
[2] AA Deutschland 131 n:o 4 Bd 6 Ausw. Amt to Rantzau 6. IX. 1917
[3] AA Dänemark 27 geheim Bd 5 p. 150 Bülow to Ausw. Amt 28. VII 1905
[4] AA Deutschland 131 n:o 4 Bd 4 note by Holstein 28. VII 1905

hagen.[1] Somehow hints of the Emperor's intentions had leaked out to the West and caused not a little apprehension, and consequently the relief was great when he dropped his idea.[2] But he was committed to the Czar and had to send a letter of excuses: "On the first day I noted a decided constraint on the part of the King & a look of apprehension on his face. The press elucubrations. . had mentioned the closure of the Baltic in times of peace against all English ships & others & intimated plans of immediate attack upon that Power . . I gathered that foreign influence had been at work, to sow discord & defiance before my arrival . . These circumstances made it impossible for me to mention the subjects we had talked about & which you kindly charged me to communicate to your Grandfather . . In the meantime through Isvolsky and also Schoen I had heard that the sensible men in society as well as in governmental circles are on their own account, little by little, coming to the conclusion, that in case of a war between us both and a foreign Powers, the latter attacking our Baltic shores, Denmark would be unable to uphold her neutrality, falling an easy prey to the foreigner. He would create Denmark his base of operations and thereby draw her on his side as his unwilling ally. Consequently. . as we would not countenance such a development of things & never allow the door of the Baltic to fall into the enemy's hands in case of an outbreak of war, these men are resigned to expect a joint occupation from us, which they would have to undergo; which however would guarantee their territory to remain undiminished & their independence to remain untouched. As this is precisely what we want the Danes to think, & as they are already on the road to it, I thought 'let well done' & said nothing: they are slowly ripening to the fruit we wish & in time to come it will fall into our laps."[3]

Of course this letter was intended as an excuse for the failure of the Emperor in his self-appointed task, and as a solace to the Czar that his hopes would be fulfilled in course of time. Perhaps there was also a certain amount of wishful thinking on the part of William himself. But as I shall point out later, William's hopes were not completely groundless, and the Germans were able to build, though only temporarily, on the basis of Danish compliance.

Then there was the strange quarrel between the Emperor and Bülow caused by the Björkö agreement. The Chancellor did not like the addition to the agreement by William of a stipulation that Russia would help Germany *in Europe* — Holstein held that the only effective help against England would be on the Indian border. Bülow resigned but by threatening suicide William kept

[1] GP 19 I p. 89 ed. note
[2] DDF 7 n. 284 Crozier to Rouvier 31. VII 1905
    DDF 7 n. 288 Crozier to Rouvier 1. VIII 1905
[3] AA Deutschland 131 n:o 4 Bd 5 n. 29 William II to Nicholas II 9. VIII 1905
    draft

his Chancellor at his post.[1] Bülow's irritation was out of all proportion to the cause he named, and has been explained as due to jealousy of his sovereign's succesful coup![2] But of course the substantial reason for Bülow opposing the treaty must have been that he did not wish Germany to court Russia to the detriment of relations with England. In his memoirs he uses an argument which had been used before, in the previous winter: "The alliance of Germany with Russia against England does not benefit us in any way, because Russia is able to help us as much as the man in the moon: she has no fleet, she cannot protect our ports and coasts, and her army is of no use against England."[3]

It was just at this time that the British fleet was coming on a visit to the Baltic. In spite of British assurances the visit was seen as a kind of demonstration in the face of rumours that had arisen about the closing of the Baltic, rumours springing in turn from uncertainty about the purpose of the Björkö meeting.[4] And Holstein saw that his apprehensions were already proving true in a more serious matter: "England now possesses authentic information on the discussion of His Majesty with the Kings of Belgium and Denmark about drawing their countries closer to Germany and England is now presenting us with the bill. As a countermove she would be ready to prepare for us a naval or diplomatic defeat in the Morocco question." Holstein hoped that even "the not very far-seeing" Lamsdorff would realize that for reasons of internal policy Russia had better to join Germany and prevent France from joining the liberal England. "Björkö shows that the Czar at last realizes what dangers collaboration with France and England causes to Czarist regime."[5] Delcassé's fall and Nichola's docility in Björkö evidently led Holstein to take an optimistic view of the future and to keep up too intense a pressure in the Morocco affair, which led to the failure of Algeciras and his own fall.

But of course Bülow and Holstein did not wish to let Russia play off Germany against England. They wanted to keep the other powers balanced against each other, and the Emperor's unexpected antics endangered that balance and caused irritation in the Wilhelmstrasse. However, the Björkö agreement was not the historic turning point which William, and Holstein in another way, had expected.

Nicholas had been on a holiday trip *ohne den Austerähnlichen Auswärtigen P. . (Der von dem Kaiser über Graf Lamsdorff gebrauchte Ausdruck entzieht sich der Wiedergabe* says the prudish editor of the Grosse Politik).[6] Afterwards

---

[1] GP 19 II n. 6230 Bülow to Ausw. Amt 2. VIII 1905
   Gp 19 II n. 6237 William II to Bülow 11. VIII 1905 ⁵
[2] Bompard p. 140
[3] Bülow p. 189
[4] AA Dänemark 37 geheim Bd 5 p. 178 Metternich to Ausw. Amt 2. VIII 1905
[5] Holstein IV n. 904 note by Holstein 31. VII 1905
[6] GP 19 II n. 6220 William II to Bülow 25. VII 1905

it was explained that he had let himself be persuaded out of "politeness" or "absentmindedness". *Le cerveau de l'empereur a été obscurci, bousculé, par tout le verbiage de Guillaume . . Sa Majesté n'a pas compris ce qu'on lui a fait signer.*[1] It was angrily rebutted that the quantity or the quality of the wines consumed during dinner had influenced his action.[2]

Nicholas did not dare to tell Lamsdorff at once, but when the minister heard of the agreement at the end of August he opposed it. His position became somewhat difficult because of the renewal of the Anglo-Japanese alliance in the autumn of 1905, which "shocked" St. Petersburg. Under the pressure of the Czar and Count Witte, Lamsdorff asked the French Ambassador whether France would eventually join a Russo-German combination, perhaps strengthened by the USA, which was beginning to turn against the Japanese.[3]

The preliminary discussion of the Russo-British understanding was also delayed.

But of course Bompard refused flatly. He was rather nervous on account of the danger of Russo-German collaboration, but the British were more sanguine because they knew that Lamsdorff personally was against such schemes.[4] In the end Lamsdorff succeeded in persuading his Emperor to see that the Björkö agreement was in conflict with the Dual Alliance, and that Russia could not pledge herself to defend German territory, especially not Alsace-Lorraine. Nicholas concurred and wrote to William that he wanted the agreement to have an additional protocol to the effect that the agreement would not be in force in case of a war between Germany and France, and that Russo-French treaties would remain in force until France joined the projected triple continental treaty.[5] Of course there was no chance of France joining, and William's coup came to nothing. Even Witte, who did not appreciate the French and wished for co-operation with the Germans, supported Lamsdorff: *C'est monstrueux! Cela* (the agreement of Björkö) *nous déshonore envers la France!*[6] France's financial resources were badly needed to "restore order" in Russia.[7] In 1906 she needed 1 200 million Frances, which Paris did not give until Russia had supported France at the algeciras Conference.[8] Russia's need of money kept her true to the Dual Alliance.

[1] Paléologue p. 140—141
[2] Bülow p. 144
    Isvolsky: *Mémoires* p. 59
[3] PRO/FO 181/841 p. 11 Hardinge to Lansdowne 11. X 1905
[4] PRO/FO 181/841 p. 50 Hardinge to Lansdowne 21. X 1905
[5] GP 19 II n. 6254 Nicholas II to William II 10/23 XI 1905
[6] Paléologue p. 140—141
[7] Isvolsky: *Mémoires* p. 68, 168
[8] Poidevin p. 72

Of course the Germans were displeased and tried to assert that the Czar's signature was binding for Russia; this caused some anxieties for the Russians later.

There is no trace of the idea of closing the Baltic in the disputes in St. Petersburg concerning the Björkö agreement. Rumours indicating such intentions were denied with resolution. It is most probable that if the Czar ever mentioned such a wish, it was inspired by the Emperor William. The matter was considered only in the Russian press. The *Rus'* was of the opinion that closing the Baltic would only be to the German advantage. If Germany succeeded in embroiling Russia in a conflict in the West as she had succeeded in the Far East, she would then be able to isolate Russia from France as much on the sea as she was doing on land. Russia would gain only in the very problematical case of a war with Great Britain, and as long as she had no navy.[1]

Novoe Vremja vrote that Germany might attempt to force a Swedish prince on to the throne of Norway in order to prepare for a Scandinavian union under her own domination. With the aid of this union Germany would be able to keep the Straits open for herself and closed for all others. Russia had every reason to oppose such schemes. As long as she had no fleet the closing of the Straits might be advantageous for her, but as soon as the fleet was rebuilt the situation would be identical with that of the Black Sea. Therefore she ought to try to prevent Scandinavia falling wholly under foreign influence. It was easy enough to do this by securing the friendship of the three Scandinavian states — she had traditionally good relations with Denmark, had recently acquired Norway's gratitude, and might win Sweden over by changing her policy in Finland.[2]

About the situation in Denmark *Novoe Vremja* wrote that the Danes feared a conflict between England and Germany and foresaw in this situation difficulties in preserving their neutrality. There was the danger of being conquered by Germany, which might be countered by concentrating the defence forces in Copenhagen and leaving the Straits exposed, or by an alliance with the Northern neighbours.[3] The *Svet* thought that it was possible and sensible for Germany to occupy Denmark, the only problem being whether to withdraw troops at the end of the conflict. As Great Britain did not possess the forces to prevent Germany, the only power able to exert pressure was Russia. That was why both London and Berlin tried to win her over. But Russia ought to stay outside the conflicts of England and Germany.[4]

The lack of enthusiasm for the closure was in harmony with the views of the leaders of Russian foreign policy, which have been discussed earlier. There was no reason for Russia to bottle herself up in the Baltic, especially if she had

---

[1] *Rus'* 2/15. VIII 1905
[2] *Novoe Vremja* 16/29. VIII 1905
[3] *Novoe Vremja* 19. IX/2. X 1905
[4] *Svet* 20. IX/3. X 1905

some hopes that the situation would develop in a more advantageous direction for her. Russia would rebuild her navy and be strong again in the Baltic. And the dissolution of the Scandinavian Union and the consequent development of Swedo-Norwegian relations promised well for her.

The Russian view on the Scandinavian conflict

When the Scandinavian Union was breaking up, the Russian vice-consul in Hammerfest Zur-Mühlen pondered upon the eventualities of the situation in Norway from what he understood to be the Russian viewpoint. Jungar has stated that these views had some weight in St. Petersburg notwithstanding Zur-Mühlen's lowly position.[1] A negative factor from the Russian point of view was the fear, expressed for instance by Sven Hedin, that Russia would attempt to take the Finmark coast now that she had been checked in the Far East. In spite of this apprehension there was not much chance of Björnstjerne Björnson's fanciful Pan-Germanism being realized. Commercial relations and the Emperor William's personal popularity were not enough to eliminate the prevalent sympathies for England and France. The most dangerous rival for Russia was Great Britain, who with her mighty fleet was the first essential for Norway's maritime commerce. Norway's co-operation with Britain created difficulties for Russia. If Russia intended to build a great naval base on her northern coast, which was free from ice the year round, the security of navigation along the Norwegian coast would be to her of essential importance. An ice-free sea, which Russia had sought for in the Far East, was in the immediate vicinity, and Russia needed only to use what she possessed. Of course it was not the moment to start new enterprises in the North when Russia was wholly occupied in solving other questions, but the internal situation in Norway was propitious for preparing future development in Russia's favour. Norway would surely appreciate Russia's sympathy and helping hand.[2] — Pohlebkin, who has published this document, has left out a couple of sentences, which Jungar has found: The gratitude of and influence on the Norwegians might help Russia to some fjord for her navy; and because Sweden was irreconcilably hostile to Russia, her weakening as a result of the dissolution of the Union was beneficial.[3] — Pohlebkin tries to show that Swedish allegations of the Russian danger were groundless, but when concealing these compromising sentences he seems to have given them too much weight. Zur-Mühlen was after all only a vice-consul, not the maker of the Russian foreign policy; it is not unnatural that during the era of imperialism he dreamed of enlarging his Fatherland in the direction

[1] Jungar p. 85
[2] Pohlebkin: *Priznanie* .. n. 2 Zur-Mühlen to the II department of the Russian F. O. 13. II 1905
[3] Jungar p. 86 note

of his own regions of activity. It does not prove anything unusually sinister about Russian policy; the vice-consul's views have importance only as far as they are in accordance with and explain Russia's later action. Of course the British would have been very much troubled if they had known of these opinions, which were exactly what the Admiralty was afraid of.(p. 67—)

In fact Russia seems to have had no intention of attacking the North during the years preceding the First World War. But naturally there was no means of knowing for sure beforehand that the Far East and the Near East would so completely absorb all Russian energy as to leave nothing over for expansion in the North-West.

After the break-up of the Union Russia set to work to gain the gratitude of the Norwegians. We have seen how the Emperors together at Björkö disapproved of the choice of Prince Charles of Denmark for the Norwegian throne and how the Czar Nicholas would have preferred Prince Valdemar of Denmark. But from Stockholm the Russian chargé d'affaires reported that no one besides Prince Charles of Denmark or Prince Charles Bernadotte had any chance of being accepted in Norway. However, any monarchy was preferable to a republic, which was a real danger, the Norwegians having strong democratic tendencies. A republic would be a danger for Russia not only in the principle of the thing but also because a republic would more easily fall under foreign, especially British influence.[1] And the Russian envoy in Stockholm Budberg wrote to Lamsdorff: "These questions have an interest for us both on account of the Straits and on account of the interest with which Finnish chauvinism observes the events in the Peninsula. ."[2] Isvolsky from Copenhagen referred to Sven Hedin's belief "that a rupture of the Union between Sweden and Norway leads to the occupation of Finmark by Russia" and warned that Hedin might find credence being well known for his personal knowledge of Russia.[3] — Thus there was every reason to handle the Norwegians carefully and drop the Russian candidate, who had no chance anyway, in order to avoid the danger of a republic in Norway. The Russian diplomats seem to have feared the danger of Great Britain closing the Danish Straits from Norway against Russia, and the bad example of the republicans in Norway on the malcontents in Finland and Russia. There was no mention of naval plans in the north.

These were the views of Russian representatives, while Lamsdorff was reticent as usual. Evidently he accepted the views of his subordinates; in any case Russia accepted the candidature of Prince Charles. Wedel thinks that Russia's revolution prevented her from attending to her interests.[4] From the foregoing it

---

[1] Pohlebkin: *Priznanie...* n. 21 Stahl von Holstein to Lamsdorff 14/27 VII 1905
[2] AVPR fond kanceljarija 1905 g. delo 111 tom I n. 274 Budberg to Lamsdorff 19. VI/2. VII 1905
[3] AVPR fond kanceljarija 1905 g. delo 35 n. 23 Isvolsky to Lamsdorff 29. VI/? 1905
[4] Wedel p. 93

seems, however, that Russia understood that winning the sympathy of the Norwegians was more important than the person of the future king, with which Wedel was pre-occupying himself.

In the critical days of June 1905 the Russian Consul-General in Christiania Tötterman asked for instructions on how to deal with the "rebellious" government, and the Government in St. Petersburg inquired as to the attitude of the other great powers.[1] From Isvolsky came a report that the powers had instructed the consuls to safeguard their compatriots and to keep aloof from the provisional government.[2] — It was important not to compromise one's nation by too eager and premature official support, but at the same time not to be left behind the rival powers by being over-cautious.

The difficulties which these relations with an unrecognized government caused were demonstrated when the Russian fishery protection ship "Bakan" returned from the North to the Baltic. She was to visit Norwegian ports, but the problem was whether she had to salute the Norwegian flag without the emblem of the Union.[3] The difficulty could not be solved, "abstention being the sole know answer for the exigencies of the actual situation"[4] and the Bakan was consequently stripped of her status as a warship which had to give the naval salute.[5] Tötterman very nearly spoiled the difficult game by accepting an official message concerning the forming of the provisional government, thereby recognizing it facto.[6] An order was hurriedly sent to Christiania to return the message and excuse the incident by referring to the consul's lack of diplomatic experience.[7] Privately the Russians then tried to repair the consequences of this mistake by explaining to the Norwegians that no insult was implied against Norway; they had only wanted to observe correct diplomatic forms. *Au contraire nous étions animés des meilleurs sentiments envers la Norvège* Budberg insisted.[8]

Les meilleurs sentiments were set to work when the Karlstad conference was interrupted.

The Franco-Russian intervention

The negotiations in Karlstad did not proceed smoothly. The Swedes demanded that the Norwegians dismantle some fortifications on the border. The

[1] Pohlebkin: *Priznanie.* . n. 9 Russian F.O. to Stahl von Holstein 21. V/3. VI 1905
[2] Pohlebkin: *Priznanie.* . n. 8 Isvolsky to Lamsdorff n. 20. V/2. VI 1905
   Pohlebkin: *Priznanie.* . n. 10 Russian F.O. to Isvolsky 21. V/3. VI 1905
[3] Pohlebkin: *Priznanie.* . 23 Varenius to Russian F.O. 10/23 VIII 1905
[4] Pohlebkin: *Priznanie.* . n. 24 Tötterman to Budberg 15/28 VIII 1905
[5] Pohlebkin: *Priznanie.* . n. 25 Varenius to Russian F.O. 21. VIII/3. IX 1905
[6] Pohlebkin: *Priznanie.* . n. 14 Budberg to Lamsdorff 28. V/10. VI 1905
[7] Pohlebkin: Priznanie. . n. 16 Budberg to Lamsdorff 30. V/12. VI 1905
[8] AVPR fond kanceljarija 1905 g. delo 111 tom I n. 270 Budberg to Lamsdorff 9/22 VI 1905

5

Norwegians regarded the demand to destroy historical fortifications as an affront and as a provocation. The Swedes thought that the Norwegians deliberately misunderstood the demand, which referred only to modern forts. After a few days of bickering the negotiations were suspended, the delegates travelled home for fresh instructions and the outbreak of war was feared.

Once more the Norwegians sought international help. In Copenhagen Nansen told Raben the Norwegian version of the facts. "Raben was afraid that Sweden was going to begin military operations . . and asked the interested powers in the interest of peace . . to ask the Swedish government to consent to settle the question of the ancient fortifications amically with the Norwegians . ." [1] Lamsdorff sent instructions to Budberg to agree immediately with the other envoys on a common démarche to the Swedish Minister for Foreign Affairs urging him to make all efforts to avert the anticipated conflict.[2] Budberg evidently understood that the Swedes would not like such a démarche — usual in Constantinople and the Balkans — and proposed instead only a simultaneous and verbal message. The German and the British representatives did not wish to participate in the démarche "having no instructions", and the French envoy had already delivered his message. Thus Budberg decided to support his French colleague by saying that "the Swedish Government would earn the gratitude of Europe if they prevented a bloody conflict".[3]

So the first step to win the gratitude of the Norwegians had been taken. There is no source showing what Lamsdorff thought of the situation. It is possible that Isvolsky's report about the threat of war made him really anxious, as it would very probably have led to intervention by Germany or Great Britain, or to a Swedish victory, while Russia had no forces to spare to send to Scandinavia.

It has been a somewhat sore point, to the Swedes, whether the démarche made Sweden consent to continue negotiations in Karlstad or whether Sweden decided independently to do so. In any case the Swedes has learned that no great power wanted an open conflict.[4]

The British wait and see

Again Johnstone advocated the Norwegian cause, even more eagerly than before. He sent a message straight from the meeting of Raben, Wedel, Nansen, the German chargé d'affaires and himself where the request for intervention was made, and in the message he said that "Nansen laid great stress on (the) influence (which the) friendly offices of His Majesty's Government would have

---

[1] Pohlebkin: *Priznanie.* . n. 26 Isvolsky to Lamsdorff 28. VIII/10. IX 1905
[2] Pohlebkin: *Priznanie.* . n. 27 Lamsdorff to Budberg 29. VIII/11. IX 1905
[3] Pohlebkin: *Priznanie.* . n. 28. Budberg to Lamsdorff 2/15 IX 1905
[4] Jungar p. 90—91

on influencing (the) Norwegian people. Two days later he tried to teach his superiors something about statesmanship: "Your Lordship will be able to judge whether the Power amongst these four who takes the lead in a friendly intervention will or will not be regarded by Norway as having a claim on their gratitude when the moment arrives for the choice of a Norwegian Sovereign".[1]

Johnstone had no success in persuading his superiors. The Foreign Office minuted: "This savours of Baron Wedel."[2] Nor was Johnstone's schoolmasterly tone liked in London: "I think he is rather too much inclined to hustle us. The policy of the Government cannot be dictated from Copenhagen". And Lansdowne concluded: ". . It is not at all likely that Norway will bear us any ill-will hereafter for having moved cautiously — we have done so in her interests".[3]

The British policy was not to be turned from its course by minor statesmen. Rennell Rodd in Stockholm acquired information as to the reasons why the Karlstad conference had broken down. From Crown Prince Gustaf he learned that the Swedes had demanded the destruction of only the outer forts, which the Norwegians had consented to dismantle but not to destroy; and that no ultimatum had been presented. There were reasonable chances of reaching a solution after the delegates had received new instructions.[4] London had no necessity to act on such an unsure ground as Johnstone's information.

Nansen visited London and judging from what he said in the Foreign Office he was evidently honestly worried by Sweden's aggressive intentions.[5] Of course it is possible that Gustaf had described to Rennell Rodd the Swedish attitude as being more peaceful than it in fact was, but it seems more probable that in the tense situation excitement and nervousness had caused the Norwegians to regard the Swedish attitude as more menacing than it was in reality. What is relevant, however, is what was believed in London. — Nansen tried to explain the Norwegian point of view in the Foreign Office. He could not see Lord Lansdowne, who was in Ireland, and the permanent officials only listened to him without promising any support.[6] Even King Edward, who had earlier so eagerly supported the policy emanating from Copenhagen, accepted the view of the Foreign Office.[7]

But of course the coldness was only on the outside. The British did not wish to stiffen the Norwegian attitude by promising support, but the Swedes felt very

---

[1] PRO/FO 22/585 Johnstone to Lansdowne 10. IX 1905
[2] PRO/FO 22/585 Johnstone to Lansdowne 12. IX 1905
[3] PRO/FO 22/584 Johnstone to Lansdowne 12. IX 1905, minutes by T. A. S(anderson) and L(ansdowne)
[4] PRO/FO 181/857 Rennell Rodd to Lansdowne 10. IX 1905
[5] PRO/FO 181/857 note by T. Sanderson 14. IX 1905
[6] PRO/FO 181/857 note by T. Sanderson 14. IX 1905
[7] PRO/FO 22/585 Lansdowne to Johnstone 13. IX 1905

well the gentle pressure of Great Britain, "in a friendly and unofficial manner."[1] Lansdowne said to Bildt, the Swedish envoy in London:".. we had refrained from sending Rennell Rodd any special instructions at this moment as we did not wish to show any want of confidence in the wisdom and moderation of the Swedish Government".[2] — It must have been delightful to show one's own considerateness after the blunder of the French and the Russians. The British press, not quite so considerate, partly inspired by Nansen, disapproved of the Swedish demands, and Swedish propaganda did not succeed in redressing this view.[3]

At this time, too, Rennell Rodd was putting forward the Swedish point of view to the Foreign Office. He thought that the Norwegians had obtained the support of the great powers on false premises[4] and that the Swedes had behaved correctly all the time in spite of provocation. He thought that, if necessary, the proposition for mediation ought to be addressed to both parties, or preferably "the powers should inform Norway that it is her duty to accept Sweden's final concessions".[5]

It has been said that the Norwegians also tried to make the Emperor William II interested in arbitrating the quarrel, but without succes.[6] In the light of what has been said earlier of the attitude of the German government it is understandable that they did not wish to intervene in the squabble.

And after all no mediation was needed. The Swedes said that from the very beginning they had referred only to the modern fortifications, and these the Norwegians consented to raze. A neutral zone was set up on both sides of the border, and an international commission was asked to supervise the work of demolition. Other questions, the rights of the Lapps for instance, did not involve "national honour" and were easily solved. It was also agreed that either states would be liable for the obligations of the Union separately and on its own behalf only.

The outcome of the negotiations in Karlstad was accepted by the Swedish Riksdag, and King Oscar vacated the Norwegian throne. Thus the independence of Norway was recognized on the 26th of October 1905. Norway survived the long crisis without direct intervention by Great Britain and without the hazardous schemes of Wedel. The relations between Norway and Great Britain and Sweden were in the main unimpaired; those of Norway and Sweden were formally correct but much time was needed to heal hurt feelings. Now was the

---

1 PRO/FO 22/585 Lansdowne to Johnstone 13. IX 1905 minutes
2 PRO/FO 73/652 Sanderson to Rennell Rodd 15. IX 1905
3 Nansen p. 25, 35, 59
  Hildebrand p. 322
4 PRO/FO 73/651 Rennell Rodd to Lansdowne 15. IX 1905
5 PRO/FO 73/651 Rennell Rodd to Sanderson 16. IX 1905
6 Lindberg: *Den Svenska.* . p. 168—

time to take up the question of securing the international position of Scandinavia by a new treaty.

The origin of the Norwegian treaty of guarantee

We have already seen that the British regarded the renewal of the Treaty of 1855 as the most appropriate safeguard for their interests in the North; but the renewal was planned in a new form, not against Russia as before. It was thought that the signature of all the powers concerned in the Northern question would prevent any one of them from invading Scandinavia.

The renewal of the treaty of 1855 was mentioned a few times during the Union crisis in the summer and autumn of 1905. Wedel discussed it, among other topics; he seems to have understood that the new treaty would be something like a reward by Great Britain for the choice of Prince Charles for the Norwegian throne [1]; that is, for the refusal of Norway to let other powers have anything to say in the matter. During the break-down of the Karlstad conference Nansen feared a sudden attack by Sweden and expressed an idea "that in order to make more evident the advantages of electing Prince Charles of Denmark as King, Gt. Britain, possibly in conjunction with other powers, should guarantee in some form the maintenance in peace & war of the neutral zone on the frontier between the two countries. ." [2] These discussions had no immediate result.

Norway survived the crisis after all without the help of Prince Charles. The offer of the Norwegian crown had originally implied that the prince ought to be the ace with which Norway would obtain the support of Denmark and Great Britain. Thus the offer could be regarded as lapsed and the constitution of Norway had to be decided anew.

At the beginning of October 1905 Nansen told Lansdowne that the republicans were gaining strength in Norway and that there was some idea of postponing the final decision until the autumn of 1906. Then he asked about the eventual renewal of the guarantee of the Treaty of 1855 — whether it would be extended to the two kingdoms after their separation, and whether such a guarantee would be more difficult to obtain if Norway adopted a republican form of government. Lansdowne explained that the renewal would depend on the relations between Norway and Sweden, and that it was not impossible for Great Britain to guarantee a republic, but "the selection of Prince Charles might predispose the public opinion here in favour of the Guarantee". [3]

---

[1] Wedel p. 52—59

[2] PRO/FO 181/857 note by Th. Sanderson 14. IX 1905
Nansen p. 14—20

[3] PRO/FO 73/649 Lansdowne to Rennell Rodd 4. X 1905
Nansen p. 75—76

Nansen was not rude à la Wedel but one gets the impression that "the stick of a republic" was once more being "shaken at" the British to obtain their support for Norway in the form of a new treaty. A little later Nansen wrote that the republican movement was not dangerous "if only we can get aid as indicated". Officially Lansdowne could not say anything before the definite abrogation by Sweden and the election of the Norwegian Sovereign, but unofficially he promised that Great Britain would recognise Norway de facto as soon as all was clear with Sweden, and would "endeavour to renew the guarantee included in the treaty of 1855". And Lansdowne promised that his communication might be used confidentially to persuade the republicans.[1] Nansen understood that the election of Prince Charles would bring Norway an immediate and obvious advantage in facilitating the renewal of the treaty of 1855.[2]

These discussions are recorded in much more detail by Wedel and Nansen than by the official documents of the British Foreign Office — after all the Northern question was only a minor factor in British policy, while for the Scandinavians it constituted essential question of independence, constitution, and foreign relations. This account of course shows how the Norwegians understood Lansdowne's words, and perhaps they understood more than was in fact implied, but there is no cause to believe that they really misunderstood or misrepresented them. Lord Lansdowne's successor, Sir Edward Grey, later admitted that Lansdowne had promised the treaty of guarantee to Norway in return for a kingdom with Prince Charles as King, and felt bound by the promise.[3] And this is easy to understand because the treaty was in Great Britain's own interest so that she did not expect to lose anything by this promise.

The practical difficulties and differencies were overcome and the republicans turned out to be not so dangerous after all. When Sweden renounced the Union on the 26th October, Prince Charles was elected King of Norway by 87 votes to 29 in the Storthing, and by 259 536 to 69 204 in the referendum. He took his oath on 27th November as Haakon VII.

The steeple-chase of recognizing Norway

The next step the Russians took in Norway was a countermove to the supposed British schemes. The Norwegian Premier Michelsen wrote to Lamsdorff after the Karlstad conference thanking him for "the invaluable services by the Imperial Government to both Norway and Sweden which helped to solve the crisis with justice". He then asked whether the Russian Government would accept Norwegian diplomatic and consular representatives and send a Russian

[1] Nansen p. 111
[2] Nansen p. 120—
[3] BD 8 n. 98 appendix, note by E. G. 19. IX 1907

envoy to Norway.[1] Lamsdorff answered that Russia would be only too happy to do so as soon as the agreement of the Karlstad conference was ratified and the separation of Sweden and Norway duly notified to all the powers.[2]

But then the Russians heard rumours about the plans for renewing the anti-Russian treaty of 1855. Budberg's French colleague had said to him that his Government had remarked 'not only on one occasion' that the ancient treaty was one of the questions on which he had to keep watch. According to Budberg the British Government was drawing Norway into the orbit of its politics and might suddenly propose to guarantee Norwegian integrity against the so-called Russian demands on Norway. Why else had Great Britain supported Prince Charles if not to strengthen her influence in Norway? "It seems to me (Budberg) undisputable that some activity is taking place". Russia had better react before it was too late. Wasn't it possible, after the Union was formally abrogated by Sweden, to add to the Russian recognition of Norwegian independence an annex which would make all thought of renewing the treaty of 1855 superfluous, gain Russia the gratitude of the new state, and strengthen Russo-Norwegian friendship, thereby preventing Norway from submitting to any objectionable influence?[3] In June 1905 the Russian Foreign Office had engaged as jurisconsult Professor Martens's pupil Baron Michael von Taube, who was to become very much preoccupied with the Northern question. He later took upon himself the honour of being the author of the Russian recognition of Norway's independence[4] — although the honour of being the initiator must go to Budberg. — Taube explained that in Sweden those who kept up the fear of the Russian danger tried to keep Sweden and Norway together by any means; this fear had to be eliminated in Norway in order to make her attitude more positive towards Russia.[5]

Lamsdorff adopted Budberg's proposition and submitted to the Czar that "England was going to take a step which was openly hostile to Russia . . had a serious significance for the Imperial Government, because they had no kind of aggressive plans against Norway, and was evidence of the notorious aspirations of England". To negative British schemes Russia had to recognize Norway as an independent state and express in a definite form Russian recognition of this new state in its territorial integrity. Russia had as soon as possible to accredit an envoy to Christiania, and this done, the envoy had immediately and confidentially to inform the Norwegian ministers that Russia looked upon the renewal of the treaty of 1855 with England as a deed not in harmony with good

[1] Pohlebkin: *Priznanie*. . n. 32 Michelsen to Lamsdorff 23. IX/6. X 1905
[2] Pohlebkin: *Priznanie*. . n. 33 Lamsdorff to Michelsen draft 28. IX/11. X 1905
[3] Pohlebkin: *Priznanie*. . n. 34 Budberg to Lamsdorff 6/19 X 1905
[4] Taube: *La politique russe*. . p. 125—
[5] = 4

neighbourly relations, especially after the recognition of Norway's territorial integrity by Russia. Then the question of the revision of the Russo-Norwegian border could be taken up with the new Norwegian Government, as agreed in 1847.[1] — All who were afraid of Russia would probably have found confirmation of their fears in the last sentence, but evidently Lamsdorff did not think of the conquest of Finmark but really of some minor revision of the border.

Immediately after Sweden had formally recognized the abrogation of the Union, Lamsdorff hurried (on 28th October) to remind Michelsen of their recent correspondence and inquired when Norway was going to ask officially for the recognition of her independence.[2] Of course the Norwegians were willing, too, and on the same day the Norwegian Minister for Foreign Affairs Lövland sent a notification of the dissolution of the Union and asked for the opening of official relations as soon as possible.[3] Lamsdorff procured by telegram the authorization of the Czar[4] and sent a message to Christiania on the 29th October recognizing Norway *'en qualité d'Etat complétement indépendent, dans tout son integrité territorielle* . .[5] Apparently the Czarist regime could move quickly when the need was there.

The Russian countermove did not kill the British plan of renewing the treaty of 1855, but the scheme was not as sinister as the Russians apprehended. The British view on the Russian guarantee was deprecating (p. 93) but evidently the Russians had collected a point in giving recognition first and in the generous form, for which "warm gratitude" was expressed by Lövland.[6]

The British picked up the next minor point. While other powers remained waiting for the election of the Norwegian King, to whom their envoys would be accredited, the British sent Mr. Herbert from Darmstadt as a temporary representative until he could present his credentials to the future King.[7] The Russians saw this as an effort to influence the election of the king.[8] Budberg wrote to Lamsdorff "the representative of Great Britain is not only nominated . . but he has already taken possession of his post. I have been told that Germany will also send to Christiania a career diplomat. . *C'est un steeplechase à qui arrivera premier et aura le pas, fait auquel au fond dans ce cas je ne comprends pas trop qu'on attache grand importance* . ."[9]

---

[1] Pohlebkin: *Priznanie*. . n. 35 Lamsdorff to Czar 6/19 X 1905
[2] Pohlebkin: *Priznanie*. . n. 37 Lamsdorff to Budberg (to Tötterman) 15/28 X 1905
[3] Pohlebkin: *Priznanie*. . n. 38 Lövland to Russian Govt. 15/28 X 1905
[4] Pohlebkin: *Priznanie*. . n. 39 Lamsdorff to Czar 16/29 X 1905
[5] Pohlebkin: *Priznanie*. . n. 40 Lamsdorff to Lövland 16/29 X 1905
  Pohlebkin: *Priznanie*. . n. 43 Pravitelstvennyj Vestnik 17/30 X 1905
[6] Pohlebkin: *Priznanie*. . n. 47 Lövland to Lamsdorff 20. X/2. XI 1905
[7] Pohlebkin: *Priznanie*. . n. 46 Benckendorff to Lamsdorff 20. X/2. XI 1905
[8] Pohlebkin: *Priznanie*. . n. 54 Tötterman to Lamsdorff 23. X/5. XI 1905
[9] AVPR fond kanceljarija 1905 g., delo 111, tom I, n. 290 Budberg to Lamsdorff 26. X/8. XI 1905

But Lamsdorff could not rest on the laurels gained through the recognition of Norway, he wanted to take part in the steeple-chase and send an envoy to Christiania to explain the reason why Norway should not renew the November Treaty of 1855. If the protest was postponed until the new treaty was signed, it would obviously be too late. Lamsdorff thought that in order to ward off the endeavours to conclude an anti-Russian treaty like that of 1855 between England and Norway alone Russia might join in a general guarantee of Norwegian integrity by all the great powers. The revision of the borders could also be postponed, according to the circumstances, to a more favourable moment.[1]

It is possible that Lamsdorff had heard of Lansdowne's views on the renewal of the November treaty. In any case he was disposed to accept the very proposition which the British Secretary of State preferred. Thus, in spite of the fact that Britain suspected Russia and Russia suspected Britain of the most sinister schemes, their plans were in practice not wholly contradictory. — A little later Isvolsky reported what Wedel had revealed about his discussions with Lansdowne: that England in fact endeavoured to make a new treaty, not with Norway against Russia, but with all the interested powers against unnamed aggressors.[2]

The instructions given to the new envoy, Anatoli Krupensky, shed light on Lamsdorff's standpoint: It ought to be easy to convince the Norwegians of Russian benevolence because their relations were good and the Norwegians had always been more friendly than the Swedes. The Imperial Government could not adopt an unconcerned attitude to the endeavours to renew the treaty of 1855, whether they were initiated in Stockholm in order to impede the progress of good relations between Russia and Norway, or whether they were "the notorious pursuits of the English government". The envoy must make the Norwegians understand their mistake in restricting their freedom of action as the first international act of their independence.

Turning from the Norwegian affairs to broader aspects, Lamsdorff remarked that there was a possibility of a Pan-Scandinavian Union. The two million Danes had been reluctant to submit to the Swedish Government which had seven million subjects in the former Union, but together the Danes and the Norwegians without any danger could balance the five million Swedes. The danger was not great at the moment, but it called forth serious attention from Russia. Coupled with this question was the problem of free navigation in the Straits, the importance of which had been shown during the war with Japan.[3] — It has already been shown what Lamsdorff thought and did about this question. But this is a useful reminder that although the Norwegian treaty of

---

[1] Pohlebkin: *Priznanie*. . n. 56 Lamsdorff to Czar 27. X/9. XI 05
[2] Pohlebkin: *Priznanie*. . n. 60 Isvolsky to Lamsdorff 10/23. XI 1905
[3] Pohlebkin: *Priznanie*. . n. 58 Instructions for the envoy in Christiania, draft 4/17 XI 1905

guarantee was being discussed, Norway was not concerned alone. We are faced all the time with the Northern alias the Baltic question, the central point of which was the problem of the status of the Danish Straits.

In December 1905 Krupensky proceeded to Christiania and hastened to say to Lövland that "now there was less ground than ever to show such lack of confidence towards Russia as the renewal of the November treaty would prove".[1] Lövland answered that personally he deemed any treaty useless — which was a lie — but if "due to some political changes or unforeseeable circumstances the Norwegian government would consider such a guarantee useful" Lövland assured Krupensky that the treaty would be not only with the Wester powers but also with Germany and especially "with the great and mighty Russia, our friendly and benevolent neighbour".[2] And Krupensky reported as a judgement on Lövland that "his intention of preserving some independence in relations with England seems to me to earn appreciation, especially as the opinion is here prevalent that Great Britain rendered a great service to Norway in preventing Sweden from starting a war against her".[3]

In March 1906 Lövland made a speech in the Storthing which gave birth to rumours that negotiations concerning the renewal of the ancient treaty were in progress.[4] Krupensky reported "without doubt the Norwegian government have decided to replace this treaty with a collective guarantee of Norwegian integrity in the form of a diplomatic act which, while achieving the aims followed by the Norwegian Government, in full measure takes into account our legitimate remarks and fears. Because the form of the replacement does not seem to have been decided on, the Imperial Government may have a dominating influence on the solving of this question".[5]

Thus, even if Russia had not been able to prevent the Norwegians from striving for the treaty of guarantee, the danger of a treaty against Russia, which Sweden and England were thought to be aiming at, seemed to be averted. In joining the eventual guarantee Russia might break the lance pointed against herself.

But before the negotiations on the Norwegian treaty of guarantee started in earnest, the Russian government was changed.

[1] Pohlebkin: *Priznanie.* . n. 66 Krupensky to Lamsdorff 8/21 XII 1905
[2] Pohlebkin: *Priznanie.* . n. 68 Krupensky to Lamsdorff 12/25. XII 1905
[3] Pohlebkin: *Priznanie.* . n. 70 Krupensky to Lamsdorff 12/25. XII 1905
[4] e.g. *Le Temps* 8. III 1906
[5] Pohlebkin: *Priznanie.* . n. 76 Krupensky to Lamsdorff 28. III/8. IV 1906

ISVOLSKY TAKES CHARGE

The background of Isvolsky's Baltic policy

The changes in the Russian machinery of government caused by the attempted revolution of 1905 led to the replacement of the leader of Russian foreign policy. The old bureaucrat Lamsdorff could not stand the thought of facing the Duma and answering for foreign policy. The envoy in Copenhagen, Isvolsky, who had expected to become ambassador in Rome *(macaroni)* or Berlin *(sauerkraut)* received the coded message *caviar* — Minister for Foreign Affairs in St. Petersburg.[1] This man has been described in contradictory words by various authors. The Russian diplomatist Rosen wrote: "He impressed me as a gifted youth of great intelligence and, for his years, a remarkably cultivated mind. In later years . . he was by long odds the ablest man in our service. His solid condition, his breadth of view, his profound understanding and thorough earnestness in the treatment of the affairs of State, his liberal mind trained in the school of Western political thought, stamped him as . . a real statesman in the European sense". This very favourable appraisal may be partly explained by the next sentence: "The telegraph has recently announced his death".[2] Lee, the biographer of King Edward VII, wrote that "Isvolsky's fashionable airs, his diplomatic monocle, his precious phraseology, oracular utterances and epigrammatic remarks often repelled new acquaintances, and even some of his friends pictured him as a self-centred pompous *petit-maître* who lacked the essential qualities of statesmanship and was fitted at most to translate simple ideas into the stately language of diplomacy. Yet he was a man of generous sympathies, of well-balanced judgement, and harmonious temper, whose extreme purity of style and language was but the outcome of a habit of clear thinking. He was a loyal friend and a magnanimous adversary, and throughout his career he maintained a high reputation of honour and integrity".[3] Edward VII and the Scandinavian statesmen who participated in the Baltic question had a different opinion: Edward said about Isvolsky that "He doesn't always tell the truth", to which Raben answered "He only sometimes tells the truth".[4] The French Ambassador Bompard said that Isvolsky was too enlightened to support the reactionary views of the Russian court; he was moderately liberal, but his snobbishness and vanity handicapped his very real abilities.[5] Bülow was of the same opinion and says that Isvolsky was as ugly as a Kalmuck, so that a woman who had refused to marry him said *Je l'ai regretté tous les jours* — because he had

---

[1] Bülow p. 294
[2] Rosen I p. 172—173
[3] Lee p. 284
[4] AA Dänemark 37 geheim Bd 17 note by Schoen 1. VII 1908
[5] Bompard p. 208

succeeded in the world — *mais je m'en suis félicitée toutes les nuits.*[1] — In the progress of this narrative we shall see how able, energetic and resourceful but also unscrupulous Isvolsky was. Evidently he acted for the best interests of Russia as he understood them, but it may be true that he went too far in identifying his personal career with the success of Russia, and his vanity with her honour.

Becoming Foreign Minister he inherited the bankrupt foreign policy of an empire near collapse.[2] The adventure in the Far East had resulted in defeat, which led to a revolutionary uprising. With difficulty the revolution was liquidated in 1906—1907, but the future was still not promising for Czarism. Russia had no more any reason to act aggressively in the Far East, and the most important task of the new minister was to disentangle Russia from Asia and from the menace of further conflicts. Japan's exhaustion and Witte's skilful performance at Portsmouth had saved Russia from the worst shame and humiliation, and it was possible to create once more tolerable relations with Japan, although long and difficult negotiations were needed up till August 1907.

But although she had done the dirty work Japan was not Russia's principal enemy. She had been financed and, according to Russian view, instigated by England. If Russia wanted to live in peace in Asia, the causes of conflict had to be settled with Great Britain, too. The moment was favourable because England herself had begun to worry about her isolation realizing that the friendship with France and Japan had not solved all her problems. She desired conciliation with her worst rival Russia, and the problem was discussed as early as 1903 and 1904. The Russo-Japanese War interrupted the discussions and at one point led Russia and England to the brink of war (the Dogger Bank incident) when the Czar Nicholas listened to the Emperor William's allurements for a continental coalition. These and Germany's other menacing gestures made England conciliatory, while Russia's defeat eliminated her threat to British interests in the Far East. Of course conciliation was not easy as the ancient animosity could not be nullified at once, and Russia's internal condition in 1906 with pogroms and the dissolution of the First Duma outraged British public opinion.[3] However, with tenacious endeavours the negotiations were carried on. The work was done mainly by Isvolsky himself and by the British ambassador Nicolson with Hardinge's (the Permanent Secretary in the F.O.) support in London. Isvolsky spent the summer of 1906 waiting for the internal situation to clear up and the next winter was needed for preparations in various directions, but during the summer of 1907 a definite step forward was made. Russia's and

[1] Bülow p. 294—295
[2] Isvolsky: *Mémoires* p. 166—167
   Holborn p. 406—
[3] Nicolson p. 206—

Britain's remaining sources of discord around India in Tibet, Afghanistan and Persia were arranged into zones of influence and an agreement was signed on 31st August 1907. The agreement was important with regard to the Turkish Straits, too. (p. 78)

But Isvolsky did not wish to remain in history only as a caretaker of a bankruptcy. He wanted success for the glory of his name. His assistant Taube says that he sought artificial opportunities to become "great" and "magnificent".[1] But it need not have been only personal ambition, for a conspicuous success would have been useful for Czarist regime[2], that is for the Russian interest as Isvolsky must have understood it. "Inability to remove the causes of revolution made Czarism seek for the aura of past glory and the power to turn people's attention away from internal problems"[3] — "an anxious wish to gather support" against the revolutionary movement.[4]

Isvolsky's plans were directed to the traditional fields of Russian ambition, the Balkans and the Turkish Straits, where the immediate aim was the right to pass through and the ultimate aim to prevent others from passing. The Russian interest in this direction could be based on arguments of commerce and navigation, of strategy, history and Slavic ties of kinship. Nicolson thought that Isvolsky had been abroad so long that he had become estranged from Russian circumstances and that he therefore overestimated the fascination of *Tsargrad* on the minds of the dissatisfied masses, and on the other hand he did not realize the strength of the nationalism of the Balkan peoples, which explains his mistakes with the Austrians in 1908.[5] Seton-Watson has expressed his astonishment at the fact that the actually not very useful Bosporus was considered so important while the more important Danish Straits were ignored.[6]

Of course it is difficult to try to measure the importance of the two passageways. Only the value of the trade carried through them can be compared numerically; the following percentages of Russian foreign trade were carried via the Black Sea and the Baltic ports:

Carried through	RUSSIAN FOREIGN TRADE			
	Import		Export	
	1905	1910	1905	1910
Black Sea	12,0 %	7,7 %	30,0 %	31,1 %
Baltic	38,9 %	32,7 %	42,4 %	43,0 % [7]

[1] Taube: *La politique russe* . . . p. 123
[2] Eckardt p. 248
[3] S. Patukanis p. 4
[4] Lederer p. 390
[5] Nicolson p. 264
[6] Seton-Watson *The Decline*. . p. 331—
[7] Schroder: *Ostsee*. . p. 61 & 107

Probably part of the commerce remained in the respective inland sea, perhaps a greater percentage in the Baltic than in the Black Sea, but the preponderance of the Baltic direction is evident in any case.

But of course foreign policy is not dictated by economics, at least not directly enough for political activities and the percentages of commerce to be in proportion. Most probably few people thought of anything but warships when the questions of the two straits were discussed. The importance of commerce in war could not be foreseen, and the problem of the straits was appraised usually from the narrow strategic viewpoint.

In any case, as shown here, far from being ignored in St. Petersburg, the Danish Straits was one of the dominant considerations of Russian Baltic policy. The lack of conspicuous Russian activity in the Danish Straits was, of course, due to the fact that there was not much that Russia could have done there. Germany was the dominant power at the Straits. If she was Russia's friend she would prevent her enemies from passing into the Baltic. If she was Russia's enemy she would close the Straits againts her. And beyond Germany there was Great Britain. Russia could not match her on sea nor in the Straits, but when she could she reacted energetically, for instance when she saw the danger of Britain closing the Straits by renewing the treaty of 1855 with Norway.

It was not in Russia's power to change the status quo in Denmark. And of course Copenhagen did not possess the religious and historical enchantment of Constantinople, nor was there in the north any Slavic kin to be freed from the tyranny of the infidel. If Isvolsky's policy was intended as a diversion for the revolutionary masses, there was no sense in choosing the Danish Straits as the aim, their commercial and strategic importance notwithstanding.

In August 1906 the Russian ambassador in Constantinople Zinov'ev sent Isvolsky his famous memorandum on the Turkish Straits urging him to act.[1] But of course Russia could not solve this question only with Turkey. Experience showed that Britain's assent, perhaps even support, was essential. This was another important reason why agreement with her was worth striving for. For the leaders of British foreign policy it was important to divert Russia's attention from the direction of India. Constantinople was a possible compensation for Russia as Morocco had been for France. In november 1906 Hardinge dropped hints about the Turkish Straits, and Isvolsky was delighted, but due to the Japanese difficulties the negotiations were delayed.[2] Later the situation changed and the British may have thought that Russia was asking too much in demanding that only Russian warships might pass the Straits. Russia on the other hand could not consent to opening them for all. The defence of the Black Sea coast

---

[1] Krasnyj Arhiv, tom LXIX—LXX p. 5—18 memorandum by Zinov'ev 25. VII 1906
[2] Carlgren: *Isvolsky und. .* p. 164—

was cheaper if the Straits were closed.[1] So the Straits were not at all mentioned in the Asian agreement which Russia and England concluded, and after that the British had no reason to present the Russians with Constantinople, until the First World War changed the situation once more.

Neither of the signatories of the Asian agreement of 1907 thought of Germany's *Einkreisung* as the Germans apprehended it, the agreement being no alliance, not even an entente. Russia got no help from London or Paris during the Balkan crisis in 1908. But the help which Austria received from Germany strengthened the opinion in Russia that she had to get closer to Great Britain. However, Persia was still a source of discord. The Russian agents would not accept the agreed limits, the Shah would have liked help from the north against his rebellious subjects, while Great Britain guarded her zone of influence jealously.[2]

Austria and Russia had in 1897 and 1903 agreed on preserving the status quo in the Balkans, both being unprepared to press their claims there. This understanding was still undisturbed in 1906 and 1907, until in 1908 the whole question was raised again and Austria manifested herself as Russia's first rival.

Isvolsky's relations with the French were cool. In Copenhagen he had been a candidate for the embassy in Berlin and he was held to be a Germanophile.[3] But the French ambassador in St. Petersburg said that it would be foolish to suspect Isvolsky's loyalty to the Dual Alliance, although the relations of Russia and France were troubled by Russian apprehension that a close relationship with republican France might have adverse effect on the internal situation in Russia.[4] To Bülow Isvolsky said that the alliance with France was and must be the foundation of Russian foreign policy, although it did not signify hostile relations with Germany.[5] The gigantic loans given by France — after Russian support at Algeciras — helped essentially to stifle the revolution, and the military convention was brought up to date in negotiations between the General Staffs in April 1906.[6]

Germany caused the greatest worry to Isvolsky; while he was negotiating with Great Britain, he was all the time glancing nervously in the direction of Berlin.[7] Germany could not afford to believe that the Asian agreement referred only to adjusting concrete causes of quarrel in the distant regions of Asia. The Germans saw the *Einkreisung* closing around them and kicked about in their distress so that it became dangerous for their neighbours.[8]

[1] Hauser p. 112
[2] Hauser p. 111
[3] BD 4 n. 219 Johnstone to Grey 27. V. 1906
[4] Bompard p. 246—, p. 273—
[5] Bülow p. 295—
[6] Salis p. 408
[7] Nicolson p. 253, 262
[8] Bompard p. 255

The conference of Algeciras made the Germans angry with the Russians, whose shortage of money compelled them to follow the lead of Paris. A rumour alleging that Russia had not supported France was disclaimed by Lamsdorff, *Le Temps* published the démenti, and the Emperor William was thoroughly upset because of this public ingratitude for the help he had given Russia during the Russo-Japanese War.[1] At the very beginning of his term as minister Isvolsky received a letter from Benckendorff, who wrote: "More than ever I think that the relations with Berlin must be preserved on, or restored to, an amical foot. On the sole condition that they do not put the knife on our throat. In Berlin imagination sweeps away reason and restraint, and they seem to have lost their head . . "[2] It was realized that Germany could close the Danish Straits and, Britain thus unable to prevent her, might transfer 150 000—200 000 men to the Russian coast. Russia had no fleet to guard her coast, and the Chief of the General staff Palicyn remarked that the Russian army was in no condition, either, to defend the country. Therefore it was of vital importance to remember that Germany was Russia's most dangerous neighbour. She must not be provoked in any way while Russia was negotiating with England.[3]

An ominous precedent was the fate of Delcassé, on whom Germany had wreaked revenge for the entente with England by ruining his career at the time of the Moroccan crisis. Germany had even more plausible ground for ill-humour now, because Britain's and Russia's agreement concerned Persia, in which Germany was much more interested than in Morocco, due to her plans for the Berlin-Baghdad railway. There were reasons enough to fear that the coup of Tangier would be repeated. So it was reasonable to try to treat Germany with consideration, and in the long run also her support might be needed in the struggle against Austria for the domination of the Balkans and Turkish Straits.[4]

In the autumn of 1906, before starting any discussions with the British, Isvolsky travelled around Europe sensing the atmosphere. In Berlin he was "able to become convinced that the *Verstimmung* dating back to Algeciras was even stronger" than he had thought, and he had "to appeal to all his calm to quieten down the first animation of the Emperor William". With energetic assurances that the negotiations "cannot in any case carry us into a political combination directed against Germany", and promises that "if our negotiations came to touch German interests, we were prepared to agree with Germany previous to any discussion" Isvolsky belived that he had succeeded: "So I believe that we can be assured that we are in the future guaranteed against all

[1] Isvolsky: *Mémoires*. . p. 40—
[2] Isvolsky: *Au service*. . n. 1. Benckendorff to Isvolsky 3/16. V 1906
[3] Trubetzkoi p. 125
  Istorija diplomatii p. 614
[4] *Istorija diplomatii* p. 617

German attempts to renew in Persia the Moroccan coup".[1] From Berlin Isvolsky proceeded to Paris but demonstratively avoided London in spite of an
invitation by Edward VII. To Clemenceau he had explained that there were
people whom he had to *ménager* until the time were ripe for the Asian agreement, and the Frenchman understood of course that William was alluded to.[2]

Notwithstanding his succes in Berlin Isvolsky naturally knew that he had to
keep the mighty neighbour constantly humoured. In March 1907 he explained
to the French ambassador that Germany was still secretly annoyed at his rapprochement with the British.[3] Evidently Berlin needed some concrete proof of
Isvolsky's good intentions towards Germany, verbal assurances were not
enough.

Subsequently we shall see Isvolsky in very intimate collaboration with the
Germans in the Baltic question. In the light of the preceding passages it is
evident that this collaboration must be interpreted as an attempt to prove in
practice that Russia had not, in spite of the Asian agreement, become England's
ally or Germany's enemy. The Baltic treaty, which Isvolsky proposed to the
Germans, was a counterweight to the Asian agreement to secure Russia against
surprises in Europe.

Lindberg sees the attempt to abrogate the humiliating servitude in the Åland
Islands as the central factor in Isvolsky's Baltic policy, in which Germany's
help against Sweden was needed. Protection against the German danger is
mentioned only as an incidental factor.[4] This view is understandable from the
horizon of Stockholm, but is it really conceivable that Isvolsky would have used
a sledgehammer to strike a pin?

Anybody backing Isvolsky?

This is a point where more than ever I must regret the self-imposed limitation of my study. The diplomatic sources seldom illuminate the factors in the
background which support or obstruct the diplomatist in his work. It is not
usual to put on official record that the minister has received bribes, or is acting
under other undue influence, and even due influence is seldom pointed at.
Amour propre prevents the minister from confessing his dependence. It is
self-evindent, however, that one man or one office is not alone the maker of the
foreign policy of an empire. It is a well-known fact that during Lamsdorff's
time the court camarilla influenced foreign policy against the minister's will —
in the Far Eastern policy with fateful consequences. Perhaps as a reaction to

---

[1] Isvolsky: *Au service.* . n. 13 Isvolsky to Nelidoff 26. X/8. XI 1906
[2] BD 8 n. 230 Bertie to Grey 22. X. 1906
  BD 8 n. 232 Bertie to Grey 25. X 1906
[3] DDF 10 n. 443 Bompard to Pichon 22. III 1907
[4] Lindberg: *Scandinavia.* . p. 100

6

this the new minister was allowed more independence, which was strengthened
by the esteem in which Isvolsky was held, and by his success in 1907. But his
star was extinguished by the Balkan storm-clouds, and Sazonov, his successor,
had difficulties even in keeping his subordinate diplomats in line.[1]

According to the Soviet historian Bestužev the agricultural and commercial
entrepreneurs with liberal inclinations supported the adjustment with Great
Britain, "because Germany's rivalry seemed to them more dangerous than that
of England, who imported Russian corn". Also Germany's invasion in the Near
Eastern market worried these people. So the liberal Kadet and Octobrist press
greeted Isvolsky's nomination with approval.[2] — This in turn strengthened
Isvolsky's position in the eyes of Britain. The more the minister could be seen
to be backed by constitutionalist forces in Russia the happier Hardinge and
Grey were in their dealings with him.[3] — It is, however, difficult to evaluate
the effect of such support. The American historian Richard E. Pipes has said
that Russia's public opinion had no practical means of influencing the foreign
policy, and that the country was too large and heterogenous to have a clear and
definite conception of the "national interest". Public opinion was mainly occupied with internal policy, which is understandable in view of the country's
overwhelming social problems. Pipes is of the opinion that foreign policy was
not dictated by commercial and financial entrepreneurs on the basis of their
economic motives and interests; the changes of balance in great power politics
determined the decisions of the leaders of the foreign policy.[4] On the foundation of the diplomatic sources it can only be said that the commercial or
economic factors were only very seldom mentioned as reasons for any action;
the factors referred to were always those of power, political influence, national
prestige and security.

It might be supposed, however, that public opinion in the press and high
society had at least some minor importance for Isvolsky. He used the press for
his own ends, manipulating it without remorse when expedient,[5] but it is also
said that a press attack could cause him a sleepless night.[6] In due course we
shall see whether the press had anything to say about the Baltic question.
Isvolsky came to the Duma only a couple of times in 1908. The members
expressed themselves on foreign policy, but this hardly had any great impor-

[1] Robert M. Slusser p. 208—
Robert C. Tucker p. 176—
[2] Bestužev p. 38—, 73—
[3] Remark by G. Maude 1974
[4] Richard E. Pipes p. 153
[5] Bestužev p. 78—
[6] Albertini I p. 188

tance for the direction of foreign policy. The Baltic question, then topical, was not mentioned at all.[1]

The support of the other ministers was much more important for the Foreign Minister. Stolypin supported Isvolsky's policy because he understood that Russia needed absolute peace to survive the revolution. He withdrew his support when he saw that Isvolsky's ambition was leading Russia into a new conflict in the Balkans.[2] Perhaps the most important factor for the Foreign Minister was the Czar's confidence in him; in spite of the Duma constitution foreign policy was the sovereign's prerogative. The liberal minister seems in fact have had the confidence of the "black sotnja" Czar, at least as far as he succeeded, thereby strengthening the prestige and position of Czarism.[3]

The court camarilla around Nicholas II did not like the courtship with constitutional England and would have preferred to work together with Germany, a country which held the monarchical principle in honour. Perhaps it was these Grand Dukes, Ministers, diplomatists and sanovniks with ready access to the Czar[4] that Isvolsky tried to appease when anxiously maintaining relations with Germany while at the same time adjusting relations with England.[5]

In 1906—1907 the direction of foreign policy was discussed in the Russian Council of Defence. The Army was anxious on account of the German might on the Western border, but it had nothing against reconciliation with England in principle. Of course the military would not have liked to pay the price of the adjustment, thinking that England was taking advantage of Russia's weakness, and they were unwilling to give up any possessions, actual or hoped for. But Isvolsky succeeded in wrenching the sanction of the Council for the concessions the British demanded, because the Army had no forces to defend those possessions.[6]

So it seems that the Czar, the Ministers and the Army saw the inevitability of Isvolsky's British policy but demanded that relations with Germany be kept tolerable. Isvolsky could even expect praise by the liberals if he succeeded in this defensive phase of his policy, but he had to undertake something more

[1] *The stenographic protocols of the III Duma*
    session 32 27. II 1908 p. 96—129
    session 36. 11. III 1908 p. 375—389
    session 49 4. IV 1908 p. 1757—1800
[2] Bestužev p. 74—
[3] Bestužev p. 75
[4] Bestužev p. 45
[5] BD 4 n. 523 Goschen to Grey 5. IX 1907
[6] *Krasnyj Arhiv*, tom LXIX—LXX
    p. 19—25 žurnal sovešanija 1. II 1907
    p. 25—32 žurnal sovešanija 14. IV 1907
    p. 32—39 žurnal sovešanija 11. VIII 1907

aggressive to gain the praise of the nationalists and to make the Czar really thankful, Russia great, and himself famous.

It is by now a well-known fact that in 1907 Isvolsky had no intention of making an alliance with England against Germany. Russia tried to balance between the Great Powers in order to be left in peace to liquidate the revolution and to gather strength.[1]

What about the Åland Islands?

In 1865 Russia had had to promise not to fortify the Åland Islands. This limitation of her sovereign rights does not seem to have hurt or disturbed Russia during the rest of the century. In 1899 at the Hague the Russians hinted at the desirability of abrogating the Åland Islands Convention. The hint was not very loud, nor was it probable that Great Britain would have consented to the wish of her main rival.[2]

In the revolutionary year of 1905 much happened also in the Baltic, making even the Åland question topical. Arms, ammunition and explosives were smuggled through Denmark and Sweden over the Baltic Sea to Finnish and Russian malcontents. The Governor General of Finland wrote to the Russian representatives in Copenhagen and Stockholm asking them to urge the Scandinavian Governments to do something because weapons were sent "in nearly every ship" that left the ports. But these liberal and constitutional governments were unable effectively to prevent private trade in weapons.[3]

Next summer it was decided to make more determined attempts to prevent the smuggling. It was deemed impossible to find the concealed weapons on the coast and islands, and therefore a vigilant patrol had to be kept on the sea.[4] This caused much work for the new Minister for Foreign Affairs. Plans were made to declare the whole Gulf of Finland a Russian territorial water, which would have given the patrolling ships the right to stop and search passing ships. Isvolsky understood that such a flagrant violation of international law would have called forth a storm of protest, and he succeeded in getting the plan cancelled. The usual customs regulations and the three-mile limit were obser-

[1] I. I. Astaf'ev: *Russko-germanskie diplomatičeskie otnošenija 1905—1911* has been most useful for the compilation of the two preceding chapters
[2] Taubert p. 618
[3] AVPR fond kanceljarija 1905 g, delo 35 n. 150 & 152
Isvolsky to Lamsdorff 19. XI & 2/15. XII 1905 (for instance; there is countless correspondence concerning the smuggling in the reports from Copenhagen and Stockholm)
AVPR fond kanceljarija 1905 g, delo 35 & delo 111 tom I & II
AVPR fond kanceljarija 1906 g. delo 44 & delo 128.
[4] AA Russland 63 Bd 1 Pourtalès to Bülow 20. VI 1906

ved.[1]

But he did not avoid all trouble. To the Åland Islands a naval squadron and an infantry battalion were sent to watch and catch the smugglers.[2] The Swedish press noted this; for instance the *Svenska Dagbladet* reported at the beginning of June that Åland looked war-like[3] and a little later more precisely that there were 400—500 infantrymen there as well the Grand Duke Aleksandr Mihailovič with his squadron.[4] The newspaper guessed that they were on the island watching the Finns and "did not wish to believe" that the Russians were going to rebuild the fortifications, because it would have been against the Paris Treaty of Peace.[5] But by the end of June the *Svenska Dagbladet* was inclined to believe that the Russians might really build a naval port in Bomarsund. It was realized that Sweden had no right to appeal to the Paris Treaty, but "the Government will surely do all they can" because "there was reason to keep one's eyes open".[6] *The Times* frightened the Swedes with the opinion that it was impossible to keep watch over Finland from Åland, so it must be only a pretext for building a naval base.[7] The *Svenska Dagbladet* feared that the befriending of Russia and Britain might lead to the British consenting to the abrogation of the demilitarization — it was all due to the dissolution of the Union: Britain had no longer any need to defend Sweden in order to keep Norway's coasts free from enemies.[8]

The Swedish Government stated soothingly that they did not take a great note of the question, but remarked that the occupation of Åland was against the terms of the Paris Treaty.[9] The German envoy reported that the Swedish Minister for Foreign Affairs Trolle believed that the Russians had wished to abrogate the Convention of 1856 de facto by creating a fait accompli by occupation.[10] Trolle regretted that in 1856 even a temporary occupation had not been prohibited.[11] The Russians on their part tried to explain that the occupation was by no means intended to break the Treaty of 1856 or aimed against Sweden "although the Swedish Government has tolerated revolutionary Russian emigrants in the country".[12]

---

[1] Isvolsky: *Au service.* . n. 10 Isvolsky to Benckendorff 22. VI/5. VII 1906
[2] Taube: *Une page inédite.* . p. 562
[3] *Svenska Dagbladet* 9. VI 1906
[4] *Svenska Dagbladet* 16. VI 1906
[5] *Svenska Dagbladet* 16. VI 1906
[6] *Svenska Dagbladet* 25. VI 1906
[7] *The Times* 27. VI 1906
[8] *Svenska Dagbladet* 30. VI 1906
[9] AVPR fond kanceljarija 1906 g., delo 218, n. 17 & 18
    Budberg to Isvolsky 9. VI & 5/18. VII 1906
[10] AA Russland 63 Bd 1 Pückler to Ausw. Amt 10. VI 1906
[11] AA Russland 63 Bd 1 Hindenburg to Bülow 18. VII 1906
[12] AA Russland 63 Bd 1 Schoen to Ausw. Amt 20. VI 1906

The Western powers also dropped polite but clear hints, so that Russia could not ignore the ancient Convention. In the British House of Commons questions were presented concerning the violation of the Treaty of 1856 and the anxiety of the Swedes. Grey answered cautiously that he did not know of any violation of the Treaty or any alarm in Sweden. But in fact Isvolsky in St. Petersburg and the Ambassador in London Benckendorff had quite a job to explain the intentions of the Russian Government to the British statesmen.[1]

After Grey's statement the *Svenska Dagbladet,* as if to show that Sweden was alarmed, published an article "Ålands as a Base for Naval action" explaining how a fort at Bomarsund would protect the flank of the Russian defende of the Gulf of Finland and close the Gulf of Bothnia. A Russian base at Bomarsund would necessitate laborious and expensive arrangements for Stockholm's defence.[2] In an interview a "Russian naval officer" tried to ridicule the rumours of fortifications — only a couple of batteries were positioned in order to test the reaction of the Western powers to the violation of the Convention of 1856.[3] — It is doubtful whether this kind of assurance really calmed the Swedes. — A "German officer" remarked that there was no appropriation for building fortifications in the Russian budget and expressed his wonder at the fear felt in Sweden — what would Russia gain if she conquered Sweden![4] The public interest in the question abated little by little, and towards the end of August a small notice was published: "The Russian troops leave Åland on the SS. 'Asia' ". Only 15 men and two officers were left to take care of a telegraphic station.[5]

Thus the reaction of the Swedish press made the Western powers notice the action of Russia on Åland and compelled the Russians to retreat. Isvolsky's position, in trying to clear up this tangle, was somewhat inglorious. He had to deal with a problem which others had caused without even bothering to ask his viewpoint.[6] As late as 1918 he showed himself still annoyed by the clumsy action of the Russian patrol forces.[7]

It seems that Isvolsky had been interested in the Åland question even before the public discussion. According to Taube he caused a memorandum to be drawn up on it immediately after entering office in May 1906. Taube does not say how the question was treated in the memorandum,[8] but he explains that

---

[1] Isvolsky: *Au service. .* n. 23 Benckendorff to Isvolsky 8/21. VIII 1906
[2] *Svenska Dagbladet* 13. VII 1906
[3] *Svenska Dagbladet* 29. VII 1906
[4] *Svenska Dagbladet* 30. VII 1906
[5] *Svenska Dagbladet* 25. VIII 1906
[6] Isvolsky: *Au service. .* n. 23 Benckendorff to Isvolsky 8/21. VIII 1906
[7] Taube: *Une page inédite. .* p. 562
[8] Taube: *Der grossen Katastrophe. .* p. 117

because the Baltic question was involved when the Scandinavian Union broke up, Isvolsky considered it reasonable to try to abolish the limitations on Russia's sovereignty before the Baltic situation were to be settled again.[1] The Åland question was no part of his grand political programme. But the regaining of Russia's full sovereignty would have been a magnificient feather in his cap, and afterwards he himself compared his endeavours with those of Gortschakoff in 1871 when the Black Sea was remilitarized. Taube is of the opinion that Isvolsky's vanity was his main motive in this question.[2]

In his effort Isvolsky had the support of the Czar, who felt painfully the diminution of sovereignty in this corner of his empire. A couple of years later he was still vexed and said to the German ambassador that before 1906 he had not known anything about the demilitarization of Åland.[3] The British also believed that the Czar had been ignorant of the Convention and that his amour-propre had been hurt by the revelation in 1906.[4] Perhaps Isvolsky's motive was not all personal vanity: satisfying the Czar's vanity and nationalistic feeling would have strengthened his position and his chances of carrying through his policy.

Indeed it does seem that there was more than vanity involved in the Åland question. We have seen that in 1906 the Russians used the Islands for watching revolutionary smugglers, and that the Swedes suspected this to be a cover for starting on work to fortify Åland. There are, indeed, some glimpses of Åland in the new plans for the defence of Russia which were made after the Russo-Japanese War. Lieutenant General Palicyn and Captain Ist Class Brusilov submitted in December 1906 a "most obedient proposition" from both services to the Czar concerning the defence of Russia in the Baltic. The supposed enemies were Germany, England and Sweden, of whom the most dangerous was Germany, especially in the very probable case of Sweden joining her. The battle on the Western border would decide the war, but it was important to secure the flank of the army and the Capital against the enemy fleet. The army could appropriate only small forces against eventual landings and therefore it was important that the fleet could answer for the coast at least to the east of the river Narva. It would be much better if the naval defence could be pushed further west, up to the line of Reval, and best of all would be the line Åland-Moonsound.[5] The Austrian military attaché in St. Petersburg reported that according to his knowledge the Russians really intended in the summer of 1906 to ignore the Convention of 1856. The fortifications in Åland would have

[1] Taube: *La politique russe.* . p. 131—
[2] Taube: *Une page inédite.* . p. 561
[3] AA Russland 63 Bd 1 Pourtalès to Bülow 29. I 1908
[4] BD 8 n. 148 Rennell Rodd to Grey 3. III 1908
[5] Šacillo p. 318—319

completed the line of defence Hanko-Dagö-Ösel, which had been planned to replace the lost fleet.[1]

The internal aspect was important, too. The smugglers caused much worry to the Russian Government, and "the excited temper of the local population" in Finland compelled the Russian Empire to prepare military operations to subjugate the eventual rising.[2] The action of the fleet in the summer of 1906 made the army hope that it might be possible to build a *'Zwinburg'* on the Finnish coast. The navy was against grand schemes of fortifications, appealed to the more pressing need to create a new fleet, and recalled the fate of Sevastopol and Port Arthur. The Defence Council and the Ministry of War refused to give up their standpoint, especially on account of Finland, which the Grand Duke Sergei Mihailovič said to be, in view of its location next to the Capital, the nearest and therefore the most dangerous enemy. — This was reported to Berlin by the German naval attaché Hintze, who supposed that the Ministry for Foreign Affairs had adopted the idea in order to break up the Treaty of 1856 by a plausible argument.[3] Later we shall see how Isvolsky defended his Åland operation with arguments referring to the revolutionary movement in Finland.

These were rumours concerning the preliminary discussions, not actual plans. The navy evidently did not like to waste in Åland the money with which they hoped to build new ships. "The navy is of the view that they do need a first-class base, that is a naval port strong enough for independent defence. Admiral Boström said to me (Hintze): We have much too many ports, and therefore the navy will be satisfied with a second or third class base, secure only against a small coup".[4] A special commission was nominated to prepare the plans. Because the Paris Convention prevented the building of naval establishments on Åland, the commission planned a floating base for torpedo and patrol boats.[5] An appropriation of 300 000 Rubels was included in the budget of 1908 for the building of the first supply ships.[6]

There is not much trace of these preparations later. In the spring of 1907 the plan of defence was revised. Coastal defence was not enough for the prestige of the empire. Conforming to the trend of the time "free naval forces" were preferred, which could be sent anywhere in the world to defend the interests

[1] HHSTA/SVA box 5 n. 88
Berchtold to Aehrenthald to Aehrenthal 14/1 XII 1907

[2] Šacillo p. 87

[3] AA Russland 63 Bd 2 Hintze to William II 13. II 1908 with a protocol of the technical committee 20. IX/3. X 1906

[4] = 3

[5] AA Russland 63 Bd 2 Hintze to William II 13. II 1908, protocol of the technical committee 20. IX/3. X 1906

[6] Šacillo p. 62

and show the flag of empire. Among others Stolypin and Isvolsky supported this plan. A detailed naval programme was completed in the summer of 1907. Together the Baltic, Black Sea and Pacific fleets would have consisted of 30 dreadnoughts. These were too big to operate in the shallow gulfs of the Baltic, but smaller ships did not count in the naval race, which was very much a question of prestige. Šacillo also says that the Minister of Marine was personally interested in getting the largest possible orders for the private docks.[1] The reluctant Duma, however, approriated the money only for four ships, and even these were not commenced until the financial situation had cleared in 1909. Later more ships were voted, but even the original four 'Ganguts' were not completed until the war, and the high seas fleet planned for 1930 never materialized.[2] Perhaps the floating base of Åland might have been part of the new plan, but Isvolsky never succeeded in freeing Russia from the servitude of the Paris Convention of 1856. In the defence plan of 1909 the line of Russian defence was drawn from Rovno to Dubno — Luck — Kovel — Brest-Litovsk — Kovno — Reval — Helsinki — Vyborg — Lake Ladoga. Warsaw and the Åland Islands, as well as Libau, were left in front of the line.[3] "A Russian official" said that without a doubt Russia was going to fortify Åland as soon as possible, but until further developments the Government had dropped the idea.[4] In 1913 a naval air base was desired for Åland, but evidently it was not very badly needed.[5] It was not until 1915 that Åland was fortified to secure transit traffic from England via Scandinavia to Finland.

Thus in 1906—1907 the Russian Minister for Foreign Affairs had good reasons for taking up the question of the status of the Åland Islands. The reasons were not of the first order, not of vital importance for the Empire, but important enough to justify the assertion that vanity was not Isvolsky's only motive. But a sense of proportion must be preserved. Formerly the Swedes thought that Isvolsky had taken up the Åland operation "to the detriment of Sweden".[6] In the sources, however, there is not a glimpse of aggressive intentions against Sweden; she is mentioned only as an eventual ally of Germany, a factor causing additional strain to the defence of St. Petersburg. Later historians have freed themselves from an exaggerated reliance on Russian aggression as

---

[1] Šacillo p. 53—
[2] Gregerer p. 11—
 Adams p. 11
[3] AA Russland 63 Bd 3 Posadowsky-Wehner to Prussian War Ministry
 11. IX 1909
 Polvinen p. 15—
[4] AA Russland 63 Bd 3 Pückler to Bethmann-Hollweg 22. VIII 1909
[5] AVPR fond sekretnyj arhiv, delo 383/390 n. 16 a memorandum by Taube 20. XI/?
 1913
[6] Söderberg: *Isvolskij's.*. p. 385

an explanation.[1] However, Lindberg is of the opinion, based mainly on Taube's memoires, that getting the Åland servitude abrogated was nevertheless the central object of Isvolsky's Baltic policy.[2] It seems, however, that viewing the question of Åland from the perspective of Stockholm has hidden from sight the most important aspect: the fear of Germany and the need to co-operate with her somewhere, albeit in the Baltic, as a counterbalance to the Asian agreement with Great Britain.

Thus the importance of the Åland question should not be exaggerated. It is only natural that Taube narrates much about the Baltic question because it was his special field of activity, but of course Isvolsky had to keep an eye on the interestes of Russia in every direction. Once commenced, the Åland question caused much work and gave much trouble for Russian diplomacy, thereby gaining importance if importance is measured with the amount of paper produced and time consumed. But this importance lasted only as long as other, more essential aspects of the foreign policy allowed. The interest in Åland was reduced at once when Austria showed signs of restlessness in the Balkans.

Isvolsky got the opportunity of raising the Åland question during the negotiations concerning the Norwegian treaty of integrity, and it gave him the occasion to collaborate with Germany which he so badly needed.

---

[1] Lindberg: *Den Svenska.* . p. 123
[2] Lindberg: *Scandinavia.* . p. 94—

THE NORWEGIANS TRY THEIR HAND IN GREAT POWER POLITICS

Lövland opens play

The renewal of the treaty of 1855 had been discussed by the British, French, Germans and Swedes, and feared by the Russians, but it was the Norwegians who took the matter up in earnest. The first move was Lövland's note to the great powers in November 1905 declaring that according to the Karlstad convention Norway did not consider herself answerable on Sweden's behalf for earlier engagements but regarded them binding on her own behalf.[1] The British answered that they were "happy" to have received the note but reserved the right to consider de novo their obligations towards the former Union.[2] At the beginning of January 1906 Lövland said to the British envoy that he assumed that the Treaty of 1855 was still in full force, being in no way affected by the dissolution of the Union. He also hoped to have the neutrality and integrity of Norway — and only Norway — guaranteed by the four great powers. Sweden "with her warlike traditions and other feelings" would not probably join in the guarantee.[3]

The British had the whole time implied that the new treaty of guarantee should cover both Sweden and Norway.[4] This design was essentially altered when the Norwegians began to arrange a guarantee for themselves only. The Norwegian Foreign Minister Lövland was said to have a "fixed idea" about an imminent naval war between Great Britain and Germany,[5] which the crisis in Morocco had brought frightfully near. The important Venstre party had favoured the idea of neutrality for a long time, and Björnstjerne Björnson had said that "Norway's foreign policy must be such that she has no foreign policy at all".[6] It was thought that with a guaranteed neutrality like that of Belgium or Switzerland Norway might ensure that she would not be drawn into the combinations of great power politics against her wish.[7]

There were some ulterior motives, too. Nansen, for instance, thought that in taking the initiative in the treaty question Norway could demonstrate her ability to deal with foreign questions without the support and guardianship of Sweden.

[1] Omang n. 3 Draft for the Norwegian note November 1905
[2] BD 8 n. 85 Lansdowne to Lövland 30. XI 1905
[3] PRO/FO 371/98/3637 Leech to Grey 22. I 1906
[4] PRO/FO 371/98/3637 minutes
[5] BD 8 p. 122 note by the Editor to Herbert's Annual Report 23. III 1908
[6] *Vårt Folks historie* p. 390
    PRO/FO 371/98/6027 Herbert to Grey 14. II 1906 reports similar opinions. Thus, Lövland was not alone advocating the policy of neutrality (Lindberg: *Scandinavia* p. 54—)
[7] Lövland p. 153

And what a triumph if Sweden and Denmark eventually had to follow her lead![1] It was therefore important to keep Sweden out of the negotiations which Norway was going to begin.[2] On the other hand, the government wished to obtain some success in foreign policy to strengthen their internal psition.[3]

In March 1906 it was thought that Lövland had made a second move. It was reported that he had said in the Storthing that negotiations were proceeding for the renewal of the treaty of guarantee.[4] In fact he seems to have only said that the question had been discussed in the press and that it was possibly to be taken up officially, too.[5]

The British, and Norwegians, too, had to answer worried inquiries on account of this misleading report. Russia's reaction has already been described (p. 71). The Swedish Crown Prince Gustaf "was unable to comprehend that negotiations could have been opened with Norway alone, and not with this country".[6] It is hardly to be wondered at that the British remarked with a certain annoyance that Lövland's communication "complicated" the treaty question.[7]

As the press, foreign powers and in Sweden seemed to take an interest in the question, Lövland deemed it best to begin preparations for the negotiations to preserve the initiative in Norwegian hands. He called the new Norwegian envoys to a conference, and the diplomats agreed that the moment was propitious. It was thought that France would be eager to replace the old anti-Russian treaty with a new one where both her friends would be guarantors. Great Britain had almost promised to participate in the treaty, and certainly she would not leave Norway alone under the influence of other powers. Russia had already shown her dislike of the old treaty and thus ought to be willing to sign a new one.[8] The Germans expressed their general acceptance, they only remarked that Norway should discuss the matter with Germany, not only with the Western powers leaving then Germany to face a fait accompli.[9]

When the Norwegian government had strengthened its position after the elections in the autumn of 1906, the time to act had come. The Norwegian envoys in London, Berlin, Paris and St. Petersburg were instructed to ask whether the governments concerned were willing to negotiate with Norway about the treaty

---

[1] AA Norwegen 7 geheim BD 1 Steubel to Bülow 20 XI 1906
[2] Omang n. 54 Nansen to Lövland 27. XI 1906
[3] Omang: *Utenrikstjeneste* p. 196
[4] PRO/FO 371/98/8214 Dering to Grey 7. III 1906
[5] Omang n. 7 Lövland's speech in Storthing 6. III 1906
[6] PRO/FO 371/98/8214 Dering to Grey 7. III 1906
[7] BD 8 n. 86 Memorandum by the F.O. 25. IV 1906, item 7
[8] Omang n. 13 & 14 A memorandum by the Norwegian Foreign Office with notes 5. V 1906
[9] AA Norwegen 7 geheim Bd 1 Steubel to Ausw. Amt 26. VI 1906

question.[1]

In Paris the Minister for Foreign Affairs Pichon answered that he had nothing against such negotiations.[2] To the British he explained that "the French Government will be glad to assist in bringing about an understanding between England and Russia on the subject, but the question of the integrity and neutrality of Norway is more important to England than to France"[3], which exemplifies the French attitude throughout the Baltic question in a nutshell.

Isvolsky answered with a promise that Russia would negotiate with the other powers about declaring Norway neutral and about guaranteeing her security.[4] The answer seemed to imply that Norway would be left out of the negotiations and only be the object of them. Isvolsky's answer was deemed at first to be a mere slip of tongue, but, as we shall see, Norway was to have difficulties in trying to lead the play of the four great powers. — To the French Isvolsky explained that Russia had already recognized the integrity of Norwegian territory, so that the new initiative was pointless as a matter of fact. Russia would, however, consent to guarantee Norway anew in order to eliminate all suspicions that she might have some designs of annexion in Norway.[5] — Isvolsky was quite right in supposing that the guarantee of 1905 did not convince the British: "The Russian declaration of November 1905 would be quite worthless as a guarantee . . If the proposed guarantee is not to be a farce, there must be a treaty . ."[6]

The German answer took a couple of weeks to arrive, but Germany promised without comment or objections to participate in the negotiations.[7]

The British were the last to answer definitely. They were the most deeply interested, and things were not proceeding according to their wishes. Great Britain would have liked to keep Norway and Sweden as closely together as possible,[8] but now the Norwegians were acting independently of Sweden and, as it seemed, wilfully ignoring and hurting the Swedes. The Norwegians had informed the Swedes of their intention of opening the discussions about a recognized and guaranteed integrity and neutrality, but the Swedes had not been invited to participate "because Sweden's policy has, as far as is known, other aims".[9] The British thought that the Norwegian decision not to keep the Swedes

---

[1] Omang n. 19 Lövland to Nansen 8. XI 1906
[2] Omang n. 21 Wedel to Lövland 9. XI 1906
[3] PRO/FO 371/98/40502 Bertie to Grey 2. XII 1906
[4] Omang n. 32 & 33 Prebensen to Lövland 14. XI 1906
[5] DDF 10 n. 324 Bompard to Pichon 29. XI 1906
[6] PRO/FO 371/98/40502 minute by EAC 3. XII 1906
[7] Omang n. 51 Tschirschky to v. Ditten 26. XI 1906
[8] PRO/FO 371/98/38228 Grey to Leech 9. XI 1906
[9] Günther p. 73
Omang n. 12 Vogt to Lövland 30. IV 1906

informed of the course of the planned negotiations was "an unfortunate attitude .. and does not augur favourably for the re-establishment of confidence
between the two countries". But on the other hand the British "doubted whether it would be advisable to catechise Norway as to her attitude towards Sweden.
It might do more harm than good".[1] It was left for the British to ask Sweden to
participate in the negotiations.

Sweden stays out

The Swedes refused. The Crown Prince Gustaf said that personally he had
always deemed the renewal of the November treaty useful, but the Norwegian
wish to have their neutrality guaranteed made it impossible for Sweden to
follow. It was unthinkable that the Swedish nation would descend to the level of
Belgium or of Switzerland.[2] Because of the acrimonious feeling in the country it
was impossible to accept even a guarantee of integrity.[3] In their bitterness the
Swedes jeered that Norway was going to hide behind the backs of the great
powers, and when the Norwegians sent their draft for the treaty to the powers
concerned, the Swedes sneered "Norway is begging around Europe".[4] A Swedes
astonishment at the Norwegians reflects in fact the attitude of the Swedes themselves: "It is a psychological puzzle that a nation so independent and cherishing
its honour as the Norwegians were so eager to get under the guardianship of the
powers. This protection might easily lead to a diminishing of self-confidence
and martial vigour".[5]

The Swedes blamed the British for having "selected Norway for opening the
negotiations, in preference for Sweden"[6] and for having "taken an initiative in
this question in their interest and that the treaty was not in the interest of the
Scandinavians themselves".[7] The growing bitterness in Sweden towards not only
Norway but also towards Britain was reflected in a statement by Trolle. He said
to the German envoy that Sweden did not want to bind herself with a treaty of
guarantee, because it would prevent her from getting closer to Germany. The
envoy was somewhat sceptical: "We must wait to see whether this, for us
satisfying, interpretation of the Swedish attitude will be confirmed".[8]

Trolle said to Vogt, the Norwegian envoy, that Sweden would not participate

[1] PRO/FO 371/98/41889 minute by CH 14. XII 1906
[2] AA Norwegen 7 geheim Bd 1 Müller to Bülow 3. XII 1906
[3] AA Norwegen 7 geheim Bd 1 Müller to Bülow 28. XI 1906
[4] Omang n. 76 Vogt to Lövland 18. XII 1906
  Omang n. 104 Wedel to Lövland 31. I 1907
[5] Reutersvärd p. 47
[6] PRO/FO 371/98/8654 Dering to Grey 7. III 1906
[7] PRO/FO 371/98/40720 Rennell Rodd to Grey 4. XII 1906
[8] AA Norwegen 7 geheim Bd 1 Tschirschky to William II 9. XII 1906

in the negotiations, and that the great powers would hardly conclude a treaty with Norway alone.[1] Evidently, Trolle wished to set the Norwegian plan at nought.

Rennell Rodd was a little troubled because the Swedes were apt to forget the "Russian danger" and to assume "that it is His Majesty's Government who have raide the question of a renewal of guarantees in the British interest".[2] That the guarantee was in the British interest was demonstrated by an article in the *Morning Post*:".. it is not territory nor rich fisheries that Russia covets.. The question is, can the 'Heir of Norway' be prevented from constructing a new and stronger Port Arthur in the Finmarken fjords, and can Norway rely on the provisions of the Treaty of 1855?"[3] This was said to be a Norwegian view, but the Foreign Office commented on it so favourably that it must have been quite near to the official British view: "The article gives a clear account ot the danger to Norway of Russian expansionist policy northwards", and Charles Hardinge remarked that "the question of integrity is far more important than that of neutralization".[4]

The last sentence shows a distinction which was to become important later. It was thought that a country which had a guarantee of integrity but not of neutrality could go to war without fear of territorial loss.[5] It was also realized "that such a guarantee need not be held to prevent one of the guaranteeing powers from temporarily occupying Norwegian territory without any intention of retaining it. Such a course might conceivably be convenient to Germany or even England in case of a war with Russia, or to Russia in the converse case".[6] As yet the British Foreign Office had no intention of preparing for the occupation of Norwegian territory and they preferred a guarantee of neutrality, which would have prevented such an occupation,[7] but the situation was to change. (p. 128)

The Swedish refusal (on the 27th November 1906[8]) did not kill the Norwegian treaty. The British would have preferred to wait much longer, so that Sweden could to some extent forget the memories of 1905, but there was the danger of antagonising Norway, who was becoming restless when the answer from London was delayed. So the British comforted themselves with the hope that Sweden would come in later, if only the door was left ajar for her.[9] There were reasons to hurry on with the answer to Norway.

[1] Omang n. 48 Vogt to Lövland 23. XI 1906
[2] PRO/FO 371/98/39654 Rennell Rodd to Grey 23. XI 1906
[3] PRO/FO 371/98/38860 Leech to Grey 16. XI 1906
[4] PRO/FO 371/98/38860 minutes
[5] PRO/FO 371/98/38361 minute by EAC 15. XI 1906
[6] PRO/FO 371/98/40405 minute by EAC 27. XI 1906
[7] Hildebrand p. 496
[8] Omang n. 53 Vogt to Lövland 27. XI 1906
[9] PRO/FO 371/98/40405 Rennell Rodd to Grey 1. XII 1906

Nansen reminded Grey that Lansdowne had promised the treaty to Norway as Haakon's dowry.[1] Much more grave was, as we have seen above, the Russian danger. Even more ominous, Germany appeared as a rival of Britain in the Scandinavian scene: "Norwegian Government have been informed by German Government that the latter are willing to negotiate on the lines of the request put forward by Norway"[2] and "the German Government had made no mention of Sweden but had simply replied to the Norwegian memorandum".[3] It seemed to Grey "curious that she should have given a reply to Norway without making any mention of Sweden".[4]

Incidentally, this was about the time that Eyre Crowe's famous memorandum about the German danger was made.[5] Germany's promptitude in answering Norway made the British suspicious and eager to prevent the Germans from realising their supposed schemes in Norway. "It behoves His Majesty's Government to arrive at an early decision on the matter. I (Grey) need hardly say that they attach the highest importance to the maintenance of the integrity of the two countries of the Scandinavian Peninsula, and would resent any interference with Sweden or Norway by any Continental Power".[6]

It is only natural that the liveliest suspicions came from Paris. It was thought that the Germans "had perhaps in mind a similar guarantee of the integrity and neutrality of Denmark and Sweden, and by such means to hold that the passage of foreign war-ships into the Baltic must be prohibited". This message was minuted in the Foreign Office: "the views as to possible ulterior motives of Germany are of interest".[7] We have already seen that the Germans wished anything but a Pan-Scandinavian neutrality; and later it will be shown how the Foreign Office reconsidered its conception of the Straits question and how it differed from this Parisian point of view. But the various details of the question are not of interest in this context; what is important is that the Norwegian question is here seen in the larger frame of the Baltic question.

Great Britain was not able to delay any more because "It is unlikely that the refusal of Sweden to come into the proposed arrangement will deter the great powers from concluding the neutrality and integrity treaty desired by Norway".[8] On the 5th December 1906 the British decided to negotiate with Norway without Sweden.[9] The method suggested was not quite what the Norwe-

[1] Omang n. 54 Nansen to Lövland 27. XI 1906
[2] PRO/FO 371/98/39484 Grey to Rennell Rodd 24. XI 1906
[3] PRO/FO 371/98/39484 Grey to Salis 23. XI 1906
[4] PRO/FO 371/98/39654 Grey to Bertie 23. XI 1906
[5] Lowe-Dockrill I p. 20
[6] PRO/FO 371/98/40328 Grey to Bertie 30. XI 1906
[7] PRO/FO 371/98/40712 Bertie to Grey 2. XII 1906, minutes
[8] PRO/FO 371/98/39969 Rennell Rodd to Grey 27. XI 1906
[9] BD 8 n. 87 a memorandum by F. O. item 10
   Omang n. 60 Nansen to Lövland 5. XII 1906

gians had thought of — a conference in Paris with the powers negotiating a join guarantee.[1] The Norwegians hastened to preserve the initiative in their hands by preparing an unofficial draft treaty for the powers as a starting point for the discussions. No conference was held, because the Germans did not like the idea of going to Paris, and the Russians seemed to detest the very idea of a conference.

The Northern question becomes the Baltic question

In the middle of December 1906 the Norwegians sent their draft to the four Powers concerned. The aim of the draft was said to be to assure the neutrality, territorial integrity, and independence of Norway. Each of the Powers was asked to conclude a treaty separately with Norway, who pledged to keep up strict neutrality, which the power in question promised to recognize and respect — not to guarantee. Norway on her part would have engaged *à ne céder à aucune Puissance partie du territoire Norvégien ni aucun droit sur le dit territoire ou sur les côtes de Norvège, et s'engage, en outre a ne premettre à aucune Puissance d'occuper aucune partie du territoire Norvégien.* — With these promises and engagements Norway hoped to obtain a position outside the field of international politics. The guarantee was asked only for the integrity of Norway: *Si l'intégrité ou l'indépendence de la Norvège venait a être menacée ou lesée, le Gouvernement NN s'engage a prêter son appui au Gouvernement Norvégien, après demande de ce dernier, at si nécessaire, après demande, a employer, à ces propres frais, ses forces de terre et de mer suffisantes pour coopérer avec les forces Norvégiennes dans la but d'assurer l'intégrité et l'indépendence de la Norvège.*[2]

In 1855 Great Britain and France had so promised to help Sweden and Norway, and it seems that Lövland did not understand that he was asking for rather much. In fact he suggested that Norway might freely dispose of the naval and military forces of the four powers, at the expense of the power in question. And this was the price asked for a mere promise of neutrality. The Russian envoy Krupensky wrote of Lövland: "His aims are respectable and understandable, but with all respect to his intellect, his means are naive".[3]

And the price he asked was all the more unreasonable because the merchandise he was offering was not "up to sample". Lövland had not forgotten the eastern neighbour. He had wished to take the lead in Scandinavian policy of neutrality, not to create an unbridgeable chasm between Norway and her neighbours. The Norwegians wanted to leave the door ajar for Sweden and Denmark

---

[1] PRO/FO 371/98/40502 Grey to Bertie 6. XII 1906
[2] Omang n. 64 Lövland to Prebensen 10. XII 1906
[3] AVPR fond kanceljarija 1907 g., delo 25, n. 4 Krupensky to Isvolsky 23. I/5. II 1907

to come in under the shelter of neutrality in the future. In promising to observe strict neutrality the Norwegian government reserved *la liberté de s'entendre avec les Gouvernements suédois et danois ou avec l'un d'eux dans le but de sauvegarder, par une assistance mutuelle, la neutralité des pays respectifs.*[1] This was the notorious "Scandinavian reservation".

The duration of the treaty was to be twenty years, renewable for further periods of twenty years if not cancelled by any of the parties.

The French were amazed at the wide demands made by the Norwegians. It had been originally thought that Norwegian neutrality would have guaranteed to the Powers that their rivals would not be able to use Norwegian territory. In consequence the powers would have no need to intervene in Norway and so could afford to bind themselves to respect her integrity. But all this was now questionable because Norway demanded the right to abstain from her neutrality if she so wished. According to the draft France should have promised to defend Norway against any enemy; if Norway had the right to side with her neighbours, an attack by any power against Sweden or Denmark might draw France into war without even the right to consider the situation — *n'est-ce pas bien grave?*. French interests in Norway were not sufficient to warrant the heavy liabilities asked for. "Public opinion would much more easily accept a joint solemn declaration by the powers to respect Norway's integrity and to guarantee her neutrality".[2]

The British Foreign Office also thought that Norway was asking for rather much. "Whether British interests in this matter are so vital as to justify her undertaking the serious additional obligations contemplated, must be weighed from a naval and military point of view"[3] — The question was referred to the Committee of Imperial Defence. — ".. probably, if France, Germany and Russia were willing to join, England would do well to associate herself with them, as the risks of collision would thereby be materially diminished".[4] A joint treaty was clearly preferable to four separate agreements. Hardinge wrote: ".. it would rest with Norway at a future date to say whether her neutrality had been infringed by any act of war of a third power, and might or might not necessitate the intervention of the other guaranteeing power.."[5] — The aim of Great Britain was to prevent any power from gaining a foothold on the Norwegian coast. The treaty suggested by the Norwegians did not achieve this

---

[1] Omang n. 31 Vogt to Lövland 14. XI 1906
  Omang n. 33 Lövland to Vogt 14. XI 1906
[2] DDF 10 n. 385 Memorandum by jurisconsult Renault 3. I 1907
  DDF 10 n. 415 Note from Quai d'Orsay to the Norwegian Legation 20. II 1907
[3] PRO/FO 371/295/1837 minute by EAC 17. I 1907
[4] BD 8 n. 88 Memorandum by Eyre Crowe 28. XII 1906
[5] PRO/FO 371/295/3568 Haakon VII to Edward VII 31. I 1907 minute by CH

aim; on the contrary it made more probable a situation which Great Britain wished to avoid. She would not be empowered to defend her interests without an invitation by Norway, who might as well invite some other, rival, power.

From the very beginning the British wished to keep in touch with the French.[1] They had discussion concerning the fate of the Treaty of 1855. The British thought that the Treaty had lapsed eo ipso when one contracting party, the Union, had ceased to exist. The French thought that the Treaty was still valid having been made with the King of Sweden and of Norway, who was by no means deceased although the two crowns were separated.[2] It was agreed to deal with the question by exchanging notes which stated that the Treaty of 1855 had ceased to exist.[3] This had no political importance, and the practical conceequences were left until later; thus the British had a convenient pretext when one was needed later to delay the negotiations. (p. 137)

A much more serious point was the Scandinavian reservation which caused concern for both partners to the Entente. "The British Government have always been ready to admit Sweden to the benefit of any guarantee that may be given to Norway, but Denmark is a continental Kingdom not forming part of the Scandinavian Peninsula, & the consequences of any guarantee given to Denmark should have to be very carefully examined beforehand".[4]

The British ambassador in Paris Bertie discussed the proposition with the French minister Pichon: "Germany might have instigated the reservation .. on the occasion of the last meeting between the German Emperor and the King of Denmark it had been arranged that in the event of Germany being at war she would be allowed to occupy Danish territory, with the view of closing the Straits between the North Sea and the Baltic against a hostile fleet." Jules Cambon had reported that earlier William II had said that nothing would induce him to agree to the neutralization of Norway. "His Majesty's change of mind must be due to some change of intentions. His unwillingness to accept the neutralization was .. due to the disadvantage which he felt it would be to Germany in the event of a war with England. His readiness now to accept it looked as though he felt that he could make sure of having the aid of Denmark in keeping out of the Baltic a hostile fleet, whilst Germany could pass her ships in and out that sea through Kiel Canal".[5] This message was "minuted" in the Foreign Office: "Germany's attitude certainly looks as if she hoped to gain

[1] PRO/FO 371/98/40663 Parliamentary Question and minutes by F. O. 27.—28. XI 1906
[2] PRO/FO 371/295/4958 Paul Cambon to Grey 14. II 1907, minutes
　PRO/FO 371/295/6196 Pichon to Bertie to Grey 22. II 1907
[3] PRO/FO 371/295/7617 Paul Cambon to Grey 6. III 1907
　PRO/FO 371/295/9654 Rennell Rodd to Grey 20. III 1907, minutes CH & EG
[4] PRO/FO 371/295/3568 Haakon VII to Edward VII, 31. I 1907 minute by CH
[5] PRO/FO 371/98/43247 Bertie to Grey 23. XII 1907

some advantage in regard to the Baltic . ."¹ Another message said that Lövland's motives were "partly historic, dating back to the end of the 18th century, when there had been a previous association in neutrality between the three countries . ."² Crowe remarked: "The allusion is obviously to the famous 'Armed neutrality' of 1780 and to the renewed treaty of neutrality of 1794 between Sweden and Denmark. These treaties had a very distinct point directed against England. They pretended, among other things, to close the Baltic to the men-of-war of belligerent powers".³

This was how the Northern question began to be seen in the larger context of the Baltic question. Hardinge wrote: "The introduction of Denmark into the neutrality question . . . entirely changes the aspect of the initial Norwegian proposal, and will require very careful consideration in all its bearings".⁴ Crowe continued: "We can take no decisive action until the draft treaty has been considered by the Committee of Imperial Defence".⁵

In the meantime we must examine what the Germans had been up to in Denmark and whether the suspicions of Bertie and Pichon were justified.

¹ PRO/FO 371/98/43247 minute by EAC 28. XII 1907
² PRO/FO 371/295/1507 Rennell Rodd to Grey 8. I 1907
³ PRO/FO 371/295/1507 minute by EAC 14. I 1908
⁴ PRO/FO 371/295/1507 minute by CH 14. I 1908
⁵ PRO/FO 371/295/1681 Herbert to Hardinge 15. I 1907, minute by EAC

DENMARK — FRIEND OR FOE?
Germany afraid of Fisher

The importance of Denmark for Germany has already been made clear. As Admiral Büchsel's statement (p. 23) clearly revealed, the Kiel Canal facilitated the German countermoves against an eventual aggressor trying to use the Danish Straits. But the Canal, built in 1895, was too narrow and shallow for Dreadnoughts, and from the strategic point of view was thus useless from 1907 until it was rebuilt in 1914.

Germany's relations with the Danes had been far from satisfactory as the Danes could not forget their defeat in 1864 nor did the Germans allow them to but kept annoying them by acts of oppression in Northern Sleswig. The Court in Copenhagen was connected with the courts of England and Russia and with the Welfs, who were not in sympathy with the Hohenzollerns.[1]But in 1901 the irreconcilable Right in Denmark lost power and the more elastic Left took office.[2] It has already been shown how the new Prime Minister Deuntzer tried to stabilize Denmark's international position and how he sought in vain to obtain the recognition of the great powers for the permanent neutrality of Denmark. Germany could not afford to bind herself by a recognition when there was no guarantee that England would let neutrality prevent her from using Denmark's territory and waters, and when Denmark was too weak to prevent her. Germany would have accepted Denmark's neutrality if it had given Germany the right to defend her neighbour, but it was deemed too dangerous to try to bring Denmark under German domination by means of a formal treaty while the Royal Navy was more powerful than the young Imperial High Seas Fleet. Too hasty an action might have provoked something umpleasant. There had been difficulties in making the Emperor remember this; after the Björkö meeting the disaster had been close.

In 1905 the Danes changed their government again. During the Rus-so-Japanese War Deuntzer's Minister of War had built fortifications around Copenhagen, without the sanction of the Folketing, and had thus made a blun-der in the defence question, which was the central problem and source of discord in Denmark's internal politics. The storm so provoked overturned the Cabinet.[3] The new régime was even more propitious from the German point of view than Deuntzer's had been.

The new Prime Minister and War Minister Christensen-Stadil understood that balancing between the powers was impossible because Russia's means of influencing Denmark's situation rested on the bottom of the Tsushima Sound,

---

[1] & [2] Herre p. 107—108
[3] Fink: *Spillet.* . p. 21—

and the German navy was strong enough to eliminate British influence in Denmark. Her only chance of survival was to arrange her relations with Germany according to the latter's wishes. The new Minister for Foreign Affairs, Count Raben, is said to have been a Germanophile, and so was Christensen's confidant, Captain Lütken, who was to play a central role in the "Play of Danish neutrality".[1] He was related to the Chief of the German General Staff, General Moltke. To him Lütken explained that Germany and Scandinavia, whom history had separated, belonged together as Germanic countries, as indeed their mutual interests also presupposed — at least Denmark could not manage alone in the rivalry of the Great powers, and Germany's friendship was her only protection.[2] King Christian had become reconciled with the Germans. "He has a decided inclination towards our most gracious master and has forgotten the past .. The old ruler is again remarkably well and has overcome his mood of dissatisfaction at the triumph of the radical party and has become reconciled with his present government .." [3] It has already been narrated how the Emperor William estimated the state of mind of the "sensible men in society" as being favourable to Germany (p. 59).

William's responsible political counsellors were reluctant to take advantage of this propitious situation, being afraid of the British reaction, but the generals and admirals around the Emperor hesitated much less. Of course they got the support of William. At the outbreak of the war the neighbours were to be asked *für oder gegen,* and *gegen* would lead to an immediate occupation. William, and also for instance Admiral Tirpitz, would have liked to ensure Denmark's complicity beforehand,[4] but Bülow answered that Denmark's subjugation was a beautiful but dangerous dream, because even an attempt would provoke other powers against Germany.[5]

Therefore the military had to take care of the problem on their own, while the politicians who accompanied them remained in the background. The Chief of the General Staff, General Moltke undertook the task. He discussed and concluded an agreement with the above-mentioned Danish Captain Lütken. Such an unofficial understanding was easy to keep secret and it could be said almost truthfully that Germany and Denmark had not concluded any treaty. It may be pointed out that in 1910 Moltke tried to discuss a similar understanding with the Swedish General Staff. And of course England's, France's and Belgium's alliance was made on the military level before the politicians "knew"

---

[1] & [2] Throughout this chapter the Danish view is presented according to Fink: *Spillet.* .
[3] AA England 78 secretissima Bd 8 Metternich to Bülow 14. VIII 1905 private
[4] Tirpitz p. 155
[5] Bülow p. 80
  Schoen p. 62 complains that the German navy had a certain inclination to cherish political ideas of their own, which were not always in accordance with the intentions of the leaders of the German foreign policy

anything of it. There has been much discussion of the validity of such semi-official understandings. It will be seen later whether the Germans had reason to be satisfied with the conclusion of their discussions with the Danes.

Moltke started the discussion at the beginning of 1906. Evidently the menacing policy of the Entente gave a definite impulse to this. The same war scare gave rise to the *Flottennovelle* of 1906.[1] In the summer of 1905 Delcassé had had to resign because he had opposed the policy of appeasement of Rouvier in the question of Morocco. In the press he defended his policy by explaining that he had not intended to precipitate France into a desperate war against Germany alone; he had had a British pledge of aid. The Royal Navy had been ready to land 100 000 men in Jutland to attack the German right flank.[2]

The Germans were particularly afraid of Admiral Fisher, who used to speak in a forcible manner resembling that of William. In 1905 Fisher did his best to frighten the Germans. He brought up the Navy to manoeuvre in the North Sea on the principle "Our drill ground should be our battleground" and took care to ensure that the Germans were aware of the fact.[3] He egged on Lansdowne to come to grips with Germany as the opportunity seemed to be a "golden" one of fighting her in alliance with France. "We should have the German fleet, the Kiel Canal, and Schleswig-Holstein within a fortnight".[4] His pet plan was "Copenhagening" (in 1807 Gambier had forced the Danish navy to surrender in the midst of peace) the German fleet before it grew too strong, which made King Edward exclaim: "Fisher, you must be mad!" Fisher also liked the idea of a landing, either on Jutland or on the Pomeranian coast. To the Germans an attack seemed imminent during the winter 1904—1905. In November 1905 the fleet was mobilized against an invasion scare, in June 1906 the Emperor said that Fisher's "great aim is to fight us", and at the beginning of 1907 the rumour "Fisher is coming" caused a panic on the Berlin bourse, and in Kiel the children were kept from school for two days.[5] In fact Great Britain had as yet promised nothing to Delcassé, though King Edward and Lord Lansdowne had mentioned eventual help and Delcassé had too hurriedly concluded too much.[6] But Bülow and Holstein are said to have been sure that a treaty of united defence had been signed by England and France.[7]

Additional factors spurring Moltke on may have been the possibility of a new peace conference in the Hague (1907) where the question of Danish neutrality might be taken up. It was important to clear up the question of the straits

---

[1] Fisher: *Krieg der Illusionen* p. 103
[2] *Gaulois* 12. VII 1905, *Le Matin* 6 & 13. X 1905
  Fink: *Spillet* p. 25—
[3] Fisher n. 24 Fisher to Corbett 28. VII 1905
[4] Fisher n. 16 Fisher to Lansdowne 22. IV 1905
[5] Marder: *From the Dreadnought.* . p. 111—114
[6] Fay p. 196—199
[7] BD 3 n. 97 Lascelles to Lansdowne 12. VI 1905

before that.[1] Besides, the Norwegians had started to procure neutrality for their country, and the Germans were afraid lest such inclinations infect the Danes, too.[2]

Perhaps Moltke, with his military way of thinking, was too impatient to be able to stand the political uncertainty which reigned in the alliance systems before the war. In 1910 he tried to force Sweden to make a decision for or against Germany, and in 1912 he wanted Italy to answer *klipp und klar* about her attitude if war broke out.[3]

Moltke's ultimatum

In February 1906 Moltke visited Denmark for the funeral of Christian IX and met Captain Lütken on board SMS Preussen. He explained Germany's aim "man to man". But what he said was to be told to the Prime Minister, and he explained that he had the approval of the Emperor and the Chancellor. In fact, therefore, his statement was not from man to man but from government to government. The general explained that a war between Germany and England was not impossible and in that case Germany could not allow her enemies to use Danish territory, a landing in Esbjerg or Limfjord being probable. Denmark had better explain unequivocally how she was going to act in such a situation. Germany would guarantee Denmark's integrity if she joined Germany and would support her with all the German might. Her fleet was strong enough to prevent British revenge, but nothing would save Denmark if she turned against Germany — not even German defeat.[4]

Moltke's greeting through Lütken made Fredrik VIII, Christensen and Raben *ganske betaget* and they thought that this initiative could not be ignored. But there was opposition, too. P. Vedel, an official of the Foreign Ministry, explained that it was dangerous to start discussions with Germany because the Western powers might get wind of it and Denmark's neutrality would be compromised. He believed that England was likely to make a direct attack on Wilhelmshaven instead of Jutland, and on the other hand Denmark would be saved if Russia imposed Danish integrity as a condition of her neutrality in the conflict. In any case it was dangerous to be too intimate with Germany because this would cause the whole Denmark to suffer the fate of Sleswig.[5] — Vedel did not understand that it was not important what the British planned but what the Germans believed them to be planning. One must also wonder at his

[1] Herre p. 112
[2] AA Dänemark 37 geheim Bd 6 p. 42 note 2. I 1907 by anon. in Ausw. Amt
[3] Fischer: *Krieg der Illusionen* p. 242
[4] Fink: *Spillet.* . n. 7 Lütken's report 19. II 1906
[5] Fink: *Spillet.* . n. 8 Vedel's notes 15. III 1906

hope that Russia would have let her decisions depend on Denmark's fate. His last sentence reflects the desperate dilemma of a small nation which has been left alone and feels powerless to protect itself from the advances of a great and mighty neighbour.

The thoughts of the Danish anti-German Right are well manifested in a memorandum written by General Kühnel, who represented the Army in the Defence Committee. He was of the opinion that Moltke was not being very sensible in fearing an invasion at Esbjerg — it was too near the German border and German defence, and too far from the object of the British, the Kiel Canal. Probably Moltke was only trying to draw the Danish forces from Sjaelland to Jutland in order to make it easier for the Germans to overwhelm Copenhagen. England was well able to wreak vengeance on Denmark by bombarding Copenhagen to ruins from the sea. Bur Germany might well be allowed to occupy Jutland while the Danes were safely waiting for the British fleet — provided only that the capital was strongly fortified landwards, which was the programme of the Right in the defence quarrel. Most probably Germany would not attack Denmark if she saw that Copenhagen was impregnable.[1] Later General Kühnel drew up a list of questions to be presented to Enland, viz. whether England would maintain a fleet in the Baltic, and if not, how long it would take for the British to arrive at Copenhagen when needed, whether England would need bases in Denmark, and what compensation England would give Denmark if she joined England in a future war.[2]

In fact, the Right was prepared to enter into similar relations with England as the Left with Germany, with the difference, as we shall see, that England was not interested.

The Left had hoped to be able to reduce the defence budget by pursuing a neutral foreign policy; at most they would have accepted fortifying Copenhagen seawards to prevent a renewal of the 1807 coup — opening the capital to attack from the hereditary enemy (Germany) and preventing the friend (England) from coming to help, according to the view of the Right. But the Left did not believe that the British were able to help Denmark when the growth of the *Hochseeflotte* was fast diminishing the chances of an intervention by the Royal Navy. Denmark had to fulfil Germany's wishes in order to save herself. Raben summed it up by saying that "Denmark's success depends on friendly and confidential relations with Germany".[3]

The Danes considered these problems so long that Moltke had to prompt them to answer.[4] Lütken visited Berlin and was instructed to underline the

[1] Fink: *Spillet.* . n. 11 Memorandum by Kühnel 25. III 1906
[2] Fink: *Spillet.* . n. 25 Memorandum by Kühnel 14. XI 1906
[3] Fink: *Spillet* n. 17 Raben to Fredrik VIII 22. VI 1906
[4] Fink: *Spillet* n. 12 Hegerman-Lindecrone to Raben 31. III 1906

importance of Germany's friendship for Denmark and to explain that Denmark was going to observe neutrality and hoped that Germany would respect it. No military alliance was possible because it would expose Denmark to Germany's enemies — without any compensation.[1] Moltke answered that Denmark's reluctance to conclude a military alliance was understandable but in any case Germany demanded that Denmark defend herself against British attack. If she yielded, Germany would be compelled to treat her as an enemy. The next day Moltke sharpened his laguage saying that Germany had no intention of respecting Danish neutrality because it was from her territory that the Straits could be closed. There was no compromise, but Denmark was free to choose *für oder gegen*. "Due to old friendship" the general advised the Danes to choose friendship because otherwise it would go *rent av ruskende galt*. As a compensation some arrangement of the border in Sleswig might be thought of, but of course only after the war. Denmark had no need to state her choice publicly because it might cause difficulties with their enemies and with Danish public opinion.[2] — On the first day Moltke seems to have thought only of the right flank of his army, and only on the second day did he remember the Straits. Perhaps the admirals had reminded him. In Fink's collection of documents only Moltke's activity is seen, nothing is shown of the forces behind him. The diplomatic documents of the German Foreign Office do not, of course, illuminate these discussions very much.

But the German diplomatists nevertheless had some work to do in this matter. If the policy sketched out by Moltke to Lütken and the Danish statesmen was to succeed, Danish public opinion had to be made more receptive for German friendship. The worst hindrance was the question of Sleswig-Holstein. Prussian officials followed a policy of germanification with their well-known tact and delicacy in the Danish regions, harassing especially the so-called Optants. In 1864 the inhabitants of the Duchies had been allowed the choice of becoming either Prussian or Danish subjects. Those who had opted for Danish nationality were liable to banishment at the whim of the authorities, and the lot of the children of the Optants was particularly unhappy, because they were stateless, having been born outside Denmark. Danish national feeling and agitation, and the measures of the Prussian authorities provoked each other. The Danes reminded the Prussians that they had in 1866 promised Austria to hold a plebiscite in the Duchies. Austria had ceased to insist in this stipulation in 1878, and the Prussian authorities of course were anyway reluctant to fulfil it, the result being evident beforehand. There are volumes on these quarrels in the German archives.[3]

---

[1] Fink: *Spillet* n. 18 Instructions to Lütken 29. VI 1906
[2] Fink: *Spillet* n. 21 report by Lütken 2—3. VII 1906
  Spillet. . n. 22 report by Moltke 3. VII 1906
[3] AA Dänemark 27 vols 1—27

As already mentioned, Tirpitz thought friendship between Denmark and Germany worth a price, a tiny bit of Sleswig in fact. Moltke agreed, and it was he who took up the matter officially. "The Chief of the Supreme General Staff Lieutenant General Moltke has repeatedly remarked that the desirable good relations with Denmark cannot be realized as long as our policy in Northern Sleswig is marked with the sharpness pursued there since Köllner's (the notorious governor 1897—1901) entering office. It has an unfavourable influence also on our relations with Sweden and Norway . . The Army and Navy give great weight to good relations with the Scandinavian north and especially with Denmark".[1] The pressure of the military had is effect: "I (Bülow) have advised H. M. to keep up the policy of germanification in Northern Sleswig but to desist from unnecessarily annoying and excessively brutal measures. Naturally the change must be done inconspicuously; King Christian and Raben might be informed but warned not to 'ring a peal of bells' about the matter" King Fredrik was "thankful"[2] but the status of the Optants and their children was still to be regulated. The problem was discussed during the year 1906 and a Convention was signed on the 11th January 1907 stipulating that the Optants were to obtain Prussian citizenship.[3] The Nationalists on both sides of the border criticized the treaty. Of course the Danes did not consent to give up their national aspirations, and the German authorities were dissatisfied at being deprived of banishment as a means of dealing with malcontents. But for Germany it was a great advantage, or so it seemed, that Denmark expressly recognized the validity of the treaties between Prussian and Austria and gave up claims on the Duchies based on the Prussia promise of a plebiscite.[4] In the end the Convention did not lead to any permanent pacification in Northern Sleswig or Southern Jutland, and after the German defeat and a plebiscite the Danish regions were annexed to Denmark in 1920. But in 1906 and early 1907 there did seem to be a chance of the issue being regulated, and this led to some of the results hoped for by Moltke.

In November 1906 William II visited Denmark with Tschirschky, his Secretary of State for Foreign Affairs, and Moltke. Raben said to his German colleague that his "mission" since entering office had been to develop relations with Germany into a real friendship. Denmark had neither army nor fleet; she could not fight even Sweden. She had very bad experiences of joining England; on one occasion the British had bombarded Copenhagen and on another they had taken away the Danish fleet. Even now England was sure to trample Denmark to death if she was not supported by a strong friend. In case of war,

[1] AA Dänemark 27 Bd 1 p. 80 note by Bülow 27. I 1906
[2] AA Dänemark 27 geheim Bd 1 p. 85 Fredrik VIII to William II 2. IV 1906
[3] AA Dänemark 27 Bd 17 p. 45 "Optant Convention" 11. I 1907
[4] AA Dänemark 27 Bd 17 p. 127 Tschirschky to William II 11. I 1907

therefore, Denmark could not but side with Germany. He assured his listener that the King and the Government were of the same opinion. King Fredrik used more general terms of speech, but Tschirschky gathered that the King really concurred in the opinion of his minister. General Moltke had spoken more "openly" with the King and repeated his point of view that it was of fundamental importance for Germany to know on which side Denmark was going to be, *Freund oder Feind?*. Germany could not wage war westwards with an insecure neighbour on her right flank. The King had answered that he hoped that the friendship with the Emperor and the joint interests of the two nations would be effectively felt even in wartime.[1] The Emperor remarked in the margin: *Sehr gut und sehr erfreulich!* In fact Raben seems to have promised very nearly what Moltke wanted, if Tschirschky has reported his words correctly; the King's words were more "diplomatic" and materially he had not said anything binding.

The Danish word of honour

Moltke was not to be satisfied with polite discussions only. He wrote to Lütken with the object of prompting the Danes to give a more decided pledge.[2] In February 1907 he drafted a treaty of a military alliance, according to which he was to leave the defence of Sjaelland and Jutland to the Danes excepting Esbjerg, which the Germans wished to defend themselves. Neither side would conclude a separate peace, and Germany was to be obliged to defend Danish interests as her own.[3] Evidently the general had not asked the opinions of the admirals as there is no mention of the Straits in the draft; only the defence westwards was considered.

The draft illuminates Moltke's worries, which were increased by an anonymous letter, which he considered important enough to be sent on to the Foreign Office in Berlin. The informant said that Denmark's export was being directed to England and with great exertions it was artificially increased in order to induce the Danes to enlarge the port of Esbjerg, where a British squadron blockading Germany would have a secure haven.[4] Bülow instructed German representatives to inform of any indications which supported the allegations of the letter.[5] Tirpitz took the matter very seriously, strengthened in his apprehensions by the information that the port of Esbjerg was to be enlarged to receive ships of 24 000 tons, which had no sense commercially. "It cannot be denied that Esbjerg can be of value as a base for a blockading force", and "it is

---

[1] AA Dänemark 27 geheim Bd 1 p. 92 note by Tschirschky 20. XI 1906
[2] Fink: *Spillet.* . n. 29 Moltke to Lütken 25. XII 1906
[3] Fink: *Spillet.* . n. 31 draft of a military convention 10. II 1907
[4] AA England 78 secretissima Bd 9 Moltke to Bülow 18. II 1907
[5] AA England 78 secretissima Bd 10 Bülow to Radolin 22. II 1907, draft

natural that England finances the enlarging".[1] The Chief of the Admiralty Staff, Büchsel, did not panic but declared that for many years to come Esbjerg could not be used except by small ships, and on the other hand it was impossible to secure against a suprise coup; so why worry? Besides, the British would not attack without the French, who did not seem bellicose at the moment.[2]

But all Germans were not equally sanguine. The negotiations between England and Russia were proceeding, and thus the Germans were hardly encouraged to abandon their fear of *Einkreisung,* which continuing fear made Denmark more important then ever, because the Straits were the line of communication between the future allies — this is how the French Ambassador in Berlin explained the German interest in the Straits.[3] In March 1907 rumours of Denmark's collaboration with Germany made the Danish envoy in London, Bille, protest that Denmark was going to observe strict neutrality,[4] which was exactly what the Germans did not wish.

There were reasons enough for Moltke to keep up his discussions with Lütken. Towards the end of March 1907 the Captain visited the General. Lütken rejected a treaty — for reasons of Danich internal policy — but explained that all the Danish leaders were convinced that Denmark could never turn against Germany. If neutrality were impossible, Denmark would be on Germany's side in a war against England.[5] Moltke reported the same discussion: "after careful deliberation Christensen has decided to join Germany in a war . ."[6] Moltke said nothing about neutrality for he took it for granted that it was impossible. Fink says that Christensen's intention was to try to observe neutrality in the first instance, but either Moltke did not understand or Lütken did not explain it clearly enough. So the General was under the misconception of having obtained the unconditional pledge he wanted.[7]

The General was satisfied and wrote to Lütken that the main problem was solved and that the written agreement could be postponed until later. He repreated his apprehensions of the threat of war and the invasion of Esbjerg, and protested his friendship for Denmark. "It would be a day of sorrow" if he were ever obliged to open fire against the Danes. He promised that Germany would buy Denmark's exports during war and compel England to pay for all damage which she might cause Denmark. The Royal Navy would hardly dare to try to force the passage into the Baltic, but it would anyway be easy to destroy it in

---

[1] AA England 78 secretissima Bd 10 Tirpitz to Tschirschky 1. III 1907
[2] AA Dänemark 37 geheim Bd 6 p. 61 note by Adm. Bussche 25. II 1907
[3] DDF 11 n. 45 Jules Cambon to Pichon 23. VI 1907
[4] *The Times* 16. III 1907
[5] Fink: *Spillet.* n. 35 Lütken's report 28. III 1907
[6] Fink: *Spillet.* . n. 36 Moltke's report 28. III 1907
[7] Fink: *Spillet:* . . p. 88

the Straits before it could do any mischief to Copenhagen.[1]

But still the Sleswig question complicated the development of neighbourly relations. Lütken complained to the General that the German authorities did not pay attention to the Optant Convention and this caused bad feeling in Denmark — could it be that German chauvinism was stronger than the Imperial Government?[2] Moltke for his part wondered how petty acts by the border authorities could influence vital questions of Danish policy,[3] but Lütken explained that what seemed a small coin to the rich was a treasure to the poor.[4] Moltke complained to the Auswärtiges Amt and described his exertions in securing the right flank of his army, in which he had succeeded so far that only a written agreement was wanted, and this was to be made as soon as Denmark's public opinion was prepared. But this propitious development was being delayed: Sleswig was for the Danes not a question of life or death, but a question of heart, and their heart was breaking as no naturalisations had taken place in spite of the Convention. Nations were in many things like children: they appreciated their possession not according to their commercial but according to their emotional value, and here the heart of Danish nationality was involved . . . If Germany would respect Danish nationality in Sleswig, the Danes could say: as a nation we have nothing to fear from Germany, and we can be politically allied with a land which is tolerant and tactful . ."[5]

The Prussian Minister of the Interior Bethmann-Hollweg proposed a conference in which the diplomatists could explain to the local authorities what the question was about, the misunderstandings being due to their having never personally met.[6] Bethmann-Hollweg, Tschirschky, Moltke, the Prefect of Sleswig-Holstein and the Envoy in Copenhagen decided that all Optants wishing to obtain Prussian nationality were to be accepted without delay, and that Danish citizens were to be allowed to travel freely provided they were no nationalistic agitators (orators, actors, singers, teachers of gymnastics), while the Danes living in Sleswig were not to be disturbed if they were not guilty of obviously provocative anti-Prussian propaganda.[7] — This decision throws an interesting light on the methods adopted so far. The Prefect (Oberpräsident) promised to break the resistance of his subordinates by 'Mactwort'.[8] The consequences were soon evident, hundreds of applications of naturalisation left pending were

---

[1] Fink: *Spillet.* . n. 38 Moltke to Lütken 27. IV 1907
[2] Fink: *Spillet.* . n. 37 Lütken to Moltke 22. IV 1907
[3] =1
[4] Fink: *Spillet.* . n. 39 Lütken to Moltke 28. IV 1907
[5] AA Dänemark 27 geheim Bd 1 Moltke to Tschirschky 3. V 1907
[6] AA Dänemark 27 geheim Bd 1 Bethmann-Hollweg to Tschirschky
    5. V 1907
[7] AA Dänemark 27 Bd 18 p. 91 protocol by Bethmann-Hollweg 12. V 1907
[8] AA Dänemark 27 geheim Bd 1 note by Klehmet

accepted. Raben was grateful for the strengthening his policy and position had received, his fellow-countrymen having accused him a few weeks earlier of having been the dupe of the Germans in the Optant question.[1]

Moltke wrote once more to Lütken describing the happy development in the Optant question, and on the other hand recounting his apprehensions concerning the visit of King Edward VII to Denmark (in April-May 1907). Lütken answered on 25th May 1905 giving his word of honour that "as long as Christensen remains in office Germany can trust Denmark".[2]

Moltke seems to have been satisfied with this word of honour. He did not demand a written agreement any longer, perhaps because the rumours of a Dano-German understanding were making foreign governments restless. In Germany Moltke, Chief of the Supreme General Staff, was an important figure; Lindberg has, in the context of Moltke's discussions with the Swedish Chief of Staff in 1910, remarked that Moltke probably saw his "opposite numbers" as more powerful than they in fact were.[3] So he may have thought that Lütken's word bound Denmark in a way in which — for constitutional reasons — it could not do. Perhaps the worst deficiency from the German point of view was the fact that the pledge was given for the time Christensen was in office. Christensen's cabinet fell in October 1908 and Lütken's word of honour became valueless.

It seems that the new Prime Minister Neergaard did not even know of the pledge. In declaring his programme he explained that Denmark's foreign policy must always have the character of strict neutrality (The Emperor's remark: "Cannot be maintained nor can we accept"). Neergaard went on to say that the new government would continue on the tried path of Christensen's; there was no mention of special relations with Germany. In a conflict of the great powers Denmark would be on neither side (The Emperor: "Then it will be occupied at once") but would fulfil all her international obligations (The Emperor: "These she cannot fulfil").[4] The Emperor's remarks underline the fact that Germany's relations with Denmark were now back at the point from which Moltke had started his operations.

In December 1908 in the shadow of the Balkan crisis the Captain and the General met again. Moltke explained the situation to Lütken: during a war between France and Germany Denmark would not be in the firing line, but England's participation would render her situation dangerous. Moltke had been accused of gullibility in believing Lütken's assurances that there was no agreement between Denmark and Great Britain in spite of the fact that the British

[1] AA Dänemark 27 Bd 18 p. 94 Henckel to Bülow 23. V 1907
[2] Fink: Spillet. . n. 45 Lütken to Moltke 25. V 1907
[3] Lindberg: *Sverige i Tysklands.* . p. 39
[4] AA Dänemark 27 geheim Bd 1 Henckel to Bülow 15. X 1908

had reconnoîtred the coast of Sleswig for a landing; but be was determined to trust his friend. Lütken reported this latest discussion to Neergaarden, stating that the atmosphere in Berlin was much colder but that Moltke was still Denmark's friend. And he promised to tell the Prime Minister everything of interest he might hear in the future.[1] Perhaps the last sentence was a shy offer to work as a private diplomatist as he did under Christensen but it was ignored. Although Neergaard had said that he was continuing Christensen's policy, in fact he was not. While his predecessor had promised to be Germany's friend, he was following the policy of traditional and internationally recognized neutrality, which Deuntzer had begun. Moltke's exertions to offer German "protection" for Denmark had been in vain.[2]

Crozier's Counterattack

The Germans and the Danes were not able to keep their relations as secret as they might have wished. The news leaked out somewhere — "the suspicions lead to the scent of the French Envoy in Copenhagen"[3] (Crozier, later Ambassador in Vienna). King Fredrik suspected that Crozier had accomplices, whom he could not name. But William could and would: "Edward and co-partner . . delightful that His Majesty has pulled off the mask of the *Halunken*".[4]

Crozier kept his government well informed on all the rumours about the Straits question. In 1904—1905 he related the German plans to close the Straits by means of Danish neutrality.[5] In January 1906 he knew of a public relations campaign by the Germans in Denmark. The Emperor himself was trying to be *liebenswürdig*, commerce was growing, Charles was not prevented from getting the Norwegian throne, Bülow had promised improvements in Sleswig-Holstein.[6] After the Royal visit to Berlin in November 1906 it was reported to Paris that the King had promised to gather all Danish forces in Copenhagen and leave Jutland and the Belts to the Germans.[7] All this was explained to be a consequence of the dislocation of the balance of power in the North, so that the feeling of being powerless and helpless forced the Danes to arrange their relations with the mighty neighbour.[8]

And it seems that Crozier did not wish to let everything go according to the

---

[1] Fink: *Spillet.* . n. 51 Lütken to Neergaard 21. XII 1908
[2] Fink: *Spillet.* . p. 153—
[3] AA Dänemark 37 geheim Bd 6 p. 128 Henckel to Bülow 14. IV 1907
[4] =3
[5] DDF 5 n. 13 Delcassé to Crozier 12. IV 1904
　DDF 7 n. 284 Crozier to Rouvier 31. VII 1905
[6] DDF 9 I n. 70 Crozier to Rouvier 26. I 1906
[7] DDF 10 n. 331 Fabre to Pichon 30. XI 1906
[8] DDF 10 n. 377 Fabre to Pichon 24. XII 1906

German plans. The French Government was not much interested in the Northern question as such, but Denmark was behind the left flank of the frontier, and if Germany could not be certain of her friendship, she would have to watch her with troops, which could not then be used on the front against France. Crozier, as also the French envoys in Stockholm and Christiania, was, understandably, more interested in the Northern question than the ministers in Paris.

Crozier seems to have told a correspondent of *The Times* of his suspicions concerning the Danish promises to the Germans.[1] On the 6th of March 1907 an article was published which stated that an entente had been concluded between Fredrik and William to mine the Straits and to deny the Baltic Sea to the Royal Navy.[2]

The Germans were alarmed that "Crozier with his bloodhounds" had found out the secret plans.[3] It is probable that this revelation partly caused Moltke to abandon his wish for a formal treaty and made him content with the unwritten word of honour which bound only Lütken and his superiors personally but not Denmark as a state. It was deemed too dangerous to awaken the suspicions of other powers.[4] The Danes tried hard to explain that the rumours were groundless. The envoy in London Bille wrote to *The Times* that Denmark had in 1857 promised to keep the fairways open *sans entrave quelconque,* and that strict neutrality was thought by King, Government and the nation to be the only policy for Denmark.[5] — Of course this statement was very much against the German wishes. — The government in Copenhagen tried their best to unmake the *Røverhistorier,* the Prime Minister himself taking up the pen: "The Danish Government have not concluded any secret treaty with Germany nor have they any intention of doing so".[6] — Of course this was true, but not the whole truth. — And Raben was sent in person to London to protest Denmark's innocence.[7] The German representatives were also instructed to "correct" the groundless apprehensions concerning a Danish promise to Germany to use Danish ports in wartime, apprehensions which were supposed to have influenced unfavourably the British attitude to the Norwegian treaty negotiations.[8] To counteract the British fears of Germany closing the Baltic the German Marine Ministry pub-

[1] Fink: *Spillet. .* p. 80—
[2] *The Times* 6. III 1907
[3] Fink: *Spillet. .* n. 33 Moltke to Tschirschky 20. III 1907
[4] Fink: *Spillet. .* n. 39 Lütken to Moltke 28. IV 1907
   n. 41 Moltke to Tschirschky 30. IV 1907
[5] *The Times* 16. III 1907
[6] Fink: *Spillet. .* p. 90
[7] Fink: *Spillet. .* p. 99
[8] AA Dänemark 37 geheim Bd 7 p. 12 Ausw. Amt to German representatives 4. VI 1907, draft

lished in *'Marine Rundschau'* an article titled *Die Ostsee — ein offenes Meer.*[1]

The commotion was at its loudest in March-April 1907 and abated later little by little.

The British are apprehensive

These rumours were heard in London, too. After the meeting at Björkö Johnstone reported from Copenhagen: "Yesterday the Empress Eugénie told me that the King of Denmark had received news which had much upset His Majesty, viz: that it was the intention of the German Emperor to propose the exclusion from the Baltic, for manoeuvering purposes, of the war vessels of all nations except those of the countries situated on that sea".[2] In the spring of 1906 Johnstone cited words which contain the gist of Raben's, and in fact also Christensen's, German policy: "He did not love Germany any more than did his countrymen, but this ought not to prevent the establishment of good relations between the two nations".[3] Johnstone suspected that "there is an arrangement or understanding that Denmark will permit Germany .. to make what use she likes of the waters of the Great Belt in case of war"[4] and that in Denmark the opinion prevailed that all Danish forces should be concentrated on the defence of Copenhagen.[5] It has already been noted how this information was discussed in the British Foreign Office at the end of 1906 when the Norwegian draft treaty was under deliberation. (p. 99—100)

After leaving Copenhagen to become ambassador in Vienna Crozier contacted British diplomats in Paris and told them about the Germanophile Danish statesmen. "M. Crozier is convinced that .. Denmark has promised to concentrate all her forces .. in the immediate vicinity of Copenhagen. . Jutland and Funen would thus be abandoned and immediately overrun by Germany — German cruisers from Kiel would swarm into the straits .. and practically close them to any fleet coming from the West .. He is of the opinion that it is now of vital importance to obtain the neutralization of the Straits .., and suggests that the question should be raised at the forthcoming Conference at the Hague .."[6]

Reports in the same tone kept coming in, stating that "Denmark's position was not an enviable one, and the German ultimatum was now ready written in

[1] AA Dänemark 37 geheim Bd 7 p. 9 Reichs-Marine-Amt to Ausw. Amt 1. VI 1907
[2] PRO/FO 22/585 Johnstone to Lansdowne 31. VII 1905
[3] PRO/FO 371/57/13695 Johnstone to Grey 18. IV 1906
[4] PRO/FO 371/57/13696 Johnstone to Grey 23. IX 1906
[5] PRO/FO 371/242/ undecipherable Johnstone to Grey 8. I 1907
[6] PRO/FO 371/242/4333 Lister to Bertie to Grey 6. II 1907

a pigeon-hole".[1] Even while trying not to believe the rumours the British diplomats reported them because "there always remains the fact that 'there is no
smoke without fire' ".[2] But the "apparent honesty with which Count Raben
disclaims the existence of any understanding with Germany makes it difficult to
surmise what that 'something in the air' may be".[3]

Some plans for counter-action were suggested, too. Originally it had been
thought that Danish neutrality would close the Straits for warships,[4] as the
Emperors William and Nicholas had planned in 1903—1905, but later it was
held that neutrality would oblige Denmark to keep the Straits free for all ships,
which made the Germans oppose it. Hardinge remarked: "The Suez Canal is
neutralized and warships can pass in time of war . ."[5] "So the only solution of
the Belt question in the event of Denmark's neutrality being guaranteed is the
neutralization of the Belts like the Suez Canal . ."[6] This was Hardinge's opinion in January 1907; it was to be modified later.

But it was thought that "the question of Danish neutrality should be allowed
to sleep"[7] because "it is clear that Germany . . is most unlikely to enter very
readily into any agreement for the recognition of Danish neutrality . . Other
powers will have little chance of preventing a German occupation of Jutland by
any means short of force or the threat of force"[8]. In other words, the proposal
for Denmark's neutralization as a check to the German schemes might mean
war against Germany, and evidently Denmark was not worth so heavy a price.

And it was quite evident that Denmark had changed her mind since Deuntzer's days and had no longer any wish to obtain neutrality. Without instructions
Johnstone asked Raben what would be the attitude of Denmark if the offer was
made to her of a guarantee similar to that requested by Norway. Johnstone's
French colleague told him "that His Excellencey had . . expressed himself
strongly about English interference and had added that all Denmark desired
was to be left in peace . ."[9] Johnstone was reprimanded because of his indiscretion,[10] but the British had learned Raben's attitude very clearly.

[1] PRO/FO 371/57/40565 Johnstone to Grey 26. XI 1906
  PRO/FO 371/242/3058 Johnstone to Grey 22. I 1907
  PRO/FO 371/242/ undecipherable Vaughan to Grey 8. IV 1907
  PRO/FO 371/242/19777 "Morning Post" 15. VI 1907
[2] PRO/FO 371/243/14609 Vaughan to Grey 23. IV 1907
[3] PRO/FO 371/243/14610 Vaughan to Grey 25. IV 1907
[4] BD 8 n. 87 Memorandum by the F. O. on the Norwegian Treaty, item 12
[5] PRO/FO 371/98/42684 minute by CH 21. XII 1906
[6] PRO/FO 371/242/3058 minute by CH 22. I 1907
[7] PRO/FO 371/242/3058 minute by CH 22. I 1907
[8] PRO/FO 371/242/4333 minute by EAC 7. II 1907
[9] PRO/FO 371/57/40566 Johnstone to Grey 29. XI 1906
[10] PRO/FO 371/57/40566 minute by EG

Then there was Sweden's negative attitude to neutrality, as the Foreign Office was reminded by Rennell Rodd.[1] The Norwegian draft treaty was causing concern in Sweden, and British support for Danish neutrality might have caused an unfavourable reaction in Sweden.

Therefore the Foreign Office was not willing to do much: "Although we must be watchful there is nothing to be done at present . . It is quite certain that France and Russia should be opposed to any closing of the straits, & as France has more to lose in being cut off from her ally than we have, the initiative . . may safely be left to her. I (Hardinge) very much doubt whether, in the event of war with Germany, our ships would want to go into the Baltic. ."[2]

The Russian point of view was not as clear as Hardinge thought nor was France as interested as he supposed, and the Admiralty had some plans of their own, all of which will be discussed later. But now it is clear that the Foreign Office did not wish to do anything about Denmark.

The British refuse to do anything

As the Northern or Baltic question was to be discussed in the Committee of Imperial Defence Sir Charles Hardinge put down his views on the Straits question in a memorandum for the committee.[3] He explained that, contrary to earlier apprehensions, the neutrality of the states situated on the coasts of the Straits would not close the passages. But Denmark showed no signs of asking for an international recognition and guarantee of her neutrality, and any guarantee would be worthless if Germany would not take part in it, and she seemed to wish for anything but neutrality for Denmark. Probably the Germans would occupy the country at the beginning of the war while the Danes would shut themselves in Copenhagen explaining that they had no power to prevent anything. The only solution which could agree with British interests would be a neutral defensive alliance of the three Northern Kingdoms, and even that might be too weak to keep the Straits open; but such an alliance was utterly impossible on account of the Scandinavian quarrel and Denmark's friendship with Germany. — Hardinge thought that the Royal Navy had no need to try to penetrate into the Baltic: in 1870 the French navy had not succeeded in doing any harm to the shallow and sparsely-populated German Baltic coast. Nor was the Suez precedent practical: the passage for warships was free but only in driblets, which could be easily destroyed in detail as they encoutered the hostile fleet waiting for them at the entrance.

---

[1] PRO/FO 371/242/4333 Rennell Rodd to Grey Jan.-Feb. 1907
[2] PRO/FO 371/242/4333 minute by CH 7. II 1907
[3] BD 8 n. 91 Memorandum by Sir C. Hardinge 18. II 1907

These views were maintained throughout the year 1907. In March Eyre Crowe remarked that "if Denmark and Sweden were to close the Straits disregarding the international law, no agreement would prevent them".[1] In June Hardinge wrote: "Such an arrangement would be regarded as a breach of neutrality on the part of Denmark in time of war & would expose her to the usual consequences".[2] In October Grey minuted "that Sweden and Denmark were sure not to make any agreement which could be said to be directed against Germany; it would be unwise to propose anything like that. They had no wish themselves to close the Straits, if they were to close them under coercion no agreement would help." [3] In May 1908 Eyre Crowe wrote "independently of all theoretical consideration" "that the straits are likely to be kept open, so far as Denmark or Sweden are concerned, so long as there are powers strong enough actively to resent and to punish such a breach of neutrality".[4]

It might be well to recall that the questions of international law were somewhat academical. The stipulations of international law did not create any security because the enemy could not be trusted to feel bound by them. It was important only to wage the negotiations so that the eventual conventions would not hinder one's own future action.

From the beginning the Foreign Office was not greatly worried on account of Denmark's secret relations with Germany, and little by little also the energetic démentis of the Danes began to take effect. Bille's letter to *The Times* in March was read "with satisfaction" in the F. O., although his conception of the Treaty of 1857 assuring the freedom of the Straits was not thought to be right: then the question had been of freeing commercial navigation from Danish customs; the question was not of the rights of belligerents.[5]

The Danish King himself sent a letter to Queen Alexandra, his sister, protesting his innocence and contending that the statements made by Crozier were all false: no political transactions had taken place during his visit to Berlin.[6] The Foreign Office was satisfied, although "A churlish critic might say that a positive denial of the existence of such an understanding would have been more to the point than a mere statement that such understanding was not discussed on a certain occasion . ."[7] — The King had chosen his words with care as he was evidently reluctant to lie. Thus Crowe was near to guessing the truth, but the Foreign Office had decided to be sceptical: "The King of Denmark has given

---

[1] BD 8 n. 104 Lascelles to Grey 7. III 1907, minute by EAC
[2] PRO/FO 371/242/19777 minute by CH 15. VI 1907
[3] BD 8 n. 108 Bertie to Grey 31. X 1907, minute EG
[4] BD 8 n. 155 Memorandum by Eyre Crowe 7. V 1908
[5] PRO/FO 371/242/8855 minutes by EAC & CH 16. III 1907
[6] PRO/FO 371/242/12568 summary of a letter by the King of Denmark to Queen Alexandra 19. IV 1907
[7] PRO/FO 371/242/12568 minute by EAC

such a categorical denial . . that I think we may safely accept it".[1]

The British were faced with the truth quite clearly but still refused to recognize it when the envoy in Copenhagen reported some press gossip concerning Captain Lütken's "pleasure trip" to Berlin.[2] The rumour was ridiculed: "If the whole fabric of the statements of the *Extrabaldet* is based on the fact of three officers having gone to Berlin about Easter-time, their foundation is very slender."[3] The conclusion was: "An alliance is, for the present at least, out of the question".[4]

British suspicions has grown since the end of 1906, fostered by the Danish King's visit to Berlin, which was followed by the Optant Convention in January 1907. By the end of April these suspicions were at their strongest, after which they rapidly diminished. The rumours were never believed into their fullest extent, but neither were the Danes fully trusted even afterwards. Rumours concerning the special relations between Denmark and Germany were heard as late as September[5] and October.[6] The suspicions lingered but the Foreign Office had decided to do nothing.

The old proposal of taking up the Straits question at the Hague Conference — revived by Sir George Clarke, the Secretary of the CID — was turned down.[7] The Foreign Office had in February asked for the views of the Admiralty, too, stating that "the Lords Commissioners will probably concur with Sir E. Grey . . that it is not desirable for Great Britain at present to raise the question of freedom of navigation in those waterways"[8] and the Lords Commissioners did concur: "they think that the question of the freedom of the Belts and Sound should not be raised at the moment". As to the rights of the belligerents in the Straits, the Admiralty considered that Deuntzer's letter (p. 36—37) gave "ampel ground for the assumption that such passage would not be hindered by Denmark on the ground of a maintenance of neutrality".[9]

Great Britain had decided to abandon Denmark to the German zone of interest: "Any activity on our part in this direction at present would be very likely to precipitate counter-action by Germany", and "we cannot make an agreement with Denmark unless we are really able to protect her from invasion

[1] PRO/FO 371/243/14610 minute by CH 6. V 1907
[2] PRO/FO 371/243/14615 Vaughan to Grey 1. V 1907
[3] PRO/FO 371/243/14615 minutes by CH & EG
[4] PRO/FO 371/243/14616 minute by EAC, initials CH & EG 3. V 1907
[5] PRO/FO 371/243/32672 Dumas to Johnstone to Grey 15. IX 1907
[6] PRO/FO 371/243/34683 Johnstone to Grey 18. X 1907
[7] PRO/FO 371/243/19562 Clarke to Hardinge 12. VI 1907
  F. O. to Clarke 15. VI 1907
  Clarke to Hardinge 17. VI 1907
[8] PRO/FO 371/242/ undecipherable F. O. to Admiralty 1. II 1907
[9] PRO/FO 371/242/15009 Admiralty to F. O. 4. V 1907

by Germany. ." [1]

After abandoning Denmark it was all the more important to prepare for counter-moves in the Scandinavian Peninsula, especially as Germany and Russia were active there, too.

No trace of Russian alarm

Russia did not protest in any way against the German schemes in Denmark. Kudašev, the envoy in Copenhagen, "had reported to M. Isvolsky his fears of an agreement having been made between Denmark . . and had sent a copy . . to Count Osten-Sacken to Berlin. The Ambassador had questioned M. Tschirschky as to the truth of the report . . The German Minister . . had given him his word of honour that no agreement had been made between the two countries".[2]

In the Russian sources no trace of alarm at Germany's schemes has been found. The intervention mentioned abover seems to have been an initiative of the representatives, not ordered by Isvolsky. This fits very well together with what has earlier been revealed of Isvolsky's views in this matter. He had been of the opinion that in her state of weakness Russia could not do anything to prevent Germany; therefore it was better to collaborate with her in order to have a hand in the game.

[1] PRO/FO 371/447/13302 Johnstone to Grey 26. V 1908, minutes
[2] PRO/FO 371/242/3058 Johnstone to Grey 22. I 1907

RUSSO — GERMAN COLLABORATION BEGINS
2 The German view of the Norwegian question

When the Norwegians sent their draft to Berlin, the Germans did not like it any more than the other powers. The British idea of a conference in Paris they detested, and it was dropped as the Norwegians were also reluctant to entertain it. They were afraid that they might not be able to hold their own when discussing simultaneously with four great powers. Norway preferred a bilateral exchange of ideas through the usual diplomatic channels.[1]

Nor was the guarantee asked for by Norway acceptable. Tschirschky stated that Germany had no interest in defending Norway *mit eigenem Blut und Gut,* a conscripted army could be used only to defend Germany's essential and vital interests.[2]

Most of all, of course, the Germans disliked the Scandinavian reservation. The Norwegian question in itself was not important to Germany, Tschirschky wrote to Metternich, the Ambassador in London, "I remind you that Norwegian neutrality does not touch our interests" [3] and "The Chief of the Admiralty Staff said that the navy had nothing against Norwegian neutrality itself, although it might give rise to certain 'considerations' if war broke out."[4]

But the Norwegian question was dangerous on account of the bad example the Norwegians were giving to their neighbours: "The treaty is undesirable as it might induce Sweden and Denmark to strive for similar treaties. And the Chief of the Admiralty Staff can under no circumstances allow Sweden or Denmark to be neutralized".[5] It became soon evident that there was no fear of Sweden following the Norwegian initiative, but the Danes were not to be so trusted. On the other hand Germany could not oppose the endeavours of the Norwegians. Tschirschky instructed the envoy in Copenhagen that in an eventual war Germany would not need Norway, and therefore she could join in her neutralization, in order not to leave the matter completely to the British and the French, and also to the Russians. But Tschirschky maintained that a corresponding neutrality for Sweden and particularly for Denmark would have grave consequences for the defence of German coasts, and therefore it was not acceptable. If Raben was to utter a wish for neutrality, Tschirschky told the envoy to try to make him abandon it, by saying that a neutralized state lost her freedom of action without having security against a power whose interests necessitated

---

[1] GP 23 II n. 8041 Tschirschky to Schoen 7. I 1907
 Omang n. 85 Lövland to envoys 24. XII 1906
[2] GP 23 II n. 8033 Tschirschky to William II 15. XII 1906
 GP 23 II n. 8036 Schoen to Bülow 24. XII 1906
[3] AA Norwegen 7 geheim Bd 2 Tschirschky to Metternich 28. II 1907
[4] AA Norwegen 7 geheim Bd 2 Chief of Adm. Staff to Ausw. Amt 2. I 1907
[5] =4

ignoring the neutrality. The British admirals had been heard to say that no neutrality would restrain them if they had the power and the need to break it. Naturally Germany could not wait until a hostile power had violated Danish neutrality and thereby given Germany the right to do likewise; Germany must know beforehand whether Denmark was friend or foe. In strict confidence the envoy was told that Raben and the Danish General Staff were already aware of these viewpoints through other channels.[1]

This was a rare hint in the diplomatic documents to the discussions and correspondence of Moltke and Lütken. It also shows the part the German diplomacy had to play in this game: to carry on the Norwegian negotiations so that the neutrality they discussed did not contaminate Denmark, while General Moltke took care of the essential question.

The Germans were able to maintain a low profile during the discussions concerning the Norwegian treaty, because they were only, so to say, negatively interested in the question, and because Isvolsky in St. Petersburg was so eager to play the leading role. This the Germans could safely leave to the Russian minister, because his views were very nearly identical with those of German statesmen: Russia had no use for Sweden's or Denmark's neutrality. So the Norwegians received no answer from Berlin to their draft, but the Russian counter-draft was in fact the result of Russo-German collaboration.

Isvolsky and Schoen at it again

In the very beginning "the Russian ambassador visited me (Tschirschky) yesterday (24. XI 1906) and asked me what attitude we were going to adopt. M. Isvolsky had instructed him to ascertain our standpoint".[2] As yet this was no collaboration, but Isvolsky's whish not to antagonize Germany by acting behind her back can be guessed at. The Imperial Governments were unanimous in seeing British schemes in Norway: "As I (Tschirschky) learn from a message by M. Isvolsky, the formulation of article 4 (concerning armed assistance in the Norwegian draft) is due to English inspiration. In fact, England is, according to the ancient British view, vitally interested in preventing any other power from establishing itself in a port on the Norwegian coast."[3] "It will be necessary to agree with Russia in these questions". And Russia was willing: "M. Isvolsky, who has many reservations against the form and content (of the Norwegian draft), and supposes that we also have doubts, would like to agree with us on the counter-proposition".[4] Tschirschky answered "that the Imperial Govern-

---

[1] AA Dänemark 37 geheim Bd 6 Tschirschky to Henckel 29. I 1907
[2] GP 23 II n. 8030 note by Tschirschky 25. XI 1906
[3] GP 23 II n. 8033 Tschirschky to William II 15. XII 1906
[4] GP 23 II n. 8034 Schoen to Ausw. Amt 17. XII 1906

ment is prepared, with pleasure, for the proposed agreement with Russia. ."[1]
Je crois qu'il ne serait pas difficile pour l'Allemagne et la Russie de s'accorder sur le sujet . .[2]

In the light of the German sources Isvolsky can clearly be seen as the initiatior of the co-operation. In the absence of Russian sources it is difficult to say how much of this was planned in advance by Isvolsky, and how much was due to the accidental harmony of interests.

But Isvolsky was not alone in initiating co-operation. His old friend from Copenhagen, Schoen, was now German ambassador in St. Petersburg. He wrote to Bülow: "I may confidentially add that I am not wholly unconcerned in the genesis of the apprehensions felt here against a too far-reaching obligation in guaranteeing Norwegian integrity, as I had already, before we had received any Norwegian draft, uttered as a personal opinion to M. Isvolsky that a certain caution seemed to necessary in regard to the concept of guarantee . ."[3]

And caution was necessary. The Norwegians might induce the Danes to try something similar, "but the question of Danish neutrality is, because here the problems of the Baltic entrances are involved, much more difficult than that of Norwegian neutrality. . Self-evidently I avoided naming Denmark here, but the objections of the Russian Government against the Norwegian draft witness that important doubts of a similar kind do exist here".[4] This comes as no surprise, because twice already, as noted, Isvolsky and Schoen had discussed the Baltic question, and the suspicion might be excused that Schoen had not avoided it completely even now, however "self-evidently" he claimed to have tried.

Isvolsky discussed the Norwegian draft with Bompard, too, "however, as M. Isvolsky assured me (Schoen), not with the intention of preconcerting united action".[5] Glimpses like this may serve to recall what was the most important aspect of the Northern question for Isvolsky: not Norway, not even the more important Straits question, but keeping Germany humoured.

The Imperial Governments discussed the counter-draft and tried to diminish the obligations of the guarantee, but not too greatly — it would have been humiliating if the Western powers had compelled them to take back some deletions.[6]

Isvolsky was willing to draft an answer to the Norwegians and the Western powers with Schoen.[7] "M. Isvolsky is prepared, with pleasure, to take the

[1] GP 23 II n. 8035 Tschirschky to Schoen 20. XII 1906
[2] AA Norwegen 7 geheim Bd 1 Tschirschky to Osten-Sacken 1/14 XII 1906
[3] AA Norwegen 7 geheim Bd 1 Schoen to Bülow 17. XII 1907
[4] GP 23 II n. 8036 Schoen to Bülow 24. XII 1906
[5] = 4
[6] GP 23 II n. 8038 Schoen to Ausw. Amt 2. I 1907
   n. 8039 Tschirschky to Schoen 4. I 1907
[7] AA Norwegen 7 geheim Bd 1 Schoen to Bülow 17. XII 1906

initiative in the further development of the Norwegian question, in such a way that he answers the Norwegian draft with a contre-convention and sends it simultaneously à titre d'information to Berlin, Paris and London. Because we are materially unanimous, Your Excellency (Bülow) will then be able to declare to the Norwegians that the Russian draft corresponds also to our views and that we approve it. M. Isvolsky thinks that it is not without risk to call the contre-convention Russo-German, because such an act would immediately provoke counter-action by the Western powers".[1]

Later it will be shown that Isvolsky was quite reasonable in trying to keep secret his liaison with the Germans, and that later his reserve made the Germans vexed and suspicious, but now "We agree with M. Isvolsky in all the points proposed by him".[2] So the counter-project came to be known as Russian and not Russo-German.

Russia takes the lead in the Norwegian question

By the middle of January 1907 Isvolsky sent his remarks on the Norwegian draft to Lövland. Russia could not accept the idea of separate treaties between Norway and each of the guarantors, because "the result would be a very cumbrous collection of treaties, nor would it agree with the precedent of Switzerland 1815, Belgium 1839, Luxemburg 1867 and the Congo 1885"[3] — Perhaps Isvolsky was reluctant to let the Norwegians make treaties with Russia's rivals without her participation, as there was no certainty about what the different powers might agree to. The apprehensions expressed by Lamsdorff as to British designs may have survived and may partly explain Isvolsky's eager activity, in addition to his German policy.

The central, most essential objection was that Norway would obtain an "unnaturally" strong position if she were allowed to choose the power she wanted to help her in need. — That power might, very probably, be Great Britain. — Krupensky had already remarked that the Treaty of 1855 was not acceptable as a model, being a treaty for war, which explained the stipulations for military help.[4] The reservation for a united defence with Sweden and Denmark was also unacceptable. If Norway absolutely wished, new countries could afterwards subscribe to the principles of the treaty.[5]

This was an unclear point, implying that Sweden and Denmark might be accepted as guarantors. It is improbable that Isvolsky would have intended to allow them to join Norway, letting develop *le germe d'une union scandinave*,

---

[1] GP 23 II n. 8040 Schoen to Ausw. Amt 5. I 1907
[2] GP 23 II n. 8041 Tschirschky to Schoen 7. I 1907
[3] Omang n. 94 appendix II *"Russisk uttalelse"* 16. I 1907
[4] Omang n. 74 Prebensen to Lövland 17. XII 1906
[5] = 3

que l'intérêt de la Russie n'était pas se provoquer.[1] Later Schoen explained to Tschirschky that the article in question was taken into the Russo-German project at his instigation, not with the intention of drawing Denmark or Sweden into the project — the German view on the inopportuneness of such an enlarging of the scope of treaty being manifested already by the elimination of the Scandinavian reservation — but hoping to offer an opportunity for other great powers to participate in the work of peace.[2] Schoen was reprimanded by Tschirschky, because the article would be understood as an inducement for Sweden and Denmark to join.

Nor would Isvolsky consent to promise military help at Russia's expense to Norway. Tschirschky would have preferred to leave out all reference to even a collective guarantee, because armed help would never be sent in any case; he proposed that instead of a guarantee the powers would speak only of assuring Norway's integrity.[3] But Isvolsky persuaded his colleague to accept the paper guarantee remarking that otherwise a gap would be left on the treaty, which other powers would note. They would be unable to avoid suspecting the intentions of those who had left the gap.[4] To the Norwegians Isvolsky said, further, that if Norway adopted neutrality, it had to be permanent neutrality. The treaty could not be temporary.[5]

With these remarks Isvolsky despatched the Russian — and secretly German — counter-draft. The Norwegians lost the initiative and Isvolsky began wielding the dominating influence of which Krupensky had spoken (p. 74). Of course it was better for Russia to be active than to wait for British initiative; also it is not impossible that Isvolsky had some kind of plan concerning the Baltic question, including the Åland question, but there is no proof of this.

In Isvolsky's draft it was declared that the object of the treaty was to safeguard Norway's independence, permanent neutrality, and integrity, concerning which objects Germany, France, England and Russia would conclude the treaty at hand. In the first article the treaty of 1855 was abrogated. In the second article Norway was declared permanently neutral within the boundaries she had at the moment of the dissolution of the Union, and in the third the powers bound themselves to respect Norway's neutrality, integrity and independence, and stated that the joint guarantee of the signatories confirmed these principles. The fourth article permitted other powers to be accepted as signatories, and the final article made the treaty perpetual. It could be abrogated only by a new and solemn treaty by the signatory powers.[6]

---

[1] DDF 11 n. 201 Pichon to French representatives 2. XI 1907
[2] GP 23 II n. 8046 Schoen to Bülow 5. II 1907
[3] GP 23 II n. 8037 Tschirschky to Schoen 29. XII 1906
[4] GP 23 II n. 8038 Schoen to Ausw. Amt 2. I 1907
[5] Omang n. 94 appendix II *"Russisk uttalelse"* 16. I 1907
[6] Omang n. 94 appendix III *"Contre-projet de convention"* 16. I 1907

Norway still doesn't give up

The Russian draft was acceptable to the great powers, the Norwegian treaty seemed ready to be signed and the Norwegian question ripe for burial in the archives. Norway would have been permanently neutral, i.e. out of the play of international politics. But the Norwegians were worried and hurt by the Russian draft. Switzerland, Belgium, Luxemburg, Cracow and the Congo were creations of the great powers, in the Norwegian view, while Norway was one of the oldest Kingdoms of Europe, which did not need la pacification du nord but only the renewal of the Treaty of 1855 to safeguard her independence.[1] The suggestion of making Sweden and Denmark Norway's guarantors was infuriating, and worrying, too, was the proposal of a treaty by the great powers without the signature of Norway.[2]

So the Norwegians were made to realize the limits of the ability of a small country to direct international affairs. Armed help and the Scandinavian reservation were clearly unacceptable to the great powers.[3] On the other hand Lövland naturally did not wish to give up his attempt, especially as he needed some diplomatic success to strengthen the internal position of Michelsen's Cabinet.[4]

The Norwegians let it be known that they accepted some of the Russian viewpoints, namely the collective form of the treaty and dropping the article concerning the eventual enlarging of the scope of the treaty. The danger of Sweden and Denmark becoming guarantors was thereby eliminated, and the Russians and Germans thought that the danger of these countries becoming guaranteed in turn was also eliminated.[5] And for his part Isvolsky wrote: "If history abounds in eternal treaties which have been broken, there is no reason to add to the number with a permanent treaty whose abrogation is stipulated in the very text! But it is perhaps not for Germany and Russia to refuse, cost what it may, this 'political experiment' if Norway insists on this point".[6] Thus Isvolsky and Schoen believed that everything was in order.[7]

But it was not. Lövland did not wish to give up the Scandinavian reservation. For him, the Northern countries were a natural unit on account of national character, kinship and centuries of common history. Norway did not wish to

[1] Omang n. 97 Memorandum by Norwegian Foreign Office 23. I 1907
[2] Omang n. 100 Memorandum by Lövland 27. I 1907
[3] Omang n. 120 Wedel to Lövland 13. II 1907
   Omang n. 121 British F. O. to Norway 13. II 1907
[4] Omang n. 100 Memorandum by Lövland 27. I 1907
[5] GP 23 II n. 8046 Schoen to Bülow 5. II 1907
[6] AA Norwegen 7 geheim Bd 2 Russian F. O. to German Embassy 20. I/2. II 1907
[7] GP 23 II n. 8046 Schoen to Bülow 5. II 1907

remain outside a future Scandinavian neutrality and defence alliance. "Norway must not deceive her kindred by retiring into the shelter of permanent neutrality." He also wanted to avoid the appearance of seeking the guarantee of the powers against Sweden.[1]

Nansen wrote from London that Norway might obtain a guarantee of integrity without neutrality. Bertie and King Edward VII had recommended such an idea, although Grey was hesitating, fearing the suspicions of the Eastern Empires.[2] This idea was to be accepted later, but at the moment the time was not propitious. Wedel had already remarked that the Swedish war party would assert that such a guarantee was pointed against Sweden.[3] On the other hand Lövland understood that neutrality without the Scandinavian reservation would seem anti-Swedish to the Swedes.[4]

So a last attempt to preserve the lead in Norwegian hands was made. The Russian counter-draft was read as if it contained only comments on the Norwegian unofficial draft, and a new draft was made trying to take the remarks into account as far as possible.

The new draft was a shock to the Empires. It is true that Norway accepted the joint treaty, in which Norway declared herself *neutral,* a status which the powers would be obliged to *respect,* and the powers further promised to respect and *guarantee* Norway's *integrity.* Their help was not to be armed but "appropriate", and Lövland thought it reasonable that Norway should be allowed to ask for aid before it was given. The treaty would be signed by the four powers and by Norway. — So the appearance of a guardianship by the powers over Norway would be avoided. All this was acceptable to the great powers. But the Scandinavian reservation remained. The powers had in their objections remarked that the Scandinavian reservation might draw the guarantors into war if Norway was allowed to defend her neighbours, whereby her integrity might be endagered and the help of the guarantors needed. Now the reservation was remade in such form that the pledge of the powers to help Norway lapsed if Norway became involved in a war because of her neighbours.[5] With this "heroic solution"[6] Lövland tried to keep the reservation and at the same time take into account the objections against it. He could not guess how repulsive the very idea of a Pan-Scandinavian alliance was to the Empires, for whom his new solution was worse than ever. On the other hand the British were now beginning to have second thoughts on Norwegian neutrality.

---

[1] Omang n. 106 Memorandum by Lövland January 1907
[2] Omang n. 111 Nansen to Lövland 5. II 1907
   Omang n. 114 Nansen to Lövland 6. II 1907
[3] Omang n. 56 Wedel to Lövland 30. XI 1906
[4] AA Norwegen 7 geheim Bd 2 Scheller to Bülow 25. II 1907
[5] BD 8 n. 93 Norwegian draft treaty 13. III 1907
[6] BD 8 n. 93 minutes, n. 7 by Hardinge

Second thoughts in London

From the very beginning the Foreign Office had been somewhat uneasy about the Norwegian proposal. Grey "saw great difficulty in recognizing the conditional neutrality of Norway, from which she would have the power to withdraw, and . . also he felt the inconvenience of recognizing the neutrality of Norway when the neutrality of Sweden might be violated".[1]

The Russian counter-proposal was greeted with satisfaction by Eyre Crowe as it "altogether eliminated the difficulties inherent in Norway's original proposition that we should furnish at own cost the armed force", the Scandinavian reservation was done away with, and the treaty would have been permanent and joint, not four separate treaties for some years. Even more important, "the Russian proposal will enable His Majesty's Government to adopt the attitude of 'following Russia's lead' in this matter, which it may for general political reasons be desirable at this moment to emphasize, and I (Crowe) think it would be an advantage if we were at once to reply to the Russian note by expressing the gratification of His Majesty's Government at finding themselves in this matter in practically complete agreement with the Russian Government".[2] — This was the time when Great Britain tried to come to an agreement with Russia on the Asian areas of conflict, but negotiations were proceeding slowly while Isvolsky was occupied in clearing away the obstacles to the treaty. — Sir Edward Grey was not quite so enthusiastic as Eyre Crowe, being worried on account of Sweden: "The four guaranteeing powers could also make a declaration amongst themselves of their readiness to admit Sweden to a similar guarantee if Sweden wished to have some intimation that the door would be kept open for her, but that point had better be reserved for the present. Someone might raise the question of whether the same should be done for Denmark, which would be awkward and would raise the Great Belt question".[3] — Once again it is seen that the question of the Straits dominated all other aspects of the Northern question.

It was the Ambassador in Paris, Sir Francis Bertie, who suggested that the neutrality of Norway might be dropped and only her integrity guaranteed.[4] Grey had discussed the situation with Nansen and had understood "that his Government would prefer a Treaty of Integrity alone rather than one which would impose neutrality without reservation"[5] (this had been Lövland's idea as early as November 1906)[6] but Grey was cautious: "it will not do for us to

[1] PRO/FO 371/295/13298 Grey to Bertie 22. IV 1907
[2] BD 8 n. 89 note by Eyre Crowe 24. I 1907
[3] BD 8 n. 89 note by Edward Grey 24. I 1907
[4] PRO/FO 371/295/4784 Bertie to Grey 12. II 1907
[5] PRO/FO 371/295/4466 Grey to Herbert 7. II 1907
[6] Omang n. 40 Lövland to Nansen 18. XI 1906

propose that neutrality should be dropped: it will make Russia and Germany suspect that we have some design".[1] Metternich did remark to Grey that if he accepted the Russian project, he could not leave the essential point out.[2] Isvolsky hoped that Grey meant to guarantee integrity and recognize neutrality, without contradicting the Russian project.[3]

These hopes were in vain. It seems that Great Britain did have "some design", and Russia and Germany did suspect her.

The Russian counter-proposal for the Norwegian treaty was discussed at the 95th meeting of the Committee of Imperial Defence on the 21st February 1907. Grey said that he was "pleased with the minimization of possible complications through the joint Treaty of Great Britain, Germany, France and Russia, proposed by Russia, instead of separate ones. He thought that in case of a joint treaty the question of the Danish straits would not arise. He supposed that Russia would insist on Norwegian neutrality and that she would not accept integrity without neutrality".[4] — It seems that Grey might have accepted the neutrality treaty in the form Russia had proposed, in spite of the eventual Swedish reaction, trusting that the Straits question would not emerge.

But the navy raised objections: "Captain Ottley from the Admiralty wanted to reserve the discussion for a later meeting because Admiral Fisher was absent; but remarked that the Norwegian neutrality might handicap Great Britain in a war with Germany — if the latter occupied Denmark, Great Britain would need to seize a Norwegian port. The terms of the treaty might involve Great Britain in war with Russia and France who would be obliged to defend Norwegian integrity".[5] (The Captain did not say that the pledge would prevent Great Britain from seizing the port which was needed!)

The second Norwegian draft was no more acceptable than the first one to the Russians and Germans, and even the British had their objections: ". . our Naval Experts would prefer the omission of all mention of the neutrality of Norway, but if all the other powers agree to it being included in this or an amended text we shall have to follow suit".[6] Grey said "We should prefer to omit neutrality unless that of Sweden and Denmark was also recognized"[7], and proposed "we might suggest that if Norway can terminate neutrality by engaging in a war of defence with one of the other Scandinavian Powers, that neutrality should also cease to be binding upon the four Powers if any of them are engaged in a war to which any of the three Scandinavian powers becomes a party".[8] — That is,

[1] PRO/FO 371/295/4784 minute by EG 12. II 1907
[2] AA Norwegen 7 geheim Bd 2 Metternich to Bülow 8. II 1907
[3] AA Norwegen 7 geheim Bd 2 Schoen to Bülow 20. II 1907
[4] PRO/CAB 2/2 minutes of the 95th meeting of CID 21. II 1907
[5] PRO/CAB 2/2 minutes of the 95th meeting of CID 21. II 1907
[6] BD 8 n. 93 note by Charles Hardinge 14. III 1907
[7] BD 8 n. 93 note by Edward Grey 14. III 1907
[8] BD 8 n. 93 note by Edward Grey 14. III 1907

if Germany were to attack Denmark, Great Britain need not respect Norway's neutrality. But this proposition was not made in earnest.

To Nansen Grey explained that there were "great difficulties" in recognizing the neutrality of Norway.[1] Nansen knew the reason; he had met Admiral Fisher in the street, and the First Sea Lord had told him that he had said to Grey that Great Britain ought not to promise to respect Norway's neutrality unless Denmark and Sweden could be made neutral, too. If Germany occupied Denmark, the Royal Navy would have to seize ports in Norway as bases for action in the Straits. Nansen remembered that the Foreign Office had in November preferred Norwegian neutrality for the very reason that it would prevent Germany from occupying Norwegian ports, but realized that the Foreign Office could not always know what the navy thought. He asked whether the Royal Navy would break through the Straits, and Fisher threatened that he would do so, adding that he had all the means for sweeping the mines, etc. As a justification for his plans the admiral mentioned the rumours about the negotiations between Germany and Denmark.[2] It was a week since Crozier's article had been published. It has already been pointed out that these were no momentary fancies but that Admiral Fisher really planned breaking into the Baltic (p. 44). The naval attaché in Berlin, Captain Dumas, thought that the first task of the Royal Navy was to destroy the Kiel Canal, and as the German defences on the North Sea end of the canal were too strong, the navy had to get through the Straits to do its work at the Kiel or Baltic end.[3] Landings on the German coast were considered, too.

A decision on the Norwegian question was not arrived at until April. Of the 96th meeting of the CID we have only a note by the secretary summarizing the conclusion of the discussion "that Great Britain must have ample guarantees as to the freedom of the passages between the North Sea and the Baltic Sea before tying her hands in any way".[4] And at the 97th meeting it was concluded that "in regard to the difficulties inseparable from any guarantee of the neutrality of Norway, it would be simpler if all mention of neutrality were dropped, integrity only being guaranteed", but "it appears impracticable to introduce a provision to this effect into any Treaty that may be negotiated".[5]

The British are suspected of ulterior motives

So the negotiations concerning the Norwegian treaty of guarantee were lagging. Rumours as to the cause of the delay began circulating, and generally it

[1] Omang n. 134 Nansen to Lövland 13. III 1907
[2] Omang n. 134 Nansen to Lövland 13. III 1907
[3] BD 8 n. 104 Dumas to Lascelles to Grey 7. III 1907
[4] PRO/CAB 4/3/102 B "Note by Secretary summarizing previous papers"
[5] PRO/CAB 2/2 minutes of the 97th meeting of CID 25. IV 1907

9

was said to be due to the British. Krupensky in Christiania said to Herbert:
"Your Government has changed its opinion from what I hear, because Sir John
Fisher has come forward and altered the whole position by pointing out that, in
case of war between Germany and England, the former would certainly occupy
some point in Denmark, and England would take a port in Norway . ." [1] The
Foreign Office was annoyed: "It looks as if Sir J. Fisher had again been
indiscreet . . . The result is unfortunate. ." [2] But the diplomatic service, too, had
men who talked too much. Raben had wondered why England did not like
Norwegian neutrality, and Johnstone had answered by hinting at the need of
bases in an eventual war.[3]

It seems that Grey really thought that he had the agreement of the Norwegians in delaying the negotiations, because the powers resented the Scandinavian reservation and the Norwegians were reluctant to abandon Sweden. "My
recollection is that Dr. Nansen himself told me that Norway would rather drop
the neutrality than have it without the reservation allowing her to join Sweden
if attacked; that he dwelt strongly on the danger of being separated from Sweden by an unreserved obligation of neutrality & that my opinion as to the
difficulty of a qualified neutrality & the inconvenience of an unconditional
neutrality was only given in accord with the opinions he expressed".[4] Sweden
had refused to participate in the negotiations but some hope was nurtured:
"Nansen seemed to have some hope that in time Sweden would become favourable . . I (Grey) said that if that was so, it might be well for Norway to wait
until Sweden was ready".[5]

It is not quite clear whether Grey himself really thought that Sweden might
come round to accepting the new treaty, or whether this was only an excuse for
trying to lead the Norwegians away from the path of complete estrangement
from Sweden. It must be remembered that Norway was not to be given neutrality without Sweden and Denmark, and Denmark's neutrality was believed neither to be possible nor desirable. The status quo was the best status from the
British point of view.

Lindberg is of the opinion that Grey thought only of the Scandinavian situation, wishing to prevent the ultimate estrangement between Norway and Sweden
and to save as much unity as possible in order to preserve the status quo. He
denies that Grey had any "ulterior motives" in regard to the Norwegian ports,
and he does not mention Denmark as being of any importance in this context.

---

[1] PRO/FO 371/295/18199 Herbert to Grey 4. VI 1907
[2] PRO/FO 371/295/18199 minute by EAC
[3] Which made Raben exclaim to the German envoy: "As if Great Britain would let the
    neutrality of any country prevent her from occupying it"
    AA Dänemark 37 geheim Bd 6 Henckel to Ausw. Amt 18. I 1907
[4] PRO/FO 371/295/18199 Herbert to Grey 4. VI 1907, minute EG
[5] PRO/FO 371/295/14809 Grey to Herbert 2. V 1907

He admits that Fisher or perhaps Hardinge may have had such plans but maintains that it was Grey who led British foreign policy, not Fisher or Hardinge.[1]

It must be admitted that Grey never spoke of the Norwegian ports but only mentioned the "difficulties" inherent in the Norwegian neutrality. He may have had no "ulterior motive".

On the other hand it seems clear from the foregoing narrative that the Committee of Imperial Defence took the naval view into account and that Grey did accept its conclusions.

It is not necessarily a sign of weak dependence if the Secretary of State for Foreign Affairs takes into account the military and naval point of view when staking out his policy, if that view is in accordance with his own aim. Grey himself said later: "The naval position underlies our European policy".[2] The decision not to grant neutrality to Norway was made in accordance with the wishes of both the Foreign Office and the Admiralty.[3] We have seen that the Danish question was of the greatest importance for both ministries and dictated the decision in the Norwegian question.

It may be that Lindberg has seen the problem too much from the viewpoint of Stockholm when he concludes that Grey's policy was in perfect accordance with Scandinavian interests. His book is concerned with *"Scandinavia* in Great Power Politics" and thus it may be that the Straits have been taken too little notice of. The importance of Sweden to Great Britain cannot be disputed, but it does seem that Lindberg bases his arguments on the situation in June when the Russian proposal concerning the Åland Islands (to be discussed later) had brought Sweden's position into the foreground and the Danish and German endeavours to cover the traces of Moltke's and Lütken's discussions had had some effect. But in fact the decision to drop neutrality had been developing during the spring months in step with the rumours concerning the Danish situation, when Sweden seemed to be sailing in calmer waters.

Isvolsky intensifies collaboration with Germany

When the Norwegians handed their new draft to the Russians in March, Isvolsky, who considered it even less acceptable than the first one, wanted to

---

[1] Lindberg: *Scandinavia.* . p. 67—80
[2] Marder I p. 429, 11. VII 1912
[3] Eyre Crowe commented very favourably on an article, the writer of which realized "the importance for Great Britain in case of war with Germany to possess a naval base close to the entrances to the Baltic". This was initialled without comment by E. G.
PRO/FO 371/529/205 Rennel Rodd to Grey 30. XII 1907, minute by EAC 3. I 1908, initials by EG

communicate with the Germans about further action.[1] He was really annoyed at the Norwegians: "Far from taking into serious consideration the Russian observations, which have happily been supported by Your Excellency (Bülow), Norway has believed itself entitled to put forward, more precisely even than in the first project, the idea of an eventual system between Norway, Sweden and Denmark of a Pan-Scandinavian guarantee of territorial integrity and neutrality".[2] This was anything but the permanent neutrality planned by the powers: "The Russian interests, and, even less, the German, cannot allow that the three Scandinavian states would carry through a rapprochement. It might easily revive the idea of a perpetually neutral Pan-Scandinavian union. Such a union, without doubt precious from the viewpoint of international law, would surely not agree with the interests of the Empires. It is evident that Russia would not gain anything by the formation, instead of three relatively weak states, of a Pan-Scandinavian union; and Germany would not like the appearance of permanently neutral states in the North, because such a combination would necessarily lead to the recognition of free navigation from the North Sea to the Baltic and vice versa for all ships of all nations and all kinds at all times, as in the Suez Canal. Russia assumes that such a project must be unacceptable to the Berlin Cabinet".[3]

It has already been noted that it was satisfactory for Russia to have got rid of the Scandinavian Union, and it is natural that she did not like the prospect of an even stronger Pan-Scandinavian combination. It may be thought odd that the opening of the Straits was said to be equally distasteful for Germany and Russia, as the freedom of the Straits had earlier been deemed to agree with Russian interests. But it must be remebered that Isvolsky had already once suggested closing the Straits together with the Germans, not as a measure dictated by the Russian interests, but because Germany was going to close them in any case so that Russia had better howl with the German wolf.

The message cited above goes on: "The Russian Government is trying to avoid all political combinations which might lead to the realization of these tendencies". Russia submitted to Germany that the new Norwegian draft was unacceptable to both Empires; that these Empires had to direct their endeavours to preserve the actual status quo between the three Scandinavian countries; and that every attempt to broaden permanent neutrality so that it would comprise the three Scandinavian Kingdoms had to be repulsed. Only the recognition of Norwegian neutrality was to be negotiated, without any participation by Sweden or Denmark. The Russian Government were prepared to

[1] GP 23 II n. 8050 Schoen to Ausw. Amt 15. III 1907
[2] AA Norwegen 7 geheim Bd 3 Russian F.O. to German Embassy 2. IV 1907
[3] GP 23 II n. 8051 Schoen to Bülow 21. IV 1907

give a pledge to Germany to follow a policy which was in accordance with the above viewpoints.[1]

Isvolsky had found the area in which he was able to state that Germany's
and Russia's interests were identical, and where treaties could be made to
counterbalance the Asian agreement with England. The promise of a pledge in
the last sentence of the message above is the genesis of the secret Baltic Treaty
of October 1907, and the policy of preserving the status quo in Scandinavia led
to the Treaty guaranteeing the Baltic status quo in April 1908. — Incidentally,
when the British mentioned the status quo they implied good relations between
Norway and Sweden with British influence predominating as had been the case
earlier. Isvolsky meant the status of 1907, with the relations of Norway and
Sweden definitely broken, which he succeeded in confirming by the Norwegian
Treaty of Guarantee in the autumn of 1907. The status quo of the Baltic
agreement of 1908 referred only to territorial possessions, not to relations
between the states.

With German help Isvolsky hoped to able to realize also his own smaller
schemes in the Baltic. Because he believed himself to have been so obliging, he
expected that "the German Government would facilitate on their part a task
which the Russian Government saw imposing itself at the moment of the regu-
lation of the Norwegian question".[2]

Isvolsky takes up the Åland question

With German support Isvolsky hoped to solve the question of watching the
revolutionary smugglers. In February 1907 he explained to Schoen "that before
long he was going to appeal to the friendship of the Imperial Government
towards Russia". Russia was going to organize an efficient service for guarding
and securing the coast, a kind of blockade, and German moral support would
be needed against the inevitable protests from Scandinavia.[3]

A month later Isvolsky explained, as Schoen had already "guessed", that the
question was mainly of the reoccupation of the Åland Islands. "Because Germany and Russia had identical interests in the Baltic and were close to each
other in their general Scandinavian policy, as the recent agreement on the
Norwegian question demonstrated, so Isvolsky believed himself to be justified
in supposing that we (the Germans) would support him, or at least make no
difficulties, in the question of the Åland Islands".[4]

Together with his note on the Norwegian draft and his pledge to agree with
the Germans on Baltic policy, Isvolsky sent a new appeal on the Åland ques-

---

[1] GP 23 II n. 8051 Schoen to Bülow 21. IV 1907
[2] AA Norwegen 7 geheim Bd 2 Russian F. O. to German Embassy 30. III 1907
[3] AA Russland 63 Bd 1 Schoen to Bülow 19. II 1907
[4] AA Russland 63 Bd 1 Schoen to Bülow 30. III 1907

tion. He explained that in Finland there were 60 000 men ready to rebel at a signal from the Russian revolutionaries. However, the Russian Government would not, after all, declare a blockade of the Finnish coastline, as the Finns were well aware that Russia would and could make a bloody end of any rebellion, and in addition the Russian revolutionary movement had abated. But the Russian Government would insist on the idea of establishing a military base on the Åland Islands.[1]

Schoen said to Bülow that Germany had no reason to prevent Russia, because it was also in Germany's interest to avoid a new revolutionary outbreak in Russia. Even the occupation of Åland by Russia could leave Germany cool; let France and England take care of their treaties.[2]

Tschirschky thought that the protest against the occupation could indeed be left to the signatory powers, but he was worried lest the occupation might frighten the Swedes into joining the Norwegian treaty of neutrality. He promised that Germany would not make any difficulties if Russia could come to an understanding with Sweden.[3] The mixing up of the Åland question with the Norwegian affair made him remark "that the question was of two completely different problems" but, of course, he did not threaten to obstruct in case Russia entered into negotiations with Sweden, "provided no harmful reaction is thereby caused in the Norwegian neutrality question".[4] — This was enough for Isvolsky, but the Germans were right in apprehending that the new Russian initiative would cause difficulties in the Norwegian negotiations.

The Norwegians learnt the Russian objections concerning the Scandinavian reservation from Isvolsky and his aide Taube.[5] At Taube's suggestion the subsequent drafts were previously discussed by the Russians and Norwegians, and then submitted to the other three powers, although the Norwegians did not quite like to act behind the back of Great Britain.[6] Evidently the Russians had decided to let in no more Scandinavian complications to the future draft.

The Norwegians had in vain waited for an answer from London, an Russia's activity was greeted with gratitude. Still, it was with a heavy heart that Lövland dropped his Scandinavian reservation. As a last effort he proposed that the possibility of a future reservation be mentioned in separate notes. Of course even this was disagreeable to the Empires, although for a while Isvolsky thought it reasonable to give in a little "in order to keep a hand in the game and to prevent Norway from initiating spontaneously a Scandinavian neutrality arrangement or agreeing thereof with only the Western powers". He might have

[1] AA Russland 63 Bd 1 Schoen to Bülow 21. IV 1907
[2] AA Russland 63 Bd 1 Schoen to Bülow 19. II 1907
[3] AA Russland 63 Bd 1 Tschirschky to Schoen 9. IV 1907
[4] AA Russland 63 Bd 1 note by Klehmet 6. V 1907
[5] Omang n. 138 Prebensen to Lövland 15. III 1907
[6] Omang n. 141 Prebensen to Lövland 1. IV 1907

consented to the proposed exchange of notes, provided the right for Norway to conclude neutrality treaties with other powers would be defined as depending on the previous consent of the four great powers. "In this way Russia and Germany would always be able to veto any Scandinavian neutrality agreement."[1] This proposition did not result in anything, but it illuminates Isvolsky's apprehensions and ingenuity. — Russia on her part desisted from demanding an eternal treaty; it was to be renewed every ten years if none of the signatories had given notice of renouncig it two years earlier.[2] Thus the hope was left open for the Norwegians that later in a more propitious situation the treaty might be revised.

After preliminary talks with the Norwegians and secretly with the Germans, Isvolsky sent the second Russian draft to all the powers concerned in June 1907. In the draft Norway declared her intention of observing neutrality in all circumstances, which the great powers promised to recognize and respect. If asked by Norway, the powers would help her to preserve her neutrality and integrity with such means as they deemed appropriate. The duration of the treaty was to be ten years, automatically renewed every decade.[3]

Isvolsky explained to the powers that Norway was, of course, free to conclude any agreements with any country, be they neutrality or defensive treaties; but it was inexplicable that these two kinds of treaty could be united in one act. And Russia could never consent to discuss with Norway a treaty concerning the vital interests of other independent states.[4]

With this note Isvolsky sent a memorandum concerning the Åland servitude. He explained that the Treaty of 1855 would disappear with the signing of the new treaty of guarantee, but it was no real satisfaction for Russia because the ancient treaty had been completely obsolete for a long time. But the price the Western powers had paid for the November Treaty, the Convention of Åland, annexed to the Peace Treaty of Paris 1856, remained. For Russia this was "self-evidently, so to say, a perpetual lesion of her most sacred rights and most legitimate interests in those latitudes;" and for the Western powers it had lost all meaning long ago. — To the Western powers Isvolsky naturally did not speak of common interests with Germany, on the contrary he remarked that the Baltic balance of power had been dislocated in consenquence of the Russo-Japanese War. How could the Baltic situation, so unfavourable to Russia and so favourable to "other powers" agree with the principal interests of France and Great Britain? Would it not be natural for the latter powers to liquidate this question of the Åland Islands now while the Northern question in

[1] Omang n. 149 Prebensen to Lövland 18. IV 1907
[2] Omang n. 157 Nansen to Lövland 2. V 1907
[3] BD 8 n. 94 appendix II *Projet de traité* 19. VI 1907
[4] AA Norwegen 7 geheim Bd 2 Russian note to powers 23. V/5. VI 1907

general was under review? [1]

The Norwegian treaty was again almost ready. Russia, Germany and Norway had already reached unanimity in May. France was prepared to sign, all the objections she had had against the Norwegian proposals having been eliminated by the new Russian draft.[2] Notes were sent to the envoys in Christiania authorizing them to sign the treaty.[3] It was now the turn of Great Britain to put on the brakes in earnest.

The whole undivided Baltic question

The Russian proposal concerning the Åland Islands changed the situation from the British point of view so that they did not discuss the second counter-draft for the Norwegian treaty at all. "The Defence Committee are of the opinion that it is impracticable to introduce a provision for the neutrality of Norway. If this view is maintained, there can be no question of our being a party to the proposed convention".[4]

Now it was Sweden that seemed to be threatened. "These new proposals emanating from the Russian Govt. appear to me (Hardinge) to place Sweden in an isolated position since, in the event of an attack upon Sweden, Norway would be precluded from coming to her assistance. . Anyhow I think we must be careful not to wound unnecessarily Swedish sentiment. . . It would be somewhat unchivalrous to abrogate our old treaty and to have Sweden to stand or fall alone after her desertion by Norway".[5]

Nansen saw Grey and was told: "I should naturally wish to do in this matter what was convenient to Norway; but the question had taken a much more serious aspect . . . If we were to guarantee the neutrality of Norway separately, and then agree to the fortification of the Åland Islands, Sweden would be placed in a most invidious position. It was clear to me now that the whole question of the Baltic was affected by the proposals which were being put forward. I did not think that was a question which should be dealt with piecemeal, and we must consult the other three Powers about it. It might be that the result would be a conference of the four Powers but time was needed for consideration."[6] To the Swedish envoy Grey explained: "It might be desirable that the place of the old arrangements should be taken by something new and comprehensive, to which all four Powers were parties."[7]

[1] BD 8 n. 95 Russian note to the powers 7/20 VI 1907
[2] Omang n. 174 & 175 Wedel to Lövland 26. VI 1907
[3] Omang n. 177 v. Ditten to Lövland 27. VI 1907
[4] PRO/FO 371/295/20728 Nicolson to Grey 24. VI 1907, minutes by CH & EG
[5] PRO/FO 371/295/20788, minute by CH.
[6] PRO/FO 371/295/21939 Grey to Herbert 1. VII 1907
[7] PRO/FO 371/295/21956 Grey to Dering 2. VII 1907

To the Russian Ambassador Grey "pointed out that, if this Treaty was signed, and the Åland Islands were fortified, Sweden would be placed in a position more disadvantageous than any where she had yet been. Sweden could be forced to look somewhere for protection, and would no doubt turn to Germany. The fact was that the whole question of the Baltic was being raised. I was quite ready to discuss this question, and I fully recognized that the French and English treaties of 1855 and 1856 no longer represented the present political situation . . . The old treaties should be replaced by new arrangements, to which all four Powers . . should be parties. But it would be necessary to deal with the Baltic question as a whole and it would require a careful consideration".[1] The British statesmen thought that the Russian "proposal will cause consternation in Sweden and will be regarded as a deadly blow to her further independence".[2] "The result would be that in a short time Sweden would become a mere annexe of Russia . . to yield to the present Russian demand would inevitably be considered in Sweden as an act of downright betrayal . . ."[3]

The old fear of the Russian danger was revived, and also the new German danger caused anxiety: Sweden might turn southwards for protection against the East.

But there was more to the German danger than that. Grey did not dwell on the difficulties that might be caused by Germany, but more light on the apprehensions of the Western powers is thrown in a report of Francis Bertie, the British Ambassador in Paris, who had discussed the problem with Clemenceau. Bertie said that the proposal concerning the Åland islands had been a disagreeable surprise to Grey. "I said that it was a curious coincidence that Russia should bring forward this demand, which would reduce Sweden to the position of a Russian Grand Duchy, at the same moment that she proposed a Treaty which would deprive Norway of the right to make arrangements with Sweden for their common defence . . There might be a renewal of the feeling in Russia and Germany for a close understanding between the Empires, and if this were brought about and a war broke out between England and Germany, and Germany got to and seized the passages from the North Sea into the Baltic before the British fleet could reach them, what would be the position of England and France, supposing that the neutrality of Norway had been guaranteed? England, even if she abstained from joining in such a guarantee, would not be able to borrow a Norwegian port to watch the approaches through the straits without raising a question in which France would be called upon to oppose England. France would be in a dilemma of having to support Germany against England or to disregard her guarantee. . I suppose that Russia must have come to some

---

[1] PRO/FO 371/297/ undecipherable Grey to Nicolson 1. VII 1907
[2] PRO/FO 371/338/22870 Rennell Rodd to Grey 10. VII 1907
[3] PRO/FO 371/338/21122 Benckendorff to Grey 25. VI 1907, minutes by GSS

preliminary understanding with Germany in regard to the Baltic, otherwise Germany would not be ready to sign the proposed Norwegian arrangement in such a hurry. . His Excellency (Clemenceau). . gave me the impression of being greatly embarrassed by the Åland Islands question and . . by the proposed guarantee of the neutrality of Norway, and of feeling the difficulty for France of opposing Russian desires. . he is extremely anxious that the negotiations between the Russian and British Governments should be brought to a succesful conclusion as soon as possible".[1] Of course Bertie tried to make the French react to the Russian proposal and may therefore have painted the picture in dark colours with hints at Russo-German collaboration, for the French were troubled about their system of alliances, not about the Baltic question proper. But evidently Bertie saw the Norwegian, the Straits and the Åland questions as parts of a larger Baltic pattern, and according to Hardinge's memoirs the Foreign Office shared these apprehensions.[2]

In Stockholm Trolle saw the situation in the same light: Norway would regret that she had been so precipitate and that she had bound her hands. "Of course I do not in the least know whether Denmark, for instance, has any secret Agreement with Germany — I don't believe she has — but she might make one for self-protection; and then, if Germany, having Denmark under her control were to turn to us and say: 'now close the Belts' what would be our situation then?" Norways's action would inevitably raise the whole question of the Baltic, where Sweden was vitally concerned, much more so than Norway.[3]

Nansen also understood that Grey was worried by Isvolsky's schemes: the Russians seemed to be trying to cut the bounds between Sweden and Norway by means of the neutrality treaty, and now the Åland proposal had shown how great the danger actually was. Nansen supposed that Åland was more of a pretext — here he erred — for refusing to guarantee Norwegian neutrality, which had worried the British for a long time — here he was right. Grey was, as we have seen, worried both because of Norwegian neutrality and of the Åland question. — Nansen added that England had found the old treaties of 1855 and 1856 to be valuable aces giving her the juridical right to have a say in the Baltic question, and she was reluctant to withdraw from that position without a replacement.[4] — Of course Nansen's thoughts are not necessarily true, but he had observed British policy during many years and his views must be accorded some weight where they do not conflict with British sources.

Grey had tried to keep open the possibility of future co-operation between Sweden and Norway: "Whether the Union existed or not, the geographical

[1] BD 8 n. 106 Bertie to Grey 9. VII 1907
[2] Hardinge, p. 129
[3] PRO/FO 371/295/23425 Dering to Grey 11. VII 1907
[4] Omang n. 191 Nansen to Lövland 5. VII 1907

situation would probably always make the community of interests felt . ."[1] But the Swedish horizon looked more and more ominous to the British view. Trolle had warned that the British plan of dropping neutrality would make the Norwegian treaty anti-Swedish: Norway "would be enabled to adopt an aggressive attitude towards her neighbour . . without any fear of retaliation . . He could not conceive that such a guarantee could be given without a correlative obligation of neutrality".[2] Then Rennell Rodd reported that the Swedish Minister for Foreign Affairs "had information as to Russian proposals respecting the Åland Islands . . He said that were the four Powers to guarantee the integrity of Norway, and were Russia as a condition to obtain abrogation of the treaties of 1855 and 1856, Sweden would be obliged to consider how she could best safeguard her position by a change of policy, which I gathered meant drawing nearer to Germany".[3] — Sometimes it seems that the Swedes magnified their anxiety in order to make the Norwegian treaty fail, and the Foreign Office commented: "the Swedes are becoming so sensitive as to be almost absurd".[4] But the French envoy in Stockholm Allizé also cautioned that guaranteeing only Norwegian integrity without the obligation of neutrality would cause "serious susceptibilities and provoke a painful impression". The prohibition on fortifying Åland was looked upon as an irreplacable cornerstone of Swedish defence. The danger really existed that Sweden might turn to Germany to seek security and the interests of the Entente in Sweden were in danger if Russia did indist on her demand.[5]

Grey had hoped that the conference he had proposed would solve the difficulties, or perhaps at least postpone the decisions till the feelings calmed down. "I think we may get out of this eventually".[6] But the idea was not acceptable to the other powers. What the Eastern Empires thought of his proposal will soon be narrated. At this point French reluctance may be noted.

It was reported that the Paris Government were prepared to accept the Russian draft treaty, and that it was impossible for them to oppose the desire of the Russian Government with regard to the Convention debarring Russia from fortifying the Åland Islands. Sweden might turn to Germany, but for France her duty towards her ally was more important. A conference would not be willingly consented to because it might bring forth thorny question.[7] The Foreign Office commented: "the readiness of the French Govt. to accede to the demand of Russia is very awkward . . We shall clearly get no help from the French Govt.

[1] PRO/FO 371/295/21956 Grey to Dering 2. VII 1907
[2] PRO/FO 371/295/15325 Rennell Rodd to Grey 7. V. 1907
[3] PRO/FO 371/295/24168 Rennell Rodd to Grey 20. VII 1907
[4] PRO/FO 371/295/15325 Rennell Rodd to Grey 7. V 1907, minute EAC
[5] DDF 11 n. 86 Allizé to Pichon 23. VII 1907
[6] PRO/FO 371/338/21122 Benckendorff to Grey 25. VI 1907, minute by EG
[7] PRO/FO 371/297/22533 Lister to Grey 6. VII 1907

— in fact if we stand out against the Russian request we shall find ourselves in opposition to them".[1]

There were reasons enough to apprehend the Swedish reaction, but on the other hand also the Norwegians were pressing the British. The French envoy in Christiania Delavaud reported that the Norwegians were surprised because Russia, whom the Norwegians had been afraid of, had turned out to be so positive in her reactions to the endeavours of Norway, and England, who had been looked upon as a friend, was obstructing Norwegian wishes. It was not Sweden that was believed to be the cause of England's refusal but Denmark, whose neutrality was the British sine qua non for Norwegian neutrality, on account of the Norwegian ports. Now England had had to put her cards on the table when Russia had not, contrary to expectations, prevented the Norwegian treaty.[2] Delavaud thought that promises given to Norway ought to be fulfilled in order to preserve the influence of the Entente and to prevent the realization of the schemes of the opposite camp. He thought that the treaty could not possibly cause any harm comparable to the harm done if the Norwegians were estranged. In that case Germany might reap an even bigger harvest because she followed docilely the lead of St. Petersburg while Great Britain opposed strongly the Russian endeavours, and France was undecided between her two friends.[3]

King Haakon himself tried to blackmail Edward VII with the standard asset: "I hope England will not make difficulties and be the cause that this affair will fall through for Norway... I need not say how much this would strengthen Germany's position in Norway that England is no longer willing".[4] — It is difficult to know how much influence the royal meddling, among other messages to the same tune, did have on the course of events.

The dilemma of British foreign policy can be sensed in the vexed tone of Hardinge's comment: "Although the Norwegian Govt. are aware of the Russian proposal about the Åland islands they still want the signature of the Norwegian neutrality convention."[5]

[1] PRO/FO 371/217/22533 minutes 8. VII 1907
[2] DDF 11. n. 61 Delavaud to Pichon 2. VII 1907
[3] DDF 11 n. 61 Delavaud to Pichon 2. VII 1907
[4] PRO/FO 371/295/22842 Nansen to Edward VII 10. VII 1907 (with Haakon's letter)
   The F. O. did not like this kind of personal politics: "Dr. Nansen must be told that such communications must in future be made through proper dipl. channels", minute by CH
[5] PRO/FO 295/371/22333 Dering to Grey 6. VII 1907, minute by CH

MUCH ADO. . .
Isvolsky's tactical retreat

Meanwhile Isvolsky had modified his plans, and the British received some intimation that the "Russian proposal is apparently not going to be pressed".[1] The next day, 11th July, the British reminded the Norwegians that Great Britain might sign a treaty guaranteeing Norway's integrity, without a guarantee of neutrality.[2] Two days later Grey informed the Russian ambassador officially that Great Britain would be prepared to accept and sign a Treaty guaranteeing the integrity of Norway, all mention of neutrality being omitted.[3] The French were "glad that the suggestion of a Conference had been dropped, for a Conference would have accentuated the differences between Russia and Germany on one side and England on the other, and France would have occupied an embarrassing position".[4]

The British knew that Sweden would not like the new form of the Norwegian proposal. Hardinge wrote: "Sweden is going to be tiresome but we cannot go back on our word to Norway."[5] Hence Lindberg's viewpoint cannot be accepted that it was mainly Sweden that Grey thought of, that it was the danger threatening Sweden from Russia through Åland that made Great Britain announce the idea of a conference, and that it was when Russia desisted from her Åland proposition that Great Britain decided to drop the conference and give Norway the integrity treaty.[6]

We have seen how the decision to omit neutrality from the treaty had emerged during the spring in step with the developments in the Straits situation. The opposition of the other powers had made the idea of a conference impossible. And the Norwegians were told of the British decision to sign the integrity treaty without neutrality on 11th July, two days before Isvolsky's official message concerning his retreat from the position he had hitherto held on Åland. No, the point at issue was to escape from the dilemma of British policy discussed in the previous chapter. The position of Sweden in the face of a Russian advance was not the only problem causing anxiety in Downing Street, although it was, of course, an important part of the problem; and the Åland proposal did not provide the deepest motivation for Grey's decisions, although it was the cause that drove him to act. The problem was the situation in the Straits, on the Baltic Sea, in Sweden, Norway and Denmark: it was the Baltic question in its entirety.

[1] PRO/FO 371/338/22870 Rennell Rodd to Grey 10. VII 1907
[2] Omang n. 196 Nansen to Lövland 11. VII 1907
[3] PRO/FO 371/295/23527 Grey to Herbert 13. VII 1907
[4] PRO/FO 371/295/23550 Bertie to Grey 14. VII 1907
[5] PRO/FO 371/295/24168 Rennell Rodd to Grey 20. VII 1907, minute by CH
[6] Lindberg: *Scandinavia. .* p. 73

The matter had not proceeded as Isvolsky might have wished, either. It had turned in the direction the Germans had warned him of; his Åland proposition had roused British suspicions, and the result had been the proposal for a Baltic conference with its incalculable consequences. Isvolsky was angry at this check to his plans and complained to the Germans that England "mixing different, essentially separate questions and under the mask of specially considering Sweden's position .. attempts to win influence and a kind of seat and voice in the discussions on Baltic questions. This aspiration is against the interests of Russia and other Baltic states and must immediately be opposed with resolution".[1] — Several times, as stated, Isvolsky sought an occasion of expressing unanimity with Germany, and this was manifestly one. But his tone was one of genuine annoyance, and we need not doubt that he really wished to keep the British out of his schemes in the Baltic, as he said to the Germans. This does not mean that he genuinely strove to close the Danish Straits. — "In order to keep Britain out of the Baltic he was prepared for the great sacrifice of giving up his attempt to solve the Åland question at the moment, thereby eliminating the grounds for Britain delaying the Norwegian question".[2]

So Benckendorff, the Russian Ambassador in London, was instructed to inform Grey that Russia could not accept the proposal to have a conference to formulate a new guarantee for Sweden, because it had been stated in the Treaty of 1855 that it could be abrogated only by the signatories. The reasons advanced by Grey were pure formalities because the Treaty of 1855 had anyway lapsed in 1905, and to enter into negotiations for its abrogation would not have responded to Russia's dignity nor to the facts of the situation. And Sweden did not wish to participate in nor to be the object of any guarantee. If the Russian proposition concerning the Convention of 1856 had caused some difficulties, Russia did not wish to connect the two questions and was prepared to discuss the Åland question at a more propitious moment. Benckendorff was, of course, forbidden to mention the "real grounds" for the Russian refusal and retreat: "our constant desire to eliminate all foreign influence from the Baltic Sea".[3]

The Germans did not like the situation at all. When the first intimation of British reluctance regarding Norwegian neutrality was received in February, Tschirschky had reckoned that Britain wished to leave Norway free to conclude neutrality treaties with her neighbours, and that was why the British viewpoint was not acceptable.[4] Now the definite proposal strengthened these suspicions. The Germans remarked to Isvolsky, who was eager to conclude the Norwegian

[1] GP 23 II n. 8064 Schoen to Bülow 13. VII 1907
[2] =1
[3] AA Norwegen 7 geheim Bd 3 Russian F. O. to German Embassy 30. VI/13. VII 1907
[4] GP 23 II n. 8047 Tschirschky to Schoen 12. II 1907

treaty for his own reasons, that Britain would be free to use the Norwegian ports if not prohibited by the declaration of neutrality.[1] Hardinge in London explained the British wish of protecting Sweden to the German Ambassador, and Metternich tried to assure Berlin of Britain's 'innocence' in his report saying that there was no proof of her intention of using the Norwegian ports, nor of creating a Northern Union of Neutrality.[2] It is hardly likely that he succeeded in reassuring his superiors in Berlin, whose suspicions were only too well grounded.

The watered down treaty accepted

In May Lövland had had to desist from his Scandinavian reservation. Now he answered that Norway would have preferred the draft negotiated with Russia, but the new British proposition could be accepted if the great powers preferred it and a proper form could be found.[3] Delavaud reported that Lövland accepted it *comme pis aller,* but was more and more surprised and dissatisfied.[4] In consequence Lövland invented the idea that after the signature of the treaty Norway might declare herself permanently neutral.[5]

Isvolsky adopted the idea to comfort the Germans, proposing that the Norwegians could be inspired to declare their neutrality "spontaneously". Germany and Russia would then recognize their neutrality, and surely France as Russia's ally would follow suit, and thus Great Britain would be compelled to submit to the fait accompli.[6] Germany, however, was not comforted by this proposal, which was too dangerously like the scheme which Martens had proposed to the Danes in 1903—04. The envoy in Christiania was instructed "that it is not desirable for us that Norway declare herself neutral after the signature".[7] The example might be contagious. Finally Lövland desisted from his idea, realizing that it was hardly proper to declare neutrality immediately after the signature of a treaty from which neutrality had been dropped. Perhaps he was also afraid that England might object to the integrity treaty if he was going to play with the neutrality.[8]

Isvolsky also thought that the British wanted to keep open the possibility of occupying the Norwegian ports.[9] Probably he did not like the prospect, either;

---

[1] GP 23 II n. 8066 v. Mühlberg to Schoen 18. VII 1907
[2] GP 23 II n. 8068 Metternich to Bülow 18. VII 1907
[3] Omang n. 199 & 200 Lövland to Irgens 17. VII 1907
[4] DDF 11 n. 92 Delavaud to Pichon 24. VII 1907
[5] AA Norwegen 7 geheim Bd 3 Scheller to Bülow 22. VII 1907
[6] GP 23 II n. 8067 Schoen to Ausw. Amt 20. VII 1907
[7] AA Norwegen 7 geheim Bd 3 Tschirschky to Scheller 26. VII 1907
[8] AA Norwegen 7 geheim Bd 3 Scheller to Bülow 29. VII 1907
[9] AA Norwegen 7 geheim Bd 3 Schoen to Ausw. Amt 20. VII 1907

British ships in Norwegian ports could not have been a pleasant vision for him. To the French ambassador he expressed his surprise at England's proposals and "was unable to understand her motives" and how integrity could be guaranteed without imposing neutrality. But "in the spirit of conciliation" he was ready to accept the proposal.[1] To the Germans he explained this spirit of conciliation: the British schemes were no reason to refuse to sign the Norwegian treaty, on the contrary it was important to conclude the negotiations in order to prevent the Western powers from elbowing into the Baltic.[2] Isvolsky had new plans for his Baltic policy, which he took up at the Swinemünde meeting which was to take place at the beginning of August 1907. His remaining aim in the Norwegian question was to conclude the confounded matter as soon as possible and with the least possible complications.

Of course Isvolsky was right in supposing that Germany did not like the Western powers mixing in Baltic questions. "We too are of the opinion that in practice the outside powers ought to be kept out of Baltic matters". Evidently Auswärtiges Amt saw the strength of Isvolsky's argument that delay would give an opportunity to Great Britain for new interventions and it was explained to Bülow that "as we were prepared to guarantee integrity *and* neutrality, there ought to be nothing against accepting only integrity".[3]

Will anybody pick the chestnuts from the fire for the British?

The Norwegians supposed that the British would obtain the adherence of the guaranteeing powers to the new proposal.[4] But Hardinge did "not quite see why we should be driven by Norway to take the initiative in this matter. We consider that the action of the Norwegian Govt. has been premature and unnecessary. We have told them & the Russian Govt. how far we are ready to go, but it is palpably the business of the Norwegian Golt. to take any further action that may be necessary".[5]

Nansen tried to make the British move: ". . it was the wishes expressed by England in 1905, as to a Treaty joined by the four Powers, and it was also the advantages in this respect held out to us by electing Prince Charles of Denmark that made us open the negotiations. . It would be difficult for the Norwegian Government to bring in this question of dropping the neutrality now, as they have already declared themselves willing to accept the Russian proposal . . the aid of England . . would turn the sympathies in that direction. . and I would

[1] DDF 11 n. 102 Bompard to Pichon 1. VIII 1907
[2] AA Norwegen 7 geheim Bd 3 Schoen to Ausw. Amt 20. VII 1907
[3] AA Norwegen 7 geheim Bd 3 Mühlberg to Bülow 22. VII 1907
[4] PRO/FO 371/295/23682 Müller to Grey 17. VII 1907
[5] PRO/FO 371/295/23682 minute by CH

consider it very unfortunate in several respects if other sympathies should get the upper hand".[1] Hardinge commented: "premature and unnecessary action . . is scarcely a valid argument for obliging us to follow them. Dr. Nansen seems to realise this and ends his letter with what might be regarded as an attempt of blackmail".[2]

Lövland, too, endeavoured to hurry the British up: his Government wished to leave the Treaty behind them as a fait accompli, as the opposition "appeared determined to turn them out at any cost".[3] He got little sympathy in London: "No sooner are the Norwegian Govt. saved from one defeat than they bring forward the imminence of another to furnish an excuse for hurriedly pushing the treaty of guarantee. The Russian reply has not yet arrived, and by the time it does, the internal affairs of Norway may have brought a change in the situation".[4] The wish of the Foreign Office to see the fall of Lövland was not fulfilled until 1908.

Meanwhile the Swedes were becoming more annoyed and worried. The Minister for Foreign Affairs Trolle said that he would not have protested if the powers had promised to *respect* Norway's integrity, but against whom but Sweden might the *guarantee* be directed? "Sweden will be tempted in the future to look eastward only and consider her connection with the west as definitely severed by the interposing of an alien State".[5] Rnnell Rodd thought that "it may . . still be worth while considering whether the new Treaty to be signed with Norway cannot be so drafted as to avoid conveying the impression here (Sweden) that it is designed to protect her (Norway) against her former partner . . and thus to leave open the door for . . future co-operation between the two Scandinavian neighbours. ."[6] So the Norwegians were asked whether the treaty could be thought of without any guarantee at all. Of course Lövland was "much disappointed at the tenour of my (Herbert) communication, and replied with considerable warmth that, if His Majesty's Government intended further to weaken the Treaty, it would be better for them to declare once and for all that they wanted to have nothing to do with it".[7] His Majesty's Government would indeed have preferred to have nothing to do with the treaty, had that only been possible. "The whole thing has become a great nuisance".[8] But it was inevitable: "The line we have taken since the separation of Norway made it impossi-

---

[1] PRO/FO 371/295/24019 Nansen to Grey 16. VII 1907
[2] PRO/FO 371/295/24019 minute by CH
[3] PRO/FO 371/295/24427 Herbert to Grey 17. VII 1907
[4] PRO/FO 371/295/24427 minute by CH
[5] PRO/FO 371/295/24703 Rennell Rodd to Grey 20. VII 1907
[6] PRO/FO 371/295/24908 Rennell Rodd to Grey 22. VII 1907
[7] PRO/FO 371/295/24803 Herbert to Grey 25. VII 1907
[8] PRO/FO 371/295/24803 minute by EG

ble for us to throw out Norway in order to be the protagonist of Sweden. Even if the course had been open to us we could not have adopted it without throwing Norway into the arms of some one else, to which there are obvious objections" Grey declared.[1] The Norwegian blackmail had not been without effect.

Desperately the British sought for a means of making the treaty fail without compromising themselves. "We can draw up a draft .. & submit it to Russia, France & Germany. If Germany should object, there will probably be no treaty and we shall be no worse off than we were before".[2] But "I (Grey) should leave the initiative to Russia & let it be a Russian draft. There was rumour that all that Germany contemplated was a promise to respect neutrality & there is still a chance that if left to other powers it may take this form".[3] The Russians were given hints of the British wishes: "I (Nicolson) observed that I was not aware whether he (Isvolsky) was desirous of limiting himself to a statement that the Powers respected the integrity of Norway .. I did not imagine that, if Russia and the other two Governments preferred the milder phrase, you (Grey) would insist on your view".[4] A warning "Sweden might throw herself into the arms of Germany" was sent through the French to the Russians — "it was for them to consider what risks were involved in the present negotiations".[5] When the Russian envoy in Stockholm was reported to have said that the guarantee would be made in the light of Swedish wishes, the Foreign Office rejoiced, prematurely as it turned out, that "Russia has apparently become aware of the danger of isolating Sweden".[6] The British could not guess that Isvolsky was working hard to isolate Sweden and to turn her towards Germany.

The third Russian draft was discussed by the Norwegian chargé d'affaires, Karl Wedel Jarlsberg, and Isvolsky's aide Baron Taube, during August.[7] In September it was submitted to the powers. In the draft Norway and the powers declared the aim of the treaty to be the independence and integrity of Norway in her actual extent, the neutral zone included. Norway pledged not to let any power occupy or otherwise to use her territory. The powers on their part promised to recognize Norway's independence and to respect it. They promised to help Norway, if she asked for it, with appropriate means, if her integrity were menaced or violated. The term of the treaty was to be ten years, to be renewed automatically for further periods of ten years if no state had renounced

[1] PRO/FO 371/338/37733 Rennell Rodd to Grey 16. XI 1907 minute by EG
[2] PRO/FO 371/295/24803 Herbert to Grey 25. VII 1907 minute by CH
[3] PRO/FO 371/295/25054 Müller to Grey 26. VII 1907 minute EG
[4] PRO/FO 371/295/27691 Nicolson to Grey 13. VIII 1907
[5] PRO/FO 371/295/25563 Grey to Bertie 29. VII 1907
[6] PRO/FO 371/295/29946 Rennell Rodd to Grey 3. IX 1907, minute by EG
[7] Omang n. 222 Karl Wedel to Lövland 16. VIII 1907
    Omang n. 226 Karl Wedel to Lövland 30. VIII 1907

the treaty two years previously.[1]

The British were disappointed but powerless. "Sweden will remain out in the cold. Hitherto we have been anxious to let the negotiations drag on in as lengthy a manner as possible because there is no reason for hurry in concluding a new treaty & partly in the hope that Sweden would think better of it & consent to come in". "It seems to me (Hardinge) a pity the Swedish view could not be met by omission but the Norwegians would not have it". "Yes, the Norwegians were told at the time when they chose a king that we should look favourably on an integrity treaty & I (Grey) renewed this later on & we cannot now take the lead in whittling it down".[2]

Sweden furious

The Swedes had even earlier remarked that a guarantee of integrity without the obligation of neutrality left Norway free to *chikanera* Sweden without fear of consequences.[3] Lövland had explained that the treaty was intended only against eventual aggressors, England or Russia, but never against Sweden.[4] But Trolle answered that the fact was that in Sweden a very bitter feeling was growing.[5] The Prime Minister Lindman explained in "a very earnest tone" that the treaty was an unearned humiliation for Sweden, who had remained peaceful in 1905 in spite of Norwegian provocation.[6] King Oscar said that he would not have consented so easily to the abrogation of the Union in 1905 had he known that Norway was going to make such anti-Swedish treaties.[7] In the Crown Council Trolle stated that the treaty was an offence against Sweden and would badly hinder the endeavours to rebuild relations between the two countries. Sweden ought to do everything to prevent the treaty.[8]

The Norwegian envoy Vogt explained that some Swedes had idealistic Scandinavian reasons for their aversion to the Norwegian treaty, hoping that the neighbours would not drift too far apart into the different camps of the great powers; others had less idealistic nationalistic reasons, wanting to keep Norway isolated and thereby obliged to follow Sweden's lead in her policy.[9] It ought to have been clear to the Swedish statesmen that the treaty was not directed

---

[1] Omang n. 228 third Russian draft 11. IX 1907
[2] PRO/FO 371/295/30451 Russian Embassy to F.O. 11. IX 1907 minutes by CH & EG
[3] & [4] Omang n. 230 Memorandum by Lövland 18. IX 1907
[5] Omang n. 234 Norw. chargé d'affaires in Stockholm to Lövland 18. IX 1907
[6] DDF 11 n. 176 Allizé to Pichon 26. IX 1907
[7] GP 23 II n. 8071 note by Tschirschky 22. IX 1907
[8] Hildebrand p. 503
[9] Omang n. 201 Vogt to Lövland 17. VII 1907
  n. 209 Vogt to Lövland 26. VII 1907
  n. 221 Vogt to Lövland 7. VIII 1907

against Sweden, but it is understandable that they were nevertheless genuinely furious. Sweden had protested against the treaty, and in spite of the protest it was to be signed. Sweden's word had not had any weight while the neighbours, former subjects and rebels, had succeeded in their endeavours to obtain the support of the great powers, who had left Sweden isolated and forsaken. The Swedish press boiled with rage, and Lindberg says that the Swedish Government would have opposed the treaty even if they knew better, because popular feeling was so incensed that the Government was in danger.[1] *Svenska Dagbladet* threw light on the real grounds of the fury: "It is the very break-up of the Union which has hurt us — no, which stands as a political crime of the worst kind!"[2] — It is probable that any success of the Norwegians, any sign that Norway needed Swedish tutorship no more would have made the Swedes angry.

The situation was most unsatisfactory from the British point of view. ". . it is impossible to get the Swedes to believe that the Treaty is not aimed against them".[3] Rennell Rodd saw through the Swedish arguments: "Sweden would not have been at all averse to holding her superior strength . . over Norway in any dispute that might arise".[4] And the Swedes continued to speak about seeking new friends, and in fact sought them, as shall be seen later. The Swedish Prime Minister, Lindman, said that ". . the action of Norway . . must inevitably produce a change. Sweden could no longer remain in the position of conspicious isolation".[5] Hardinge wrote: "The Norwegian treaty is a very tiresome affair as Sweden is making such a fuss over it. I cannot imagine why the Russian Government never realized the danger of throwing Sweden into the arms of Germany and did not propose a draft Treaty by which the integrity of Norway would be respected but not guaranteed by the four powers. However it is now too late . ."[6] Rennell Rodd said: ". . it will be most unfortunate if this really succeeds in widening the existing breach between the two halves of Scandinavia".[7] But Hardinge concluded: ". . We shall have to sign this Treaty to which we are greatly opposed".[8] The British aim, of trying to maintain a Union which had disappeared, had proved impossible. The tactics of "wait and see" left the field free for others who were more active.

[1] Lindberg: *Scandinavia.* . p. 110
[2] *Svenska Dagbladet* 26. IX 1907
[3] PRO/FO 371/295/30821 Rennell Rodd to Grey 14. IX 1907
[4] PRO/PO 371/295/31244 Rennell Rodd to Grey 15. IX 1907
[5] PRO/FO 371/295/32335 Rennell Rodd ro Grey 28. IX 1907
[6] BD 8 n. 100 Hardinge to Nicolson 2. X 1907 private
[7] PRO/FO 371/295/31221 Rennell Rodd to Grey 14. IX 1907
[8] BD 8 n. 100 Hardinge to Nicolson 2. X 1907 private

Germany passive

The Germans thought that "it was difficult to discover how Sweden is able to see a point against herself" in the guarantee of Norwegian integrity.[1] A little morosely they added that up to this the Swedes had let England take care of their interests, so that it was a little late to expect that Germany would endanger the result of the Norwegian negotiations just to please Sweden.[2] The reception of the Swedish overtures was thus not enthusiastic; the change of direction in Swedish policy was not believed in. It was suspected that British influence was "evidently" hidden behind Sweden's demands.[3] The whole excitement in Sweden was seen as inspired by Rennell Rodd, who was also compelling the French to support Sweden.[4] The German explanation of British reluctance in the Norwegian question was Britain's misgivings about the Russo-German Baltic policy[5] which will be discussed later.

So, at least in September, the Germans did not appreciate the chance of strengthening their influence in Sweden which the British were afraid of, and which Isvolsky hoped to use to further his own schemes. Without trying the Germans succeeded where the British failed, for by November they were able to congratulate themselves: the Swedes "have not avoided noticing that we have kept aloof the whole time, and they suppose that we could not help signing (the Norwegian Treaty) in the end".[6]

Final attempts to satisfy Sweden

The French envoy in Stockholm Allizé was worried on account of the diminution of the influence of the Entente in Sweden. In a discussion with Prime Minister Lindman a suggestion was made, it is not known whether by Allizé or by Lindman,[7] that Sweden might become a guarantor, too.[8] This was a splendid solution from the Swedish point of view, as she would then have been an equal of the great powers, and this would have been a humiliation for Norway. Allizé conveyed this proposition to this government, arguing that the solution would bring moral and commercial advantages to the Entente powers.[9] Pichon in Paris "having no illusions about the reception which this proposition would

[1] GP 23 II n. 8071 note by Tschirschky 22. IX 1907
[2] GP 23 II n. 8072 Tschirschky to Jenisch 25. IX 1907
[3] GP 23 II n. 8081 Bülow to William II 5. XI 1907
[4] AA Norwegen 7 geheim Bd 4 Scheller to Bülow 15. X 1907
[5] GP 23 II n. 8077 v. Hindenburg to Bülow 21. X 1907
[6] AA Norwegen 7 geheim Bd 4 Müller to Bülow 12. XI 1907
[7] BD 8 n. 101 Hardinge to Nicolson 14. X 1907
[8] DDF 11 n. 176 Allizé to Pichon 26. IX 1907
[9] = 8

meet in Christiania, instructed the French representatives in London and St. Petersburg to inquire as to the views of the Ministers for Foreign Affairs".[1]

Hardinge wrote "I think they (the Norwegians) ought to be made to accept it as a solution to the whole question, but we, for dynastic reasons, are unable to apply the pressure required".[2] "The idea of Sweden joining in a guarantee of Norwegian integrity would be too galling for Norwegian pride".[3] Of course nothing could induce the Norwegians to submit to the tutelage of neighbours from whose control they had so recently broken free.[4]

Another hope lay in the old treaties: "If the Swedes make objections to abrogating the Treaty of 1855 .. that might serve as an excuse for France or Russia to make some new proposal to Norway in which we (the British) could perhaps associate ourselves".[5] As expected, the Swedes made objections. At first they promised to abrogate the Treaty of 1855 on condition that the Norwegian Treaty was revised in a manner acceptable to Sweden, and as it was not so revised, they refused categorically to abrogate the old Treaty (October 15th 1907).[6] Trolle hoped that "the abrogation of the Treaty of 1855, although it was a dead letter as a result of the excellent Russo-Swedish relations, was a good object of exchange with the Norwegians who drew on their feet against accepting the Swedish signature on the treaty although all the powers had consented to that".[7]

This hope also failed. Lövland said that according to the Convention of Karlstad the Treaty of 1855 could be abrogated only on Norway's behalf, without the participation of Sweden.[8] The British held that he overlooked "the consideration that in a question of this sort Scandinavia cannot be considered piecemeal, one half living under one treaty arrangement, the other half under a different one .. consequently M. Lövland's theories are not of much account".[9]

But since it was Isvolsky's wish that Scandinavia should be considered piecemeal and Sweden isolated from the West, Lövland's theories were of much account. Isvolsky proposed that the Treaty of 1855 be abrogated only as far as Norway was concerned, whereby Sweden's refusal would not prevent the signing of the Norwegian Treaty.[10] Up to this time the British had supposed that

---

[1] DDF 11 n. 201 Pichon to French representatives 10. XI 1907
[2] BD 8 n. 101 Hardinge to Nicolson 14. X 1907
[3] PRO/FO 371/295/31244 Rennell Rodd to Grey 15. IX 07 minutes
[4] AA Norwegen 7 geheim Bd 4 Treutler to Bülow 29. X 1907
    DDF 11 n. 194 Delavaud to Pichon 18. X 1907
[5] PRO/FO 371/296/32420 Rennell Rodd to Grey 30. IX 07 minutes
[6] Hildebrand p. 504
[7] AA Norwegen 7 geheim Bd 5 Hindenburg to Bülow 30. X 1907
[8] AA Norwegen 7 geheim Bd 4 Treutler to Bülow 23. X 1907
[9] PRO/FO 371/296/34147 Müller to Grey 6. X 1907 minute CH
[10] PRO/FO 371/296/undecipherable Nicolson to Grey 25. X 1907

Isvolsky's energetic exertions in this matter had been due to his wish to get rid of the old treaties, so his move seemed somewhat odd.[1] Of course he had his own schemes, but the British saw no more any reason to be *plus royaliste que le Roi*.[2] It had been deemed that "the only hope lies in either France or Russia letting the matter drop".[3] No hope remained, as the French also hastened to promise the Norwegians their signature on the new treaty regardless of the abrogation of the old one. So the British were "regarded by the Norwegian Government as being the obstacle". King Haakon once more threatened "an increase of German influence and deprecates any delay in signing this treaty".[4] In Norway the Treaty of 1855 was declared lapsed in 1905 as a result of the disappearance of one of its signatories, the Union, but in Sweden it remained in force — "there the matter rests and the old treaty remains in a most curious situation" Hardinge sighed.[5]

"Sweden's last chance, a poor one"[6] remained: "the Norwegian Minister for Foreign Affairs may be able to persuade his Government to listen to the strong appeal made to him by the Swedish Prime Minister".[7] This was wishful thinking by Rennell Rodd after Trolle's last, desperate attempt to induce the Norwegians to give up their strong position. Lövland answered by stating that it was a little too late in the day to hope to remake the treaty on a new basis as everything was agreed to by the powers and ready to be signed. But to "demonstrate his willingness to conciliate" he gave 48 hours to the Swedish Government to make their proposition.[8] Of course this was only play-acting, there being no chance of Norway accepting any essential changes the Swedish trip to Canossa was doomed to fail. The Swedish envoy answered that it was useless for him to bring forth any new propositions, as Norway had not accepted Sweden as a guarantor. And, as if to confirm the break-up of relations, he stated that it was of no use for the Norwegians to repeat that the Treaty was not directed against Sweden once Sweden had stated that it was so.[9]

The Treaty was signed on the 2nd November 1907 according to the third Russian draft. Later the Swedish Government declared their consent to the abrogation of the old Treaty,[10] but this was not done until the Baltic Treaty was signed the following spring.

[1] BD 8 n. 102 Hardinge to Nicolson 30. X 1907 private
[2] =1
[3] PRO/FO 371/295/32420 Rennell Rodd to Grey 30. IX 1907 minutes
[4] PRO/FO 371/296/34148 Müller to Grey 8. X 1907
[5] BD 8 n. 102 Hardinge to Nicolson 30. X 1907 private
[6] PRO/FO 371/296/33539 Rennell Rodd to Grey, minute by CH
[7] PRO/FO 371/296/33209 Rennell Rodd to Grey 7. X 1907
[8] AA Norwgen 7 geheim Bd 4 Treutler to Bülow 29. X 1907
[9] AA Norwegen 7 geheim Bd 5 Günther to Lövland 1. XI 1907 translation into German
[10] PRO/FO 371/296/38451 Rennell Rodd to Grey 18. XI 1907

Russian schemes

The French proposal to accept Sweden as a guarantor of Norway was most unwelcome to Isvolsky. He expressed his displeasure to the German chargé d'affaires wondering at the *nation amié et allié* who had acted behind Russia's back on Sweden's behalf disregarding the fact that Russia had all the time led the negotiations.[1] There was more to it than a question of amour-propre.

Isvolsky had no wish to satisfy the Swedes. The Russian envoy in Stockholm Budberg reported how hurt and bitter the Swedes were on account of Norway's success. Isvolsky adviced the envoy to blame everything on Great Britain, who could be accused of having prevented Russia's proposals to defend Sweden's interests. Russia had only wished to soothe Sweden and protect her, as had also Germany. The envoy might add that an exchange of views between the three powers might be useful. — This was in preparation for the Baltic treaty, which will be discussed later. — Confidentially Isvolsky added that there was no reason to aim at satisfying Sweden; indeed she should be compelled to go on noticing that her only comfort was in collaboration with the eastern Empires. "The state of mind of the Swedish Minister for Foreign Affairs, created by the success of the Norwegians, is not wholly against Russia's interest".[2]

In November the German chargé d'affaires in Norway reported that the Russian envoy Krupensky had spurred the Norwegians on heedlessly, in order to cause the humiliation of the Swedes.[3] At the same time the British, looking back, noticed ". . the curious divergence of attitude . . of the respective Russian Ministers in Christiania and Stockholm. While the former has exhibited actual impatience in hurrying on the signature, the latter has shown an apparent anxiety to consult Sweden, and submitted a draft of the treaty to the Swedish Government at a moment when the Norwegian Government insisted on maintaining secrecy. The knowledge of its contents thus acquired really occasioned the ineffectual action of the Swedish Government in seeking to obtain modifications, and eventually involved them in the final rebuff from Norway under which they are smarting. The Russian Government showed a decided disinclination to modify the text, while their Agent here (Stockholm) seems to have assured the Swedish Government that it was only Great Britain who at that stage of the proceeding could do anything for them. Finally, when there was at last a prospect of direct negotiations between the Swedish and Norwegian Governments, the Russian Government, which had it in its power to prolong the period of negotiations by maintaining the position first adopted with regard to the preliminary abrogation of the Treaty of 1855 by Sweden, abandoned their

---

[1] GP 23 II n. 8076 Miquel to Bülow 5. X 1907
[2] AVPR fond sekretnyj arhiv, delo 380 n. 49 Isvolsky to Budberg 8. IX 1907
[3] AA Norwegen 7 geheim Bd 5 Müller to Bülow 12. XI 1907

position and thus made signature inevitable and further prospect of mediation impossible. It is, perhaps, unnecessary to seek for an explanation of the apparent inconsistencies of Russian diplomacy, but were one to be looked for, it must seem justifiable to conclude that Russia had a definite object in accentuating the differencies between the two Scandinavian Kingdoms, and in placing new obstacles in the way of their ultimate reconciliation, thus more effectually isolating Sweden with a view to rendering her more malleable in the future".[1] — Rodd's report has been cited at length because in the light of Isvolsky's letter to Budberg it seems to describe the activity of the Russian representatives substantially correctly.

The "odd" behaviour of the Russians will be explained in connection with the discussion of Isvolsky's Baltic policy. During the autumn of 1907 the British Foreign Office received some warnings but was slow to give heed to them. On the remark "M. Kroupensky seems to entirely disregard the possibility that his excess of zeal might leave his Government open to the suspicion of working for the isolation of Sweden aiming to the consequent strengthening of Russian influence there"[2] Hardinge commented "M. Kroupensky is well known in London & we can well afford to ignore him".[3] Concerning Budberg, Hardinge thought "the Russian minister seems to have played a curious role",[4] but when the French warned that "Sweden does not desire to have her integrity guaranteed, but it was by no means unlikely that she should come to some arrangement with a Baltic power in regard to certain eventualities affecting both of them", the message was commented on: "M. Pichon gives no idea of what he means".[5] We shall later see that the British were in fact reluctant to the end to believe the worst of Isvolsky's politics because he was the man of conciliation in Asia. It seems that the British fear of the Russian danger had greatly diminished since the signature of the agreement of August 1907.

The British were inclined to favour the very solution which Isvolsky secretly planned. Grey believed "that the best end to the whole business would be for Russia to approach Sweden direct & negotiate some reassuring treaty with her, which she would accept in exhange for the abrogation of the 1855 & the Åland Island treaty. It is to the interest of Russia to be on as advantageous terms with Sweden as Germany can be with Denmark. Russia cannot secure this by force, but can do it with diplomacy".[6] This was in September and October, and November was far advanced before any doubt was felt "that some project was

[1] PRO/FO 371/338/37733 Rennell Rodd to Grey 13. XI 1907
[2] PRO/FO 371/296/36542 Müller to Grey 31. X 1907
[3] PRO/FO 371/296/36542 minute by CH
[4] PRO/FO 371/296/35938 Rennell Rodd to Grey 28. X 1907, minute by CH
[5] PRO/FO 371/296/36845 Bertie to Grey 7. XI 1907, minutes
[6] PRO/FO 371/296/31892 Rennell Rodd to Grey 20. IX 1907, minute by EG

in the air" because Isvolsky had said that "Sweden could not appeal to Germany without addressing herself at the same time to Russia".[1]

The result appraised

Norway had got her Treaty of Guarantee. For two years Lövland had energetically worked towards this goal and had reached it, in spite of Sweden's rage and England's reluctance, with the help of Russia's interest. However, it cannot be called a diplomatic victory: compared with Norway's first draft of 1906 the final Treaty seems rather meagre. It did not save Lövland's Cabinet in March 1908. In 1909 Lövland wrote that the Treaty had "more value than people seem to realize", it made clear Norway's international position and its significance could be measured by the anger it aroused among the *storsvenskarna*.[2] Others were not so appreciative. Lövland's successor Christophersen said that by concluding the integrity treaty Norway's weakness was openly admitted, although it had been sensible to take the facts into account.[3] In 1911 Sigurd Ibsen wrote that in a war between the great powers paper guarantees of integrity signified very little (the Emperor William's comment: "Right!"). If some power needed a base on the Norwegian coast, the treaty would not be heeded. (William: "Right!") Norway had got a useless treaty which lessened her international status, as was shown when she was not accepted as a signatory to the North Sea Convention. This diplomatic *Meisterstücke* made Norway dependant on the four powers and made Sweden bitter against her.[4]

It was no victory for Norway, but the defeat for Sweden was bitter. Sweden's protest seemed to have been ignored by the great powers, she felt forsaken by Great Britan and humiliated by Norway; internationally she felt isolated. There was no danger or hope of Scandinavianism for many years to come. Great Britain was accused of being the instigator of the Norwegian Treaty and the power really responsible for it.[5] The disappointment of the British Foreign Office can be felt in the tone of their comment: "The Norwegian Government have throughout acted on purely selfish lines. If they could get their integrity treaty they would not mind how much they embittered their own relations with Sweden or the relations of Sweden with other foreign powers".[6]

Nor were the French happy with the result. Pichon said "that it was very difficult for them to oppose the wishes of Russia, and that he had hoped that

[1] PRO/FO 371/296/38723 Nicolson to Grey 18. XI 1907
[2] Lövland p. 271
[3] AA Dänemark 37 geheim Bd 16 p. 169 Treutler to Bülow 2. V 1908
[4] AA Norwegen 7 Bd 6 Obeerndorff from Christiania to Bethmann-Hollweg 7. III 1911
[5] PRO/FO 371/296/undecipherable Grey to Rennell Rodd 30. X 1907
[6] PRO/FO 371/296/35938 Müller to Grey 8. X 1907, minute by CH

His Majesty's Government would have delayed the signature on account of Sweden".[1] They tried to save something by blaming the British: "France had acted as a sympathetic interpreter towards the other powers of the wishes of Sweden to take part in the Treaty .. but .. the Norwegian Government made a strong representation to England and succeeded in inducing that power to sign the treaty without the participation of Sweden". The Foreign Office commented: "It is scandalous that the French should thus deliberately misrepresent the attitude of His Majesty's Government".[2] — In fairness to the French it must be said that from the outside it was difficult to see the British in any other light. The inside picture can be seen only when reading the documents and the minutes of the Foreign Office. Of course it might be asked whether assuring one's wish to aid and lamenting one's powerlessness to do so was enough to make good the fact that Great Britain had in practice regarded Norway as more important than Sweden.

The break-up of the Union and the policy of Isvolsky had made the option inevitable. Great Britain had opted for Norway, and Sweden was left out in the cold. Isvolsky had succeeded. Now it is time to see what was in Isvolsky's mind, and therefore we must return to the sunny days of the summer of 1907.

---

[1] PRO/FO 371/338/27617 Bertie to Grey 13. XI 1907
[2] PRO/FO 371/296/36981 Rennell Rodd to Grey 6. XI 1907, minutes

THE RUSSO—GERMAN SECRET
Swinemünde

At the beginning of August 1907 the Emperor William II received the Russian Czar Nicholas II as his guest at Swinemünde. The meeting was attended by the foreign policy-makers of both Empires. Here Isvolsky reached the zenith of his success, uniting threads from many skeins into a beautiful rosette.

Germany, powerful and jealous, had made the Russians afraid. Isvolsky explained to his aide Baron Taube how useful it was for Russia to adjust her quarrels with Great Britain in Asia, but emphasized that it must not lead to scheming against Germany *à la Edouard*. Russia must strive to act sincerely in concert with Germany, on a strong and concrete foundation, which would guarantee Russia against all surprises from the West. But he did not like "sentimental and vague" agreements like that of Björkö, which might lead Russia and even France under German domination. He preferred an entente on practical questions, similar to the Asian agreement with England. Asian and Baltic questions were geographically separated and therefore politically not connected; so there was nothing contradictory in planning a Baltic treaty with Germany which was downright undesirable if not hostile to the British. If Baltic questions were politically not as important as Asian problems, they were closer geographically.[1]

In the progress of the Baltic question Northern Europe had turned out to be the natural area of Russo-German co-operation, where the interests of the two countries often seemed to converge. We have seen how Great Britain would have liked a union of neutrality of the three Northern Kingdoms to keep the Danish Straits open and Scandinavia free from outside influence. The British aim was distasteful to Germany, who needed the Straits for her defence and who did not like the idea of Danish or Swedish neutrality. Nor did Russia like to contemplate an eventual reunion of Sweden and Norway. As to the Danish Straits the hypothesis here adopted is that Isvolsky had resigned himself to German domination of the Straits and even supported it in order to keep a hand in the game. Once Grey upset Isvolsky's Åland operation, Isvolsky really wanted to keep Great Britain out of the Baltic.

The visits of the Royal Navy in the Northern waters, demonstrating that the Baltic was no mare clausum, gave no satisfaction to the Russians[2], especially since they could be seen as an encouragement to the Russian liberals.[3] This may have been an additional motive for Isvolsky.

---

[1] Taube: *La politique russe.* . p. 115—, 134—
[2] Bülow p. 145, 152
[3] DDF 10 n. 145 Bihourd to Bourgeois 10. VII 1906
  DDF 10 n. 148 Bompard to Bourgeois 12. VII 1906
  GP 25 n. 8512 Mühlberg to Schoen 7. VI 1906

Russo-German co-operation had been cultivated during the Norwegian nego-tiations, but already as an envoy in Copenhagen Isvolsky had privately dis-cussed common interests with Schoen (p. 29, 41). In the absence of Russian sources it is not possible to know when these deliberations hardened into a definite plan of action. In the note of 21st April (p. 132) there is the first official offer by Russia of Baltic co-operation. Although the Germans had not liked Isvolsky's mixing of the Åland complication with the Norwegian affair, they were unanimous in disapproving of British obstructionism: ". . other influ-ences, excepting those of the coastal powers, must be kept out of the Baltic. ." [1] Isvolsky had good reasons to suppose that the Germans would accept his offers.

The inspiration for the Baltic treaty came from the Mediterranean. Spain agreed on the 17th May 1907 with France and with Great Britain to respect and, if need be, maintain the territorial status quo on the coasts of the Western Mediterranean and the adjacent Atlantic. The Treaty was concluded to counter-balance German influence in Spain, which had worried the Western powers.[2] The Germans did not like the Treaty nor the fact that an international agree-ment had been completed without their participation.[3] Isvolsky said: "These arrangements have not contributed to the badly needed purification of the at-mosphere in Berlin; on the contrary they have recharged it with electricity." [4] It was of course a dismal matter for Berlin to see agreement after agreement eliminating the very quarrels the irreconcilability of which had been the foun-dation of Holstein's and Bülow's belief that time worked for Germany.

The Western diplomatists reported even before the meeting at Swinemünde that something was in the air. "Of the few words which M. Isvolsky said to me (Bompard) I think I can infer that Germany, desiring to escape her isolation and to oppose convention with convention, is thinking of an entente among the coastal states of the Baltic Sea, and has even made suggestions to this effect to the Cabinet of St. Petersburg."[5] It was easy to guess what the Germans had in mind: ". . to prevent the success of the negotiations now in progress between England and Russia. Germany wants to draw Russia into an agreement with the object of closing the Baltic . . the consurrence of Sweden and Denmark is assured . . . an elegant counter-coup to that of the Mediterranean."[6] — We know that it was Isvolsky and not Germany who was planning this agreement. It is possible that "the few words" to the French Ambassador were some kind

[1] GP 23 II n. 8066 Mühlberg to Schoen 18. VII 1907
[2] Hardinge p. 135
   DDF 11 n. 2 Paul Cambon to Pichon 17. V 1907
[3] DDF 11 n. 38 Jules Cambon to Paul Cambon 19. VI 1907
   DDF 11 n. 48 Jules Cambon to Pichon 23. VI 1907
[4] DDF 11 n. 51 Bompard to Pichon 27. VI 1907
[5] DDF 11 n. 30 Bompard to Pichon 15. VI 1907
[6] DDF 11 n. 45 Jules Cambon to Pichon 25. VI 1907

of reinsurance; Isvolsky put the blame on the Germans before proposing the agreement to them, in case the secret might leak out. In fact it did leak out, but the insurance was not enough to make him immune from French accusations. Then the fact that France and Great Britain had made the treaty with Spain without informing Russia was an essential part of Isvolsky's defence. Then the French realized that even Isvolsky and not only the Germans had been annoyed at the treaty made behind their back.[1]

The first record of a draft for the plan to be presented to the Germans at Swinemünde dates from sometime in June 1907. The object of the operation was declared to be that of excluding England from the Baltic, and the means thereto was to be to guarantee Sweden in her territorial extent "on the basis of excluding non-coastal powers from the Baltic" — that is, only Russia and Germany would have guaranteed Sweden. It has already been narrated how, during the Norwegian negotiations, Isvolsky worked to demonstrate to the Swedes that they were abandoned by all other powers and had to arrange matters with the Baltic Empires. To the Czar Isvolsky remarked that this principle of excluding from the Baltic all outside influence had been the principle of Nicholas's Great Ancestor Catherine II.[2] This memorandum is marked as "being without consequences", but is illuminates Isvolsky's anger at the British having compelled him to retreat in the Åland question, so that he was prepared to contemplate closing the Baltic by force — Catherine had led the "Armed neutrality". But the "being without consequences" proves that Isvolsky recovered his senses.

Yet another memorandum was intended for the Germans, and this illuminates the proposals which Isvolsky actually made at Swinemünde. In the memorandum it was stated that Britain had tried to delay the Norwegian negotiations, but unexpectedly for the London government Norway had accepted their proposal of a treaty without neutrality, which would be a hindrance for the British plans of Pan-Scandinavian neutrality. Therefore Britain had tried to take up the "Swedish aspect" of the Northern question and to prevent the abrogation of the Treaties of 1855—56, which would have signified the end of her juridical right of intervening in the political combinations of the Baltic. That was diametrically opposed to Russian policy. Germany might remember that Russia had always opposed the attempts of outside powers to introduce themselves into the Baltic, which belonged only to the coastal powers, namely Germany, Russia, Sweden and Denmark. Probably Germany had only one objection: the incompatibility of Russian intentions on Åland with Sweden's interests. But Russia, in aiming at the abrogation of the Convention of 1856, was not following aims hostile to Sweden. Russia's only motive, excepting for the moral

---

[1] DDF 11 n. 251 Bompard to Pichon 24. I 1908
[2] AVPR fond sekretnyj arhiv, delo 380, n. 1 "Secret memorandum" June 1907

satisfaction of ending the servitude, was her wish to have an observation post to watch the Finns. Because Sweden could not be satisfied with verbal assurances of amity, she ought to be given a real and formal guarantee of the status quo. And Russia was able to give that, having no designs on Sweden's integrity. Therefore Russia, Germany and Sweden should make a treaty to guarantee Sweden her actual territorial status quo, on the secret basis of excluding in general all foreign influence from Baltic affairs.[1] This memorandum was not sent to the Germans, but it served as a basis for Isvolsky's oral propositions at the meeting of Swinemünde and after. It shows clearly how Isvolsky combined his general wish for co-operation with the Germans with his special aim of restoring Russian sovereignty on Åland and with the idea of a new Baltic entente. The question of Åland was the concrete detail which made his wish for co-operation plausible to the Germans and helped him to avoid "sentimental and vague" general agreements.

It is hardly likely that Isvolsky would have had very much support in public opinion for his policy of closing the Baltic with the Germans. At the turn of the year 1907/08 there were rumours in the air, which gave occasion for the Russian press to state their views. Both conservative and liberal organs took a negative attitude to the scheme. The *Novoe Vremja* wrote of the rumours under the headline "The Newest Manoeuvre of the German policy"[2] and explained that it would be foolish to suspect Russia of such intentions, because, due to Russian weakness, the *mare clausum* would be *mare teutonicum*. Of course Germany would like the idea, but Russia never nor the Northern countries either. Most probably Germany had let loose the rumour in order to disturb Russia's relations with other powers.[3] The liberal press wrote in the same tone, remarking that closing the Baltic would harm Russia because her future fleet would be left in a trap.[4]

Once again Schoen was eagerly supporting Isvolsky's afforts to promote Russo-German co-operation. Schoen had been in Copenhagen with Isvolsky, then he served as Ambassador in St. Petersburg and in the autumn of 1907 he was promoted State Secretary of the Auswärtiges Amt. Before the meeting at Swinemünde he sent to Berlin an unreservedly positive report on Isvolsky, drawing a picture of an eager and sincere Germanophile. After entering office, so Schoen's report ran, Isvolsky had, as the very first step, visited the German Embassy to underline the value of the traditional good relations between Berlin and St. Petersburg, and to wipe away the disagreeable memories that had dis-

---

[1] AVPR fond sekretnyj arhiv, delo 380, n. 4
Russian F. O. to German Embassy, draft without date and signature, not sent
[2] *Novoe Vremja* 1/14 I 1908
[3] *Novoe Vremja* 9/22 I 1908
[4] *Reč* 10/23 I 1908
Svet 9/22 I 1908

turbed them. They had had occasion for concrete co-operation only to small
extent, first in the question of the Baghdad Railway, and then in the Norwegian
question. In the latter the co-operation had succeeded in nullifying the Norwegian dreams of a Pan-Scandinavian Union and the British efforts to confuse the
Norwegian and Baltic questions. The Russo-German disagreements due to Morocco and disarmament — an idea of socialists, Jews, and hysterical women,
according to Isvolsky — were deplorable but only interludes. Isvolsky was no
Anglomane, even though he was more liberal than Russian statesmen as a rule.
His attitude towards France was cool, because he disliked the radical spirit,
which threatened to invade even Russia.[1]

There is no evidence in the Russian nor in the German sources of preliminary collaboration between Schoen and Isvolsky, but of course one may doubt
whether they could really refrain from falling into their old habits. Nicolson
had heard some gossip: "I was informed confidentially . . that negotiations were
proceeding here between M. Isvolsky and the German Ambassador"[2] ". . as to
an accord to which Sweden would be asked to adhere for maintaining status
quo in the Baltic on lines similar to those on which the Anglo-Spanish accord
has recently been made".[3]

The forecaste was favourable. The weather and the mood at Swinemünde
turned out to be splendidly sunny. *Unser allergnädigster Herr* treated Isvolsky
with benevolence, Bülow said. The Czar Nicholas underlined to the Emperor
William the importance of close contacts between the Empires and explained
that the monarchistic principle could be upheld only if the three Empires united
their efforts to subjugate the revolutionary movement.[4]

Isvolsky and Bülow agreed to "continue" in the spirit of the Björkö agreement and to try to solve its "inherent difficulties", "although without undue
haste".[5] — Thus the dead agreement, whose ghost had haunted the Russians,
was buried and allowed to rest in peace. The Germans had looked upon the
agreement *stillschweigend als zu Recht bestehend,* William II not having accepted Nicholas's additions as to the French concurrence.[6] Evidently Bülow
understood that it was impossible to keep up an agreement, however *stillschweigend,* which the other party did not wish for. There was no sense in
pressing the Russians, as Isvolsky was otherwise eager to please the Germans.

All the topical questions were discussed, Morocco, Macedonia, and the Second Hague Peace Conference. Bülow expressed his "complete understanding"

---

[1] GP 22 n. 7377 Schoen to Bülow 25. VII 1907
[2] PRO/FO 371/338/20725 Nicolson to Grey 18. VII 1907
[3] PRO/FO 371/338/20160 Nicolson to Grey 17. VII 1907
[4] GP 22 n. 7378 note by Tschirschky 7. VIII 1907
[5] GP 22 n. 7378 note by Tschirschky 7. VIII 1907
[6] GP 22 n. 7376 Tschirschky to Bülow 25. VII 1907
   GP 22 n. 7375 Mühlberg to Bülow 22. VII 1907

to Isvolsky's explanation concerning his Japanese policy. Speaking about the agreement with England Isvolsky emphasized that it was concerned only with Tibet, Afghanistan and Persia, and that Russia did not aim at a general political treaty with England. He assured Bülow of his loyalty towards Germany, citing as an example the neutral zone in Persia: Russia had refused to divide the coast of the Persian Gulf into zones of interest because other powers had interests there, too. To this explanation Bülow listened without protesting, although it must have been disheartening for a man whose policy had been based on the assumption of the irreconcilability of Russian and British interests, a situation which ought to have accorded the splendid role of *arbiter mundi* to Germany.

Then Isvolsky turned to the Northern question. The Norwegian negotiations seemed to be proceeding after all, in spite of England's obstructionism. Isvolsky disapproved also of Britain's meddling in the Baltic question on the pretext of caring for Sweden's interests, so that Russia had had to desist from the abrogation of the Åland servitude. Having thus once more prepared the ground Isvolsky presented to the German Chancellor his proposal, the main features of which have been already explained: that all powers excepting Germany, Russia, Sweden and Denmark ought to be excluded from Baltic questions. Then Russia with German support would guarantee Sweden, who thereafter would consent to the abrogation of the Åland servitude. Isvolsky emphasized that Russia had no intention of fortifying Åland against Sweden or anybody else, she only needed a police station to watch the *schwungvolle Waffenschmuggel* to Finland. In addition to these practical questions the honour of Russia demanded the end of the servitude. If Sweden consented, France, Russia's ally, would surely not resist, and in isolation England would have to follow suit. Bülow did not promise anything but agreed emphatically that Great Britain was not wanted in the Baltic. Isvolsky's propositions concerning Baltic collaboration would be studied most attentively and he would be informed of the result through the Imperial Ambassador.[1]

Isvolsky could return home satisfied. No discord had clouded the sunny days of Swinemünde. The Germans had swallowed their annoyance at the Asian agreement and Isvolsky had been given the green light. The agreement with the British was signed at the end of August 1907. The Baltic treaty with the Germans, which he had offered as a counterbalance had now to be carried through; its byproduct, Åland, could then be secured.

---

[1] GP 22 n. 7378 note by Tschirschky 7. VIII 1907
  AVPR fond sekretnyj arhiv, delo 380, n. 16
  Isvolsky to Russian representatives 31. VII/12. VIII 1907 draft
  AVPR fond sekretnyj arhiv, delo 262/263 n. 34
  "A most loyal address" by Isvolsky 31. VII/12. VIII 1907

11

The German reception

In St. Petersburg Isvolsky hurried to present to the Germans a draft for the treaty. The complete concurrence of the interests of the Empires in the Baltic was stated in the preamble, and the aim of the treaty was declared to be the strengthening of the centuries-old good relations of the neighbours. Their common object was to preserve the status quo by excluding all foreign political forces from the Baltic. The Empires mutually guaranteed their possessions on the coasts and islands in the Baltic area. They bound themselves not to recognize any interests in Baltic affairs as legitimate but those of the coastal powers. The other two Baltic powers could be admitted to participate in the maintenance of the status quo and territorial integrity, in separate accords.[1] — The undefined terms of international law caused much confusion on the discussion of these questions. When the closing of the Baltic Sea was spoken of in the press, it usually implied the closing of the Danish Straits, as indicated earlier. Now Isvolsky's term of "excluding foreign political forces" from the Baltic did not refer to navigation but to juridical right to participate in Baltic negotiations. The emphasis on this aspect was due, of course, to the Treaties of 1855 and 56, which had given the Western powers the pretext for demanding a "seat and voice" in Baltic questions.

The Germans were not as eager to accept Isvolsky's anti-British proposition as he might have supposed. In spite of Schoen's recommendation Isvolsky had not won the confidence of the statesmen in Berlin. Holstein wrote in his diary: "Isvolsky is more open and clever than the deceitful Lamsdorff; in Swinemünde he estimated the internal situation very pessimistically and was therefore thoroughly friendly." [2]

In the German Foreign Office *Vortragender Rat* Jagow studied the Russian draft. He was of the opinion that the principle of status quo was acceptable, but, although Germany in practice might try to keep foreign powers out of the Baltic, it was impossible to make written treaties on it. The Baltic was not a *mare clausum,* the Western powers had the formal right to act there. Isvolsky's proposition was directed against England, and Germany had every reason to avoid such agreements. If she signed it, the British might get wind of it; the Russians might tell them in order to put the odium on Germany, to have a trump against her, or the Swedes might let slip their tongue. (Bülow remarked in the margin: *Gewiss!)* The Mediterranean precedent could be taken advantage of in the Baltic: in practice the mutual guarantee by the coastal powers excluded foreign influences, and accusations of closing the Baltic could be answered by appealing to the Mediterranean analogy. Therefore, Jagow thought, the answer to Isvolsky ought to be negative, with an accompanying explanation that

---

[1] GP 23 II n. 8083 note by Tschirschky 7. VIII 1907
[2] Holstein IV p. 438, n. 1046 Diary 13. VIII 1907

an openly anti-British treaty was undesirable as Sweden might reveal everything and cause grave difficulties, and that status quo in itself implied the exclusion of foreigners. Isvolsky could be given a verbal promise that foreign states were to be kept out of the Baltic, but nothing in writing. And whatever was agreed on must be published in order to avoid the dangers due to an eventual indiscretion.[1]

The German Ambassador in Vienna, Karl von Wedel, wrote to Berlin in October that in his opinion the proposed treaty was so important for Russo-German relations that Germany ought to use all her influence in Sweden to help the Russians and gain thereby Russian gratitude; but in Berlin Tschirschky wrote in the margin: "what does Russia give us for it?" [2] It seems that the statesmen in Berlin did not appreciate such agreements on concrete detail. It has been said that Bülow and Holstein waited for the great upheaval of the alliance system when Russia's implacable hostility would compel Great Britain to fall into Germany's arms. What in fact happened was that the surrounding powers, without any intention of *Einkreisung,* built an Entente around Germany with agreements on practical details, and Germany was left isolated, waiting for the great chance which never came.[3]

Jagow went on in his memorandum to propose that Germany should invite Great Britain to sign the Baltic treaty. Russia probably would not consent, as she had so strongly disapproved of British meddling in Baltic affairs. Thus the Western powers would learn that Germany had proposed but Russia had refused to include England in the Baltic agreement. Germany would have a trump card against Russia and a proof of friendship towards Great Britain.[4] — Thus Jagow proposed to do exactly what he suspected the Russians of scheming, and evidently his great aim was to prevent the Russo-British understanding, which was near conclusion. He went on enlarging the scope of his proposition: Germany might suggest an analogous agreement on the status quo of the North Sea to be signed by Germany, Great Britain, Denmark, Norway and Holland. The guarantee of the territorial status quo of the small neighbours would eliminate suspicions of the imagined German plans of annexation, and the world would receive a proof of Germany's peaceful, non-expansionist policy.[5]

Tschirschky, the State Secretary, adopted the views of Jagow. He was suspicious of Russian intentions and accepted the proposed answer to Isvolsky. He also estimated highly the value of an analogous agreement with England, the very fact of which would have a favourable influence on Germany's general political situation — Tschirschky seems to have hoped to break the *Einkreisung*

---

[1] GP 23 II n. 8084 note by Jagow 11. VIII 1907
[2] GP 23 II n. 8094 Wedel to Bülow 5. X 1907
[3] Salis II p. 414
[4] GP 23 II n. 8084 note by Jagow 11. VIII 1907
[5] GP 23 II n. 8084 note by Jagow 11. VIII 1907

or at least to separate England from France — and would permanently improve Germany's relations with Holland and Denmark.[1] The chargé d'affaires in London Stumm reported a few weeks later that "here in some places the thought is being cherished of reaching a general agreement with us. It may be that a Baltic treaty can play a role in this. ." [2] Compared with such chances of carrying out the basic aspiration of German foreign policy, Russia's anti-British proposal was not very alluring and had to be handled with caution. This was the genesis of the North Sea Treaty, which will be discussed later.

By the end of August Schoen was given instructions to communicate the German fears to Isvolsky. He was to emphasize the danger of British reaction to the closing of the Baltic. If this dangerous point was left out, the treaty could be published, and defended by reference to the Mediterranean analogy, and it would facilitate Russia's efforts in Åland, as Swedish public opinion would become aware of the superfluousness of the ancient Convention; and there would be no danger of the Western powers answering by closing the Mediterranean. "We believe that also the Russian Government, who are striving for the elimination of points of friction with the British, will see the advantages in the German proposition. ." [3] Schoen was authorized to give oral promises of German concurrence in Russian wishes, but nothing was to be put in writing. In the German draft the signatories only declared their wish to maintain the actual status quo in the Baltic regions, on the mainland and on the islands.[4] The importance of keeping the preparations secret from the British was underlined in the remark that the British intention of participating in a Baltic treaty could be avoided only by the fait accompli of a signed treaty. Therefore the Russo-German agreement must be made first, and then Sweden and Denmark might be invited to participate.[5] — Evidently, the sooner the treaty was signed and published, the less was the danger of Isvolsky being able to realize his sinister schemes of compromising Germany in British eyes.

The secret Baltic treaty

It seems that Isvolsky was not very sorry to receive the German refusal to close the Baltic against British influence. He thanked the Germans for their consent to the principle of status quo and concurred in their objections concerning the dangers of the project.[6] — In Swinemünde he had achieved his most important aim, Germany's acquiescence in his Asian policy. The proposition

[1] GP 23 II n. 8085 Tschirschky to Bülow 13. VIII 1907
[2] AA England 78 secretissima Bd 11 Stumm to Ausw. Amt 13. IX 1907
[3] GP 23 II n. 8086 Tschirschky to Schoen 23. VIII 1907
[4] GP 23 II n. 8086 appendix, German draft treaty
[5] GP 23 II n. 8087 Tschirschky to Schoen 23. VIII 1907
[6] GP 23 II n. 8088 Schoen to Ausw. Amt 25. VIII 1907

for closing the Baltic had thus served it purpose, it had been a proof of Is-volsky's anti-British and pro-German feelings.[1]

Perhaps it is too categorical to say that it had no other significance, seeing that Isvolsky had been rather annoyed at the British in the summer, and that he wanted to isolate Sweden for his Åland operation. But he had no hurry to conclude an agreement, because Grey had revoked his demand for a Baltic conference and it was reasonable to suppose that he would not renew it very soon. Evidently Isvolsky reckoned that he had time to solve the Åland question at leisure.

He therefore answered the Germans, who had not at all mentioned Åland in their draft, that before the four Baltic powers proceeded to guarantee the status quo, the Åland question had to be solved lest the servitude be reinforced as part of the status quo they were going to guarantee. The Norwegian Treaty also had to be signed before the Baltic one, to eliminate the November Treaty of 1855 which the Western powers might otherwise use as a pretext to meddle in Baltic affairs. He also proposed making the Baltic treaty with Sweden and Denmark, too, as merely associating them with it afterwards might offend them.[2] And the Russians wanted to keep the preparations secret. Taube wrote to Isvolsky: ". . it is evident that any direct Russo-German agreement on this question, however inoffensive its text, cannot, if it is published, facilitate our task, in London, of getting the Åland convention abrogated. ."[3] Taube was right in his apprehensions, as will be seen later.

To calm Isvolsky's apprehensions Tschirschky proposed that Russia and Germany should sign a separate protocol stipulating that the guarantee of status quo was no prejudice to the abrogation of the Åland servitude.[4] Isvolsky adopted this idea, which later gave much trouble in the negotiations between Russia and Sweden; but in itself it was not enough for him. The Germans were pressing for the agreement on the status quo which Isvolsky did not want before he could be sure of Swedish acquiescence in the abrogation of the Åland servitude. So he tried to find a compromise.

He explained to the Germans that the Russo-German agreement might disagreeably surprise England and France and they might cause difficulties in the Åland question. That was why he had asked that the Baltic treaty be kept secret until further notice. It was to be hoped that England could be kept ignorant of it, but if not, her eventual reaction could perhaps be averted by the presentation of the fait accompli. Therefore he would consent to a Russo-German agreement, which was to be kept secret as long as possible. The public agreement

[1] Remark by J. J. Astaf'ev, Moscow 1970
[2] GP 23 II n. 8088 Schoen to Ausw. Amt 25. VIII 1907
[3] AVPR fond sekretnyj arhiv, delo 380 n. 29 Taube to Isvolsky 29. VIII/11. IX 1907
[4] GP 23 II n. 8089 Tschirschky to Schoen 29. VIII 1907

between the four Baltic powers would be concluded after the Norwegian and
Åland questions were cleared up.[1]

Isvolsky's attitude to the German refusal to close the Baltic and his reluctance to conclude the Baltic Treaty before the abrogation of the Åland Convention is further proof that he did not regard the closing to be in Russia's interests
but only a means of being at one with Germany in a question which he thought
to be advantageous for the mighty neighbour. The importance of this matter for
Isvolsky can be roughly measured by the fact that after the conclusion of the
Asian agreement on 31st August he left St. Petersburg on holiday, leaving the
Baltic question in the care of Taube, Gubastov taking charge of the Foreign
Office.[2] On his trip to Central Europe, however, he naturally kept in touch with
St. Petersburg and met a few important statesmen.

In Karlsbad he saw the Swedish Minister for Foreign Affairs Trolle and
started the Åland operation, to be discussed later. Jagow, too, stayed in Karlsbad and heard anew Isvolsky's reasons for his Baltic activity. Isvolsky dwelt on
Russia's wish to regain her sovereignty in the Baltic and her need for a police
base on Åland, and the advantages of the Empires giving satisfaction to Sweden
who was hurt by the Western powers. He was still reluctant to conclude the
Baltic treaty before the Åland one, and said that the matter could be dealt with
after he had returned to office at the beginning of the following November.[3]

Tschirschky was already becoming nervous at this delay. He had thought that
the North Sea proposition should be presented to the British immediately,
irrespective of what was going on in regard to the Baltic. His idea was to
forestall an eventual British proposition, in order to show to the Dutch and
the Danes that Germany did not covet their territory. But there was, too, the
danger of Britain pushing herself into the Baltic, which Germany did not like,
of course; Jagow's idea of proposing it had only been meant to be refused by
Russia. Therefore the Baltic treaty had to be hastened to its conclusion as soon
as possible. The North Sea proposal might be secretly disclosed to the Queen of
the Netherlands in order to make her a "crown witness" to the fact that Germany had been there before Great Britain, just in case the latter was to come
forward with a similar proposal.[4]

The State Secretary very nearly sent an ultimatum to Isvolsky. He said in the
draft that the dilatory Russian attitude to the Baltic proposition seemed to
indicate that the Russians did not like the idea any more. Without a clear
answer to the question of whether they were going to have the proposed treaty,
Germany would be entitled to assume that Russia had let the question drop.[5]

[1] AA Norwegen 7 geheim Bd 4 Miquel to Bülow 30. VIII 1907
[2] AA Norwegen 7 geheim Bd 4 Miquel to Bülow 30. VIII 1907
[3] GP 23 II n. 8092 Jagow to Tschirschky 20. IX 1907
[4] GP 23 II n. 8091 Tschirschky to Bülow 9. IX 1907
[5] AA Dänemark 37 geheim Bd 8 p 12 Tschirschky to Schoen, draft 4. X 1907, not sent

This strong draft was not sent, but of course the Russians were informed of Berlin's displeasure. Jagow in Karlsbad tried to make Isvolsky hurry on the conclusion of the Baltic treaty, and Isvolsky promised to see whether the matter might be attended to before the end of his holiday.[1]

As the Germans disapproved of delay, and Isvolsky feared the consequences of making the agreement public, it was logical to accept as a compromise his idea of a secret treaty to be immediately concluded only between Germany and Russia. It was evidently difficult for the German statesmen to understand how important the Åland question seemed to Isvolsky and how he based his policy on the isolation of Sweden, which made it obligatory for him not to rouse suspicions in the West. His emphasis on keeping the agreement secret made the Germans more suspicious and even jealous: *'Die Russen wollen eben nichts publizieren was sie mit uns machen'.*[2]

Taube edited the text of the compromise agreement with the Germans, and after Isvolsky had accepted it,[3] it was signed by Schoen and Gubastov on the 29th (16th) October 1907. Germany secured her rear by making the Dutch Queen a crown witness as Tschirschky had planned. Wilhelmina and her Prime Minister were "proud and happy", but remarked that without Great Britain they would not sign any treaty.[4] The Russians secured their flank with the special protocol stipulating that changes in the status of the Åland Islands represented no change in the status quo.[5]

When the French got wind of this secret, they thought in their fright that it signified an upheaval of the alliance system, as we shall see later. In fact it was very far from anything so serious. For the Russians it was a means of securing German aid in the Åland question, for the Germans it was a reinsurance against Russian treason. Mutual mistrust, which later was to grow even greater, prevented it from becoming anything more.

Immediately after the signature of the secret Baltic treaty Schoen left St. Petersburg to succeed Tschirschky as State Secretaty. Isvolsky was satisfied. He wrote to Taube that the most pressing affair was to get the Norwegian treaty signed and then with German help to secure sufficient pressure on Stockholm to induce Sweden to "enter our point of view"... "In this regard the advancement of Schoen to Minister cannot but be useful for us, because he seems to share our views completely".[6] But in spite of that, and Swinemünde notwithstanding, the Asian agreement made Schoen's superiors annoyed and suspi-

---

[1] GP 23 II n. 8092 Jagow to Tschirschky 20. IX 1907
[2] GP 23 II n. 8094 Wedel to Bülow 5. X 1907, margin by Tschirschky
[3] AVPR fond sekretnyj arhiv, delo 380 n. 34 Isvolsky to Taube 26. IX/9. X 1907
[4] GP 23 II n. 8101 German Envoy in the Hague to Ausw. Amt 13. XI 1907
[5] GP 23 II n. 8095 Schoen to Bülow 29. X 1907
[6] AVPR fond sekretnyj arhiv, delo 380, n. 63 Isvolsky to Taube 29. IX/12. X 1907

cious. "The situation is not without danger and demands all our (Russian) vigilance".[2] It seems that in Berlin even Schoen began to have second thoughts on Isvolsky's Baltic policy. Taube had "hoped that Russia and Germany would always walk hand-in-hand in Baltic questions", which Miquel, the German chargé d'affaires reported adding that "there was no doubt of his honesty" but recalled that Russia first of all wanted German help in the Åland question.[2] Germany was being taken advantage of by Isvolsky, it seemed.

Success within Isvolsky's grasp

The forecast seemed favourable for Isvolsky's Åland schemes. "In 1907 there undoubtedly existed here (Sweden) an inclination to enter into closer relations with Russia",[3] an inclination which was due to the Norwegian affair.[4] Sweden felt bitter and isolated, and Isvolsky knew how to sharpen this feeling. "As a sign of special benevolence" the Russians kept the Swedes informed of the various phases of the Norwegian negotiations,[5] thus rubbing in the fact that the Western powers ignored her protests. The Swedes "must understand that it was morally impossible for us to avoid the insistence on Norway's part". The only means of giving satisfaction for Sweden would have been to insist on Norwegian neutrality, but Sweden knew who had refused that . . . And every time Isvolsky blamed Great Britain he also hinted that Russia and Germany were anxious to reassure Sweden and spoke of an exchange of ideas about an agreement to secure Sweden against all eventualities.[6]

Isvolsky had also some difficulties in his relations with Sweden. The Prime Minister, Lindman, was full of wrath against Norway but did not see the value of Russian assurances.[7] Budberg, the Russian envoy in Stockholm, was a *fainéant des fainéants* whom nothing could induce to work.[8] And Sweden's envoy in St. Petersburg was the obstinate General Brändström who was not at all receptive to Isvolsky's allurements.

But the most important Swedish statesmen surprised Taube by being remarkably "abordable", for instance the envoy in Berlin Count Arvid Taube, as well as King Oscar and Crown Prince Gustaf, and especially the Minister for Foreign Affairs Trolle.[9] In addition to the Norwegian affair, the interval of

---

[1] AVPR fond sekretnyj arhiv, delo 380, n. 126 Osten-Sacken to Isvolsky 16/29 XI 1907
[2] AA Russland 63 Bd 1 Miquel to Bülow 5. X 1907
[3] AA Russland 63 Bd 3 Pückler to Bülow 30. VI 1907
[4] Rennell Rodd p. 85—
[5] AVPR fond sekretnyj arhiv, delo 380, n. 28 Isvolsky to Budberg 27. VIII 1907
[6] AVPR fond sekretnyj arhiv, delo 380, n. 48 Isvolsky to Budberg 3/16 IX 1907
[7] AVPR fond sekretnyj arhiv, delo 380 n. 50 Budberg to Isvolsky 11/24 IX 1907
[8] Taube: *Der grossen. .* p. 149—150
[9] Taube: *Der grossen. .* p. 148

repression in Finland may have lessened the traditional feeling against Russia in Sweden.[1]

On the 24th September in Karlsbad Isvolsky saw Trolle, who was "extremely irritated" on account of the Norwegian Treaty and tried to persuade Isvolsky to nullify the success of the Norwegians. Of course Isvolsky gave no solace but tried to add to the discomfort of the Swedes in the spirit of his instructions to Russian representatives (p.?).[2] Then he explained that he did not approve of violence against loyal Finland, but if she wanted "something more", he was ready to crush her. A base in Åland was badly needed against the smugglers of arms, but not for fortifications. The discussion was continued a little later in Paris, where Isvolsky revoiced his theme that it was his absolute duty as Russian Minister for Foreign Affairs to eliminate the remnants of restrictions on Russia's full sovereignty over her possessions. Russia might guarantee the territorial status quo in the Baltic in order to dispel Sweden's apprehensions, and if she were afraid of being left alone with Russia, another power, for instance Germany, might be asked to participate in the guarantee treaty.[3] Isvolsky wrote to St. Petersburg that Trolle personally was clearly disposed to agree with Russia and had promised to take up the matter in Stockholm.[4] — The exchange of views having been oral there remained the possibility of misunderstanding, and it was not quite clear what they had agreed to. Isvolsky remembered that Trolle had been favourably disposed towards his Åland wishes, and Trolle remembered mainly that Isvolsky had promised not to fortify Åland. This was to cause much ado later.

Crown Prince Gustaf visited Berlin at the beginning of November and opened the discussion of a treaty of guarantee, explaining that he had the support of the King and the Government. At his own initiative he proposed to leave England out.[5] Evidently the Swedes were making earnest of their threats to seek support "elsewhere" if abandoned by Great Britain; and also seeking support in order to be not left alone with Russia. Schoen on his part "successfully" reassured the Swedes about the Russian intentions in Åland. Satisfied, he wrote to the Russians that the situation was favourable and that the state of mind of the Swedes ought to be taken advantage of.[6] Gustaf was told that the matter had been *angeregt* with the Russians, but of course nothing was said of the secret Baltic treaty which was already signed. — Because the Crown Prince had taken up the question with Schoen, there has existed a mistaken notion that

[1] Sten Carlson p. 270—

[2] AVPR fond sekretnyj arhiv, delo 380 n. 63 Isvolsky to Taube 28. IX/12. X 1907

[3] Hildebrand p. 525

[4] AVPR fond sekretnyj arhiv, delo 380, n. 70 Isvolsky to Taube 10/23 X 1907

[5] AA Dänemark 37 geheim Bd 8 p 58 William II to Bülow 8. XI 1907

[6] GP 23 II n. 8100 Schoen to Pourtalès 8. XI 1907

Gustaf was the initiator of the Baltic Treaty.[1]

The Germans tried to fulfil their promise of moral support to Russia. Gustaf reported that the Emperor William had supported the Russian wishes and explained them justified.[2] There is also a story how William, with his usual outspokenness, explained to the Swedish envoy that there was no military reason whatever that Sweden should not withdraw her objections.[3] The Auswärtiges Amt was informed that the German Admiralty Staff had no objections against Russia watching smugglers and revolutionaries from Åland.[4] The Germans urged the Swedish Government "to view the question with calm and not to cause difficulties. The answer was that in Stockholm neither the Court nor the Government had an intransigent point of view, but they had to habituate Swedish public opinion, which up to that had been badly prepared".[5] — Later we shall see how the habituation of the Swedes succeeded. —

The Swedish Government felt powerless to oppose Russia. Trolle explained to Brändström that he did not wish to withdraw from the discussion, at least not in the very beginning. Pichon had said that France could not oppose Russian wishes, and Great Britain was not to be trusted either, having recently concluded a treaty with Russia. It was practically certain that Russia would liberate herself from the Convention of Åland even without Sweden's consent.[6] "The recent days have shown how helpless we are".[7] Rumour had it that Trolle had admitted that a Russian naval base in the Åland Islands was a grave matter, but that it might be allowed if Russia offered a sufficient guarantee of Sweden's security.[8] It seems that in the autumn of 1907 the Swedish Government would really have consented to Russia fortifying Åland. Although later some reservations were "remembered",[9] no reservations are on record from the time in question.

At the beginning of November Trolle wrote to Isvolsky saying that the matter had been submitted to the King, who did not wish for anything else but good relations with Russia, had supported the plan of a guarantee of the Baltic status quo, and had decided to ask the advice of his council. Therefore Isvolsky was asked to send a draft agreement in order to have the details clear for the discussion.[10]

[1] Lagercrantz p. 328
[2] Hildebrand p. 530
[3] PRO/FO 371/745/31301 Spring-Rice to Grey 17. VIII 1909
[4] AA Russland 63 Bd 1 note by "v. G." 10. IV 1908
[5] AVPR fornd sekretnyj arhiv, delo 380, n. 88 Benckendorff to Islovsky 31. X/13. XI 1907
[6] Hildebrand p. 530
[7] Lindberg: Den svenska. . p. 200—
[8] HHStA/SVA n. 131 Esterjesy to Aehrenthal 17. I 1908
[9] Lindberg: Scandinavia p. 158
[10] AVPR fond sekretnyj arhiv, delo 380, n. 82 Trolle to Isvolsky 6. XI 1907

Isvolsky, well content, told the Germans that Trolle had written to him, and that he was going to start the discussions. His plan of proceeding was: 1. to sign in Stockholm the two declarations (Russo-Swedish and Swedo-German), 2. to publish the said declarations, but only after the publication of the Norwegian Treaty to preserve the appearance of the declarations being the natural sequel to it; 3. the abrogation of the Treaty of 1855 on Sweden's behalf and 4. the abrogation of the Convention of 1856 by Russia, France and England. 5. In view of Danish reluctance and for the general political considerations, well-known to the Berlin Cabinet, it was advisable to put off the negotiations with Denmark until later. "That is evidently a question of a most delicate political nature, which must be touched on with the greatest circumspection, and which in any case needs a preceding period of diplomatic preparation". He sent the draft agreement to be appraised by the Germans, adding that it might serve as a model for the Swedo-German declaration, without, of course, the clauses referring to the abrogation of the Treaties of 1855 and 1856. He planned to make the Guarantee Treaty in three separate agreements, of which the Russo-German one was already signed, because such a procedure followed the Mediterranean example.[1]

The preamble of the draft was identical to that of the secret Russo-German agreement. In the text it was said that as the Treaty of 1855 had ceased to have effect in consequence of the dissolution of the Union, Russia and Sweden recognized the principle of the territorial integrity of Sweden within the boundaries existing at the moment of the said dissolution. On their part the Swedish Government declared that they did not look upon the abrogation of the Convention of 1856 as being against the principle of Status quo.[2]

The Germans remarked that the mentioning of the Union might be distasteful for the Swedes, and Isvolsky left it out. Otherwise the Germans agreed with the draft.[3] After Nicholas had been pleased to give his most gracious consent, the draft was given to be studied by the swedish Government. Isvolsky thought, satisfied, that succes was within his reach.[4]

The secret disclosures

Russia and Germany were not able to keep their relations as secret as they could have wished. In May Tschirschky had discussed the Norwegian Treaty

[1] AVPR fond sekretnyj arhiv, delo 380, n. 111 Russian F.O. to German Embassy 13. XI 1907
AA Dänemark 37 geheim Bd 8 p. 94 Russian F. O. to German Embassy 14/27 XI 1907
[2] AVPR fond sekretnyj arhiv, delo 380, n. 114 *projet de declaration* 13. XI 1907
[3] AVPR fond sekretnyj arhiv, delo 380, n. 189 Russian F. O. to German Embassy 27. XI 1907
[4] AVPR fond sekretnyj arhiv, delo 380, n. 203 Isvolsky to Budberg 29. XI 1907

with Jules Cambon and had said that Germany "marched entirely in accord with Saint-Petersbourg, who had the conduct of the affair". The French Ambassador was disturbed at "the care with which he underlined the accord with Russia".[1] After the Swinemünde meeting rumours began circulating about the agreements made there, but nothing was known for certain as yet. In the summer everything was seen as being initiated by Germany; it was hoped "that M. Isvolsky would not get involved in a combination which would appear to public opinion as an indication of a new orientation in Russian politics".[2]

It was not until autumn that the Entente powers got any precise knowledge. The French Ambassador in Rome, Barrère, who had known Isvolsky, "observed that M. Isvolsky was very false, and he felt sure that he had either come to some arrangement or was negotiating one with the German Government. ." Of course Barrère was angry with Russia because "the Alliance between Russia and France being in restraint of Germany, the Russian Government had no right to enter into an agreement with the German Government detrimental to the interests of France . ."[3] The British Ambassador Bertie thought that "the French Government must be in possession of some reliable information . . that an Agreement or understanding regarding the Baltic has been concluded . ."[4] Pichon thought that Isvolsky's observations about "the Mediterranean understanding having been concluded without the knowledge of the Russian Government" "might be intended to prepare the French Government for some arrangement between Russia and Germany without consultation with the Quai d'Orsay . . What he considered possible was that Germany and Russia had come to an understanding to maintain the status quo . . there might be some understanding about the Åland Islands also".[5]

By the end of December 1907 Bertie reported that Clemenceau had got written proof that Isvolsky had initiated the negotiations between Germany and Russia, and that an unsigned agreement existed, with secret articles, which went beyond the mere questions of status quo.[6]

The British had heard something, too. In July Nicolson reported "It has been intimated to me that negotiations are pending between Russia and Germany as to an accord to which Sweden would be asked to adhere for maintaining the status quo in the Baltic on lines similar to those on which the Anglo-Spanish accord has recently been made".[7] This was a couple of weeks before Swi-

[1] DDF 10 n. 495 Jules Cambon to Pichon 10. V 1907
[2] DDF 11 n. 42 Pichon to Bompard 21. VI 1907
[3] PRO/FO 371/338/36543 Bertie to Grey 1. XI 1907
[4] PRO/FO 371/338/37617 Bertie to Grey 13. XI 1907
[5] PRO/FO 371/338/38141 Bertie to Grey 16. XI 1907
[6] BD 8 n. 135 Bertie to Grey 28. XII 1907
[7] PRO/FO 371/338/20160 Nicolson to Grey 17. VII 1907

nemünde. Somebody who knew of Isvolsky's preparations must have been Nicolson's informant.

Isvolsky himself strengthened these suspicions. He mentioned to Nicolson that, in view of the Mediterranean agreement, "Germany might contract what he termed a 'counterbalancing agreement'. . he might have been alluding to a Baltic agreement".[1] While the French were nervous about a Russo-German agreement in itself, regardless of contents, as portending the end of the Dual Alliance, the British took a more relaxed attitude to the rumours: "The maintenance of the status quo in the Baltic would be satisfactory to us; it would be better still if it were extended to include Denmark & the Belts & the Sound".[2] The Admiralty was a little worried lest a status quo agreement might close the Baltic — if the Royal Navy attacked its enemy on the Baltic Sea, would such action be regarded as ipso facto altering the status quo in the Baltic, and would all the Baltic powers join that enemy?[3] Of course the Foreign Office was not able to inform the Admiralty as to the details of the rumoured treaty, but Hardinge explained that "The status quo in the Baltic is the free passage of the Belts & Sound & so long as no power closes them or seizes territory within the Baltic the status quo would not be disturbed".[4] — This was the British definition, but of course "the status quo" is a vague term and could be construed in different ways.

The Swinemünde meeting roused no suspicions in London, although "the dream of reconstituting the Alliance between the three Emperors undoubtedly exists in some quarters . . Isvolsky is generally credited with not being adverse to Russia following such a course".[5] The British were not given to such hypothetical combinations; they took note of the satisfactory practical result: "Isvolsky's description was excessively couleur de rose. He seemed to have found the Emperor William and the Chancellor in the most amiable disposition", and Germany had shown the green light to Isvolsky's Asian policy.[6] In September the Japanese chargé d'affaires told Nicolson that at Swinemünde the Baltic question had been discussed and that unanimity had been reached in regard to mutual assistance in the defence of Russo-German interests in the Baltic, but Nicolson does not seem to have taken this very seriously.[7]

When more information was received in November the Foreign Office was still reluctant to believe that Isvolsky had done anything shady. The rumours concerning the German plans in Denmark were well remembered, but it was

[1] PRO/FO 371/338/20725 Nicolson to Grey 18. VII 1907
[2] POR/FO 371/338/20160 minutes
[3] PRO/FO 371/338/24768 Admiralty to F. O. 24. VII 1907
[4] PRO/FO 371/338/24768 minute by CH 24. VII 1907
[5] PRO/FO 371/261/26680 Cartwright to Grey 7. VIII 1907
[6] PRO/FO 371/326/27686 O'Beirne to Grey 10. VIII 1907
[7] BD 8 n. 107 Nicolson to Grey 7. IX 1907

deemed that "the closing of the Baltic cannot possibly be a Russian interest as long as she remains the ally of France, & it is improbable that if any understanding has been arrived at it is to that effect . . I (Hardinge) very much doubt it there is any real foundation for the rumoured treaty".[1] The co-operation of Schoen and Isvolsky in 1905 was remembered [2], but since the Asian agreement Isvolsky was a man of conciliation in the British eyes, not the dangerous Germanophile he was seen to be from Paris. "M. Pichon is apparently quite unable to suggest a *subject* for the hypothetical agreement which would be objectionable to France. It looks as if it is the possibility of an agreement on any subject whatever between Russia & Germany which he considers detrimental to France".[3] So Pichon did consider, and the British were unable to understand such an attitude.

It was not until Rennell Rodd in Stockholm began to wonder at the behaviour of the Russian envoys during the Norwegian negotiations (p. 152) that the British became thoughtful.[4] The idea began to dawn on them that "Russia and Germany are playing a very subtle game".[5] Nicolson sent more information from the same informant he had used in July [6] and by the end of November Hardinge and Grey deduced that "It is evident that so far nothing has been concluded, but it is probable that discussions as to the maintenance of the status quo in the Baltic, and some special provisions as to the Åland Islands have been in progress".[7] And "the Swedish Govt. would be well disposed to make an agreement with Russia & Germany . . , in order to give them the moral prestige which they consider they have lost through the recent Norwegian Treaty".[8]

Because "except by direct enquiring it seems difficult to get at the truth"[9] Hardinge tackled the secretary of the Russian Embassy Poklevsky. Hardinge said that an arrangement between Russia, Germany and Sweden with the object of maintaining the status quo in the Baltic would probably leave Great Britain unmoved, but the impression would be more unfavourable if the agreement aimed at closing the Baltic, which was, anyway, useless for Russia. If war broke out between France and Germany, Russia would automatically be at war with the latter, and consequently all Russian Baltic arrangements would be nullified. The only means for Russia to obtain liberty of action in regard to the Åland Islands was to negotiate directly with Sweden, giving her some guaran-

[1] PRO/FO 371/338/63055 Bertie to Grey 31. X 1907 minutes
[2] PRO/FO 371/338/37617 Bertie to Grey 15. XI 1907 minutes
[3] PRO/FO 371/338/38141 Bertie to Grey 16. XI 1907 minutes
[4] PRO/FO 371/338/37733 Rennell Rodd to Grey 13. XI 1907
[5] PRO/FO 371/338/37733 minutes 16. XI 1907
[6] PRO/FO 371/338/38715 Nicolson to Grey 11. XI 1907
[7] PRO/FO 371/338/38935 Bertie to Grey, minutes CH 26. XI 07
[8] PRO/FO 371/338/39049 Rennell Rodd to Grey 22. XI 1907, minutes CH 27. XI 1907
[9] PRO/FO 371/338/37305 Nicolson to Grey 11. XI 1907 minutes

tee. Hardinge said that England would probably not object to the change of the status quo on these islands after such negotiations, but the English standpoint would be totally different if the change were to be obtained at the price of closing the Baltic.[1] — Clearly the Åland Islands had no importance for Great Britain, and their importance in relation to the direction of Swedish policy did not emerge until later. But Hardinge realized their importance to Russia, and tried to use them to prevent Russia from agreeing to the alleged German schemes for closing the Straits. Hardinge was of the opinion that the Royal Navy should not enter "the Baltic trap" if war broke out, but of course he was not ready to acquiesce in the closure of the Straits during peacetime.

After a few days Hardinge spoke to the Ambassador himself in the same tone. He let Benckendorff understand "that Germany was forcefully trying to make the Russians suspect in the eyes of the London Cabinet . ."[2] — The British architect of the Russo-British understanding did not wish to estrange the Russians by accusing them, but hinted at the possibility that it was the Germans who were playing the "subtle game" to the detriment of the recent understanding between England and Russia.

Benckendorff had also to answer questions concerning the Baltic when he saw the French Ambassador Paul Cambon, who reminded him of Schoen's and Isvolsky's plans in 1905 and said that "this project, modified or not, has now been taken up again and has produced results". Benckendorff wrote to Isvolsky:". . it is as clear as day that indiscretions have been committed".[3]

It has never been definitely cleared up where the leak occurred: probably there were several of them. It seems that the French had some secret proof they could not show to the British, Nicolson had an informant in St. Petersburg, and Rennell Rodd in Stockholm either drew his conclusions or heard something confidentially. What is significant is how the Germans and Russians were ready to suspect each other. The Wilhelmstrasse thought that Isvolsky himself had talked too much in Paris, either in order to compromise the Germans in the West, or just carelessly.[4] On the other hand the Russians suspected that the Germans had given the information in order to break up the Dual Alliance or the Triple Entente.[5]

The Germans were eager, for their own reasons, to inform London of the Baltic project. Up to this time Isvolsky had demanded strict secrecy, but now it was evident that something had to be told the British.[6] He emphasized that the

[1] AVPR fond sekretnyj arhiv, delo 380, n. 106 Poklevsky to Benckendorff 8/21 XI 1907

[2] AVPR fond sekretnyj arhiv, delo 380, n. 119 Benckendorff to Isvolsky 14/27 XI 1907

[3] AVPR fond sekretnyj arhiv, delo 380, n. 108 Benckendorff to Isvolsky 13/26 XI 1907

[4] GP 23 II n. 8016 Metternich to Ausw. Amt 30. XI 1907

[5] AVPR fond sekretnyj arhiv, delo 380, n. 226 Nelidoff to Isvolsky 13/26. XII 1907

[6] AVPR fond sekretnyj arhiv, delo 380, n. 122 Russian F.O. to German Embassy 15/28 XI 1907

secret Baltic treaty of 16/29th October must in any case be kept secret, the information to be given concerning only the negotiations with Sweden. Russia and Germany were to speak separately and only for themselves, Russia as if continuing the earlier exchange of views about the Åland Islands. Nothing was to be said about Denmark.[1] — All semblance of Russo-German co-operation was thus to be avoided. The Russian reluctance to touch on the Danish question will be discussed later.

To Nelidoff in Paris Isvolsky sent a letter to help the Ambassador in his encounter with the French. For his defence he explained that "it was clear that no satisfactory solution of the Åland question was possible without an exchange of views with the Government in Gerlin". He stressed the analogy of the planned Baltic declarations to "those which had been signed last spring between Spain, France and England". Of course the object was not to close or to neutralize the Baltic but only to maintain the actual territorial status quo, which would inspire in Sweden a sense of security, which in turn "would permit her to envisage with equanimity the eventual revocation of the restrictive clauses concerning the Åland Islands . . Such an accord could not . . provoke any objection on the part of France . . A parallel exchange of views is actually taking place between Sweden and Germany, if we are well informed, and I have every reason to believe that we are so" — this was the nearest that Isvolsky came to confessing the existence of the secret Baltic understanding. — "It pleases me to believe that the French Government will see in the present communication a new proof of our amicable sentiments towards them. ."[2] — This was very nearly irony as it must have been clear to Isvolsky that the French Government would see his message as something else.

The West reacts

Isvolsky's proof of friendly sentiment was received with reproof in Paris. Pichon said that an agreement between Russia and Germany, which guaranteed the status quo in the Baltic, was contrary to the Dual Alliance because it prevented Russia from acting against Germany in the Baltic area. There had been nothing about any Russo-German agreement in Isvolsky's message[3], but Pichon knew of it from his own sources and therefore Isvolsky's line of defence was difficult to maintain. The analogy of the Mediterranean treaty was brushed aside on the ground that it was no concern of Russia, "while all questions having regard to German or Russian territories were unavoidably correlated

---

[1] AVPR fond sekretnyj arhivdelo 380, n. 130 Russian F.O. to German Embassy 17/30 XI 1907
[2] AVPR fond sekretnyj arhiv, delo 380, n. 154 Isvolsky to Nelidoff 22. XI/5. XII 1907
[3] AVPR fond sekretnyj arhiv, delo 380, n. 170 Nekludov to Isvolsky 24. XI/7. XII 1907

with France's relations with the Government of the Czar". And if the question was only of Sweden, why had not France been asked, wasn't she a signator of the Convention of 1856? Such goings-on were harmful for the Dual Alliance and the Paris Government was worried because Russia "has on several instances had a tendency to orientate towards Germany, or at least to give guarantees to Berlin to make them excuse the happy result of the recent (Russo-British) negotiations".[1] Paul Cambon explained that it would be difficult to make the public opinion believe that Russian collaboration with Germany in the Baltic did not signify a revolution in the system of alliances.[2] The President of the French Republic, Fallières, gave a lecture to the Russian Ambassador Nelidoff: "The Russian Government had no right to enter with another Government into any arrangement affecting in any way the interest of France without consulting the French Government . . France expected Russia to act as loyally towards her as she did to Russia. ." [3]

The Russians blamed the Germans for this onslaught. Pichon's inquietudes "were probably excited by the insinuations of our enemies" [4] and about the French "indubitable piece of information" it was thought "that it cannot originate anywhere but from" Jules Cambon, the Ambassador in Berlin [5], who had got it from the Germans, of course. These suspicions were preliminaries to those to be aroused by the German North Sea proposal. The honeymoon after Swinemünde was nearing the beginning of its end.

Isvolsky stuck to his guns. He was "painfully surprised" by the reception of his communication, and he was "unable to understand" how a declaration to reassure Sweden could harm the Dual Alliance. Russia had too well proved to be faithful that she might be suspected. "An alliance is like the wife of Caesar — she must not be suspected". The Czar Nicholas wrote "excellent" on the margin of this letter.[6] It would be fun to know what the French thought who knew that Caesar's wife had a secret liaison outside the alliance.

The British received similar information from the Russians. Isvolsky reassured Nicolson "that nothing had been definitely concluded, and that the discussions which have taken place do not relate to the closing or neutralization of the Baltic. ." He gave the well-known explanations about Sweden's security and Åland, and the Mediterranean treaty. With Germany he had gone only so far in the discussion as to satisfy her amour-propre, and "there had been no earlier

[1] AVPR fond sekretnyj arhiv, delo 380, n. 191 Nelidoff to Isvolsky 28. XI/11. XII 1907
[2] AVPR fond sekretnyj arhiv, delo 380, n. 183 Benckendorff to Isvolsky 27. XI/10. XII 1907
[3] BD 8 n. 115 Bertie to Grey 6. XII 1907
[4] AVPR fond sekretnyj arhiv, delo 380, n. 191 Nelidoff to Isvolsky 28. XI/11. XII 1907
[5] AVPR fond sekretnyj arkiv, delo 580, n. 184 Benckendorff to Isvolsky 27. XI/10. XII 1907
[6] AVPR fond sekretnyj arhiv, delo 380, n. 218 Isvolsky to Nelidoff 6/19 XII 1907

occasion to speak to the Western powers". Nicolson said that Isvolsky had been somewhat embarrassed when rattling off these excuses.[1]

The comments from Downing Street were much more unperturbed than from the Quai d'Orsay. "As long as the negotiations have nothing to do with either the closing or neutralization of the Baltic our interests cannot suffer by them".[2] Isvolsky's game was difficult to see through, in spite of the leak, with its different agreements written and unwritten with Germany and Sweden. His communication did not clear up the mystery, but the British remembered that "we can show ourselves recalcitrant about the abrogation of the treaty about the Åland Islands until we know the actual situation in the Baltic".[3] When the French said that these "negotiations are seriously to the prejudice of the Franco-Russian alliance", the British thought that "the French will make a mistake if they extend their objections to the substance; these should be confined to the manner of the negotiations"[4] because "If Russia can come to terms with Sweden about the Åland Islands it can only be a matter of satisfaction to all concerned".[5] So the reproof from London was very mild compared to that which Nelidoff had to endure in Paris: Grey said to Benckendorff that "it was surprising that we should have heard nothing more till matters had got so far"[6], "having himself made on the subject of this question a proposition which he had thought to be advantageous for Russia he had hoped that in consequence Isvolsky would have sent him some communication on the subject of the projects for further negotiations on this same question".[7]

The British thought that "the Russian contention that France has no ground of complaint is scarcely justified . . but there is no reason for Sir A. Nicolson to discuss this question at present".[8] The British were not angry, rather they thought that "it was stupid of Isvolsky as the French have the whip in the Åland question".[9] When Nicolson conjectured that perhaps Isvolsky had after all lied[10], Hardinge answered "I am not at all of the opinion that Isvolsky has been deceiving us over the Baltic question . . being in reality without experience of 'les grandes affaires' he made the mistake of opening negotiations with Sweden and Germany without informing us and France merely because it had

[1] PRO/FO 371/338/39907 Nicolson to Grey 4. XII 1907
[2] PRO/FO 371/337/39907 minute by CH
[3] BD 8 n. 111 Hardinge to Nicolson 12. XI 1907
[4] PRO/FO 371/338/40334 Bertie to Grey 6. XII 1907 minute CH & EG
[5] PRO/FO 371/338/40292 Nicolson to Grey 4. XII 1907 minute CH
[6] PRO/FO 371/338/40600 Grey to Nicolson 17. XII 1907
[7] AVPR fond sekretnyj arhiv, delo 380, n. 179 Benckendorff to Isvolsky 27. XI/10. XII 1907
[8] PRO/FO 371/338/40671 Nicolson to Grey 11. XII 1907 minutes
[9] BD 8 n. 122 Hardinge to Nicolson 11. XII 1907 private
[10] BD 8 n. 123 Nicolson to Grey 23. XII 1907

not occurred to him that it was necessary to do so".[1]When the German Ambassadors made their proposal about the North Sea Treaty they let slip some words that disclosed Russo-German collusion, but even this was explained away so as to save the image of Isvolsky as an honest friend.[2] "I (Hardinge) do not see why M. Isvolsky's word may not be accepted. .." [3]

In France Clemenceau was wild with rage, which made the British somewhat worried. It was reported that "What he cannot put up with is that Russia, the ally of France, should enter into compacts with Germany behind the back of France respecting matters in which French interests are included". "If the Russian Government repudiate the proceedings of which he has accused them, he will present them with German written proof of the truth of the accusations . . Clemenceau roundly abused Isvolsky and said the means must be found of getting rid of him." And he thought that he had an efficient weapon: Russia "is at the present moment anxious to obtain an advance of £ 10 000 000. She will not get it until she has given assurances about mending her recent conduct. .." [4] Lister, the British chargé d'affaires, added that "Clemenceau may be playing Germany's game and she may once more find herself in her old position of *tertium gaudens*. ."[5] Even Pichon had second thoughts: "he did not by any means intend to play the game of Germany by quarrelling with Russia over the matter".[6] Clemenceau was more impulsive and difficult, and had to be handled carefully "to insinuate your (Grey's) views into C's mind".[7] Grey thought that "the French should not be too much carried away be information written or otherwise from a German source".[8] Perhaps the formidable man thought it over himself and realized that the sources of information in Berlin might have some ulterior purpose; when Bertie "called on Clemenceau (he was) quite satisfied. He says that the result of the French representation at Petersburg has been to knock on the head the projected Agreement between Russia and Germany".[9] — Of course Clemenceau was too satisfied for the moment, but in fact the Russo-German relations were beginning to cool.

Germany had maintained a rather low profile during the long Norwegian negotiations, but now the suspicions against her began to flare up again. Instead of Russian deceit the British saw German schemes behind the Baltic and North Sea propositions, which "were evidently devised with the purpose of isolating

[1] BD 8 n. 133 Hardinge to Nicolson 24. XII 1907 private
[2] PRO/FO 371/338/40768 Nicolson to Grey 12. XII 1907, minutes CH & EG
[3] PRO/FO 371/338/41220 Nicolson to Grey 16. XII 1907 minute CH
[4] PRO/FO 371/527/1167 Bertie to Grey 23. XII 1907
[5] PRO/FO 371/527/1167 Lister to Grey 18. XII 1907
[6] PRO/FO 371/338/40769 Lister to Grey 11. XII 1907
[7] PRO/FO 371/527/1167 Lister to Grey 18. XII 1907
[8] PRO/FO 371/527/1167 Grey to Bertie 30. XII 1907
[9] PRO/FO 371/527/1167 Bertie to Grey 2. I 1908

France from her ally Russia & her friend Great Britain. Had she succeeded she would have been able to adopt a high-handed attitude towards France, & perhaps compel the latter to follow a German policy".[1] Grey averted this danger by compelling Germany to accept France as a participant in the North Sea negotiations (p. 190) Now to destroy the Baltic scheme the French proposed "to drown these arrangements *à deux* by an arrangement *à quatre* .. by an Arrangement between the four Powers Pichon hoped to remove the venom out of the Arrangements between Russia and Sweden, and Russia and Germany".[2]

Also the British Admiralty was worried on account of the rumours concerning the Baltic arrangements and reminded the Foreign Office "that it would be to the interest of Great Britain to give such support to Sweden as would succeed in preventing her from falling entirely under Russian influence. It is, however, of cardinal importance that all the Northern Powers (= Russia and Germany included) should recognize that under no circumstances can Great Britain acquiesce in any Arrangement which has for its object the exclusion of the British fleets from the Baltic either in peace or war".[3] After the picture had somewhat cleared, the Admiralty sent another message to the Foreign Office suggesting that "it would appear to be desirable that the question of the Baltic and the North Sea .. should be dealt with as a whole, and not by means of separate Agreements. A single Agreement, which included as contracting powers Russia, Germany, Norway, Sweden, France, Denmark, Belgium, Holland and Great Britain, would be preferable. The crucial point .. is the approach to the Baltic .. and no Agreement can be satisfactory to Great Britain as a naval Power which omits this region, including the Danish Islands. ."[4] — Once more the central importance of the Straits in the Baltic question is emphasized.

The Foreign Office was not very eager to accept these suggestions. In fact the Admiralty's propositions had in a way been answered in November in a letter by Grey to the First Lord of Admiralty, Lord Tweedmouth. Grey explained, first, that Russia and Germany could not be prevented from making agreements about closing the Straits between them. Second, France "cannot undertake obligations in favour of Sweden, directed against both Russia and Germany, and we cannot ourselves tell Sweden that she may reject any overtures from Russia and Germany, and rely upon us to protect her against them and prevent Åland from being fortified". It might have been well to have the Danish Straits neutralized, but it was impossible to get all the powers to agree. "I doubt whether I could do more than to keep us free from any international entanglements so that in time of war we should be free to do what we pleased

---

[1] PRO/FO 371/338/40769 Lister to Grey 11. XII 1907 minutes
[2] PRO/FO 371/338/40769 Lister to Grey 11. XII 1907
[3] PRO/FO 371/338/41616 Admiralty to F.O. 19. XII 1907
[4] PRO/FO 371/527/879 Admiralty to F.O. 8. I 1908

at our own risk".[1] — This sentence seems essential for the understanding of British policy in the Northern question. The treaties "in vogue" were looked upon as a nuisance, to be made as harmless as possible if it was impossible to avoid them altogether.

Grey was anxious not to hurt even the Germans unnecessarily, nor was he inclined to see their schemes as Satanic as the French did. "If Germany wishes to make agreements about the Baltic which are in themselves harmless, I do not want to make a grievance with her about it, or affront her by upsetting the German apple-cart for the sake of *amour-propre*. It may well be that all Germany desires is to gratify her *amour-propre* by appearing before the world as a party to some Agreements .. and so demonstrating that she is not isolated."[2] "If we are to quarrel with Germany, let it be for something worth quarrelling about, and not for *amour-propre;* and let us humour her in things that don't matter."[3] "On the other hand, it is possible that there is something going on with Germany and Russia behind the scenes about Baltic, which goes further than we have been told. I am therefore quite willing to make it a condition of the abrogation of the Åland treaty that Russia should make a clean breast." Thus German prestige would not be upset, Russia would be given a lesson and it would be demonstrated that France and Great Britain could not be ignored.[4] One cannot but admire Grey's common sense and good nerves in this far from clear situation, not committing himself to anything rash but being prepared for every possibility. And always keeping uppermost the most important aspect: "If there is a suggestion of closing the Baltic, we should reconsider our attitude."[5]

The Germans and the Russians insisted on keeping the Agreements separate, the British consented to it, and the French had to acquiesce. Jules Cambon thought that Grey planned to put the responsibility for the eventual failure of the North Sea project on France. Therefore it was better for the French to stop protesting. "It will be dangerous if Russia and England are able to wash their hands of the guilt of failure. .. it would be very bad for us (the French) if we had shown malevolence." Again, the French were not interested in the details of the Baltic question but in the combinations in the system of alliances: "Something is forming which will succeed the state of affairs created by the coexistence of the triple alliance and double alliance and the isolation of England."[6] But alone France was not able to prevent the new combinations between the Russians and the Germans.

In the summer of 1907 Grey had been frightened at Isvolsky's Baltic plans

---

[1] BD 8 n. 112 Grey to Tweedmouth 19. XI 1907
[2] BD 8 n. 136 Grey to Bertie 29. XII 1907
[3] PRO/FO 371/527/1167 Grey to Lister 16. XII 1907
[4] BD 8 n. 136 Grey to Bertie 29. XII 1907
[5] = 4
[6] DDF 11 n. 236 Jules Cambon to Pichon 7. I 1908

and had tried to stop all negotiations. In the winter it was said that "we are quite calm over the Baltic".[1] One explanation is, of course, the Asian agreement. Further, the British had saved what could be saved in Norway by dropping neutrality and so keeping open the possibility of an appropriate reaction to an eventual crisis in the Straits question. Isvolsky's eagerness in the Åland question had disclosed to the British the value of the Convention of 1856 as a juridical weapon in the Baltic affairs. Isvolsky's anger with the Germans over the Baghdad Railway, Persia and the North Sea project made him all the more reliable from the London point of view. "Therefore he is a Minister who should be supported by England and France since his tendency will be to lean more and more on us than on Germany".[2] — There were great difficulties indeed in Russo-German relations, although it was not until renewed Austrian activities in the Balkans that Hardinge's hopes were quite fulfilled.

[1] BD 8 n. 122 Hardinge to Nicolson 11. XII 1907
[2] BD 8 n. 139 Hardinge to Nicolson 21. I 1908

WHEN THE THIEVES FALL OUT

Germany plans the North Sea agreement

Schoen accepted Isvolsky's conditions for the message to be given to the Western powers (p. 176), but he did not show the text of the German message to the Russians as Isvolsky had asked.[1] Thus Isvolsky did not learn anything of the German North Sea project until afterwards.

The Germans were in agreement with the Russians that the Western powers were to be kept out of the Baltic, although they did not dare to leave written proof of this wish in Isvolsky's hands. In the autumn of 1907 it looked as if it was going to be easy to win Denmark and Sweden over by a surprise assault, which would leave them no time to get support from the West, and after the signature of the treaty, which had been secretly agreed to with Russia before-hand, the Western powers would not be able to make any countermoves. Sweden was not expected to get so nervous over Åland as she did in fact in 1908, the new guarantee of status quo was thought to give better security than the obsolete servitude, which no one was interested in keeping in force. It was very well understood that Great Britain would not like the Baltic agreement, but the projected North Sea agreement was intended both as a weapon to prevent her from elbowing into the Baltic, and as a sop to compensate for her being left out. The Russians being unreliable friends it was also useful to have evidence of good intentions towards England in case Isvolsky tried to use the Baltic secret to incriminate the Germans in British eyes. A treaty with Great Britain would also demonstrate to the world that Germany was not isolated, and it would show to Holland and Denmark that there was no ground for the fear of German annexation, caused by the propaganda of the Pan-Germans.[2]

It had been agreed with Isvolsky that the Baltic project had to be kept secret until all was clear with Sweden and Denmark, but by the end of November it began to be clear that the secret had leaked out. The Germans were sure that the Russians were to blame.[3] Isvolsky's wish to keep the Baltic agreement between Germany and Russia permanently secret had already made the Germans suspicious, and his conditions for informing London only deepened these suspicions. "It is to be seen from Isvolsky's total behaviour that he is trying to get closer to the British while pretending to be inclining to us ... Isvolsky has authorized Poklevsky to inform King Edward of the Russo-German Baltic treaty .. Therefore Isvolsky's proposal for Germany to speak in London about

---

[1] AA Dänemark 37 geheim Bd 8 p. 81 Miquel to Ausw. Amt 29. XI 1907
    AA Dänemark 37 geheim Bd 8 p. 108 Schoen to Miquel 3. XII 1907
[2] GP 23 II n. 8096 Metternich to Bülow 29. X 1907
    AA Russland 63 Bd 1 Metternich to Bülow 1. XI 1907
[3] GP 23 II n. 8106 Metternich to Ausw. Amt 30. XI 1907

a new Baltic treaty between the four Baltic powers was designed to strengthen Grey's belief in Germany's duplicity because Grey would know that there already existed a Baltic agreement. Isvolsky's wish to make the démarche separately was due to his fright that the Germans might see through his game. But Isvolsky's scheme might be neutralized by referring to the discussions between Russia and Germany about the Baltic as a fact, when informing the British of their intention to conclude a Baltic agreement *à quatre.*"[1]

This memorandum explains the "slip of the tongue" of Metternich and Radolin when they made the communication concerning the Baltic project in Paris and London. Both Ambassadors referred to Russo-German talks on the theme as a matter of fact. This confirmed the Western statesmen in their belief in the secret agreement about which they had received various information, even though Isvolsky energetically denied its existence.

As far as known, Isvolsky had no intention of betraying Germany's confidence, but the Germans could not afford to trust the architect of the Asian agreement. Their countercoup made Isvolsky in turn suspicious and dissatisfied. The friendship which had begun over the Straits question and the Norwegian negotiations floundered in the Baltic project, with which Isvolsky had intended to crown the co-operation.

When the thieves fall out

Tschirschky would have preferred to be honest with Isvolsky and to have told him about the North Sea project.[2] Nothing had come of it, which is easy to understand when the essence of Berlin's attitude to Isvolsky was distrust and fear of his intentional indiscretions. It is inexplicable why Schoen, Isvolsky's confirmed accomplice, adopted so soon and so completely the suspicious attitude prevalent in Berlin. After Metternich had proposed the North Sea project to the British at the beginning of December, Schoen only told the Russian Ambassador Osten-Sacken how he regretted Prince Gustaf's indiscretion. After his visit to Berlin (p. 169) Gustaf had evidently told Rennell Rodd everything he had heard, and "this indiscretion had worked on English susceptibilities and the suspicion of our going to declare the Baltic a 'mare clausum' "Schoen had considered that the best means of eliminating the consequences of this incident had been to explain everything frankly, which Metternich had been instructed to do. The démarche had succeeded, and Schoen congratulated himself on the result.[3]

---

[1] AA Dänemark 37 geheim Bd 8 p. 110 note 3. XII 1907 anon.
[2] AA Dänemark 37 geheim Bd 7 p. 44 Tschirschky to Schoen 17. VIII 1907
[3] AVPR fond sekretnyj arhiv, delo 380, n. 159 Osten-Sacken to Isvolsky 23. XI/6. XII 1907

This seems to have been a most inadequate narration of Metternich's interview with Grey, for in this interview Metternich had proposed the North Sea Treaty. It is easy to imagine Isvolsky's feelings when he learned through the French of the German proposition. He "did not wish to make recriminations" but made them anyhow: it was odd that Belgium had been left out of the North Sea project, thereby depriving Russia of the right, as a guarantor of Belgian neutrality, to participate. Germany had, as Isvolsky understood, proposed a joint treaty of the coastal powers of the North Sea, which was not analogous to the Mediterranean exchange of notes and which made it difficult to prevent the Western powers from claiming the right to participate in the Baltic project. And the main point: when proposing to England and France an agreement which accorded Denmark a guarantee for her Western coasts, had not Germany given to these powers an occasion to raise the question of a general act of guarantee for Denmark? Even if the Baltic powers could maintain that the Eastern coast of Denmark did not interest outside powers, the same could not be said of the Straits, which had been internationally regulated by the Treaty of 1857. Isvolsky's tone was somewhat vexed: "The result is that the new German project has considerably complicated the question." The Russian minister had grown suspicious of the reliability of his summer friends: "It is only after elucidating the points mentioned above that the Imperial Government will feel itself able to pronounce on its attitude in regard to the opening of negotiations with the Danish government".[1] Raben, in his innocence, proposed that England "might even be asked to participate in it (Denmark's guarantee), which would doubtlessly enhance enormously the importance of the measure to be taken"[2], which must have added to Isvolsky's irritation.

There was material enough for Nicolson's report: "Isvolsky is much annoyed with Germany over several matters (others were Persia and the Baghdad Railway), and thinks that she has not treated him well in the Baltic and North Sea questions."[3] Isvolsky explained to Nicolson: "By the impetuous and hasty action of Germany .. the whole question had become confused"[4] being now "enlarged from a simple understanding with Sweden, which was natural and desirable, into an arrangement affecting the whole of the Baltic, and thereby that would occur which he wished to avoid, namely the opening up of the whole Baltic question"[5] Eyre Crowe remarked, surely not unsatisfied: "When the

[1] AVPR fond sekretnyj arhiv, delo 380, n. 207 Russian F. O. to German Embassy 4/17. XII 1907
[2] AVPR fond sekretnyj arhiv, delo 380, n. 224 Raben to Isvolsky 9/22 XII 1907
[3] BD 8 n. 138 Nicolson to Grey 16. I 1908
[4] PRO/FO 371/527/2043 Nicolson to Grey 13. I 1907
[5] PRO/FO 371/527/2042 Nicolson to Grey 13. I 1907

thieves fall out . . !"[1]

In the preceding summer the opening up of the whole Baltic question had made Grey demand a Baltic conference, which had caused the hasty retreat of Isvolsky in the Åland question. It was self-evident that in a conference he had no possibility of keeping Sweden isolated, nor of defending Russian interests in the Straits question. Privately Hardinge and Nicolson played with an idea to take advantage of the situation by inviting Russia to join the North Sea project, which "would certainly please Isvolsky".[2] But "treating as a whole" the Baltic and North Sea affairs and "saving Sweden from German domination"[3] were not as alluring ideas as the British thought, because Isvolsky was not quite so angry with Germany as was believed. And the Germans were trying to patch up their mistakes.

The rift patched up

In his interview with Metternich Grey had remarked that the Baltic and the North Sea projects were parts of the greater Northern question.[4] Hints like this brought home the danger of the British elbowing into the Baltic, a danger which both Isvolsky and the Germans were afraid of.

So the Germans sought to answer Isvolsky's accusations and apprehensions: in the North Sea separate declarations were planned just as in the Baltic and the Mediterranean. Belgium was left out because it was permanently neutral and thus unable to take up any obligations. "The German Government is also of the opinion that it would agree as well with German as with Russian interests not to introduce the question of the Straits into the actual discussions. The Berlin Cabinet believes also that if Russia and Germany are firmly resolved, this matter can be kept out".[5] "We are keeping to the standpoint that only coastal powers are to take part in the Baltic agreements."[6] The Empires might avert the Western schemes by keeping together and not quarrelling — a reproof to Isvolsky for his irritability. The German project did leave the question of the Straits and the Kattegat open, but they could be dealt with later. The Treaty of 1857 concerning the Sound dues did not give France or England any right to intervene in other questions because it referred only to the customs.[7] Denmark could well be guaranteed from the East and from the West leaving the Straits

---

[1] PRO/FO 371/527/1397 Nicolson to Grey 13. I 1908, minute EAC
[2] BD 8 appendix II Nicolson to Hardinge 2. I 1908 private
[3] BD 8 n. 137 Hardinge to Nicolson 7. I 1908 private
  BD 8 n. 130 Nicolson to Grey 16. XII 1907
[4] BD 8 n. 125 Grey to Salis 12. XII 1907
[5] AVPR fond sekretnyj arhiv. delo 380, n. 235 German Embassy to Russian F.O. 17/30. XII 1907
[6] AA Dänemark 37 geheim Bd 9 p. 57 Schoen to Miquel 16. XII 1907, draft
[7] AA Dänemark 37 geheim Bd 9 p. 86 Schoen to Pourtalès 24. XII 1907

uncovered. — Of course the Germans hoped to "deal with" the Straits later, and without the participation of the Western powers. One might doubt that they were very eager to let the Russians have a say in the matter, either.

Isvolsky answered the Germans by expressing doubts about whether the Danish negotiations could be kept within the limits they would have preferred.[1] Nor could he convince himself that it was possible and practicable to leave the Straits out of all agreements. He believed that in spite of their promises to Germany the Danes would strive for a general guarantee of their territorial integrity on all sides. Or, as the French tried to participate in the North Sea project on the strength of the fishery treaty of 1882, they were sure to use the pretext of the Sound Dues Treaty of 1857 to elbow into Danish and Baltic affairs.[2]

Schoen tried to calm his former friend by saying that the best way to avoid the broadening of the scope of the Baltic treaty was to sign the declarations with Sweden and Denmark as soon as possible. The formulation the Germans had proposed *possessions continentales et insulaires dans les régions de la mer Baltique,* of which the territorial status quo was to be guaranteed, would prevent the Straits from being taken into the agreement. If the Sound and the Kattegat were to be parts of the Baltic, then why not even the Skagerrak, and then Norway, too, would be a Baltic power — it was clearly nonsense.[3]

Evidently Isvolsky let himself be assured. He tried to hurry on the Åland negotiations with Sweden, for which he still needed German support.

Denmark invited to join

Denmark had been left out of the negotiations concerning the Norwegian Treaty in the autumn of 1907, because "the idea . . did not occur to anybody".[4] Isvolsky had wished to keep Denmark out of the Baltic negotiations until later and concentrate on forcing Sweden to accept his Åland proposal. His reluctance to inform Denmark is often attributed to his fear of the Western powers using Denmark as a pretext to intervene in the Baltic question. In the preceding summer Great Britain had caused his first Åland attempt to fail, and by great exertions he had succeeded in isolating Sweden from the West before making a renewed attempt. If Denmark were invited to join the negotiations, it would be impossible to keep the Western powers out because they had a legitimate interest in the Straits question. The isolation of Sweden would be broken, and

[1] AVPR fond sekretnyj arhiv, delo 380, n. 238
   Russian F.O. to German Embassy 20. XII 1907/2. I 1908
[2] AA Dänemark 37 geheim Bd 10 p. 10 Pourtalès to Bülow 2. I 08
[3] AA Dänemark 37 geheim Bd 10 p. 21 Schoen to Pourtalès 6. I 1908
[4] PRO/FO 371/296/37893 Johnstone to Grey 14. XI 1907, minute CH

supported by the West she would refuse to give up her stand on Åland. There was, however, also another aspect of Isvolsky's attitude to Denmark, but this will be narrated later. Isvolsky's reluctance to include Denmark in the negotiations explains also his wish to make separate agreements between each pair of Baltic powers:[1] Denmark could not be omitted from a general Baltic agreement, but the separate agreements could be negotiated one by one.

The British, too, had been reluctant to take up the Danish question. The status quo in the Straits was in accordance with British wishes, and Grey had no intention of taking up the question of Denmark's position lest a violent German reaction be provoked.

Nevertheless Denmark could not be kept out of the negotiations concerning the Baltic and North Sea declarations. When Rennell Rodd in November travelled home from Stockholm via Copenhagen, he saw Johnstone and told him what he knew of Russo-German collaboration and the Russian schemes concerning Sweden.[2] Johnstone conveyed everything that he had heard to Raben.[3] For this indiscretion he got a severe reprimand from Grey: "Sir A. Johnstone should not have started it without instructions .. I think after the warning given last year he should not have stirred up this matter. ." [4] But the matter had been revealed and the Danes took great fright.

Raben was sure that Sweden and Germany had agreed that Sweden should lend her aid to Germany and receive the Danish islands as a reward, Germany contenting herself with Jutland.[5] Nervous out of all proportions, he returned to the question many times, but after the warning Johnstone did not say anything. Raben saw also the Russian envoy Kudašev and was 'un peu froissé' because Russia had not informed him of the project.[6] In drafting the message to be given to the British about the Baltic negotiations Isvolsky had still thought that Denmark ought to be left out and only Sweden mentioned.[7] Now Denmark could no longer be left completely out, and because also the Germans preferred taking the Danes along — for reasons of their North Sea project, of which Isvolsky was as yet ignorant — Isvolsky reluctantly gave way, underlining the need to be cautious.[8] Kudašev received a copy of the message which was sent to the Foreign Office with the "explanation" that "for reasons which it would take too long to explain here, it has not been so far possible to take Denmark into

[1] AA Dänemark 37 geheim Bd 8 p. 85 Miquel to Bülow 27. XI 1907
[2] PRO/FO 371/338/37894 Johnstone to Grey 14. XI 1907
[3] PRO/FO 371/338/39543 Johnstone to Grey 28. XI 1907
[4] PRO/FO 371/338/39543 minute by EG
[5] PRO/FO 371/338/39543 Johnstone to Grey 28. XI 1907
[6] AVPR fond sekretnyj arhiv, delo 380, n. 117 Kudašev to Isvolsky 14/27 XI 1907
[7] AVPR fond sekretnyj arhiv, delo 380, n. 130
  Russian F.O. to German Embassy 17/30. XI 1907
[8] AVPR fond sekretnyj arhiv, delo 380, n. 135
  Russian F.O. to German Embassy 21. XI/4. XII 1907

the sphere of the negotiations".[1]

Kudašev thanked Isvolsky for "having kept me informed on these matters, which has put to sleep all the bad blood and inquietude of poor Mr. Raben caused by that imbecile Johnstone, who always wants to be important and keeps talking to Raben with sinister and mysterious airs".[2] But it seems that Russian reluctance left a bad impression in Denmark, and according to Johnstone "Raben is hurt at Russia's whole attitude in this question and also does not hesitate to blame M. Isvolsky"[3], Schoen having been more disposed to disclose the secret to the Danes.[4]

After the Russo-German quarrel concerning the North Sea proposition had been patched up, Isvolsky promised to Raben to enlarge the circle of participants in the Baltic negotiations and to introduce Denmark "once the matter had been thoroughly examined".[5] When it had become clear that the Baltic and the North Sea agreements were to be kept separate, it was time to invite Denmark to participate officially. In the middle of January 1908 the Danes received the draft for the Baltic declaration[6], and at the beginning of February they were given the North Sea draft.[7]

Raben declared himself satisfied with these proposals, especially the North Sea one. It brought Germany and England closer to each other, which diminished the danger that the Danes were most afraid of.[8] He was satisfied also with the definition of the status quo as a territorial term, which allowed the fortifying of Copenhagen.[9] The Danish government had no material objections; they only preferred joint declarations instead of separate ones.[10]

Evidently it was comforting for the Danes to be the subject of international interest after being left alone with the Germans for so long a time. And it was satisfying to participate in a treaty on an equal footing with the Swedes, instead of being left out to be sneered at as the Norwegians were.[11] Raben only hoped that the North Sea declaration would be signed simultaneously with or before the Baltic one, to avoid being left alone with Russia and Germany.[12]

---

[1] AVPR fond sekretnyj arhiv, delo 380, n. 145 Isvolsky to Kudašev 22. XI/5. XII 1907
[2] AVPR fond sekretnyj arhiv, delo 380, n. 181 & 177
  Kudašev to Isvolsky 27. XI/10. XII 1907
  Kudašev to Isvolsky 26. XI/9. XII 1907
[3] PRO/FO 371/447 Annual report 1907 for Denmark by A. Johnstone, paragraph 28
[4] PRO/FO 371/447 paragraph 17
[5] AVPR fond sekretnyj arhiv, delo 380, n. 238 Isvolsky to Raben 20. XII 1907/2. I 1908
[6] AA Dänemark 37 geheim Bd 10 Schoen to Henckel 18. I 1908
[7] AA Dänemark 37 geheim Bd 11 Schoen to Raben 2. II 1908
[8] AA Dänemark 37 geheim Bd 12 Henckel to Bülow 6. II 1908
[9] AA Dänemark 37 geheim Bd 12 Raben to Schoen 11. II 1908
[10] AVPR fond sekretnyj arhiv, delo 381 n. 303 Kudašev to Isvolsky 19. I/1. II 1908
[11] AVPR fond kanceljarija 1908 g, delo 33 n. 1 Kudašev to Isvolsky 5/18 I 1908
[12] AA Dänemark 37 geheim Bd 11 Henckel to Bülow 31. I 1908

THE BALTIC QUESTION IN THE NORTH SEA

The German broth watered down

When Metternich came to propose the North Sea Treaty, Grey "did not see much object in it", but then he was struck by the "suggestion that it might remove the suspicions which might be entertained in some quarters with regard to German designs on Holland" which would have a beneficial effect. "Count Metternich said that this had been merely an incidental remark of his, and must not be regarded as the main object or motive of the proposed Agreement".

But it soon turned out that, apart from this, there was not much sense left in the project. Grey directed the discussion on to the question of what scope the arrangement ought to have: he wanted France in. This led to a duel of wits where even herrings were used as weapons — Grey argued that in the Convention on North Sea Fisheries of 1882 there was a "definition of the limits of the North Sea which included a straight line drawn from Cape Griz-Nez in France. This definition therefore included part of the French coast as being on the North Sea". It did not avail the German Ambassador to point to the map and explain that France bordered only upon the Channel and not on the North Sea. "It seemed to me (Grey) impossible to conclude an Arrangement about the North Sea to which France was not a party".[1] Metternich tried his best, but Grey was not to be moved. Bülow instructed the Ambassador that "for reasons of general policy" France had to be accepted.[2]

The value of the project was thereby materially minimized for Germany, "the broth was watered down" as Schoen says in his memoirs. He wonders whether Grey's insistence really was caused by the wish for a general pacification or by a reluctance to conclude a treaty with Germany which might be understood as a political entente.[3] — The fact is that by leaving France out and agreeing with Germany, Grey would have killed the Entente of 1904.

So the German Ambassador in Paris Radolin went to tell Pichon of the project and to ask the French to participate. Pichon found it natural that France should join the North Sea project, being a North Sea power on the strength of the 1882 Fishery Treaty, as well as legitimately interested in Baltic affairs as a signatory of the Convention of 1856. He said that the general political situation would be greatly improved if France and Germany could join in signing an agreement of this kind.[4]

The British were satisfied that they had prevented an attempt to break the Entente. Hardinge wrote: "The German idea was, I believe, to be able to show the French that their ally Russia was negotiating a Treaty with the German

[1] PRO/FO 371/338/40665 Grey to Salis 9. XII 1907
[2] GP 23 II n. 8114 Bülow to Metternich 10. XII 1907
[3] Schoen p. 59
[4] GP 23 II n. 8117 Radolin to Ausw. Amt 14. XII 1907

Govt. about the Baltic, and the British Govt. about the North Sea, French interests in both cases being entirely ignored. The object being to show that the French had been deserted both by their ally and friend." [1] Hardinge estimated it to be "a clumsy proposal" and "a feeble attempt to attempt a new grouping of the Northern Powers".[2] But "we frustrated the attempt, France is deeply grateful".[3]

Schoen's words indicate that he may really have thought of something like this, and Metternich's insistence points in the same direction. Bülow's and William's views are not known, evidently they were not interested in commenting upon a failure. The North Sea Treaty lost its *raison d'être* from the very beginning. "The whole business seemed to (Jules Cambon) to be becoming an absurdity since thanks to Sir Edward Grey, the one object of the Germans, to make a grouping of Northern and Western Powers without France, has failed." [4] But of course the project still had its propaganda value in Holland and Denmark, and its importance in the context of the Baltic question.

And since he had broken the edge of the attempt and saved the Entente, Grey had no reason for refusing the toothless treaty, and no wish to offend German *amour-propre* by such a refusal. Thus both the Baltic and the North Sea Treaties failed to fulfil the intentions of their initiators and in fact were useless. They survived because nobody wished to take the odium of killing them. Grey submitted to the Cabinet his opinion that "obviously we cannot refuse . . if we were to refuse, our refusal would be attributed either to a desire on our part to keep our hands free to alter the status quo, or else to reluctance on our part to enter into any Arrangement to which Germany was party . . I think it very desirable that we should not refuse an innocent arrangement of this kind with Germany".[5] The Cabinet accepted the plan in principle on the 12th February 1908, the main characteristics of the agreement being a reciprocal pledge to respect the territorial status quo, to be declared jointly by all the signatory powers.[6] But as far as the details were concerned there was much to be negotiated to keep the agreement really innocent and acceptable to all participants.

Belgium and Norway left out

The first question to be discussed was the scope of the agreement. France had been taken into the group of signatories, but Belgium and Norway were left out.

[1] PRO/FO 371/527/2043 Nicolson to Grey 13. I 1908 minute CH
[2] BD 8 n. 122 Hardinge to Nicolson 11. XII 1907
[3] BD 8 n. 139 Hardinge to Nicolson 21. I 1908
[4] PRO/FO 371/527/1167 Salis to Grey, January 1908
[5] PRO/FO 371/528/6741 Grey to Cabinet 16. I 1908
[6] PRO/FO 371/528/5103 Grey to Lascelles 12. II 1908

Perhaps the Germans were reluctant to give new guarantees to Belgium because they were sure that England and France would not respect her integrity in any case, and that she would resist an occupation only with platonic protests.[1] Schlieffen had made his plans accordingly, and the Emperor's "friend or foe"-ultimatum has already been referred to.

The British explained that "the neutrality of Belgium being guaranteed by the powers, there could be no question of a change in the status quo of the Belgian coast". So Belgium was not invited to join, although "personally" Hardinge would not have had anything against it.[2] Nor werw the Belgians interested, explaining that this was due to the fear of "giving rise to the suspicion that Belgium was dissatisfied with the guarantee which she now enjoyed, and which afforded her far greater security than would be provided by the proposed declaration".[3]

The Norwegians were kept entirely out of the status quo-negotiations. They asked in Copenhagen for information about the Baltic declaration, and were answered "very shortly; firstly, Norway was not a Baltic littoral Power, and that, secondly, as she had chosen to make her own integrity treaty without consulting either Denmark or Sweden, she could not expect to be consulted in her turn. ."[4] The Foreign Office concurred: "Count Raben's tit-for-tat to Norway is amusing".[5]

Lövland tried to be brave about it, "Norway was not anxious to take part in any negotiations". It was not, however, pleasant, and Lövland was criticized for his foreign policy, which was unfavourably compared with his home politics[6] — the whole affair had turned upside down, as originally diplomatic success was hoped for as a trump card for home policy. So the Norwegian chargé d'affaires in London pointed out that Norway, not being neutralized, was in a position to take part in other treaties. Grey did not discuss this point but gave "a piece of advice privately . . Norway ought to remain content for the time. The Norwegian Government might impress upon the Norwegian public opinion that they had had great diplomatic successes, and could not expect a new one every year".[7] It seems that Grey was rather fed up with the Norwegians and all the difficulties they had caused him.

Norway's exclusion was made definite when it was decided to take Sweden into the North Sea Treaty, because "Sweden was very anxious that Norway should not be included in this latter agreement".[8] When the Norwegians won-

[1] Bülow p. 77

[2] PRO/FO 371/527/2373 Grey to Hardinge 24. I 1908, minutes

[3] PRO/FO 371/528/5402 Lascelles to Grey 12. II 1908

[4] PRO/FO 371/527/1585 Johnstone to Grey 13. I 1908

[5] PRO/FO 371/527/1585 minute by EAC

[6] AVPR fond kanseljarija 1908 g., delo 27, n. 7 Krupensky to Isvolsky 3/16 III 1908

[7] PRO/FO 371/528/4980 Grey to Herbert 11. II 1908

[8] PRO/FO 371/528/3946 Vaughan to Grey 4. II 1908

dered at Sweden being a coastal state of the North Sea, Grey answered coldly
that "no definitions had been proposed as to what the limits of the North Sea
were".[1] Lövland's successor Knudsen was interested in the North Sea Treaty, so
that the Swedes had the satisfaction of declaring to the Norwegian envoy "that
it would be too late to consider the question of Norway joining in the North Sea
declaration".[2]

Evidently the British could well afford to snub the Norwegians this much. In
spite of the threats in the years 1905—1907 of turning to Germany, Norway's
vital interests remained directed to the West.

Dutch apprehensions

The Dutch had been the very first to share the secret of the North Sea
proposition. When asked officially they naturally accepted "appreciating the
proposal as a proof of the Emperor William's good intentions". They could not
have accepted a neutrality treaty because of their great past, but they could well
sign the status quo agreement, as co-equal with the other powers.[3]
But there was one point which the Dutch did not like: in the German draft it was
declared that the intention of the signatories was 'status quo aufrechtzuer-
halten'. If the treaties were to be separate, one between each pair of powers, it
would mean that, if the British were to attack Hamburg or Bremen, Holland
would be obliged to go to the assistance of Germany. "On no account would
Holland give up her right to remain neutral".[4] The British took up this point
with the Germans in order "to encourage them (the Dutch) to believe that we
are anxious, wherever we can, to promote their interests. It may make all the
difference in our relations with Holland if it is we, rather than the Germans,
who have been of help to her in the present matter, however small that matter
may appear in our eyes".[5]

And for the French it was no small matter. Pichon said that "the French and
British Governments would have to be very careful not to place themselves in
a position entailing a guarantee by France and England of German territory on
the North Sea".[6] "Public opinion could not but see in such an arrangement the
first step towards the definitive consecration, under the form of a reciprocal
guarantee, of the state of affairs created by the Treaty of Frankfurt".[7]

[1] PRO/FO 371/528/7554 Grey to Herbert 2. III 1908
[2] PRO/FO 371/529/13615 Rennell Rodd to Grey 16. IV 1908
[3] DDF 11 n. 286 Pellet to Pichon 17. II 1908
[4] PRO/FO 371/528/4979 Grey to Howard 10. II 1908
[5] BD 8 note by Ed. p. 172—, minute by EAC
[6] PRO/FO 372/527/3382 Bertie to Grey 30. I 1908
[7] DDF 11 n. 263 Pichon to French representatives 30. I 1908
13

The Germans had hoped to be able to calm the small North Sea powers by promising to maintain the status quo. They were of the opinion that it did not imply an obligation to maintain it with armed force[1] and thought it "remarkable"that the British wanted only to "preserve intact" their own rights. But as the Dutch and the Danes accepted, and in fact preferred, the weaker alternative, the Germans gave way.[2]

Grey also proposed that there ought to be only one treaty to be signed jointly by all the powers concerned. This was much more simple as it was reckoned that there would have been 15 separate treaties.[3] The Germans had no such reasons to keep the agreements separate as Isvolsky did, and they accepted,[4] hoping that the moral effect in regard to the small powers would thereby be enhanced.[5]

The fear of compromising their neutrality did not, however, leave the minds of the Dutch. They tried to make the powers accept an addition to the text of the agreement to the effect that the declaration did not prevent any power from observing neutrality during the war. This was not accepted[6] but the Dutch tried to make the other small powers join in their attempt. The Danes evidently adopted the idea[7] but the Swedish Government declined to support the proposal.[8] Schoen says in his memoirs that "in the twelfth hour, when everything was ready to be signed, the Dutch and the Danish envoy came to propose the addition of a few words about the agreement not preventing them from declaring themselves neutral in case of war". Schoen answered that both states were free to declare themselves neutral eventually, but if they aimed at a permanently recognized neutrality, he was ready to drop the Treaties and to enter into new discussions with the North Sea and Baltic powers if the Danish and Dutch governments proposed it officially. At this threat the envoys dropped the proposition and claimed that the initiative was not theirs nor of their governments; they blamed the Dutch envoy in Copenhagen, whose lively imagination was guilty of everything.[9]

We have already seen what the Germans thought about the idea of neutrality of their small neighbours. Even if Holland was not so directly involved in the

---

[1] GP 23 II n. 8131 Schoen to Metternich 3. II 1908
[2] GP 23 II n. 8138 note by Schoen 21. II 1908
[3] PRO/FO 371/527/2806 minutes by F.O. to the German draft 24. I 1908
  BD 8 n. 140 Grey to Lascelles 24. I 1908
[4] PRO/FO 371/528/5894 Grey to Lascelles 18. II 1908
[5] GP 23 II n. 8128 Metternich to Bülow 24. I 1908
[6] PRO/FO 371/528/8360 Grey to Lascelles 9. III 1908
[7] PRO/FO 371/529/13856 Johnstone to Grey 22. IV 1908
  AA Dänemark 37 geheim Bd 16 p. 34 Danish envoy to Ausw. Amt 22. IV 1908
[8] PRO/FO 371/529/13461 Rennell Rodd to Grey 20. IV 1908
[9] Schoen p. 61

German plans as Denmark and Belgium, the idea of drawing her closer to Germany existed. There was no reason to encourage such ideas in any country bordering Germany.

Grey thought that "there is no objection to such a reservation though it is quite unnecessary".[1]

The territorial status quo only guaranteed

The Baltic agreement very nearly failed on the definition of the status quo, but for the North Sea this was an easy question.

Metternich, the German Ambassador in London, wondered whether the status quo could be understood as referring only to unalterable borders, or whether the projected treaty would entitle Great Britain to protest if Holland drew closer to Germany when "the Dutch confidence in Germany" grew. The naval status quo in the North Sea would be markedly altered if the Dutch estuaries came under German dominations.[2] The Germans wondered whether they might have acquired Heligoland in 1890 if the territorial status quo had been guaranteed then. There was the question of Denmark's position in case of war, too; and, on the other hand, the British were suspected of schemes regarding to Esbjerg which might be touched on by the new treaty. In the end it was concluded that it was better not to discuss this problem, because even a hint of it would arouse grave suspicions in London.[3]

The British also thought that "it might perhaps be left as it was",[4] since they had worries of their own in this respect, for instance "the deepening of the Sound might be interpreted as an alteration of the status quo".[5] It was important not to close the Baltic by defining the status quo as signifying the naval situation, which would be altered when a British fleet attacked in the Baltic: "it is better not to show our hand at this stage, but to stick to the word territorial"[6] so that "the rights and privileges of foreign shipping in the Baltic remain untouched".[7]

The term status quo was defined as referring only to territorial possessions, and the definition was added to the North Sea agreement in a special memorandum.[8] The British and the Germans were able to agree with each other in this

---

[1] PRO/FO 371/529/13856 Johnstone to Grey 22. IV 1908, minute by EG
[2] GP 23 II n. 8096 Metternich to Bülow 29. X 1907
[3] GP 23 II n. 8128 Metternich to Bülow 24. I 1908
   GP 23 II n. 8129 Schoen to Metternich 29. I 1908
[4] PRO/FO 371/528/4182 Grey to Lascelles 5. II 1908
[5] PRO/FO 371/527/1591 Rennell Rodd to Grey 15. I 1908
[6] PRO/FO 371/527/1591 minute by EG
[7] PRO/FO 371/527/2732 Cartwright to Grey 23. I 1908 minutes
[8] = 3

question, although their aims were contradictory.

Can the North Sea and Baltic questions be kept separate?

The survey of the problem of defining the term status quo shows that when the discussion became earnest, it was concerned with Baltic and not with North Sea problems. The North Sea project never succeeded in acquiring independent importance. It had been born as an excrescence of the Baltic treaty, to keep out the Western powers and to reinsure Germany against eventual Russian perfidy. Grey had killed what independent importance it might have had. The greatest, the only real difficulties in the North Sea negotiations were due to the Danish Straits. The agreement remained all the time a part of the Baltic question, in spite of the manifold exertions of Russia and Germany to keep the two questions separated.

It has been narrated already how the French, and the British Admiralty, would have liked to unite the two agreements. The British Foreign Office was satisfied when they learned that Denmark had been invited to join in the Baltic negotiations.[1] If the status quo was understood as the British did — as the free passage through the Straits — they had no reason to object to Germany signing a treaty which guaranteed the status quo in the Straits. The guarantee of the territorial status quo might even prevent the occupation of Denmark by Germany. The Germans on the other hand understood that maintaining the status quo implied restoring Danish territory to Denmark without reductions after a war in which she had been on Germany's side, as Moltke had promised.

Paul Cambon prompted the British to induce the Danish Government to propose an arrangement by which all the Northern powers could be brought into a general agreement[2], and Raben was favourably disposed to this plan.[3] The British liked this idea, too, because it would make easier to raise the question of the passages between the two seas.[4] This solution was suggested in the press,[5] which gave Grey an occasion to take the suggestion up without compromising himself. But Metternich let Grey understand that Germany would absolutely oppose uniting the two projects,[6] although Isvolsky was blamed for this.[7] Metternich argued that it was not sensible to bind the agreements together as the Baltic project was being delayed, perhaps interminably,

[1] PRO/FO 371/527/803 Egerton to Grey 8. I 1908 minutes
[2] PRO/FO 371/527/2286 Grey to Bertie 24. I 1908
[3] PRO/FO 371/527/2171 Vaughan to Grey 17. I 1908
[4] PRO/FO 371/527/879 Admiralty to F.O. 8. I 1908 minutes
[5] *Daily Graphic* 18. I 1908
[6] AA Russland 63 Bd 1 Metternich to Ausw. Amt 30. I 1908
[7] PRO/FO 371/527/2286 Grey to Bertie 24. I 1908

and would thereby make also the more hopeful North Sea Treaty fail. In fact he was worried and dissatisfied with Russia, who was losing time with the Åland question, worthless from the German point of view. Metternich apprehended new complications, in fact just those that the French hoped for.[1] We have already seen that Grey felt it important not to antagonize Germany in vain, and the Foreign Office thought that "it is not for England to move in the matter".[2] England could afford to remain outside the Baltic agreement when she was sure that it did not imply closing the Straits, and she had always the Convention of 1856 as juridical asset which entitled her to a seat and voice in the Baltic councils if she so needed.

Jules Cambon's secretary Hermite made a gaffe when Schoen, trying to keep the French out of the Baltic, referred to the fact that Germany had not been allowed to participate on the Mediterranean treaty. Hermite, evidently not understanding the complications, said that he saw no reason why Germany should not participate in the southern arrangement. With alacrity Schoen promised to take France into the Baltic at this price, because in this way the Mediterranean treaty would have been watered down completely to the gain of Germany. Embarrassed, the French had to explain that everything was due to Hermite's "impulsiveness", and his offer had to be made void.[3]

The Baltic and the North Sea agreements remained separate documents because of the insistence of Russia and Germany and the compliance of Great Britain. But consequently there arose the question of the boundary of the "jurisdiction" of the two treaties.

Where is the boundary line between the Baltic and the North Sea?

Somehow the Danish Straits had to be provided for. One point to which Grey attached importance was that, if there were to be two separate agreements, one about the Baltic and the other about the North Sea, there should be no gap between them, and the areas covered by the arrangements should be so defined that one began where the other left off.[4] It proved very difficult to define the line of demarcation in this way.

It is clear that the British preferred the dividing line as far east as possible so that the North Sea agreement would have covered the Straits. Thereby Germany

---

[1] GP 23 II n. 8123 Metternich to Bülow 10. I 1908
[2] PRO/FO 371/527/2171 Vaughan to Grey 17. I 1908 minute EAC
[3] GP 23 II n. 8118 Schoen to Radolin 16. XII 1907
  GP 23 II n. 8121 Radolin to Ausw. Amt 8. I 1908
  GP 23 II n. 8122 Schoen to Radolin 10. I 1908
  AA Dänemark 37 geheim Bd 10 p. 48 Radolin to Ausw. Amt 13. I 1908
[4] PRO/FO 371/527/2790 Grey to Rennell Rodd, end of January 1908

would have admitted that Great Britain was entitled to participate in the governance of the Danish Straits. Hardinge thought of a line from Kiel to Trelleborg.[1] When the exact geographical demarcation proved difficult, the British proposed that the North Sea agreement should cover "the North Sea and the entrances to the Baltic".[2]

Of course the Germans wished to keep the British out of the Straits. They agreed that there should be no gap, but their "Government felt that they could not put before the German public an Agreement which covered the Eastern entrances to the North Sea but contained no guarantee as regards the Western entrances".[3] As the British and the French on their part had no intention of letting Germany regulate the affairs of the Channel, "the entrances to the North Sea" on either side were left out of the document.

The Germans would have liked a line from Denmark to Norway, for instance as in 1882 when the limit of the North Sea had been agreed on as being between Lindesnes and Hanstholm.[4] Without a gap between the two seas this would have made Norway a Baltic country. The German Admiralty had found some geographical handbooks which maintained that on account of depth, water density, salinity and temperature the Kattegat was part of the Baltic, and that there was no unanimity about whether the Skagerrak was part of the North Sea.[5] Perhaps it is due to misunderstanding these discussions that the Swedish envoy in Copenhagen says in his memoirs that Norway wanted to take part in the Baltic Treaty [6], of which there is no trace in the sources. — These views were of no help in deciding the line of demarcation, which was a political and not a geographical question. The British chargé d'affaires in Copenhagen Vaughan suggested that the Belts should be included in the North Sea Treaty and the Sound in the Baltic one.[7] The Foreign Office found this an ingenious idea, but confessed "to much doubt whether it would prove acceptable".[8]

The Danes would have preferred the Straits to come under the North Sea Treaty,[9] which was due to their reluctance to be left alone with the Baltic Empires, especially at the time when Russo-Swedish negotiations seemed to have broken down, which implied that Sweden might be left out of the Baltic Treaty. "No matter how innocent such an arrangement might prove to be, he (Raben) should certainly be represented by sections of the Danish press as

[1] BD 8 n. 142 Hardinge to Nicolson 5. II 1908
[2] PRO/FO 371/527/2806 British draft 25. I 1908
[3] PRO/FO 371/528/5894 Grey to Lascelles 18. II 1908
[4] GP 23 II n. 8131 Schoen to Metternich 3. II 1908
[5] AA Dänemark 37 geheim Bd 17 p. 82 Adm Staff to Ausw. Amt 24. IV 1908
[6] Lagercrantz p. 331
[7] PRO/FO 371/527/3166 Vaughan to Grey 28. I 1908
[8] PRO/FO 371/527/3166 minute by CH
[9] PRO/FO 371/528/10510 Johnstone to Grey 27. III 1908

having involved Denmark in an alliance with Germany, and, in fact, having sold the country to the Germans."[1] — Happily for Raben, it was agreed that both treaties were to be signed simultaneously. When the great powers could not agree on the exact line of demarcation, Raben said that "Denmark understands the Baltic sea according to its geographical definition — no one could say that the Baltic did not touch the east coast of the Danish islands, but neither could it be said that either Belts or Sound were included in it".[2] This was not a good solution for either group of great powers. The British said that "the idea is very feeble".[3] When Isvolsky heard that Denmark wished to leave the passages out of the Baltic treaty he hastened to remind Schoen that they had agreed to keep the Western powers out of the Baltic, and wondered where Russia would be left if the other powers supposed that she had voluntarily given up her rights in the Straits.[4] Under Russian pressure Denmark had to give up all ideas of her own. The Russian attitude to the Straits will be discussed later.

No line of demarcation, acceptable to both groups of powers, could be found. The Germans suggested that a formulation be accepted — based on Grey's words at the very beginning — that "one began where the other left off": "the Baltic begins where the North Sea ends, and vice versa, so as to leave no gap between them".[5] This was accepted and added to the annexed memorandum in which the status quo was also defined. Everybody was satisfied, as the line could be thought to lie wherever one wished. "The delimitation between the North Sea and Baltic may be 'indeterminate' but there can be no doubt that one agreement or the other covers the Straits".[6] In fact this was symbolic of the whole of the Baltic question during the years 1903—1908. The diplomatists were unable to solve any real problems; all they managed to do was to make the agreements void of any substance so that everybody with equal indifference might accept them.

Sweden joins the North Sea powers

It was mainly due to the Straits question that Sweden was taken into the circle of signatories of the North Sea Treaty. At first she had not been thought of, from the first British draft she had been struck out together with Belgium

[1] PRO/FO 371/527/2431 Vaughan to Grey 17. I 1908
[2] PRO/FO 371/529/12268 Johnstone to Grey 9. IV 1908
[3] PRO/FO 371/529/12268 minutes
[4] A VPR fond sekretnyj arhiv, delo 381,
   n. 381 Kudašev to Isvolsky 28. III/10. IV 1908
   n. 404 Kudašev to Isvolsky 29. III/11. IV 1908
   n. 410 Russian F.O. to German Embassy 2. IV/15. IV 1908
[5] PRO/FO 371/528/5894 Grey to Lascelles 18. II 1908
[6] PRO/FO 371/529/15018 Acton to Grey 29. IV 1908 minutes

and Norway.[1] But then it was understood that if the Straits were to be kept under the surveillance of the North Sea treaty, if Norway was not to be a Baltic power, Sweden would have to be taken in. "The proposal that the agreement should cover the entrances to the Baltic clearly gives Sweden a locus standi." [2] And Sweden was most welcome from the British point of view because she was anxiously trying to strengthen her right of participating by arguing that the Straits did belong to the North Sea [3], "Trolle was most anxious that the entrances to the Baltic should be dealt with in the North Sea Agreement".[4] — Thus, if the question of the line of demarcation was to arise in the future, Great Britain would have documentary evidence signed by Germany that the Swedish coast was washed by the North Sea. — Then there was another point in favour of Sweden's inclusion: "the inclusion of Sweden in a North Sea agreement . . will remove the bad impression prevalent in Sweden with regard to our (British) attitude during the Norwegian negotiations".[5] So the British undertook to propose to the Germans the inclusion of Sweden.[6] Somewhat reluctantly the Germans accepted [7]; evidently they did not like the idea but had no wish to estrange the Swedes with a refusal.

A third agreement?

The treaties were to be signed simultaneously. This was according to the wishes of Denmark and Sweden,[8] who did not like the prospect of being left alone with the eastern Empires. Great Britain, too, wanted it in order to be sure that the gap between the Treaties would not reappear after the signature of the North Sea Treaty.

The details of the North Sea treaty had been negotiated during January and February 1908 and the agreement seemed ready for signature at the end of February. But meanwhile the Baltic negotiations seemed to miscarry on account of the Åland question and a deadlock was reached by the end of February. The Germans suggested that the North Sea Agreement be signed but not published before the Baltic one was ready, but Grey did not consent, explaining that he could not keep Parliament in the dark so long.[9] So the Baltic muddle very nearly killed off its Western offspring.

[1] PRO/FO 371/527/2806 British draft 25. I 1908
[2] PRO/FO 371/528/4609 Rennell Rodd to Grey 7. II 1908 minute EG
[3] PRO/FO 371/528/4605 Rennell Rodd to Grey 4. II 1908
    PRO/FO 371/529/11630 Rennell Rodd to Grey 5. IV 1908
[4] PRO/FO 371/528/7853 Rennell Rodd to Grey 3. III 1908
[5] PRO/FO 371/528/4620 Vaughan to Grey 7. II 1908
[6] PRO/FO 371/527/4856 Grey to Rennell Rodd 10. II 1908
[7] PRO/FO 371/528/5104 Grey to Rennell Rodd 13. II 1908
[8] PRO/FO 371/528/5104 Grey to Rennell Rodd 13. II 1908
[9] PRO/FO 371/528/8360 Grey to Lascelles 9. III 1908

This fact revived a proposal which the French had thought of. For a while they had been of the opinion "that the best solution of the two questions would be one which had been suggested by M. Jules Cambon, viz. that the powers concerned in them should restrict themselves to a declaration to insure the free passage at all times of the Straits . ."[1] Grey had not consented, being unwilling to snub the Germans.[2] Now this proposal for a third agreement was taken up when the original treaties were in difficulties: if the Baltic one failed, the North Sea one might be saved with the Straits treaty. Jules Cambon had spoken with Schoen of the idea, but the Secretary of State had not been very enthusiastic,[3] for natural reasons. The project of a third agreement was also discussed in St. Petersburg. The Scandinavians, who were used to seeing Isvolsky in the worst possible light after their experiences in the Åland question, thought that Isvolsky had inspired the French in order to make the Baltic agreement fail altogether because he was not able to succeed in the Åland question.[4] This seems a little far-fetched, although of course not entirely impossible. There is no proof for or against such a hypothesis, but Isvolsky's interest in the third agreement was of a different kind, as we shall see later.

The British were not officially involved in the question: "Such an agreement would presumably not conflict with the views of His Majesty's Government but we are not called upon the express any opinion so far. ."[5] "but we need have no objection".[6] The Germans were given to understand that the British "were ready to fall in with such arrangement; otherwise the German government might feel, even if they were disposed to entertain the suggestion, that, having come to an Agreement with us on another plan, they ought not to reopen the question".[7]

Then, after all, the need to discuss the third treaty disappeared when Isvolsky retreated in the Åland question and the Baltic powers could proceed with their agreement.

Happy end after all

In his memoirs Schoen says that the treaty very nearly failed on the opposition of the German naval leaders, who saw in it a limitation on their freedom of action in war. However, these doubts were succesfully dispelled.[8]

The Chief of Naval Staff, Count Baudissin, had already uttered these doubts

---

[1] PRO/FO 371/527/3383 Bertie to Grey 30. I 1908
[2] PRO/FO 371/527/3383 minutes by CH & EG
[3] AA Dänemark 37 geheim Bd 14 Schoen to Henckel 21. III 1908
[4] AA Norwegen 4 geheim Henckel to Bülow 19. III 1908
[5] PRO/FO 371/528/9729 Rennell Rodd to Grey 17. III 1908 minutes
[6] PRO/FO 371/528/10195 Rennell Rodd to Grey 24. III 1908, minute by CH & EG
[7] PRO/FO 371/529/11264 Grey to Lascelles 31. III 1908 minutes
[8] Schoen p. 62

in February 1908. He had said that he had nothing against the Baltic project, but the participation of France and Holland made the North Sea Agreement a bit dubious, because the powers were thereby given grounds for legitimate protest if Germany were compelled to "take preventive messures" in the Dutch and Belgian ports and the entrance of the Baltic.[1] At the last moment before the signing of the Agreement in April the Admirals came again and protested to Schoen, saying that Great Britain had no such need to violate the neutrals in a war as Germany had, and therefore the North Sea Agreement would be injurious for Germany. It was especially so when Denmark and Holland were participating; England's participation alone would not have been so detrimental, but now all the advantages accrued to the power who was stronger on sea.[2]

How did Schoen manage to "succesfully dispel" these naval doubts? He explained that the North Sea Agreement would produce a calming effect which Germany wished.[3] Also it was too late to make the treaty void, because the failure of an agreement proposed by Germany would be a grave check to her. It had been impossible to avoid making the proposal, for England had to be prevented from forcing herself into the Baltic agreement, and an agreement with England alone would not have prevented this. There were also great political advantages to be obtained by better relations with France, England, Holland, Denmark and Sweden. The Admirals admitted these advantages and stated that the military doubts were not strong enough to justify a refusal to sign in these circumstances. A concluding argument by Schoen was a statement that in the *Ernstfalle* Germany, like all the other powers, would ignore all agreements which stood in the way of military necessity.[4] — This needs no comment indeed.

All worries concerning the Danish Straits were not due to the treaty negotiations. The British Admiralty would have wished to urge Sweden to deepen the Sound "to take the largest-sized battle-ships", which at that time could use only the Great Belt.[5] The Foreign Office did not accept this suggestion, because it was quite certain that any such proposal would have been violently opposed by Germany; at most Sweden could privately and discreetly be encouraged.[6] When Sir Alan Johnstone returned from vacation to his post in February 1908 he at once took up the Baltic and North Sea negotiations in a discussion with Raben. Exasperated, Hardinge minuted: "We must not encourage Sir. A. Johnstone. We have already had to restrain him twice, and these conversations with Count

---

[1] AA Dänemark 37 geheim Bd 12 note by Schoen 9. II 1908
[2] AA Dänemark 37 geheim Bd 16 Schoen to Jenisch 20. IV 1908
[3] AA Dänemark 37 geheim Bd 12 note by Schoen 9. II 1908
[4] AA Dänemark 37 geheim Bd 16 Schoen to Jenisch 20. IV 1908
[5] PRO/FO 371/338/41616 Admiralty to F. O. 19. XII 1907 and F.O. to Admiralty 1. I 1908

Raben are quite useless."[1] But Johnstone needed no encouragement: without it
he submitted a plan to urge Sweden and Denmark to deepen the Sound. Grey
was appalled: "It would never do to start an intrigue about the Sound while the
Baltic and North Sea negotiations were in progress."[2]

The German Admiralty Staff would not indeed have liked the idea if they
had known of it. The deepening of the Sound would have compelled the divi-
sion of German defence forces into two directions, and the concentration of
forces would have been impossible.[3]

Their own past also came back to haunt the British. The Library of the
Foreign Office discovered that in 1854 England herself had demanded that
Denmark close the Sound (which was too shallow for the British ships drawing
25 feet but deep enough for Russians with 23 feet of draught). The Danes
refused, pleading neutrality. Thus both the British and the Danes had in theory
attributed to Denmark the right to close the Sound. Happily everybody had
forgotten this; however "it is awkward that we have once asked for the Straits
to be closed; it is fortunate that we were refused; we must in future. . . stand
upon the ground on which the refusal was based".[4]

During all the years of the Baltic question the British and the French kept in
close touch, informing each other of their views before committing themselves.
The Entente seemed to work rather well in spite of occasional hitches. Most
often they could state that their opinions were in complete accord, as for
instance before authorizing their envoys to sign the North Sea Agreement.[5]

So Denmark, England, France, Germany, Holland and Sweden solemnly declared their wish to maintain peace and good neighbourly relations, to respect
the status quo and to preserve intact their sovereign rights in their respective
possessions. If the status quo were menaced, the powers were to communicate
in order to concert their measures to restore the status quo. In a memorandum
annexed to the declaration the status quo was defined as territorial and therefore in no way limiting the sovereign rights of the signatories. The North Sea
was described as reaching in the east to the point where the Baltic commenced.[6]

[1] PRO/FO 371/528/6021 Johnstone to Grey 20. II 1908 minute CH
[2] PRO/FO 371/528/9326 Johnstone to Grey 17. III 1908, with minutes by EG
[3] AA Dänemark 37 geheim Bd 6 Büchsel to Tschirschky 12. III 1906
[4] PRO/FO 371/529/15693 *Memorandum Respecting the Passages into the Baltic Sea*
   6. V 1908, with minute by EG
[5] PRO/FO 371/529/13102 Stumm to F.O. 15. IV 1908 minutes
[6] BD 8 n. 152 Declaration and Memorandum between the Unites Kingdom, Denmark,
   France, Germany, the Netherlands, and Sweden, concerning the maintenance of the
   States quo in the Territories bordering upon the North Sea. Signed at Berlin, April
   23. 1908

ISVOLSKY'S FAILURE IN THE BALTIC

Victory slips out of Isvolsky's reach

On the 23rd December 1907, after King Oscar's death, the King's council met in Stockholm, King Gustaf presiding. The Minister for Foreign Affairs Trolle explained Swedish foreign policy. The Treaty of 1855 had lost its effect when the Union broke up. France would not support Sweden against Russia, and even Great Britain seemed to have lost interest. In such a situation a possibility of arriving at a mutual agreement with Russia must necessarily be greeted with satisfaction. But the Russian draft (p. 171) could not be accepted as such. In a bilateral relation the smaller country could easily fall into dependence on the larger; it was therefore important to have Germany and Denmark in. The simultaneous project of the North Sea Treaty was useful because it took away all appearance of an anti-Western edge from the Baltic project. And Sweden wanted to be an equal partner in the Treaty, she did not wish for a unilateral guarantee by Russia. And "even while wholly appreciating the peace-loving intention of the Russian Government it was impossible not see a danger for Sweden's independence in the fortifying of Åland". If Sweden signed the declaration, the Western powers would think that Sweden had consented to the abrogation of the Convention, and such a declaration Sweden could not give.[1]

King Gustaf turned to William II to enlist his help in influencing the Czar. Schoen supported the Swedish aspirations, and William wrote to Nicholas prompting him to instruct Isvolsky to accept the model of the secret Russo-German treaty, which did not contain anything undesirable for the Swedes.[2] The Emperor opposed only the wish of the Swedes to have the declaration signed by the sovereigns, explaining that only treaties of alliance were so loftily signed.[3] Gustaf had said that the question of the Åland Islands was better dealt with separately in notes to be exchanged between Russia and Sweden.[4] Evidently he did not explain clearly enough, or did not understand, Trolle's words in the Council. William urged Nicholas to hurry on with the signature, because the well-disposed Swedish government might be changed before long[5], and Schoen reminded Isvolsky that delay might lead to the very complications feared by Isvolsky in the Straits (p. 185).[5] No complications were foreseen by the Russians, either, excepting those pertaining to the North Sea declaration, which

---

[1] Hildebrand p. 533—

[2] AVPR fond sekretnyj arhiv, delo 393/402 n. 2 William II to Nicholas II 13/28. XII 1907

[3] AVPR fond sekretnyj arhiv, delo 38 n. 232 Nicholas to William II, draft
   n. 240 *projet d'aide-mémoire à la Legation Royale de la Suède*

[4] AA Dänemark 37 geheim Bd 9 William II to Nicholas II, draft 23. XII 1907

[5] AA Dänemark 37 geheim Bd 9 Schoen to Pourtalès 26. XII 1907

caused bad blood between Germany and Russia. It was hoped that the final draft of the declaration could be signed before the 15th January 1908.[1]

Everything seemed clear until Isvolsky received a letter from Trolle, repeating the identical remarks that had been sent through Gustaf and the Germans, but with additions. Trolle explained that Sweden preferred a joint declaration by all the Baltic powers instead of the twelve notes to be exchanged between them. To the undoubted dismay of Isvolsky Trolle said that his King had mentioned the project to King Frederic VIII (at King Oscar's funeral) who had been favourably impressed.[2]

But much more dismay must have been caused by the matter of Åland. Trolle reminded Isvolsky that he had promised in Karlsbad and Paris that the Islands were not to be mentioned in the declaration — which Isvolsky surely had not said — and that Russia had no intention of fortifying them — which Isvolsky had really said, on every possible occasion. Trolle explained that mentioning the Convention of 1856 in the declaration would alarm public opinion in Sweden, and therefore they had better leave it out.[3]

When informing the Germans about the Swedish answer Isvolsky was a bit subdued because Sweden had brought up new wishes to complicate the negotiations. He denied categorically that he had promised anything about binding Russia not to fortify Åland — his aim was to regain Russia's sovereignty, not to diminish it anew in regard to Sweden. But anyway he hoped that these difficulties might be overcome.[4]

"With pleasure" Isvolsky hastened to accept Trolle's remarks regarding the need to omit the Russian guarantee of integrity for Sweden. But he opposed Trolle's wish for a joint declaration, for reasons which have been already explained (p. 188), but stating aloud: "this was in order not to give the Western powers occasion to make a similar joint treaty in the Mediterranean".

It was especially in the Åland question that the Imperial Government had "certain reservations": "Could a complete silence on this point, which constituted the only moral obstacle for a solid and sincere friendship between Russia and Sweden, could a silence suffice to convince the Cabinets of London and Paris that Sweden would not regard the abrogation of the Convention of 1856 as a hostile action?"

This sentence shows that Isvolsky really thought that Trolle had promised more in the Åland question than he himself understood or remembered. Isvolsky evidently believed that Trolle was anxious to consent to the Russian wishes, the only obstacle being his fear of the reaction of Swedish public

[1] AA Dänemark 37 geheim Bd 9 Nicholas II to William II 15/28. XII 1908
[2] AVPR fond sekretnyj arhiv, delo 393/402 n. 3 Trolle to Isvolsky 26. XII 1907
[3] =2
[4] AA Dänemark 37 geheim Bd 10 p. 13 Pourtalès to Bülow 2. I 1908

opinion, to which Trolle had referred. Isvolsky tried to help Trolle: ".. The
problem is to find a formula satisfying the aspiration of the Russian Government without being disagreable to the Swedish Government.. The only solution was to sign a secret protocol on the Åland question, which would never be
published and the only purpose of which would be to prove to the signatories of
the Convention of 1856 that no misunderstanding reigned in this question between Russia and Sweden".[1] For Trolle personally Isvolsky added that he had
no hesitation in assuring him that Russia had nothing against Sweden, but "this
assurance can in no case be interpreted as any kind of restriction on our liberty
of future action concerning the Åland Islands".[2]

Isvolsky tried to hurry the Swedes on, to make them leave Denmark's participation for later discussion, and to sign immediately the separate declarations
between Sweden and Russia, and Sweden and Germany.[3]

Isvolsky's proposition of a secret protocol was discussed and rejected in the
Swedish King's Council on the 11th January 1908. Trolle explained that because it was not certain at all that the Convention was to remain in force,
Sweden might consent to its abrogation. But Russia ought to engage, in the
same protocol, not to fortify the Islands in the future. This solution would be
even better than the old servitude which the Western powers had maintained,
because then Russia could not fortify without Sweden's consent. And in any
case the situation would then be clarified as Russia's refusal would indicate her
intention to fortify.[4] — This viewpoint was hardly a sensible one. It was against
all psychology to ask a great power to surrender voluntarily her sovereignty.

Evidently the attitude of Swedish statesmen had hardened since autumn.
Some Swedes think that this is partly an illusion, because in Karlsbad and Paris
Isvolsky had spoken of the Åland question in such veiled words that Trolle and
Gustaf did not understand him. Therefore their consent implied only the gua-
rantee of the status quo. When they received concrete proposals in writing from
St, Petersburg, they were freightened by the clauses concerning Åland.[5]

It is difficult to pronounce a definite judgement, but it does seem that the
Swedes were really discouraged in October when the Norwegian Treaty was
brought to its conclusion in spite of Sweden's protests — perhaps Isvolsky
would have succeeded then if he had had a treaty written ready to be signed.
Gustaf's words in Berlin indicate that he at least was prepared to accept in a

[1] AVPR fond sekretnyj arhiv, delo 380, n. 240
　Projet d'aide-mémoire à la Légation Royale de la Suède
[2] AVPR fond sekretnyj arhiv, delo 380, n. 245 Isvolsky to Trolle, private, draft
[3] AVPR fond sekretnyj arhiv, delo 380, n. 240
　Projet d'aide-mémoire à la Légation Royale de la Suède
[4] Hildebrand p. 536
[5] Hildebrand p. 528
　Anon. p. 435— Svensk Historisk Tidskrift 1935

separate protocol the abrogation of the Åland servitude. But by the end of the year the Swedes had recovered a little and were able to examine the price the Empires demanded for the support they offered in place of the "lost" British aid. Reutersvärd, the biographer of the Swedish envoy in St. Petersburg, General Brändström, gives a great part of the merit for this national revival to his hero.[1] In the very beginning the General had seen the Åland question implied in the Baltic status quo, and he did not at all believe that Isvolsky was in earnest when speaking of smugglers — in the summer of 1906 eighty ships had been patrolling without finding one single gun.[2] He understood that the Russian Defence Committee had found Libau to be unfit for a naval base. Åland was needed instead, and the diplomatists had been given the task of making its fortifying legal. Brändström was worried on account of the danger to Stockholm and of the cost of its defence, he was even afraid lest Sweden decline into dependence on Russia.[3] At the funeral of King Oscar the Swedish envoys discussed the Baltic question with Trolle. Brändström fiercely demanded that the government should not make, behind the back of the Swedish people, any agreement with Russia which would involve even the least thought of consenting to the abrogation of the Åland servitude. Unlike the statesmen in Stockholm he was sure of eventual British support and therefore felt he could afford to oppose the Russian proposals so rigidly.[4]

However that may have been, Trolle in any case sent Isvolsky a message on the 12th January 1908 about the decision of the previous day. He accepted the principle of status quo, but explained that Sweden had not signed the Convention of 1856 and therefore she could not express any opinion on it. But a fortification in the immediate vicinity of the Swedish capital would call forth inquietude in the population, which would eliminate the confidence which had grown up between Russia and Sweden. As the Russian government had assured Sweden that they had no intention of fortifying the islands, Russia might insert in the same protocol a declaration to that effect as a "natural complement" to the Swedish consent to the abrogation of the ancient Convention. This would be no restriction on Russian sovereignty but a voluntary obligation.[5]

Isvolsky tried once more to explain his views on the Åland question. The proposal for the secret protocol had been an attempt to consider Swedish interests together with Russian aims. But the Swedish interest — security in regard to Russia — surely did not entitle Sweden to more than an assurance by Russia

[1] Reutersvärd p. 70
[2] AA Dänemark 37 geheim Bd 10 Pourtalès to Bülow 2. I 1908
HHStA/SVA n. 119 Berchtold to Aehrenthal 2/15 I 1908
[3] Reutersvärd p. 51—
[4] Reutersvärd p. 51—59
[5] AVPR fond sekretnyj arhiv, delo 393/402 n. 7 Trolle to Isvolsky 12. I 1908

that the eventual fortifications in Åland would not be directed against Sweden. It was too much to ask that with the guarantee of the status quo Russia should for ever sanctify a stipulation which she had always regarded as a grave moral wrong. It was even questionable whether the Convention of 1856 could logically be held to remain in force after its parent Treaty of 1855 had lapsed, in the opinion of England and France, as a consequence of the dissolution of the Union. Because Sweden had said that she could not express an opinion on a Convention which she had not signed, the only way to save the Russo-Swedish declaration was that Russia would annex to it a unilateral declaration to the effect desired by her, which needed no reply by Sweden.[1]

This document resembled the explanation added to the secret Russo-German treaty and the memorandum annexed to the North Sea declaration: "The Imperial Government understands the term status quo, the maintenance of which is the object of the agreement, exclusively in the sense of the territorial integrity of actual possessions, continental and insular, of the high contracting parties in the basin of the Baltic, and consequently the abrogation of the Convention of 1856 cannot in any case be envisaged as an infringement of this principle." [2]

Isvolsky said to Brändström that Russia was unusually friendly in discussing the matter with Sweden, as she might easily have the Convention abrogated by turning direct to the signatory powers. — Of course this was a lie, as Isvolsky had seen in the summer when he had asked France and England, and Grey had blocked his attempt. — Brändström answered that it was impossible for King Gustaf to start his reign by turning the Swedes against himself by giving up in so vital a matter.[3]

To the Germans Isvolsky explained that he had gone to the utter limits to meet the wishes of the Swedes [4] and that he hoped that Germany would support his solution of a unilateral explicative note.[5] The Emperor William agreed, with the comment that King Gustaf was a big *Jammerlapp* and his standpoint was the complete opposite to that of October, in Berlin. — The German mediation will be discussed a little later.

One cannot but admire Isvolsky's inventiveness and tenacity. His new proposal frightened the Swedish government, being a logical counter-move to Sweden's answer and therefore difficult to counter. But if Sweden had let it be realized, the Western powers would have read Sweden's silence as meaning her consent, and the consequences would have been fateful for Sweden.[6] The

[1] AVPR fond sekretnyj arhiv, delo 392/401 n. 18 *projet d'aide-mémoire* 8/21 I 1908
[2] AVPR fond sekretnyj arhiv, delo 392/401 n. 21
projet de declaration du plenipotentiaire russe
[3] AA Dänemark 37 geheim Bd 10 Pourtalès to Bülow 18 I 1908
[4] AA Russland 63 Bd 1 Pourtalès to Bülow 26. I 1908
[5] AA Dänemark 37 geheim Bd 10 Pourtalès to Bülow 18. I 1908
[6] Hildebrand p. 536

Swedes planned to answer, if they could not persuade Russia to drop the Åland question, with a counter-declaration to the effect that the Swedish government would refrain from any statement on the correctness of Russia's interpretation of the principle of the status quo, but that an eventual fortification of the Åland Islands would prevent the development of friendly relations between the countries[1] — i.e. would be a hostile act. This counter-declaration would have been an unambiguous protest on the abrogation of the servitude, so that Isvolsky could never say in London and Paris that Sweden had consented.

By the end of January it had become clear the neither party could accept the standpoint of the other; the negotiations were in a blind alley. Feelings were becoming heated. Raben knew that "from the very first exchange of views M. Isvolsky had made misrepresentations to M. de Trolle, and that Russia had played a double game. Other nations deceive each other now and then, but with Russia it was the rule to do so, and not the exception. He considered she was a thoroughly demoralized nation".[2] — Clearly there had been some complaint by Trolle, who either had misunderstood Isvolsky's hints in the autumn, or was frightened at what he had let loose;

The quarrel becomes public

There was less than ever a chance of the Swedish government retreating once Isvolsky made the question public. This was interpreted as an attempt to expedite progress and force the Swedes to submission by making the matter a question of prestige.[3] Isvolsky himself explained that he was only trying to correct the false statements which the well-known journalist Lucien Wolf had published in the *Daily Graphic*. These allegations of schemes for closing the Baltic and proposals for uniting the Baltic and North Sea project had "touched him painfully". Isvolsky's communication stated that the guarantee of Norwegian integrity had led to a discussion concerning a mutual guarantee of possessions in the Baltic, and nothing more.[4]

In the middle of January the Swedish press, too, was given an intimation that something was afoot by Trolle himself.[5] The *Svenska Dagbladet* told its readers that negotiations were in progress with St. Petersburg and Berlin about a guarantee of the Baltic status quo to replace the November Treaty of 1855.[6] After a few days the same paper said that it had had an intimation from St. Petersburg that the negotiations included Russia's endeavours to fortify Åland.

---

[1] Hildebrand p. 537
[2] PRO/FO 371/527/3683 Vaughan to Grey 31. I 1908
[3] AA Dänemark 37 geheim Bd 10 Pückler to Ausw. Amt 17. I 1908
[4] AA Dänemark 37 geheim Bd 10 Pourtalès to Ausw. Amt 13 I 1908
[5] HHStA/SVA n. 121 Esperjesy to Aehrenthal 19. I 1908
[6] *Svenska Dagbladet* 24. I 1908

14

Public opinion now began to take a lively interest in the question, and by the beginning of February a real press storm was raging in Sweden. Hjalmar Branting's article in the *Social-Demokraten* represents the views of the time: If the prohibition on fortifying Åland were abrogated, Russia's might would move closer to the heart of Sweden. It would mean an upheaval in the balance of power in the Baltic. A reborn Russian fleet in a new Port Arthur at a distance of a few hours from Stockholm — the Russian colossus would be threatening in a different way than hitherto, the Russian envoy's word would weigh as in a vassal state, and soon nobody would be able to call Sweden independent or neutral. Sweden must not submit to this. She must try to appeal to England, whose aim was the freedom of the seas and who consequently could not be indifferent to the closing of the Gulf of Bothnia. And Sweden must appeal to France, in spite of her being Russia's ally. Sweden must not remain silent as in the 1830's when the Russians built Bomarsund. The Russians and all others must not be allowed to remain in the belief that the matter did not mean anything to the Swedes. "We are all against it".[1] — This article was unusually significant, because the author was a *Social Demokrat,* no nationalistic or militaristic alarmist. For once the conservatives and the leftists were unanimous.[2] Captain E. Söderhielm explained the strategic implications of Russia's plans and concluded: "Fortifications on Åland are a sword-point directed against Sweden's heart".[3] All papers wrote on this theme on identical lines. The envoys of the great powers sent home thick bunches of newspaper cuttings which expressed Sweden's horror at Isvolsky's observation post on Åland, now grown into a mighty and ominous naval base on the horizon of Stockholm.

The alarm extended to the Riksdag. Staaff put a question to the Government on the 22nd February referring to the news concerning the Baltic status quo and the abrogation of the Åland Convention, which had led to *att en icke ringa oro bemäktigat många svenska sinnen.* Trolle answered that Sweden did not wish for any guarantee for her neutrality or integrity, for she tried to avoid dependence on the guaranteeing powers. But the Baltic agreement could not endanger Sweden in any way, as its only aim was to preserve peace and the status quo. Trolle did not say anything about the negotiations about Åland, because they were still continuing, but he assured the Riksdag that Sweden's interests would be well looked after. Staaff thanked him for the reassuring answer and remarked that the true intention of the interpellators had been to bring out the feelings of Swedish public opinion in the Riksdag.[4]

---

[1] Branting p. 183
[2] *Svenska Dagbladet* 10. II 1908
  Svenska Dagbladet 1. III 1908
[3] E. Söderhielm p. 114
[4] Westman p. 47 (protocol of II chamber 22. II 1908 and protocol of
  I chamber 25. II 1908)

The German envoy in Stockholm reported that press opinion was unanimous, and wondered whether it could be so without a lead from above.[1] It seems clear, however, that the press, from the conservatives to the socialists, could not be manipulated so completely; the press storm was caused by a genuine and natural apprehension as to Russian intentions on Åland. — The fierce state of public opinion made it definitely impossible for the Swedish government to comply with Isvolsky's wishes.

There was some discussion in the Russian press, too. *Novoe Vremja* disapproved of the groundless fear of Russia in Sweden, explaining that Russia had no aggressive intentions. Russia simply did not wish to deprive herself of sovereignty on Åland by the new agreement. She had no intention of fortifying the islands; at most a post of observation was needed. The matter had no material importance for Russia, but a moral importance it did have, having reference to the sovereign rights which Russia had had to renounce temporarily at the Paris Conference in 1856.[2] — *Novoe Vremja* reflected Isvolsky's views quite closely, perhaps inspired by the Foreign Ministry.

The liberal *Reč* saw the matter in a different light: it was stupid of Russia to take up the Åland question. The smallest hint of fortifications on the Åland Islands would inevitably call forth a firm resistance in Sweden, who had not been soothed by Russia's platonic assurances of friendship nor by the offer of a guarantee of the status quo. Sweden could not believe that Russia was not going to fortify the Islands if she was so keen on getting the servitude abrogated, nor could Sweden comprehend that the prohibition tarnished Russia's honour. If Russia disputed long enough with Sweden, the latter would say in the end *hvatit!* and join Germany, which was much more dangerous to Russia than the absence of fortifications on Åland. *Reč's* solution came quite close to the Swedish proposal: Russia might promise Sweden not to fortify the Islands. The humiliating international servitude would disappear thereby, but Sweden would have the identical security. Russia had no wish to fortify, it was the French and British jurisdiction over an area of the Empire that hurt Russia's pride.[3]

Novoe Vremja had already found an answer to propositions of this kind. This paper was "unable" to understand Sweden's apprehensions and deemed the agitation a childish selfishness which did not take the other's rights into account. In Russia the ministers were not answerable to parliament; but if the Minister for Foreign Affairs gave up Russia's rights on Åland, it was certain thet he would not be sitting many minutes longer in his office on Palace Square.[4]

[1] AA Russland 63 Bd 2 Pückler to Bülow 13. II 1908
[2] *Novoe Vremja* 2/15 II 1908
[3] *Reč* 19. II/3. III 1908
[4] *Novoe Vremja* 15/28 II 1908

If it is true that *Novoe Vremja's* articles were sometimes inspired by the Russian Foreign Office, Isvolsky was here apparently exposing his whole career because of Åland. Of course he had no intention of giving up either Åland or office, the article must be understood as strong pressure upon Sweden. If it was not an inspired article, it represented in turn strong pressure upon Isvolsky by the nationalists.

The Russo-Swedish negotiations were in a blind alley. Making the quarrel public had turned differences of opinion into questions of prestige, which made it nearly impossible for either party to retreat from its position.

But Sweden's situation face to face with Russia turned out to be not so desperate after all. At this stage she began to receive support which she had thought impossible earlier.

Åland as a British asset

When Rennell Rodd had reported on the "very subtle game" that Russia and Germany were playing in sowing discord between Norway and Sweden and drawing Sweden into the Baltic agreement, it was deemed very doubtful whether anything the British could do would be able to prevent Sweden from gravitating to Germany. Grey thought that alone Great Britain was unable to give Sweden any guarantees of support about the Åland Islands, and France would not join with Great Britain in it against both Russia and Germany.[1] We have also seen that the Foreign Office had been "quite calm" as regards the Baltic question, and had thought that if Sweden was going to agree on something with Russia, it was all the better for Great Britain. It was regrettable that Great Britain had lost the friendship of Sweden, but Grey thought: "It is more unfortunate for Russia than for us that Sweden should turn to Germany".[2]

But little by little Downing Street began to see some opportunity to further British interests as the negotiations did not proceed as smoothly as Isvolsky might have wished. At first the British thought only of the Straits: ". . these difficulties . . cannot well be supposed to arise in connection with a scheme for closing the Baltic"[3] — that is, there was no cause for worry in London. The first intimation of Sweden's need for British support was given by her envoy in London, Wrangel: Sweden would be grateful to know that the British would not regard with favour the fortification of the islands . .[4] It was some kind of a promise when Grey said that Great Britain could not discuss the abrogation of the Åland servitude before seeing the text of the Baltic treaty. Of course this was dictated by British interest in the Baltic agreement, and by way of a quid

[1] PRO/FO 371/338/37733 Rennell Rodd to Grey 13. XI 1907 minutes
[2] PRO/FO 371/491/2230 Herbert to Grey 12. I 1908 minutes by CH & EG
[3] PRO/FO 371/527/99 Rennell Rodd to Grey 1. I 1908 minute by EAC
[4] PRO/FO 371/527/836 Grey to Rennell Rodd 6. I 1908

pro quo Grey asked that the Swedish government should say something to remove the impression that England's action in the course of the Norwegian negotiations had been in any way less favourable to Sweden.[1] — The occasion to say so never arose since there was no discussion in the Riksdag on this subject.

For a while the British could not learn the reason for the drawing out of the Russo-Swedish negotiations, and they were afraid lest the result be kept secret from them.[2] But by the beginning of February the Åland Island question was recognized as the stumbling block in the negotiations[3] and Rennell Rodd reported that the whole Swedish press was alive to the danger, and all shades of opinion urged united opposition to the national danger.[4]

Isvolsky, too, poured out his heart to the British: "The close propinquity of Finland to St. Petersburg was becoming a cause of serious embarrasment to the Russian Government, as in that country the gravest conspiracies were organized . . the Finnish authorities were exceedingly lax and afforded little assistance . . the Finns were intractable. ."[5] The British did not quite believe him: "If all that Russia wants is a post of observation & a place of refugee for patrol vessels there is no need for fortifications."[6] It was reported that Russia intended to fortify the Åland Islands in any case, believing that France would make a formal protest only and that Great Britain would "bluster and make a great fuss, but she would do nothing".[7] Grey could not believe Russia to be so mean[8] but a little later this danger was not deemed completely improbable.

By the middle of February the British Foreign Office was alive to the Russian danger in Sweden and to the possibilities that it offered the British. "The Russian plan is to get England and France to abrogate the treaty provided Russia gives Sweden an assurance that she will not fortify the islands. Anyone familiar with Russian diplomacy and its method of dealing with 'assurances' must sympathize with Sweden in her reluctance to accept such an agreement."[9] A couple of months earlier the British had regarded such an assurance quite sufficient, but now there could be "no question of the abrogation of the Treaty

[1] PRO/FO 371/527/2791 Grey to Rennell Rodd 22. I 1908
[2] PRO/FO 371/527/1221 Johnstone to Grey 9. I 1908 minute EAC
    PRO/FO 371/527/1867 Rennell Rodd to Grey 22. I 1908
[3] PRO/FO 371/528/3776 Rennell Rodd to Grey 31. I 1908
    PRO/FO 371/528/4605 Rennell Rodd to Grey 4. II 1908
[4] PRO/FO 371/528/4906 Rennell Rodd to Grey 10. II 1908
    PRO/FO 371/528/6684 Rennell Rodd to Grey 22. II 1908
[5] PRO/FO 371/528/3627 Nicolson to Grey 22. I 1908
[6] PRO/FO 371/528/3627 minute by EG
[7] PRO/FO 371/528/5077 Rennell Rodd to Grey 11. II 1908
    PRO/FO 371/528/5149 Grey to Rennell Rodd 13. II 1908
[8] PRO/FO 371/528/5149 Grey to Rennell Rodd 13. II 1908
[9] PRO/FO 371/528/5687 Bertie to Grey 15. II 1908 minutes

of 1856 until Sweden is satisfied with the guarantee offered by Russia".[1]

Then there was the other Imperial power in the Baltic. Wrangel told Grey that Germany had been doing what she could to promote an arrangement between Russia and Sweden.[2] Rodd said that if Germany were to succeed in such an object, she would not only secure the gratitude of both parties concerned but she would also get rid of the privileged position held by Great Britain and France as factors in Baltic questions by the existence of the Convention of 1856 in which they were participants.[3]

But if it was "an object of British policy to prevent Sweden being drawn into a position of dependence on Germany and at the same time to retain to some extent a right to have a voice in Baltic questions",[4] the problem was how to achieve this object. Lagercrantz, the Swedish envoy in Copenhagen, had the answer: "Sweden looks to Great Britain to uphold the Treaty of 1856."[5] Count Wachtmeister, former Minister for Foreign Affairs, added: ". . intense anxiety prevails in Sweden for support of England . . Sweden may otherwise be driven to a yet closer union with Germany, as a protection against Russian aims".[6]

This provoked a somewhat acid comment from the Foreign Office: "It seems to be a common thing in Scandinavia to threaten us with an increase of German influence if we do not meet their wishes — as was done by both Sweden and Norway during the negotiations for the Integrity Treaty" and "considering the way their Press treated us about the Norwegian Treaty they have not lost much time in coming back to us".[7] But of course the Foreign Office took advantage of the situation. A question in Parliament gave occasion for Grey to calm the Swedes with some measured support. He was asked whether he was aware that alarm had been occasioned in Sweden by the report of Russia's intention to demand release from her treaty obligations, and what was the attitude of His Majesty's Government upon this question.[8] Hardinge advised that it would be more prudent to answer that no statement could be made, but Grey thought that "we had better make some statement; there is a Swede working up agitation".[9]

There is no clue as to who the Swede might have been, but Grey's sentence confirms the apprehensions of the Germans who were certain that it was no chance that the interpellations in the Swedish and British parliaments were simultaneous.[10] It was only natural that the Swedes did their best to ensure the

[1] PRO/FO 371/528/3391 Rennell Rodd to Grey 31. I 1908, minute CH
[2] PRO/FO 371/527/2791 Grey to Rennell Rodd 22. I 1908
[3] PRO/FO 371/528/6415 Rennell Rodd to Grey 20. II 1908
[4] PRO/FO 371/528/6415 Rennell Rodd to Grey 20. II 1908
[5] PRO/FO 371/528/3946 Vaughan to Grey 4. II 1908
[6] PRO/FO 371/528/5917 Rennell Rodd to Grey 16. II 1908
[7] PRO/FO 371/528/5917 minutes
[8] PRO/FO 371/528/6522 Parliamentary question 20. II 1908
[9] PRO/FO 371/528/6522 minutes CH & EG
[10] AA Norwegen 7 geheim Bd 4 Scheller to Bülow 15. X 1907

support of the British public opinion. It has not been possible in the scope of
this study to investigate how far the British press was inspired by the Swedes.
(A pro-Finnish and anti-Russian tradition, since 1899, may have had some
inportance in 1908, too.[1])

But the inspiration, if there was any, was only a contributory factor: the
opinion in support of Sweden was so unanimous that it must have been based
on a genuine worry concerning Britain's own interests. The *Daily Telegraph*
was of the opinion that Britain had no reason to oppose Russia's endeavours in
the Baltic Sea,[2] but it was said that this opinion was the only one in favour of
Russia.[3] Hardinge wrote to Nicolson that the Government was obliged to defend Swedish interests because the strong and unanimous public opinion would
have caused difficulties, being opposed to leaving small countries "on the ten-
der mercies" of Russia.[4] There was a report of an initiative by the Sheffield
Chamber of Commerce, who had the intention of making an appeal to the
Government not to abrogate the Convention of 1856, in order to prevent Russia
from making the Gulf of Bothnia a *mare clausum*. This was based on the
argument that the steel industry of Sheffield was dependent on Swedish iron.[5]
This one glimpse is sufficient to remind us that British industry had a sufficient
interest in Sweden to put pressure on the Foreign Office not to forsake the
Swedish cause, but of course it is not enough to enable us to measure the
strength of the pressure. — Sir Edward Grey was unusually independent for a
parliamentary minister. Perhaps he would not have let any pressure influence
his policy against the British interests as he understood them, but evidently in
this question there was no contradiction.

In Parliament Grey gave as much support to Sweden as he could without
pledging Britain to anything definite, which was in accordance with his well-
known methods. He said: ". . it is not at the present moment necessary for His
Majesty's Government to come to any decision. . If and when this is necessary,
we shall, of course, consult with both the other parties to the treaty and take
into account the feeling of Sweden . . before coming to any decision".[6]

Grey thought that this was enough. When rumours were reported concerning
new mediation by Germany, who desired to play her part of "honest broker"
and to do all she could to gain the confidence of the Swedes, Grey remarked

---

[1] Maude *Finland and Britain.* p. 173, 234, 255, 306
[2] *Daily Telegraph* 14. II 1908
[3] *Senska Dagbladet* 15. II 1908
   Pro-Swedish articles for instance in
   Morning Post 20. II 1908
   Standard 20. II 1908
[4] BD 8 n. 149 Hardinge to Nicolson 3. III 1908
[5] AA Russland 63 Bd 3 Metternich to Bülow 26. III 1908
[6] PRO/FO 371/528/6522 Parliamentary question 20. II 1908 and answer 21. II 1908

that Sweden knew that Great Britain would not come to any decision to abrogate the Åland treaty without consulting her, which strengthened her position.[1]

By the end of February Russia made a new proposal to define the term *status quo,* as the North Sea powers had done, that it did not signify limiting the sovereign rights of either State over their own territory. Trolle feared a trap — it might be utilized afterwards by Russia to support a contention that Sweden had assented to remove the restriction respecting the Åland Islands.[2] — Of course it was no *trap* because such was Isvolsky's explicit intention! "It was difficult to accept" and therefore it was sent to London to be submitted to Grey.[3] In other words, Trolle asked Grey's help.

The Secretary of State answered that it was not possible for Great Britain to give an unconditional promise that she would under no circumstances agree to a modification or abrogation of the Åland Islands treaty.[4] Wrangel explained that as Sweden could not sign the Baltic agreement without such a pledge, matters were in an impasse.[5] Grey remarked to his aide: "A pledge not to abrogate the 1856 Treaty would put us in the position of having to declare war on Russia if she fortified the Åland Islands, for if Sweden in the faith of such a pledge signed this agreement we could not honourably content ourselves with a mere protest if Russia denounced the Treaty without our consent." [6] — Grey had lost his faith that Russia could not do anything so immoral.

The fear that Russia might some day do something like that was strengthened by *Novoe Vremja's* argument that the disappearance of the parent Treaty of 1855 had eo ipso made the Convention of 1856 void.[7] *Novoe Vremja's* articles were often regarded as at least inspired if not semi-official, and were "in the worst style of Russian argumentation in favour of the thesis that no treaty is binding on Russia which she does not like".[8] — The Foreign Office felt no sympathy towards the Russian wish to free herself from the servitude, which was not "an unexampled humiliation".[9]

In Stockholm Rennell Rodd, however, tried to find a way out of the impasse, and to avert the German danger by giving more concrete support to Sweden. He proposed that "If Russia were prepared to give Sweden definite and sufficient assurances as to the innocence of her future intentions in the Åland Islands, Great Britain and France might become parties to any instrument placing these assurances on record. This would retain to Sweden the right to

[1] PRO/FO 371/528/6845 Nicolson to Grey 27. II 1908 minutes
[2] PRO/FO 371/528/6673 & 6861 Rennell Rodd to Grey 25. II 1908
[3] =2
[4] PRO/FO 371/528/6933 Grey to Rennell Rodd 26. II 1908
[5] BD 8 n. 145 Wrangel to F. O. 25. II 1908
[6] BD 8 n. 145 minute by EG
[7] *Novoe Vremja* 2/15 II 1908
[8] PRO/FO 371/528/7147 Nicolson to Grey 28. II 1908 minutes
[9] PRO/FO 371/528/7129 Nicolson to Grey 26. II 1908 minutes

appeal to these two in case of any threatened violation of Russia of her undertaking .. while it would enable Russia to get rid of the appearance of a servitude. ."[1] The Foreign Office guessed that this would have been unpalatable to
Russia, who desired to get rid of Great Britain and France altogether in this
agreement, but Rodd was instructed to ascertain what the Swedes thought of the
proposal, as a personal suggestion of his own.[2] Trolle received the suggestion
thankfully[3] but it was made obsolete by Isvolsky's retreat and was dropped: "It
is probably now unnecessary for the British Govt. to move further in the
matter."[4]

The Russian retreat at the beginning of March 1908 was held to be due to
British support. "The considerable advance in the direction desired by Sweden"
was attributed by Trolle "in a great measure to the attitude of His Majesty's
Government and to that of the press in England"[5] which, it was believed, the
Emperor Nicholas was in the habit of reading.[6]

Afterwards, during his journey to Sweden with King Edward in April and
May 1908 Hardinge was able to reap the harvest of gratitude due to British
policy in the Baltic question, which made good the loss of sympathy that had
occurred during the Norwegian negotiations. "The support of Grey and the
British press in the Åland Islands question had changed the whole political
atmosphere and the cordial admittance of Sweden to the North Sea treaty
restored the conviction of the friendly attitude of His Majesty's Government."[7]
Rodd's successor in Sweden, Spring-Rice, agreed: "we appear to have regained the sympathies of Sweden, and she seems now to have returned to her
ancient policy of impartial neutrality and armed independence".[8]

The honest broker

It has been supposed that Germany was interested in seeing Isvolsky's operation carried through to a succesful conclusion in order to get rid of the Convention, which gave the Western powers the juridical right to intervene in Baltic
affairs.[9] It seems, however, that this interest was only of secondary importance.

It has already been related how the Emperor William had done his share to

[1] PRO/FO 371/528/6415 Rennell Rodd to Grey 20. II 1908
[2] PRO/FO 371/528/6415 minutes
[3] PRO/FO 371/528/7853 Rennell Rodd to Grey 3. III 1908
[4] PRO/FO 371/528/7853 Rennell Rodd to Grey 3. III 1908 minutes
[5] PRO/FO 371/528/9729 Rennell Rodd to Grey 17. III 1908
[6] PRO/FO 371/528/10431 Rennell Rodd to Grey 24. III 1908
[7] BD 8 n. 154 Rennell Rodd to Grey 28. IV 1908
[8] PRO/FO 371/745/ undecipherable Annual report for Sweden 1908 by Spring-Rice
[9] Gihl p. 353

support Russia and how the Germans helped to start the discussion in December 1907. In January Schoen continued the support saying that he hoped that Sweden would not feel it necessary to keep up the Convention once the Baltic declaration gave her a more general security,[1] and he explained that the Åland servitude was a question of amour-propre to the Czar, not only a whim of the Foreign Minister.[2] Rumour had it that the Emperor William had said that if Sweden did not secure her territory now when the opportunity was offered, she might be swept away completely when the conflict came.[3] Evidently this pressure made Germany, seen from Stockholm, to be more Russophile than she in fact was. The Russians also made the Swedes apprehensive by speaking of *nos conjurés de Berlin*.[4]

The Swedo-German declaration — which in the end was submerged in the joint Baltic declaration — was planned according to the model of the secret Russo-German Baltic Treaty, and Germany proposed that identical pairs of notes be exchanged between each pair of Baltic powers. This caused further irritation between Russia and Germany, as Isvolsky was "surprised" at this proposal and recalled that they had agreed to keep the secret treaty secret.[5] The Germans had to explain that there was no question of disclosing the secret, but of a new declaration, identical and simultaneous with those between the small Baltic powers, in order to avoid hurting them and arousing their suspicions, which would have been unavoidable if they were treated ifferently from Russia's and Germany's treatment of each other.[6] Isvolsky admitted the validity of the German argument but wished, however, to postpone the said declaration.[7] Taube explained that Russia must take her ally into consideration — which was certainly understandable, remembering the violent criticism he had received from the French in the autumn. Schoen remarked to Pourtalès that it was "characteristic" of Isvolsky to be shy of agreeing to the declaration with Germany.[8] But Pourtalès recommended accepting Isvolsky's point of view and delaying the Russo-German declaration. Thereby Isvolsky could be made accustomed to concluding treaties secretly from the French.[9] — This has no importance from the point of view of the outcome of the Baltic treaty, which was made, after all, jointly and not in pairs. But it illuminates the degree to which Russo-German relations had deteriorated as a result of mutual distrust, worsened by the snags of the North Sea proposition.

---

[1] AA Russland Bd 63 Bd 1 Schoen to Pourtalès 10. I 1908
[2] Hildebrand p. 537
[3] Reutersvärd p. 57
[4] Reutersvärd p. 57
[5] AA Dänemark 37 geheim Bd 11 Pourtalès to Ausw. Amt 31. I 1908
[6] AA Dänemark 37 geheim Bd 12 Schoen to Pourtalès 11. II 1908
[7] AA Dänemark 37 geheim Bd 13 Pourtalès to Bülow 26. II 1908
[8] AA Dänemark 37 geheim Bd 12 Schoen to Pourtalès 11. II 1908
[9] AA Dänemark 37 geheim Bd 13 Pourtalès to Bülow 7. II 1908

So the pressure, which the Swedes felt so depressing and which made Germany seem Russia's *conjurée* cannot have been very serious.

At the beginning of January the Germans still tried to mediate cautiously. The German envoy in Stockholm was instructed to calm the Swedes by saying that the Russians were known to be planning only a second-class base to watch the smugglers,[1] and Schoen "with evident success" assured Count Taube of Russian innocence.[2] But these efforts were not so earnest as Isvolsky might have hoped. Pückler explained to his Austrian colleague in Stockholm that he was by no means on Russia's side, he only wanted to be an *ehrlicher Makler,* a bit inclined to Sweden's side. The Russian envoy complained to the same Austrian that he had received little support from the Germans.[3] For Pückler's "personal information" Schoen wrote that an eventual failure of the Baltic agreement would only benefit the German North Sea negotiations.[4]

Again we can see Schoen's inexplicable change from being almost a colleague of Isvolsky into being the "honest" broker. He seems to have lost all faith in Russian friendship, so that even the "watered-down broth" of the North Sea agreement, a question of mere prestige, was more important to him than Baltic co-operation with Russia.

Pückler, by the middle of January, was already warning that the German efforts to calm the Swedes as to Russia's intentions might lead them to believe that Germany supported the Russian wishes more warmly than those of Sweden in St. Petersburg. The Russian envoy himself had expressed his apprehensions that Sweden might seek and find support in England and France.[5] Isvolsky's policy was endangering Germany's interests in Sweden, and this may have been an additional reason for Schoen's change of mind.

Of course Schoen did not wish to act openly to the detriment of Russian interests, in spite of all the bad blood, and so he had to balance between the two disputants. He urged the Russians to conclude the Russo-Swedish negotiations before the British Cabinet took up the North Sea project and with it probably also the Baltic question. He supported the Swedish proposal of signing the secret protocol, with the supplement of a Russian pledge not to fortify the Åland Islands.[6] On the other hand, when Isvolsky proposed the unilateral note which the Swedes planned to answer by their own unilateral declaration, the Germans advised them emphatically to drop the idea.[7]

As the bilateral discussions between Russia and Sweden ended in an impasse, the Germans began to seek a way out. They suggested a simple declaration to

[1] AA Dänemark 37 geheim Bd 10 Schoen to Pückler 6. I 1908
[2] AA Dänemark 37 geheim Bd 10 Schoen to Pourtalès 6. I 1908
[3] HHStA/SVA n. 139 Esperjesy to Aehrenthal 22. I 1908
[4] AA Dänemark 37 geheim Bd 10 Schoen to Pückler 6. I 1908
[5] AA Dänemark 37 geheim Bd 10 Pückler to Bülow 13. I 1908
[6] AA Dänemark 37 geheim Bd 10 Schoen to Pourtalès 16. I 1908
[7] AA Dänemark 37 geheim Bd 11 Schoen to Pourtalès 30. I 1908

respect the status quo, and a supplementary memorandum stipulating that the status quo implied only actual territorial possessions. Consequently the changes which the High Contracting Parties were to make in their fortifications and naval or military dispositions could not be held as infringing the status quo. "This would in fact completely correspond to the Russian wishes but would avoid their unilateral character and naming the Åland Islands which the Swedes did not like." [1]

Isvolsky received this draft coolly, saying that it would not seem any more acceptable to the Swedes than the earlier ones.[2] Then he consented to consider the suggestion. He dropped the reference to fortifications, and substituted a stipulation that the guarantee of the status quo in no way prevented the "full enjoyment of sovereign rights on the continental and insular possessions" of both participants.[3] He promised to take this new initiative, provided the Germans were able to ensure that he would not be exposed to a new refusal.[4]

Schoen discussed the matter with Count Taube, and the Swede found the way acceptable, provided that Sweden's consent to the memorandum was not interpreted as a consent to fortifying the Åland Islands. He said that it would be easier to maintain that the memorandum was only a definition of the status quo if a similar memorandum was added also to the North Sea declaration (which in fact Germany and Great Britain had already agreed to do) and to which Sweden would "of course" join.[5]

Together the Secretary of State and the envoy drafted the documents, and then Taube proceeded to Stockholm to make his government accept them. His intention was to continue his journey to St. Petersburg to negotiate with Isvolsky. "With his influence in Sweden he is the man to carry he matter to a succesful conclusion" Schoen hoped.[6] Evidently the obstinate General Brändström was to be put aside. Isvolsky was surprised to hear of Taube's journey. *C'est une bonne nouvelle que vous me donnez* he said to Pourtalès, but he was still doubtful because he knew Swedish resistance to the abrogation of the Åland Convention to be strong and vocal.[7]

In Stockholm Taube said to his government, according to what he told Pückler, that Sweden could not take the responsibility for causing the failure of the Baltic Agreement, and thus eventually also of the North Sea Agreement. It was reasonable now to accept the proferred guarantee, and to give up the Åland Convention. Later anyway the Convention might be annulled without any com-

[1] AA Dänemark 37 geheim Bd 11 Schoen to Pourtalès 30. I 1908
[2] AA Dänemark 37 geheim Bd 11 Pourtalès to Bülow 2. II 1908
[3] AA Dänemark 37 geheim Bd 12 Pourtalès to Bülow 7. II 1908
[4] AA Dänemark 37 geheim Bd 12 Pourtalès to Ausw. Amt 11. II 08
[5] AA Dänemark 37 geheim Bd 12 note Schoen 10. II 1908
[6] AA Dänemark 37 geheim Bd 13 Schoen to Pourtalès 23. II 1908
[7] AA Dänemark 37 geheim Bd 13 Pourtalès to Schoen 26. II 1908

pensation to Sweden. Taube said that the King was compliant, but the Prime Minister Lindman less so, being apprehensive of public opinion. Taube was not very sure of the success of his mission.[1]

Then Isvolsky's retreat changed the situation, as will be narrated in the following chapter.

The Germans had grown weary of mediating. Metternich had in January already been of the opinion that Russia ought to drop her differences with Sweden, in order not to render her open to any Anglo-French allurements, which were dangerous to Germany and disagreeable to Russia.[2] In February Schoen sighed that Russia ought to carry out the difficult task herself she had undertaken, "it is mindless to blame Germany for the lack of success".[3] Pückler, the envoy Stockholm, warned repeatedly against supporting Russia too far, "it would be a misfortune if Germany lost sympathy in Sweden to the advantage of the British"[4]; Rennell Rodd had very good cards in his hands and was striving hard to draw Sweden nearer to England.[5] Similar warnings arrived from London[6] and even from St. Petersburg, where the Swedish Legation was anything but satisfied with German attitude.[7]

Schoen tried to repair as much as possible. He instructed Pückler to say to the Swedes that there was no agreement concerning Åland between Russia and Germany — which was untrue, of course — and to explain that Germany had not guessed how great an importance Sweden gave to the ancient Convention — which was true. Germany, he went on, had only wished to help the Czar to get rid of the stipulations which Russia felt so irksome. Germany had been surprised at the violent reaction in Sweden, and had tried to advise Russia to stop the pressure on Sweden. He also tried to get part of the credit for Isvolsky's retreat for himself.[8] — Lindberg is of the opinion that Schoen had secretly prompted Sweden to seek British support against Russia, in order to make the Baltic treaty fail and thus cease disturbing the North Sea project, which was of prime importance to Schoen.[9] This seems a little far-fetched, on the sole proof that Schoen was "reluctant" to support Russia, which can be adequately explained by his wish not to estrange Sweden; there was no reason for him to push Sweden towards Britain.

[1] AA Dänemark 37 geheim Bd 13 Pückler to Bülow 29. II 1908
[2] AA Russland 63 Bd 1 Metternich to Bülow 13. I 1908
[3] HHStA/SVA n. 172 Szögyeny to Aehrenthal 4. II 1908
[4] AA Dänemark 37 geheim Bd 13 Pückler to Ausw. Amt 24. II 1908
   AA Dänemark 37 geheim Bd 13 Pückler to Bülow 29. II 1908
[5] AA Dänemark 37 geheim Bd 14 Pückler to Schoen 25. III 1908
[6] AA Dänemark 37 geheim Bd 12 Metternich to Bülow 12. II 1908
[7] AA Dänemark 37 geheim Bd 13 Pourtalès to Bülow 3. III 1908
[8] GP 23 II n. 8146 Schoen to Pückler 11. III 1908
[9] Lindberg: *Scandinavia.* . p. 208

Schoen dropped his endeavours to mediate after Count Taube had taken to Stockholm the proposal they had prepared together. He instructed Pourtalès to this effect, adding: "let us see how Russia and Sweden succeed in their negotiations, to us all propositions are acceptable".[1] The question was about the explanations and counter-explanations which Russia and Sweden wanted to add to the Baltic declaration, after Isvolsky's retreat. The Germans only carried messages between Russia and Sweden [2], and believed that "we are obliged to desist from any more attempts at influencing" the course of events.[3]

According to Pückler the mischief had been done already. He said that the decisive turning point in the Russo-Swedish quarrel was the moment when Sweden learned for certain that England was not going to abrogate the Convention without Sweden's consent.[4] Parallel with Count Taube's discussions in Berlin there had been negotiations in London resulting in this *Rückversicherung* [5], and King Edward was coming to visit Sweden, accompanied by Sir Charles Hardinge, to complete the scheme.[6] Stumm, the chargé d'affaires in London, expressed a similar fear.[7]

Isvolsky loses support and interest

Sweden had won British support, and the honest German broker was of no great help to Isvolsky. Then Isvolsky found further stumbling-blocks in his way. At the end of February 1908 King Gustaf V sent a letter to Nicholas II about the marriage plans of the royal families. (Prince Wilhelm of Sweden and Maria Pavlovna were about to start their unfortunate alliance). In the same letter he begged the Czar's understanding in the Åland question: "Personally I understand perfectly your point of view, but on the other hand I must ask you take into kind consideration the feelings of my country in this sore question. ."[8] Baron Taube has said that it was due to this letter that Isvolsky was obliged to give up his Åland operation. Nicholas had commanded his minister to an audience, had shown Gustaf's letter to him and said that he had already answered the King. He had promised that Åland would not be mentioned in the agreement and that the matter would be put off until a more suitable occasion. Isvolsky came from the audience pale with rage.[9]

[1] AA Dänemark 37 geheim Bd 14 Schoen to Pourtalès 24. III 08
[2] AA Russland 63 Bd 2 Schoen to Pourtalès 7. III 1908
[3] AA Dänemark 37 geheim Bd 14 Schoen to Pourtalès 24. III 08
[4] AA Russland 63 Bd 3 Pückler to Bülow 2. I 1909
[5] AA Dänemark 37 geheim Bd 13 Pückler to Bülow 4. III 1908
[6] AA Dänemark 37 geheim Bd 14 Pückler to Bülow 3. IV 1908
[7] AA Russland Bd 3 Stumm to Bülow 14. V 1908
[8] AVPR fond sekretnyj arhiv, delo 381, n. 355 Gustaf V to Nicholas II 26. II 1908
[9] Taube: *La politique russe.* . p. 167

Lindberg has denied the truth of Taube's tale, on the strength of the argument that when writing his memoirs Taube had no documents of the Foreign Ministry at his disposal, and that he had put the scene with the King's letter and the Czar's surrended as occurring in April, at the moment, that is, when Isvolsky definitely gave up.[1] But it was as early as 1913, when he was still in the service of the Russian government and consequently had all the documents at his disposal, that Taube wrote a memorandum in which he gave decisive importance to the said letter, and at the right moment, at the end of February and beginning of March.[2] This was the time when Isvolsky gave up his attack and when the defensive phase of the Åland operation began. And there is no discernible reason to suppose that Taube would have lied in this question.

Isvolsky was "pale with rage", but it was no light matter for Nicholas II, either. He explained to the German military attaché that the abrogation of the servitude was for him a question of honour.[3] It had been a disagreeable surprise to learn, in 1906, that Russia was deprived of the right to fortify Åland — what would the Swedes say if they were not allowed to rule and reign on Gotland as they would. "They say that Åland is too near Stockholm, but I cannot carry it farther away."[4] Diplomatic gossip had it that the Swedish marriage and the attitude of the British press made Nicholas stifle the dictates of pride.[5] It is a pity that there is no first-hand source to illuminate the Czar's attitude.

It was the British attitude that was of central importance to Isvolsky, too. The Western powers had the might to maintain or abrogate the Åland servitude, the operation with Sweden was only a preparation for a request to London and Paris. The opinion of the British press and Grey's answer in the House of Commons made it clear to Isvolsky that he had little hope of reaching his aim, especially as British influence was perceived also in the stiffening Swedish attitude. General Brändström had acted so positively and resolutely towards Isvolsky that the minister could not believe it possible without a secure promise of British support. "Taking England into consideration we must give up" Isvolsky had written to Kudašev. — This is related by Lagercrantz, who is perhaps not the most reliable of witnesses, but the story fits in the pattern.[6]

Perhaps the decisive occurrences that emphasized the importance of Great Britain for Isvolsky's plans took place in the Balkans. Up to this time Austria

[1] Lindberg: *Scandinavia.*. p. 279
[2] AVPR fond sekretnyj arhiv, delo 383/390 n. 9
   Spravka po voprosu ob alandskih ostrovah 1. VI 1913
[3] Lambsdorff p. 269
[4] AA Dänemark 37 geheim Bd 11 Pourtalès to Bülow 29. I 1908
[5] GP 23 II n. 8141 Pourtalès to Ausw. Amt 4. III 1908
   BD 8 n. 148 Rennell Rodd to Grey 3. III 1908
[6] Lagercrantz p. 330

had worked together with Russia to maintain the status quo in the Balkans, against the wishes of Great Britain and Italy, who strove for reforms in Macedonia. But the status quo was secure no more, and by the end of the year 1907 Aehrenthal decided to move, having secured German support and quieted down the quarrelsome Magyars. Aehrenthal's ultimate aim was probably to subjugate the Serbians and to clear up the nationality problem that menaced the existence of Austria. His immediate aim was to build a railway through the Sanjak of Novibazar and to connect it with the Adriatic ports, for this would have given to Austria economic dominance in the Balkans. Aehrenthal procured the concession from the Sultan and made public his plan on 27th January 1908. This was Aehrenthal's notorious bomb at Isvolsky's feet. In the Council of Russian Ministers on 3rd February Isvolsky demanded counter-moves, but the other ministers would not allow this because Russia lacked forces to back any diplomatic action. At the beginning of March Isvolsky appeared "elegic" about his chances of remaining in office as Foreign Minister. Nevertheless he stayed on, but he had been made to realize that it was not possible to defend Slavic interests without a conflict with Austria-Hungary. Thereafter it was even more important than ever before to get British support against the Germanic empires. The Asian agreement of 1907 was no alliance, but the British royal and naval visit to Reval in the summer of 1908 was already an omen of an entente.[1]

It is obvious that these great and serious matters compelled Isvolsky to turn his attention from his Baltic schemes and the particular problem of Åland.[2] The political importance of the Northern question could not be compared with the exciting and inflammable problems of the Balkans and the Tsargrad at the mouth of the Turkish Straits.

Isvolsky gives up

Isvolsky gave up his attack on the Åland front. He had against him the furious public opinion of Sweden, the unyielding Swedish government, and these had behind them British support. Germany as an honest broker was of no great help. His own Emperor had forsaken him, and anything might happen in the Balkans at any moment. There was no chance any more of getting the servitude abrogated, and it was useless to waste time in the hopeless quest. But it was not very easy to retire from the exposed position to which he had brought himself.

He was prepared to accept the "Swedish" proposal (of Taube and Schoen), the question of Åland was to be completely divorced from the question of the Baltic status quo.[3] To the Swedish envoy Isvolsky explained that a reassuring

[1] Carlgren: *Isvolsky und* . . . p. 263—
[2] Lindberg concurs: *Scandinavia* p. 227
[3] AA Dänemark 37 geheim Bd 13 Pourtalès to Ausw. Amt 4. III 1908

article was to be published in the official *Rossija*. The question of Åland was thereby being put off to the future, and he hoped that the article would calm all excited minds. Trolle related this information in the Council in Stockholm on the 2nd March, and concluded that Sweden had no reason any longer to obstruct the progress of the Baltic status quo agreement.[1] — So it was not wholly due to Count Taube's influence that his (and Schoen's) compromise proposal was adopted, at least not so completely as he let Berlin understand.[2]

On the 5th March *Rossija* published the promised article. It stated that the rumours were groundless which attributed to Russia the intention of fortifying the Åland Islands. It was also not true that Russia had turned to the signatory powers to ask them to abrogate the servitude.[3] This article was read as Isvolsky's admittance of defeat and as a public and official promise not to fortify the Islands.

Isvolsky had given up his hopes of seeing the Åland servitude abrogated in the imminent future. But the means to attain this unattainable goal had been launched and had achieved a life of their own: the Baltic agreement had been proposed, and the proposal could not very well be annulled, in spite the fact that its *raison d'être,* from Isvolsky's viewpoint, had disappeared. And although he had given up the hope of getting the servitude abrogated, he naturally did not wish to get it renewed as part of the status quo which was to be guaranteed.

When Isvolsky had explained to Brändström his article, the General had answered "rudely" that no articles in *Rossija* could calm Sweden.[4] Trolle was surprised to hear of the envoy's behaviour, because he thought that there was nothing more in the way of preventing Sweden from signing the Baltic agreement. Trolle's aide Ehrensvärd said that Sweden would do everything to make Russia's retreat easier.[5] Trolle admitted that there might be some difficulties with public opinion or some ministers, but these could be overcome if Russia would accept some reassuring explanations to the memorandum annexed to the agreement.[6] Isvolsky accepted the form of a joint declaration — his reasons for opposing it had become obsolete, as the Western powers had resigned themselves to being left out of the Baltic agreement and on the other hand Great Britain had succeeded in blocking his Åland operation nevertheless. But he remarked that if Sweden were to add explanations in the memorandum, Russia reserved the right to add counter-explanations.[7]

---

[1] Hildebrand p. 544
[2] GP 23 II n. 8140 Schoen to Pourtalès 3. III 1908
[3] *Rossija* 22. II/5. III 1908
[4] Reutersvärd p. 64
   AA Dänemark 37 geheim Bd 13 Pourtalès to Ausw. Amt 5. III 1908
[5] AA Russland 63 Bd 3 Pückler to Bülow 2. I 1909
[6] AA Dänemark 37 geheim Bd 13 Schoen to Pourtalès 7. III 1908
[7] AA Dänemark 37 geheim Bd 14 Russian F.O. to German Embassy 23. II/7. III 1908

15

The Swedish explanations were put forth in an aide-mémoire which stated how happy the Swedish government was at the spirit of moderation and benevolence of which the Imperial Government had given proof by dropping a question which was of so vital and worrying a nature to Sweden. *Le Gouvernement du Roi ne saurait, en effet, se dissimuler que la creation éventuelle sur les îles d'Aland, à toute proximité de la capitale et de la côte suédoise, d'établissements militaires ou maritimes plus importantes ne laisserait que d'entretenir les inquiétudes en Suède et d'entraver par là le developpement de l'amitié et de la confiance absolues mutuelles . .* [1] — that is, although Isvolsky had promised to drop the attempt to abrogate the servitude, the Swedes wished to state officially that such an abrogation would be regarded as a hostile act.

Isvolsky then sent his counter-explanations in the form of a new draft for the annex memorandum of the Baltic agreement. He had added to the memorandum the words which he had been reluctant to accept when the Germans first proposed them: the status quo was to be understood as referring only to the territorial possessions so that eventual alterations in the military or naval establishments would not be in conflict with the principle of the status quo.[2]

This was a disappointment to the Swedes. It is evident that the "rude" General Brändström had understood the limits of Isvolsky's retreat more realistically than the government in Stockholm. King Gustaf complained: "It is not very easy to deal with the Russians because they have a rich treasury of words, and it is not always easy to harmonize what they say to-day with what they said yesterday." [3] — In fact there was no ambiguity in Isvolsky's policy. It seems that the Swedes were given to excessive fears and hopes alternatively, and Isvolsky's fault was, if he had any, that he failed to make the Swedes understand what he had intended from the beginning, and what he had given up.

The situation was by the end of March nearly identical with that of January. The Swedes wished to get some guarantee that their signature in the memorandum could not be used as a proof of their consent to the abrogation of the Åland convention; and Isvolsky wished to get the Baltic agreement concluded without renewing the servitude.

The difference between the situation in January and March was in the intentions of Isvolsky — what he meant to do after the agreement was signed. In March he did not aim at the immediate abrogation of the servitude. Therefore he did not need any proof of Sweden's consent to be shown to the Western powers; what was needed was a formula which left his hands free in the future. Schoen had proposed that the Baltic memorandum be identical with the one added to the North Sea declaration. So the reference to the military and naval establishments was dropped from the text, the status quo was defined as not

[1] AA Russland 63 Bd 2 copy of the Swedish aide-mémoire 7. III 1908
[2] Hildebrand p. 546
[3] AA Russland 63 Bd 3 Pückler to Bülow 3. IV 1908

preventing the enjoyment of sovereign rights, and that was all.[1]

Now Isvolsky had gone back to the starting point. The Swedes, too, gave way a little. Count Taube explained that the latest Russian proposal was quite acceptable, provided Sweden were allowed to add an explicative aide-mémoire stipulating "that this accord cannot be interpreted as prejudicing the existing treaties".[2] This document did not need any answer by Russia, nor did it imply a threat of an unfavourable reaction if the Åland question were to be taken up later, but no one could say that Sweden's signature signified consent to the abrogation.

Of course Isvolsky did not like this mentioning of the old treaties [3], which in a way reinforced them. But a refusal might have led to the failure of the Baltic agreement with unfavourable consequences for the international "climate of opinion". Notwithstanding their reluctance to intervene the Germans seem to have put a mild pressure on both disputants in this last phase.[4] — The British had refused to sign the North Sea Agreement before the Baltic Agreement. — Isvolsky, and the Czar, "hurried" to accept without "any objections"[5] the Swedish aide-mémoire and everything was ready to be signed.

In Great Britain Isvolsky's counter-explanation, in fact a last desperate attempt to save something, strengthened the prevalent suspicions against Russia: "Sweden may consider that she is effectually covered by the memorandum which she proposes to put in on the side. But Russia is a slippery customer, and I (Crowe) suspect that Sweden will ultimately find herself cheated."[6] But these explanations were not essential: "Whatever Sweden accepts can hardly affect our position towards the Treaty of 1856" was the final opinion of the leaders of British foreign policy.[7]

All the difficulties had succesfully been avoided and put off until later. The Baltic treaty with its addenda had been made void of any significance. It was now acceptable to all participants. The Swedish government approved the cluster of documents on the 8th April 1908.[8] It was decided to abrogate the old Treaty of 1855 simultaneously with the signing of the Baltic and North Sea Agreements.[9] The Swedes preferred to state that the Treaty ceased to exist when the Baltic Agreement was signed, but the British were of the opinion that

[1] AA Dänemark 37 geheim Bd 13 Schoen to Pourtalès 6. III 1908
[2] AA Dänemark 37 geheim Bd 14 Schoen to Pourtalès 2. IV 1908
[3] AA Dänemark 37 geheim Bd 14 Pourtalès to Ausw. Amt 3. IV 1908
[4] AA Dänemark 37 geheim Bd 14 Schoen to Pourtalès 2. IV 1908
[5] AVPR fond sekretnyj arhiv, delo 381, n. 393 Isvolsky to Brändström, draft 25. III 1908 (probably Old Style)
[6] PRO/FO 371/528/11027 Rennell Rodd to Grey 31. III 1908, minute EAC
[7] PRO/FO 371/528/11027 minute CH, initialled EG
[8] Hildebrand p. 548
[9] PRO/FO 371/529/13271 Rennell Rodd to Grey 16. IV 1908

it had lapsed in 1905. To save Swedish amour-propre the date was not mentioned at all; it was only stated that the ancient treaty had lapsed.[1]

Russia and the straits again

Due to Germany's mediation the Baltic and North Sea declarations were nearly identical, and this went, too, for the definition of the term status quo as referring only to territorial possessions. But the Baltic declaration had no reference to the line of demarcation between the two seas, which caused so many problems in the North Sea negotiations.

It has already been related how Isvolsky was averse to starting the negotiations with Denmark, and angry with Germany for drawing the Western powers into the discussions about the North Sea project. This was explained by his wish to deal with Sweden alone in the Åland question. But there was more to it.

That "more" was, however, hardly what Raben supposed. He told the British that Kudašev had explained that Russia's reluctance to have the North Sea and Baltic agreements combined was due to Russia's unwillingness to be party to any instrument with England.[2] The Foreign Office commented: "Raben talks nonsense"[3] and the explanation a week later did not make any more sense: the aversion was due to religious reasons. England had been the ally of the Turks and of the Japanese, and she reigned over millions of Muslims. As the Russians divided the world into Orthodox and Infidel, the British were par excellence of the latter.[4] — It is difficult to imagine that Isvolsky could have uttered anything like this, it can only have been the product of Kudašev's genius. Isvolsky said of him: "He is a brave boy, but in spite of two months of efforts I have not succeeded in making him comprehend my ideas."[5]

The very idea of a treaty covering Denmark seems to have made Isvolsky apprehensive. In January 1908 he warned the Germans that the signatories of the Treaty of 1857 might "complicate matters" and make an effort to guarantee the whole of Danish territory in a general European treaty.[6] The Germans tried to calm him by assuring him that the North Sea project did not in any way affect the older treaties about the Straits. The status quo -agreements would guarantee Denmark only on her North Sea and Baltic coast, leaving the Straits open.[7] Isvolsky was not to be soothed. His apprehensions grew when the discussions began to lead to a joint declaration about the North Sea, instead of the

---

[1] AA Dänemark 37 geheim Bd 16 Stumm to Ausw. Amt 21. VI 1908
[2] PRO/FO 371/527/2838 Vaughan to Grey 26. I 1908
[3] PRO/FO 371/527/2838 minute by CH
[4] PRO/FO 381/527/3683 Vaughan to Grey 31. I 1908
[5] AA Dänemark 37 geheim Bd 14 Henckel to Bülow 2. IV 1908
[6] AA Dänemark 37 geheim Bd 10 Pourtalès to Bülow 18. I 1908
[7] AA Dänemark 37 geheim Bd 9 Pourtalès to Bülow 18. XII 1907

separate notes which Isvolsky had advocated. When the suggestion to this effect was made, he was "worried lest his fears prove well grounded and the joint project would indeed comprise the Straits. In that case Russia would be compelled to insist on participating in the (North Sea) project".[1]

The fear of being left out when the question of the Straits was decided is evident here. The central and essential aspect of the Baltic question was the problem of the Danish Straits. This hard fact has been covered by the froth of the discussion concerning the Åland Islands, which has hitherto prevented the importance of the Danish Straits from being appreciated.

When the French proposed the third agreement, which would have covered only the Straits and was to be signed by all the powers interested in the North Sea and Baltic negotiations, the Danes attributed this proposition to the schemes of Isvolsky. They supposed that because he had not succeeded in his operation, he was now trying to bring down both the North Sea and Baltic projects in order to get a new chance in Åland.[2] This view illuminates the distrust of Russian policy which was felt in Copenhagen, but of course it is no evidence of the Russian attitude. In fact this explanation seems to have reversed the true order to the facts. If the French proposal was inspired by the Russians, it was due to Isvolsky's wish to have a word in the Straits question, which seemed to be coming up unavoidably. There is, however, no proof that the French were so inspired; on the contrary, they were very suspicious of Isvolsky. It seems, from what he said to the Germans, that Isvolsky would have preferred to leave this important question altogether out.

This explains the indifference which Isvolsky professed in regard to the problem of the demarcation of the seas. When Berlin informed St. Petersburg of the agreement with London that the Baltic commences where the North Sea ends, the Russians did not show any interest. They only said that they would accept anything that Germany accepted.[3] The Swedish Minister for Foreign Affairs Trolle complained to the British envoy that "some difficulty had been created by the attitude of Russia in expressing her entire indifference at the question of the limits to be assigned to the Baltic". When Rennell Rodd pointed out that this did not complicate but rather simplified the question, "M. de Trolle agreed that this should be so, but he appears now to have acquired a profound mistrust of M. Isvolsky. ."[4] — Apart from testifying to the nature of Isvolsky's image in Sweden, this report is clear evidence of Isvolsky's professed indifference. But this indifference was not very profound.

[1] AA Dänemark 37 geheim Bd 13 Pourtalès to Bülow 29. II 1908
[2] PRO/FO 371/528/10510 Johnstone to Grey 27. III 1908
[3] AVPR fond sekretnyj arhiv, delo 392/401
   n. 23 German Embassy to Russian F.O. 20. II 1908
   n. 24 Russian F. O. to German Embassy 23. II/7. III 1908
[4] PRO/FO 371/529/12298 Rennell Rodd to Grey 7. IV 1908

Isvolsky was in fact opposed to the said article in the North Sea memorandum, which defined the limitation of the seas. He complained to the Germans that it was too indefinite and might give the French an occasion to take up the question of the Straits. He would have preferred dropping the question altogether.[1] Isvolsky was afraid that the Straits question would be decided in the period of Russia's weakness, which had dictated his Danish policy since 1905. When Bompard actually hinted at an interpretation according to which the Straits would be included in the North Sea, Isvolsky reminded the Germans of his intention of insisting on Russia signing the North Sea Treaty in order *d'avoir voix au chapitre*.[2]

The Danes, too, frightened Isvolsky in this question. Raben tried to define the line of demarcation more exactly than the great powers, and said to Kudašev that he thought of a line running from Helsingör to Aarhus. Isvolsky was afraid that Germany had given up the hazy formula hitherto adhered to and that the whole of Kattegat was being left to the North Sea.[3] Even worse was the Danish idea of defining the limitation by the term "geographical". When Kudašev asked what Raben meant with his "strictly geometrical definition of the term *régions de la Mer Baltique*", Raben answered that *ce terme comprendrait l'exclusion des détroits*.[4] Thoroughly worried Isvolsky reminded the Germans that he had always wished to keep the Straits question out of discussion, and that Germany had promised to keep the other powers in check. If the signatories of the North Sea Agreement were to accept the Danish idea, the Straits question would be put out of the Russian sphere of influence.[5]

In this question Russian and German interests were still parallel. Schoen answered Isvolsky that Germany was never going to accept the Danish definition. The line of demarcation had been left undefined expressly because it would have caused too many difficulties. Now the question remained open until an eventual practical need would cause the powers to take it up again.[6]

But Isvolsky remained disturbed because the two Danish thrusts towards defining the line had threatened to leave Russia out of the game as regards the Kattegat and Skagerrak. A week before the signing of the agreements he once more warned the British that the areas named did not belong to the North Sea. He might later strive for an international arrangement concerning them. It would have been better if the demarcation line of the 1882 treaty could have

[1] AA Dänemark 37 geheim Bd 13 Pourtalès to Ausw. Amt 9. III 1908
[2] AA Dänemark 37 geheim Bd 14 Pourtalès to Bülow 19. III 1908
[3] AVPR fond sekretnyj arhiv, delo 381, n. 388
   Russian F.O. to German Embassy 24. III 1908
[4] AVPR fond sekretnyj arhiv, delo 381, n. 404 Kudašev to Isvolsky 28. III/10. IV 1908
[5] AVPR fond sekretnyj arhiv, delo 381, n. 410
   Russian F. O. to German Embassy 2. IV/15. IV 1908
[6] AVPR fond sekretnyj arhiv, delo 381, n. 413
   German Embassy to Russian F.O. 5./18 IV 1908

been used, but he understood that this was difficult, Sweden being a participant in the North Sea Agreement. "He was compelled to maintain that the international situation in respect to all the questions regarding the Straits would not be simplified after the signature of the new projected agreements." [1]

The scope of the Baltic agreement could be interpreted as defining Russia's sphere of interest in this direction. There was no reason for Isvolsky to accept a definition of the limitation of the seas which might be held as leaving the entrances to the Baltic beyond Russia's jurisdiction. The participation of Sweden in the North Sea declaration made this danger more threatening still. Isvolsky's "indifference", as expressed to the Swedes and Danes, masked a decision to leave the obnoxious definition out of the Baltic agreement, so that it could be discussed anew later, when Russia would be powerful again.

In spite of the unsatisfying definition, the possibility of a new international treaty was left open. It was no mere academic[2] interest that led Isvolsky to discuss the problem with Nicolson after the agreements had been signed. "He did not quite understand the wording of the North Sea Agreement .. the phraseology was vague, and did not necessarily include the straits, which were governed by international acts. He did not in any way wish to raise the question, and his remarks were merely academical, but he thought that it might be possible hereafter that there might be a variety of interpretations. The limits of the North Sea had been defined by a Convention in 1883 (1882?), and the straits did not come within the definition, while the Baltic, in the general acceptance of the term, did not certainly include the straits. It had been proposed to him in regard to the Baltic Arrangement that some similar phraseology should be employed, but he had declined to adopt it, as he considered the straits were a question apart, and being regulated by international Acts, could only be dealt with by the signatories of these acts."[3]

It seems clear that here Isvolsky wished to put on record the Russian point of view, so that in future it would not be possible to say that Russia had acquiesced in renouncing her right to have a say in the Straits question. He had not accepted the definition used in the North Sea arrangement in order not to be left out of the Straits; thus Russia could appeal to other international acts, which she had signed with other powers and which thereby gave her the right to participate in future decisions concerning this problem. The British did not understand what international acts Isvolsky was referring to. According to their view the only known act, that of 1857, concerned simply the freeing of shipping from the Danish Sound dues. But in fact it was this Treaty the Russians referred to; according to their view the Treaty abolished the Sound dues *and*

---

[1] AA Dänemark 37 geheim Bd 15 Pourtalès to Bülow 15. IV 1908
[2] nor mischievous, as Sweet says, p. 476.
[3] PRO/FO 371/529/14250 Nicolson to Grey 22. IV 1908

opened the Straits to unimpeded navigation for ships of all nations.[1]

Because the question never arose, we do not know how Isvolsky or his successors would have used the possibilities that remained open after 1908. Ultimately it was no treaty but the German navy that prevented Russia from having a say in the Straits question.

Polemic about Åland

The Baltic Agreement led to a discussion in the press of St. Petersburg which illuminates the attitude of the various Russian circles to the matter. The *Reč* of the Kadet party and the *Slovo* of the Octobrists were of the opinion that the Convention of 1856 was still in full force. The Agreement of 1908 had annulled the Treaty of 1855; but in 1856 Sweden was not at Paris, and because only signatories were able to alter their agreements, the Treaty of 1908 had altered nothing in the question of Åland. Sweden had recognized Russia's sovereignty, but this fact did not free Russia from obligations in regard to England and France.[2]

The *Novoe Vremja* generally defended the greatness of the Empire and had close relations with the Foreign Ministry. In some articles there are arguments nearly identical with the statements of Baron Taube (p. 234), and they may be regarded as attempts of the Foreign Office to account for their endeavours to the home public. The basis of *Novoe Vremja's* thesis was that the dissolution of the Scandinavian Union made the obligations lapse which had been made in the Union's favour. Therefore the declaration of 1908 could not have annulled the Treaty of 1855, which had already disappeared in 1906 (1905?). The Stockholm declaration only stated the fact of the situation. Now that the Treaty of 1855 had been nullified, there could not be a single piece left of the Convention of 1856, which had been concluded to complete the former Treaty. Did Russia have the right to fortify the Åland Islands? If England and France had been released from their obligations to defend Sweden, and if Sweden herself had no rights in regard to Åland — only the signatories of 1856 had these rights — there was no doubt of Russia's right to enjoy her full sovereignty.[3]

The *Reč* wrote: regrettably we are dealing with persons who in their pseudo-patriotism turn the facts and acts upside down.[4] Fortifying Åland was like levelling a gun at Sweden's head — it was nice to know that the gun was in the

---

[1] AVPR fond sekretnyj arhiv, delo 395/405
   n. 66 Memorandum on the question of the Danish Straits 14. IV 1905
   n. 89 *Rapport succinct sur la neutralisation du Danemark* 22. II 1909
[2] *Reč* 12/25 IV 1908
   Slovo 13/26 IV & 16/29 IV 1908
[3] *Novoe Vremja* 19. IV/2. V 1908
[4] *Reč* 16/29. IV 1908

hand of a friend (the *Novoe Vremja* had emphasized its friendly feeling towards Sweden) but it was much nicer if no gun were to be levelled at all.[1] *Slovo* remarked that too much fuss in this matter would only harm Russia, who had no reason to push her neighbour into Germany's arms, especially as the question was academic, for the *Novoe Vremja* had emphasized that Åland was not to be fortified in any case.

The *Novoe Vremja* stated that its opponent seemed to write in the capital of Sweden and not in that of Russia. The *Reč* and *Slovo* answered that common sense should be enough to enable one to understand the situation, but as the *Novoe Vremja* could neither understand it nor prove its standpoint, it now used the argument which had already been expected of it: its opponents were unpatriotic.[2] The *Novoe Vremja* answered that evidently the *Slovo* felt unpatriotic, because "we have not said so; we have spoken only of political blindness and juridical helplessness, to which is now added falsity".[3]

This polemic was remarkably voluble, here only the most essential arguments are presented. The papers continued to abuse each other without adding anything relevant, both parties naturally keeping their ground. *Novoe Vremja* tried to illuminate its standpoint by imagining what might happen if a war broke out: Russia would naturally fortify Åland to close the Gulf of Bothnia. Sweden would protest. If either Miljukov or Fedorov (leaders of the Kadets and Octobrists) became Russian Minister for Foreign Affairs, Russia would evidently desist from fortifying the Islands. But because God was still apparently protecting Russia, Miljukov and Fedorov were not ministers. Thus Russia would fortify and would answer Sweden that the situation was understandably unpleasant for her, but would equally ask by what right she made her protest. Hadn't she given up her right to protest in 1908? Now Miljukov or Fedorov would advise Sweden to appeal to the Treaty of 1856. But Russia had made that Treaty with England and France! Sweden ought to turn to London and Paris. If Miljukov and Fedorov had happened to be ministers in England and France, the Western powers would prevent Russia from fortifying. But the actual ministers would answer Sweden that in 1856 they had promised to defend the Union, which had disappeared in 1905. No help would be forthcoming, and the Convention of 1856 was irrevocably dead. Poor *Slovo* and *Reč* could not understand this; they gazed stupefied like fools at the fact that it had not been formally declared annulled.[4]

As a last phase the *Wiener Politischer Korrespondenz* published an article from "official St. Petersburg sources, which stated that the Scandinavian Union

[1] *Reč* 18. IV/1. V 1908
[2] *Reč* 19. IV/2. V 1908
  Slovo 20. IV/3. V 1908
[3] *Novoe Vremja* 27. IV/10. V 1908
[4] *Novoe Vremja* 25. IV/8. V 1908

had been dissolved and the Treaty of .1855 had been declared to have lapsed with it, but that discussion was continuing as to the validity of the Convention of 1856. But the matter was easily solved: because France and England had been freed from the obligations of the Treaty of 1855 to defend the Union, they had been freed also from the Convention of 1856, which had been made to fulfil these obligations. Thus Russia was fully entitled to enjoy her sovereign rights on Åland, although the Paris Convention was formally yet not annulled. The polemic was unnecessary, and Russia knew very well what she must do in the future to carry the matter to conclusion.[1] — So the "official" view was very nearly identical with that of the *Novoe Vremja*'s. But both had had to admit, as the *Reč* pointed out, that formally the Convention was not abrogated, and Russia had still to do something in this question, before she had the right to fortify the Islands.[2]

Afterwards, in 1913 Baron Taube tried to maintain the standpoint which the *Novoe Vremja* had presented: the servitude could not be juridically valid because its political foundations had disappeared. The guarantee to Sweden by several powers in 1908 had changed the situation so completely that Russia had no reason to refrain from erecting any military or naval establishment (a base for aerial observation was in question) in Åland. But Taube had to admit that formally the Convention of 1856 had not been abrogated and that the Western powers might protest platonically.[3]

Taube had been active in making the Baltic agreement of 1908, and it is possible that he tried to interpret the result of his exertions as more favourable to Russia than in fact was the case. Another official of the Foreign Ministry, Baron Nolde, wrote a memorandum, too, in which he said that the Åland Convention was still in full force. The political situation had very much changed since the year 1856, but political changes had no importance juridically, and certainly not from the point of view of Åland's neutralization. Nor had the Agreements of 1908 any effect on the Convention of 1856, Nolde added. It was true that in the Baltic Agreement it was stated that the Agreement did not restrict Russia's sovereign rights, and it had been necessary to state this in order not to incorporate the servitude in the status quo which was confirmed in 1908. But the Agreement could not be used to even prove that Sweden might have given up the neutralization of Åland. Because she had never had any juridical relation in regard to the Convention concerning the status of the archipelago, she could not have given up any such rights in 1908. The prohibition on fortifying the Åland Islands remained therefore, concluded Nolde, in full force.[4]

[1] *Wiener Politischer Korrespondenz* 15. V 1908
[2] *Reč* 6/19 V 1908
[3] AVPR fond sekretnyj arhiv, delo 383/390 n. 16/19 a memorandum by Taube 20. XI 1913
[4] AVPR fond sekretnyj arhiv, delo 383/390 n. 21 a memorandum by Nolde 4. III 1914

Isvolsky had completely failed in his quest for this feather in his cap.

These feelings were reflected in a wrangle concerning decorations. Isvolsky was given, in spite of Brändström's protests, the highest Swedish Order of the Seraphin, but Trolle got only the Russian third, Alexander Nevsky, and that without brilliants.[1]

In 1909 the *Novoe Vremja* frightened the Swedes by reminding them that Russia wished to fortify the Islands in order to defend herself against a powerful Germany.[2] When Isvolsky visited Sweden in 1909 on his journey to Western Europe, he could not help speaking of Russian difficulties with the smugglers of arms. "Russia could not continue for an indefinite time to consent to a diminution of her sovereign rights." When the Swedes remonstrated and remarked that "this would be a step backward in the relations between the two countries", Isvolsky promised not to take up the question in the West without previously informing Sweden.[3] This gave occasion for the Swedes to repeat to the British the well-known sentence: ". . . if England and France do not continue their resistance to Russia's demands, Sweden will have to turn elsewhere".[4]

— It is probable that Isvolsky did not really intend to take up the question but only wished to recall that it was still open in order not to give the impression that Russia had abandoned her position. Isvolsky lost much of his fame in the Bosnian crisis; when a vacancy occurred in Paris in 1910, after Nelidoff left the Embassy, Isvolsky was moved there from the office of Foreign Minister. After that the Åland question was not taken up publicly, and nothing happened in Åland until the Great War came.

Appraisal

The conclusion of the negotiations and the signing of the agreements did not cause very much comment. The diplomats had expressed their views on the matter so many times during the endless discussions that there was little left to be said.

Schoen estimated his own work thus: "The value of the declarations must not be exaggerated, but they were useful to Germany because they reassured both participants and outsiders, and because they diminished the fear of Germany in the neighbouring countries. Regardless of the content of the agreements it was important that Germany had succeeded in concluding them, especially with

[1] AA Russland 63 Bd 3 Jacobi to Bülow 18. V 1908
[2] *Novoe Vremja* 3/16 & 4/17 1909
[3] Hildebrand p. 564—
[4] PRO/FO 371/745/29656 Spring-Rice to Grey 3. VIII 1909

England and France." [1] Reports from the Hague and Copenhague also underlined the reassuring effect of the declarations.[2] Everybody was unanimous in
that "their importance was not be exaggerated", but, as Trolle remarked, a few
years earlier it would have been impossible to carry to a succesful conclusion so
large a complex of agreements between the European powers.[3] Nobody dared
say that the agreements had any value in themselves, or that they would have
solved any problems.

The tone of the comments of the press, as reported by the diplomatists, was
similar. The agreements were not regarded as remarkably important, but they
were greeted as signs of a general will for peace and as indicating a calming
down of the general political situation since the crises of the previous years.
The small countries around Germany were reassured about the benevolence of
their mighty neighbour. The North Sea Agreement in particular was greeted as
the first sign that Germany and the Entente powers were getting closer to each
other.[4] In Denmark the conservative *Vort Land* deplored Danish resignation in
the status quo of Southern Jutland, and the radical *Politiken* stated that the
guarantee of status quo made armaments superfluous[5] — two examples of the
influence of partiality on the appraisal. The Swedish press was satisfied with
the proof of the will for peace, with the fact that small states had been accepted
as signatories to the treaties on an equal footing with the great ones, with the
fact that the Covention of 1856 had not been upset, and with the fact that
Norway had been left out.[6]

There were some critical comments, too. *The Standard* stated that it was a
diplomatic triumph for Germany to have succeeded in keeping Great Britain
out of the Baltic, and the *Daily Graphic* deplored this fact, which did not
correspond with political reality, the Baltic and North Sea questions being
inseprable.[7] The radical *Berliner Tageblatt* was "rather inclined to mock at the
importance of the whole thing. On the whole, the Agreements produce a pleasant impression, and any one may rejoice at their conclusion; but it asked why it

---

[1] GP 23 II n. 8154 Schoen to William II 13. IV 1908
[2] GP 23 II n. 8158 German envoy in the Hague to Bülow 30. IV 1908
   Herre p. 132
[3] Hildebrand p. 550
[4] AVPR fond sekretnyj arhiv, delo 384, n. 12 & 13 Osten-Sacken to Isvolsky 18. IV/1.
   V 1908
   HHStA/SVA n. 318 Szögyeny to Aehrenthal 28. IV 1908
   GP 23 II n. 8157 Stumm to Bülow 30. IV 1908
[5] AVPR fond sekretnyj arhiv, delo 384, n. 10 Kudašev to Isvolsky 14/27 IV 1908
[6] AVPR fond Kanceljarija 1908 g., delo 124, n. 11 Budberg to Isvolsky 15/28 IV 1908
[7] AA Dänemark 37 geheim Bd 16 Stumm to Bülow 27. IV 1908

should have taken the diplomatists of seven nations so long to arrive at a draft satisfactory to all parties in a matter apparently so simple".[1] In 1912 Hanotaux jeered at the whole string of declarations of status quo and treaties of arbitration, where the powers by solemn words manifested their will to keep what they had.[2]

Stumm's conclusion of the attitude of the British press might serve as a balance: "World peace is not built on the foundation of paper agreements, but these declarations cannot cause any harm." [3]

Almost immediately after its conclusion, the Baltic question was buried in the archives and there it has rested, its documents gathering dust, disturbed only by some historians in "their desperate search for a theme of a thesis". Only a few of the participants have bothered to mention the question in their memoirs; only the most thorough textbooks devote a couple of sentences to it.

[1] PRO/FO 371/529/15131 Lascelles to Grey 27. IV 1908
[2] Hanotaux p. 126—
[3] AA Dänemark 37 geheim Bd 16 Stumm to Bülow 27. IV 1908

CONCLUSION

"Since the days of Lord Nelson it has been the policy of the British Navy to strike first and strike at once, not to wait to be attacked. In the event of a naval war with Germany or Russia it is therefore of cardinal importance that the British fleet should have free access to the Baltic, and the question of the passage of the Sound and the Belts has always been of the greatest interest to this country." [1] The course of time had changed many aspects of the question since the days of Lord Nelson, but in the story narrated here it has become evident that the question of the Danish Straits was, indeed, the central aspect of the Baltic question, which affected all the other aspects.

The Baltic or the Northern question was, for Great Britain, the problem of maintaining British influence in the Baltic and the Northern countries. The growth of the German might, the dislocation of the Baltic balance of power, and the dissolution of the Scandinavian Union made it impossible for the British to preserve a dominant position in the whole of Northern Europe. But Great Britain succeeded in keeping the opposite coast, the most important spot, clean of hostile influences. In spite of the threats in the years 1905—1907 of turning to Germany Norwas's vital interests remained directed to the West, and in 1914—1918 she was Britain's "neutral ally". In theory British influence was felt in the Baltic, too. It was unsatisfactory that Britain had been left out of the Baltic Treaty, but the Convention of 1856 gave her still a juridical right to have a say in Baltic matters. But no theoretical juridical right could have compensated for German naval might, and the Foreign Office was more discerning than the Admiralty in realizing that in case of war Great Britain could not force the Straits and that Denmark had to be abandoned to her fate. Therefore it was important to keep Norway in hand in case of an emergency. It was a hopeless attempt to try to keep Norway and Sweden together and both attached to Great Britain. Unwilling to choose, the British resorted to their policy of "wait and see", thereby giving the Norwegians the chance to bungle the question of the treaty of guarantee. This in turn gave Russia an opportunity to contribute to making the Scandinavians irreconcilable for many years.

Germany wanted to defend her Baltic coast in the Danish Straits. This aim was not attainable by normal diplomatic means, which could not be used for fear of an eventual British reaction. But the Germans were satisfied that the informal discussions and words of honour between the military leaders were enough. They were not very much interested in Scandinavia, leaving Norway under British influence and acting the role of honest broker in Sweden. The story of Swedish neutrality before and during World War I is not part of the Baltic question proper. It was not until the new phase of Russification in

[1] PRO/FO 371/529/15693 *Memorandum respecting the passages into the Baltic Sea,* May 6, 1908

Finland and the cooling down of Russo-German relations that some attempts were made to get Sweden closer to Germany.[1] But in the end Sweden as well as Denmark decided to keep to neutrality.

The Baltic question, once the Straits seemed to be secured, was important for Germany only as far as it offered opportunities for co-operation with Russia and/or England. Russia was not trusted, in spite of all monarchical solidarity, especially after Isvolsky had concluded the Asian agreement with Great Britain. Isvolsky's eagerness to co-operate with Germany was interpreted as a wish to take advantage of her in the Åland operation, and eventually to compromise her in British eyes. The attempt to separate England from France with the North Sea agreement failed, and estranged Russia. But perhaps its couclusion brought some goodwill and prestige to Germany.

Russia preferred to keep the Straits open. An exception was the Czar Nicholas who, under William's influence, apprehended a Japanese or British attack through the Baltic. Isvolsky's plans to close the Straits were no exception. He only understood that after defeat and revolution Russia had no means of realizing her preference and of preventing Germany from closing the Straits. And Isvolsky wanted further to show agreement with Germany in some question, in order to reinsure Russia against German jealousy born from the Russo-British Asian arrangement; and he hoped to gain German support for his plans in the Balkans and the Turkish Straits. Russia rejoiced at the Scandinavian quarrel, and did her best to weaken a hostile Sweden by isolating her from Norway and Great Britain. But just as the good-will she won in Norway was not enough to eliminate British influence, so, too, what chances Russia had in Sweden Isvolsky spoiled with his unsuccesful Åland operation. Traditional fear of Russia and cultural ties drew Sweden towards Germany, but not enough to make her give up her neutrality in the end.

It was the German might in the Baltic and the British might in the Atlantic which the Baltic states had to reckon with during the years 1914—1918. The Central powers were able to close both the passageways which had connected Russia with the rest of the world. The Scandinavian countries were economically dependent on their transoceanic imports. Therefore England held a sway over them which more than compensated for the geographical closeness of German influence.

France was not so immediately interested in the Baltic question as the other three powers, only so far as this question affected the system of alliances. The French envoys in the Northern capitals were naturally more immediately interested in the local aspect of the question, but the Government in Paris was apt to leave the details to the British. In the beginning the French, as well as the

---

[1] Lindberg: *Svensk-Tyska generalstabsförhandlingarna.*. Carlgren: *Neutralität oder Allianz.*.

British, had hoped that the Baltic question would draw the members of the Entente closer to each other. Isvolsky's double game in the Baltic led to the unexpected result that the British had to patch up the relations of the French and the Russians. The French had a powerful weapon in their financial might, but nevertheless for a long time they were apprehensive *propter trahison russe*. Even small signs of Russo-German co-operation were seen as a new Björkö.[1]

In spite of the co-operation of Isvolsky and Schoen the Baltic question did not lead to the *grand tournant* which the French feared. Isvolsky was not able to master all complications of his political game, which was, however, an interesting example of Russian attempts to balance between the Entente and the Central powers.

Austria and Italy were not interested in the Baltic question, for natural reasons.

To repeat, the Danish Straits were the underlaying, dominant theme of the Baltic policy of every participating power. That this was not openly mentioned every time was due to the delicacy and danger of the question. The most unimportant and uninteresting aspects, the Norwegian Treaty of Integrity and the Convention of Åland, caused the greatest production of documents. This fact has led previous students of the Baltic question to ignore the Straits and to concentrate on the other aspects, which were closer to their respective countries. The Baltic question was not a dominant problem of world politics; it did not dictate the relations of the The Great Powers to each other, as for instance the rivalry in the Balkans influenced Russo-Austrian relations. In a way this means that the diplomatists were succesful in dealing with the Baltic question.

The Baltic and North Sea declarations had no real point, nor had the Norwegian Treaty of Integrity much more. Why should the various countries promise to maintain their possessions when it is a notorious fact that no state has ever given up its territories voluntarily? And if they were forced to cede their provinces, how could a paper pledge not to do so help them? The importance of the Baltic question cannot be measured by the documents which were the result of the long negotiations that went on about it. The diplomatists used all their ability to formulate the treaties so that they did not touch on any point at which the interests of the powers were really involved and, consequently, opposed to each other. Examples abound: the neutrality of Norway, the demarcation of the Baltic and North Sea, the status of Åland were put off to be discussed anew later when they could not ultimately be avoided any more. The powers were able to reach unanimity and to sign treaties because these were void of any content.

The diplomatist were left to deal with the Baltic question without disturbance by the *forces profondes* for the very reason that they succeeded in avoiding the

---

[1] DDF 12 n. 229 Touchard to Pichon 22. VI 1909

real problems. The projects that made one power afraid of another were in fact never very seriously intended, for instance the Russian base in Norway.[1] Even the freedom of the Danish Straits was an academic question because of the German naval might, as Isvolsky and the British Foreign Office realized. The vital interests of the great powers were not involved in the Baltic question, and therefore no one had any reason to raise a public hue and cry. That is also the reason why this question has not been accorded more lines in the textbooks of history: the potentially interesting questions never saw the light of day. On the whole the status quo was maintained, and maintaining the status quo does not make exciting history. There were exceptions: Swedo-Norwegian relations excited opinion in both countries, as did the Åland question on Sweden. In both cases we saw that the diplomatists were quite powerless to lead policy against the irrational outburst of national feelings.

But in general, in spite of the dissolution of the Scandinavian Union, the situation was not so labile as it was, for instance, in the Balkans. The Northern states were one thousand years old, without aggressive nationalistic aspirations. The spheres of interest and influence of the great powers were comparatively firmly established, and there was no immediate threat to vital interests nor a chance of easy victory alluring them to rash action. The great powers only tried to ensure that they had their hands free for eventual action, should the need arise, unhampered by the various agreements under discussion.

[1] Remark by G. Maude 1974

16

SOURCES

AA AUSWÄRTIGES AMT. POLITISCHES ARCHIV, ABT. I A

Europa generalia 88 Die Verbindung der Ostsee mit der Nordsee
Deutschland 131 geheim Die Verhältnis Deutschlands zu Russland
Deutschland 131 n:o 4 Deutsch-russische Verhandlungen über Abkommen anlässlich des russisch-japanischen Krieges
Deutschland 136 Die Beziehungen zwischen Deutschland und Schweden
Deutschland 137 Allgemeine deutsche Politik
Deutschland 148 geheim Verhandlungen mit England wegen Abschluss eines Allianzvertrages zwischen Deutschland und England
Deutschland 165 Herbeiführung einer Annäherung in gewissen Fragen unter den Continentalmächten Deutschland, Italien, Russland und Frankreich gegenüber England
Dänemark 27 geheim Die Beziehungen Deutschlands zu Dänemark
Dänemark 27 Die Beziehungen Deutschlands zu Dänemark
Dänemark 37 geheim Die Neutralität Dänemarks und der Schutz der Ostsee
Dänemark 38 Die Beziehungen Dänemarks zu Schweden
Dänemark 43 Die Beziehungen Dänemarks zu Russland
Dänemark 44 Die Beziehungen Dänemarks zu England
England 78 secretissima Die Beziehungen Deutschlands zu England
England 83 geheim Die Beziehungen Englands zu Russland
England 93 Die auswärtige Politik Englands
Norwegen 4 Die Beziehungen Norwegens zu Schweden
Norwegen 4 geheim Die Beziehungen Norwegens zu Schweden
Norwegen 7 geheim Verhandlungen über Unabhängigkeit und Integrität Norwegens
Norwegen 10 Die Beziehungen Norwegens zu Russland
Norwegen 12 Die Beziehungen Norwegens zu England
Russland 63 Die Aalandsinseln
Russland 98 Der Deutsche Militärbevollmächtigter in Petersburg und seine Berichterstattung
Schweden 45 Die Beziehungen Schweden zu Russland
Schweden 56 Die Stellung Schweden-Norwegens im Falle eines Krieges. Neutralitätsfrage
Schweden 57 Die Beziehungen Schwedens zu England

PRO PUBLIC RECORD OFFICE

PRO/CAB 2 Minutes of the Committee of Imperial Defence
PRO/CAB 4 Memoranda, Miscellaneous (CID)
PRO/CAB 37/ 74—96 Cabinet Papers 1905—1908

PRO/FO Foreign Office, General Correspondence
PRO/FO 22/578 Denmark 1904 Diplomatic
PRO/FO 22/584 Denmark 1905 Diplomatic
PRO/FO 22/585 Denmark 1905 Diplomatic
PRO/FO 73/649 Sweden—Norway 1905 Diplomatic
PRO/FO 73/650 Sweden—Norway 1905 Diplomatic
PRO/FO 73/651 Sweden—Norway 1905 Diplomatic
PRO/FO 73/652 Sweden—Norway 1905 Diplomatic
PRO/FO 73/654 Sweden—Norway 1905 Diplomatic
PRO/FO 109/1 Norway 1905 Diplomatic, Consular, Commercial, Treaty
PRO/FO 181/857 Russia 1905 Diplomatic

PRO/FO Foreign Office, Political Correspondence
PRO/FO 371/57 Denmark 1906
PRO/FO 371/98 Norway 1906
PRO/FO 371/125 Russia 1906
PRO/FO 371/242 Denmark 1907
PRO/FO 371/243 Denmark 1907
PRO/FO 371/295 Norway 1907
PRO/FO 371/261 Germany 1907
PRO/FO 371/296 Norway 1907
PRO/FO 371/297 Norway 1907
PRO/FO 371/326 Russia 1907
PRO/FO 371/338 Sweden 1907
PRO/FO 371/447 Denmark 1908
PRO/FO 371/491 Norway 1908
PRO/FO 371/527 Sweden 1908
PRO/FO 371/528 Sweden 1908
PRO/FO 371/529 Sweden 1908
PRO/FO 371/745 Sweden 1909
PRO/FO 371/980 Russia 1910
PRO/FO 371/1218 Russia 1911
PRO/FO 371/1478 Sweden 1912

HHStA
HAUS-, HOF- UND STAATSARCHIV, WIEN
Ministerium des Äusseren
Politisches Archiv
"Frage der Behandlung der Ostsee im Kriegsfalle und Absicht, Fortifikationsverbot auf den Alands-Inseln aufzuheben (Nordsee-Uebereinkommen)"
(Xerocopies in Suomen Valtionarkisto, National Archives of Finland, SVA "Itävallan Valtionarkisto", box 5)

АВПР АРХИВ ВНЕШНЕЙ ПОЛИТИКИ РОССИИ

(Историко-дипл. Управл. МИД СССР)

фонд канцелярия министра

1905 г дело	24	(Christiania)
	дело	35	(Copenhagen)
	дело	111	(Stockholm)
1906 г дело	34	(Christiania)
	дело	44	(Copenhagen)
	дело	128	(Stockholm)
1907 г дело	25	(Christiania)
	дело	36	(Copenhagen)
	дело	118	(Stockholm)
1908 г дело	27	(Christiania)
		33	(Copenhagen)
		124	(Stockholm)

фонд секретный архив министра

дело	262/263	(Swinemünde)
дело	380	(Baltic question 1907)
дело	381	(Baltic question, Danish point of view)
дело	383/390	(Aland question 1908—1914)
дело	384	(Newspaper cuttings)
дело	392/402	(Aland question, Russian point of view)
дело	393/402	(Aland question, Swedish point of view)
дело	394/403	(Aland question, point of view of Great Powers)
дело	395/405	(Danish neutrality)

PRINTED DOCUMENTS

BD *British Documents on the Origins of the War,* 1898—1914ed. by G.P. Gooch and Harold Temperley
Vol 3. *The Testing of the Entente 1904—1906.* London 1928
Vol 4. *The Anglo-Russian Rapprochement 1903—1907.* London 1929
Vol 5. *The Near East 1903—1909.* London 1928
Vol 6. *Anglo-German Tension 1907—1912.* London 1930
Vol 7. *The Agadir Crisis.* London 1932
Vol 8. *Arbitration, Neutrality and Security.* London 1932

DDF *Documents diplomatiques français 1871—1914*
2e série 1901—1911
Ministère des affaires étrangères
Comission de publication des documents relatifs aux origines de la guerre de 1914
tome 5. 9. IV—31. XII 1904. Paris 1934
tome 6. 2. I—6. VI 1905. Paris 1935
tome 7. 7. VI—28. IX 1905. Paris 1937
tome 8. 29. IX 1905—15. I 1906. Paris 1938
tome 9. I 16. I—1. III 1906. Paris 1946
tome 9. II 2. III—7. IV 1906. Paris 1946
tome 10 10. IV 1906—16. V 1907. Paris 1948
tome 11 15. V 1907—8. II 1909. Paris 1950
tome 12 9. II 1909—26. X 1910. Paris 1954

GP *Die Grosse Politik de Europäischen Kabinette* 1871—1914 Sammlung der Diplomatischen Akten der Auswärtigen Amtes
Im Auftrage des Auswärtigen Amtes herausgegeben von Johannes Lepsius, Albrecht Mendelssohn Bartholdy und Friedrich Thimme
Bd 19 I—II *Der Russisch-Japanische Krieg.* Berlin 1925
Bd 22 *Die Österreich-Russische Entente und der Balkan.* Berlin 1925
Bd 23 II*Die Zweite Haager Friedenskonferenz, Nordsee- und Ostseeabkommen.* Berlin 1925
Bd 25 *Die Englisch-Russische Entente und der Ostsee.* Berlin 1925

Fink: *Spillet . .*
Troels Fink: *Spillet om dansk neutralitet 1905—1909* L. C. F. Lütken og dansk udenriks- of forsvarspolitik (Skrifter udgivet af Jysk selskab for historie, sprog og literatur 6) Aarhus 1959

Fisher
Fisher of Kilverstone: *Fear God and Dread Nought* The Correspondence of Admiral of the Fleet Lord Fischer of Kilverstone. Selected and Edited by Arthur J Marder London 1953

Holstein
Die geheimen Papiere Friedrich von Holsteins Herausgegeben von Norman Rich und M. H. Fischer, Deutsche Ausgabe von Werner Frauendienst Bd IV Briefwechsel 10. Januar 1897 bis 8. Mai 1909. Berlin-Frankfurt 1963

Isvolsky: *Au service. .*
Alexandre Isvolsky: *Au service de la Russie*
Correspondance diplomatique Recueillie par Hélène Isvolsky Introduction et notes de Georges Chklaver. Paris 1937

Omang
Reidar Omang: *Norge og stormaktene 1906—1914* vol I 1906—1907 (Skrifter utg. av det kgl. utenriksdep. arkiv 3). 1957

Siebert
> *Graf Benckendorffs Diplomatischer Schriftwechsel* Herausgegehen von B. von Siebert
> Neue stark vermehrte Auflage der Diplomatischen Aktenstücken zur Geschichte der
> Ententepolitik der Vorkriegsjahre Bd I 1907—1910. Berlin und Leipzig 1928

Государственная Дума
> Третий созывъ
> Стенографические отчеты 1907—1908 гг
> сессия первая 1—3 С. Петербургъ 1908

Красный Архив
> Исторический журнал Том 2—3/1935 (69—70) Москва 1935

Похлебкин
> *Признание Россией норвежского независимого государства*
> Сборник документов
> Составитель кандидат исторических наук В. В. Похлебкин

BIBLIOGRAPHY

Adams Charles E. Der Wiederaufstieg der russischen Kriegsmarine in den Jahren 1905—1914 (deutsch: Joachim Röscher). *Marine Rundschau* 1/1964

Albertini Luigi. *The Origins of the War of 1914.* transl. & ed. by Isabella Massey. Vol. I The European relations from the Congress of Berlin to the eve of the Sarajevo Murder. Oxford 1965

Annuaire diplomatique de l'Empire de Russie pour l'année 1906. St. Petersbourg 1906

Annuaire diplomatique de l'Empire de Russie pour l'année 1907. St. Petersbourg 1907

Annuaire diplomatique de l'Empire de Russie pour l'année 1908. St. Petersbourg 1908

Apunen Osmo. *Suomi keisarillisen Saksan politiikassa 1914—1915.* Mit einer deutschen Zusammenfassung: Finnland in der deutschen Politik der Jahre 1914—1915. Helsinki 1968

Assmann Kurt. Deutsche Seestrategien in zwei Weltkriegen. *(Die Wehrmacht im Kampf, Bd 12 II/1957).* Heidelberg 1957

Barros James. *The Aland Islands Question.* Its Settlement by the League of Nations. New Haven and London 1968

Biörklund E. Det ryska anfallsföretaget mot Sverige år 1914. Nya dokument om det kritiska läget under de första augustidagarna *(Svensk tidskrift* 1936 p. 213—255) Uppsala 1936

Bompard Maurice. *Mon ambassade en Russie 1903—1908.* Paris 1937

Bourgeois Émile. *Manuel historique de politique etrangere.* tome IV. La politique mondiale (1878—1919) Empires et nations. Paris 1926

Branting, Hjalmar. *Tal och skrifter V.* Svensk Försvars- och fredspolitik. Stockholm 1927

"Britannicus" The Northern Question *(The North American Review,* August 1908 pp. 237—247)

Bülow Bernhard (Fürst von) *Denkwürdigkeiten.* Zweiter Band: Von der Marokko-Krise bis zum Abschied. Berlin 1930

Carlgren W. M. *Isvolsky und Aehrenthal.* Russische und österreich-ungarische Balkanpolitik 1906—1908. Uppsala 1955

Carlgren W. M. *Neutralität oder Allianz.* Deutschlands Beziehungen zu Schweden in den Anfangsjahren des ersten Weltkrieges (Acta Universitatis Stockholmiensis, Stockholm Studies in history 6) Uppsala 1962

Carlsson Sten. Försvars- och utrikespolitik i stormaktsalliansernas skugga 1905—1914 *(Den Svenska Historien 9* Industri och folkrörelser) Stockholm 1968

Colban Erik. *Stortinget og utenrikspolitikken.* Oslo 1961

Danielsen Egil. *Norges utenrikspolitikk ovanfor Sovjetunionen 1914—1940.* Oslo 1964

Dockrill see Lowe

Duroselle J. B. L'Europe de 1815 à nos jours. Vie politique et relations internationales *"Nouvelle Clio" n. 38.* Paris 1964

Eckardt Hans von. *Russland* (Provinzen der Weltwirtschaft und Weltpolitik) Leipzig 1930

Emeljanoff Nikolaj. *Rysslands framträngande till Atlanten och de Rysk-Svenska relationernas framtid.* Svar på "ett varningsord" af Sven Hedin. Helsingfors 1915

Emeljanoff N. B. *Existerar den "Ryska faran"?* Stockholm 1916

Eskola Seikko. *Suomen kysymys ja Ruotsin mielipide.* Ensimmäisen maailmansodan puhkeamisesta Venäjän maaliskuun vallankumoukseen. With an English Summary Helsinki 1965

Eyck Erich. *Das persönliche Regiment Wilhelms II.* Politische Geschichte des Deutschen Kaiserreichs von 1890 bis 1914. Erlenbach-Zürich 1948

Fahlbeck Pontus. *Svensk och Nordisk utrikespolitik.* Stockholm 1912

Fast Bertil. *Stormakterna och Norden*. Politiska och militära relationer under fyra decennier. Lund 1942

Fay Sidney Bradshaw. *The Origins of the World War*. Vol. I Before Sarajevo: Underlying causes of the War. New York 1929

Fink Troels. *Deutschland als Problem Dänemarks*. Die geschichtlichen Voraussetzungen der dänischen Aussenpolitik (Die Deutsch-Dänischen Bücher 2) Flensburg 1968

Fink Troels *Spillet*. . see printed documents

Fink Troels. *Ustabil balance*. Dansk udenrigs- og førsvarspolitik 1894—1905 (Skrifter udgivet af Jysk selskab for historie, sprog og literatur 9) Aarhus 1961

Fischer Fritz. *Griff nach der Weltmacht*. Die Kriegszielpolitik der kaiserlichen Deutschland 1914/18. Düsseldorf 1961

Fischer Fritz. *Krieg der Illusionen*. Die deutsche Politik von 1911 bis 1914. Düsseldorf 1969

Friedjung Heinrich. *Das Zeitalter des Imperialismus 1884—1914 III*. Berlin 1922

Futrell Michael. *Northern Underground*. Episodes of Russian Revolutionary Transport and Communications through Scandinavia and Finland 1863—1917. London 1963

Gihl Torsten. *Den svenska utrikespolitikens historia 4* (1914—1919) Stockholm 1951

Gjerløv Olaf. *Norges politiske historie*. Høires innsats fra 1814 til idag I—II. Oslo 1934—1935

Gregerer René. *Die Russische Flotte im ersten Weltkrieg 1914—1917*. München 1970

Goriainov Serge. *Le Bosphore et les Dardanelles*. Etude historique sur la question des detroits. D'aprés la correspondance diplomatique déposée aux Archives centrales de Saint-Pétersbourg et à celles de l'Empire. Préface de m. Gabriel Hanotaux. Paris 1910

Grey of Fallodon (Viscount) *Twenty-five years* 1892—1916 vol I. London 1925

Günter Ernst. *Minnen* från ministertiden i Kristiania åren 1905—1908. Stockholm 1923

Haberman Wilhelm (= Öhquist Johannes) *Åland*. Schwedische Stimmen über die militärpolitische Bedeutung der finnischen Inselgruppe. Altenburg 1916

Hanotaux Gabriel. *La politique de l'équilibre 1907—1911*. Deuxieme édition. Paris 1912

Hardinge of Penshurst (Lord) Reminiscences. *"Old Diplomacy"*. London 1947

Hassel Ulrich von. Tirpitz' aussenpolitische Gedankenwelt *(Berliner Monatshefte*, April 1939)

Hauser M. Henri see Renouvin

Hauser Oswald. *Deutschland und der englisch-russische Gegensatz 1900—1914* (Göttinger Bausteine zur Geschichtswissenschaft 30) Göttingen-Berlin-Frankfurt 1958

Herre Paul. *Die kleinen Staaten Europas und die Entstehung des Weltkrieges*. München

Hildebrand Karl. *Gustaf V* som människa och regent. Kronprinstiden och de första kungaåren. Unionskrisen och utrikespolitik. Malmö 1945

Holborn Hajo. Russia and the European political System (see Lederer: *Russian foreign.* .)

Hubatsch Walther. *Der Admiralstab un die obersten Mainebehörden in Deutschland 1848—1945*. Wiesbaden 1958

Hubatsch Walther. *Die Ära Tirpitz*. Studien zur deutschen Marinepolitik 1890—1918 (Göttinger Bausteine zur Geschichtwissenschaft 21) Göttingen 1955

Høyer Liv Nansen. *Eva og Fridtjof Nansen*. Oslo 1954

Isvolsky: *Au service*. . see printed documents

Isvolsky Alexandre (ancien ambassadeur de Russie à Paris 1906—1910), *Mémoires* Pré face de M. Gabriel Hanotaux. Paris 1923

Jungar Sune. *Ryssland och den Svensk-Norska unionens upplösning*. Tsardiplomatı och rysk-finländsk pressopinion kring unionsupplösningen från 1880 till 1905 (Acta academiae Aboensis ser. A, Humaniora vol 37 nr 3) Åbo 1960

Kruck Alfred. *Geschichte des Alldeutschen Verbandes* (Veröffentlichungen des Instituts für europäische Geschichte Mainz, 3) 1954

Lagercrantz Herman. *I skilda världar*. Herman Lagercrantz berättar om sina minnen. Stockholm 1944

Lambsdorff Gustaf (Graf von, Generalleutnant a.D.) *Die Militärbevollmächtigten Kaiser Wilhelms II am Zarenhofe 1904—1914*. Greifswald 1937

Lederer Ivo J. Russia and the Balkans see Lederer: *Russian*. .

Lederer Ivo J ed. *Russian Foreign Policy*. Essays in Historical Perspective. Binghamton N. Y. 1962

Lee Sir Sidney. *King Edward VII*. a Biography. Vol II. The Reign (22nd January 1901 to 6th May 1910) London 1927

Lindberg Folke. Bakom borggårdskrisen. Tyskland föreslår militär konvention med Sverige 1910 *(Dagens Nyheter 11. VIII 1954)*

Lindberg Folke. Sverige i tysk politik 1905—1914 (Summary of a lecture published in *"Pohjoismainen historiantutkijain kongressi Turussa 1955"*, Turku 1955)

Lindberg Folke. De svensk-tyska generalstabsförhandlingarna år 1910 *(Historisk Tidskrift 1957)*

Lindberg Folke. *Scandinavia in Great Power Politics 1905—1908* (Acta universitatis stockholmiensis, Stockholm Studies in History I) Stockholm 1958

Lindberg Folke. *Den svenska utrikespolitikens historia III: 4* 1872—1914. Stockholm 1958

Lindberg Folke. *Kunglig utrikespolitik*. Stockholm 1966

Lowe C. J. and Dockrill M. L. *The Mirage of Power*. British Foreign Policy. Vols. 1—3 London-Boston 1972

Løvland J. *Menn og minner* fra 1905 av statsminister J. Løvlands papier utgitt av Torkell J. Løvland. Oslo 1929

Marder Arthur J. *From the Dreadnought to Scapa Flow*. The Royal Navy in the Fisher era 1904—1919 vols. I—V. London 1961—1965

Martens F. de. La neutralisation du Danemark *(Revue de Deux Mondes* 15. XI 1903, LXXIIIe annee, V periode, t. 18 II, Paris)

Maseng Einar. *1905 og 1940. En leksjon i maktpolitik*. Oslo 1953

Maseng Einar. *Utsikt over de nord-europeiska staters utenrikspolitikk i de siste århundrer* Del II Nasjonalismens århundre 1800-tallet. Oslo 1967

Maude George. *Finland and Britain 1854—1914* (Univ. of London Ph. D. thesis) 1970

Maude George. Finland in Anglo-Russian relations 1899—1910 *(The Slavonic and East European Review*, October 1970)

Michon Georges. *L'alliance franco-russe 1891—1917*. Contributions nouvelles. Paris 1931

Moltke Generaloberst Helmuth von. *Erinnerungen Briefe Dokumente 1877—1916*. Ein Bild von Kriegsausbruch, erster Kriegsführung und Persönlichkeit des ersten militärischen Führers des Krieges. Herausgegeben und mit einem Vorwort versehen von Eliza von Moltke. Stuttgart 1922

Monger George. *The End of Isolation*. British Foreign Policy 1900—1907. 1963

Moorehead Alan. *Gallipoli*. New York 1955

Müller Günther. *Die Schliessung der Ostsee* (sogenannte Neutralisation). Inaugural-Dissertation zur Erlangung der juristischen Doktorwürde der Rechts- und staatswissenschaftlichen Fakultät der Philipps-Universität zu Marburg. Pitzwalk 1929

Nansen Fridtjof. *Dagbok fra 1904*. Med innledning av Jacob S. Worm-Müller. Oslo 1955

Nekludoff A. *En diplomats minnen 1911—1917*. Stockholm 1921

Nicolson Harold. *Sir Arthur Nicolson*, Bart., First Lord Carnock. A Study in the Old Diplomacy. Glasgow 1937

Nissen Bernt A. Nasjonal vaekst *(Vårt folks historie VII)* Oslo 1964

Numminen Jaakko. Mauri *Vuoden 1908 Itämeren sopimuksen synty* (Yleisen historian laudatur-kirjoitus 1951 Helsingin Yliopistossa)

Omang see printed documents

Omang Reidar. *Norsk utenrikstjeneste*. Grunnleggende år. Oslo 1955

Paléologue Maurice. *Un grand tournant de la politique mondiale 1904—1906.* Paris 1943

Paléologue Maurice. *Guillaume II et Nicolas II.* Paris 1935

Parkes Oscar. *British Battleships.* Warrior to Vanguard, a History of Design, Construction and Armament. London 1957

Paul Johannes. *Europa im Ostseeraum.* Göttingen-Berlin-Frankfurt 1961

Pipeş Richard E. Domestic Politics and Foreign Affairs. see Lederer: *Russian...*

Poidevin Raymond. *Finances et relations internationales 1887—1914* (Collection U 2, Série "Dossiers pour l'Histoire contemporaine", dirigée par Georges Dupeux, professeur à la Faculté des Lettres et Sciences humaines de Bordeaux) Paris 1970

Polvinen Tuomo. *Die Finnischen Eisenbahnen in den militärischen und politischen Plänen Russlands vor dem ersten Weltkrieg.* Helsinki 1962

Rauch Georg von. Russland im Zeitalter des nationalismus und Imperialismus (1856—1917) *(Schriften des Arbeitskreises für Ostfragen 8)* München 1961

Reinach J. P. *Le traité de Bjoerkoë 1905.* Un essai d'alliance de l'Allemagne, la Russie et la France. Paris 1935

Renouvin Pierre. Le système des ententes europèennes de 1905 à 1909 *(Histoire diplomatique de l'Europe 1871—1914* publ. Henri M. Hauser) Paris 1929

Renouvin Pierre. L'apogée de l'Europe *(Histoire des relations internationales,* publiée sous la direction de Pierre Renouvin. Tome sixième: Le XIXe siècle II: De 1871 à 1914) Paris 1955

Renouvin Pierre et Duroselle Jean-Baptiste. *Introduction à l'histoire des relations internationales.* II ed. revue et corrigée. Paris 1966

Renouvin Pierre. Les relations franco-russes — a la fin du XIXe at au début du XXe siècle. Bilan de recherches *(Cahiers du monde russe et sovietique 1, Mai 1959)*

Reutersvärd Pontus. *Generallöjtnanten och envoyen Edvard Brändström.* Svenskt sändebud i Ryssland 1906—1920. Stockholm 1947

Robbins Keith. *Sir Edward Grey.* a Biography of Lord Grey of Fallodon. London 1971

Rodd Sir James Rennel, G. C. B.. *Social and Diplomatic Memories.* Third Series 1902—1919. London 1925

Ropponen Risto. *Die Kraft Russlands.* Wie beurteilte die politische und militärische Führung der europäischen Grossmächte in der Zeit von 1905 bis 1914 die Kraft Russlands. (Dissertationes historicas I edidit societas historia Finlandiae. Historiallisia tutkimuksia LXXIV julkaissut Suomen Historiallinen Seura) Helsinki 1968

Rosen Baron. *Forty Years of Diplomacy I—II.* New York 1922

Salis J. R. von. *Weltgeschichte der neuesten Zeit Bd II.* Zürich 1955

Schebeko N (ancien Ambassadeur de Russie à Vienne) *Souvenirs.* Essai historique sur les origines de la guerre de 1914. Paris 1936

Schoen (Freiherr von) *Erlebtes.* Beiträge zur politischen Geschichte der neuesten Zeit. Stuttgart 1921

Schroeder Herbert. *Russland und die Ostsee.* Riga 1927

Seton-Watson Hugh. *The Decline of Imperial Russia 1855—1914.* London 1952

Seton-Watson Hugh. *The Russian Empire 1801—1917* (Oxford History of Modern Europe) Oxford 1967

Siebert see printed documents

Siewert Wulf. Der Ostseeraum (Heft *8 "Macht und Erde",* Hefte zum Weltgeschehen, Hrsg. von Dr Karl Haushofer, prof. a.D. Univ. München, Generalmajor a.D.) Berlin 1938

Slusser Robert M. The Role of the Foreign Ministry. see Lederer: *Russian...*

Stieve Friedrich. *Iswolski und der Weltkrieg.* Leipzig 1924

Stieve Friedrich. *Deutschland und Europa 1890—1914.* Ein Handbuch zur Vorgeschichte des Weltkrieges mit den wichtigsten Dokumenten. Berlin 1928

Sweet David W. The Baltic in British Diplomacy Before the First World War *(The Historical Journal,* XIII" 3, 1970)

Söderberg Verner. Aftalen om Nordsjön och Östersjön *(Det nya Sverige,* Tidskrift för nationella spörsmål) Stockholm 1908

Söderberg Verner. Isvolskij's misslyckade Ålandsmanöver *(Svensk Tidskrift 1925)*

Söderhielm E. Kapten. Ålands befästande och Sveriges försvar *(Det nya Sverige,* Tidskrift för nationella spörsmål) Stockholm 1908

Söderhjelm J. O. *Demilitarisation et neutralisation des Iles d'Aland en 1856 et 1921* Helsingfors 1928

Taube Baron M de. Une page inédite de l'histoire moderne du problème Baltique. Les îles d'Aland et le mémorandum de Saint-Petersbourg du 23 april 1908 *(Revue générale de droit international public, doits des gens — histoire diplomatique — droit penal — droit fiscal— droit administratif.* Deuxième série Tome V) Paris 1923

Taube Baron M. de. Mémoires. *La politique Russe d'avant-guerre et la fin de l'empire des tsars 1904—1917.* Paris 1928

Taube Dr Michael Freiherr von. Erinnerungen. *Der grossen Katastrophe entgegen.* Die russische Politik der Vorkriegszeit und das Ende des Zarenreiches 1904—1917 (Zweite umgearbeitete und erweiterte Ausgabe) Leipzig 1937

Taubert Siegfried. Die Aland-Frage *(Berliner Monatshefte Juli 1939)*

Taylor A. J. P. *The Struggle for Mastery in Europe 1848—1918* (Oxford History of Modern Europe) Oxford 1957

Tcharykov N. V. *Glimpses of High Politics* through war and peace 1855—1929. The autobiography of N. V. Tcharykov, serf-owner, ambassador, exile. Foreword by Sir Bernard Pares K. B. E. London 1931

Thulstrup Åke. *Svensk politik 1905—1939.* Från unionsupplösningen till andra värlskriget Stockholm 1968

Tingsten Lars. Åland ur militärisk och politisk synpunkt från 1808 till våra dagar *(Kungl. Krigsvetenskaps-akademiens handlingar och tidskrift. Bihäfte n:r 1)* Stockholm 1925

Tirpitz Alfred von. *Erinnerungen.* Leipzig 1919

Trubetzkoi Fürst G. *Russland als Grossmacht.* Übersetzt und eingeleitet von Josef Melnik Stuttgart und Berlin 1913

Tucker Robert C. Autocrats and Oligarchs see Lederer: *Russian.* .

Urbye Andreas. *Karlstadsförhandlingene 1905.* Referat fra de møter hvor sekretærene var til stede. Av den norske delegasjons sekretær (Skrifter utgitt av Det Kgl Utenriks-departements arkiv 1) Oslo 1952

Wedel Jarlsberg F. *1905 Kongevalget.* Oslo MCMXLVI

Weibull Jörgen. *Inför unionsupplösningen 1905.* Konsulatfrågan. Stockholm 1962

Weibull Jörgen. Kronprins Gustaf inför unionsupplösningen 1905 *(Scandia.* Tidskrift för historisk forskning, p. 167—227 Band XXVI Årgång 1960)

Westman Karl Gustaf. *Sverige inför Östersjöfrågan.* Tal hållet i Uppsala den 7. dec. 1917 samt Handlingar och uttalanden i Ålandsfrågan 1856—1917. Uppsala 1917

Wilhelm II (Kaiser) *Ereignisse und Gestalten* aus den Jahren 1878—1918. Leipzig 1922

Vogt Benjamin. *Indtil 1910.* Oslo 1941

Worm-Müller Jacob S. Prins Carl blir Konge i Norge *(Haakon 7.* Utgitt til 75-årsdagen 3 august 1947 av den norska regjering) Oslo 1947

Worm-Müller see Nansen

Svenska Dagbladet VI—VIII 1906, 1907, I—VI 1908

The Times 1907, I—VI 1908

Separate newspapers as indicated in the notes

Астафьев И. И. Балканская политика царизма и русско-германские отношениа накануне босниского кризиса 1908—1909 годов. (*Вестник Московского Университета*, серия 9 история 3. отдельный оттиск) Москва 1965

Астафьев И. И. Вопрос о черноморских проливах в период босниского кризиса 1908—1909 годов. (*Вестник Московского Университета*, серия 9 история 1. отдельный оттиск) Москва 1967

Астфьев И. И. *Русско-германские дипломатические отношения 1905—1911 гг.* (От портсмутского мира до потсдамского соглашения) Москва 1972

Бестужев И. В. *Борьба в России по вопросам внешней политики 1906—1910.* Москва 1961

Бовыкин В. И. *Очерки истории внешней политики России.* конец 19. века — 1917 года. Пособие для учителя. Москва 1960

Ефремов П. Н. *Внешняя политика России* (1907—1914 гг) Москва 1916

Зайончковскии. *Подготовка России к мировой войне в международном отношении.* с предисловием и под редакцией М. П. Павловича. (Штаб РККА управление по исследование и использованию опыта воин 16) Ленинград 1926

Игнатьев А. А. *Пятьдесят лет в строю.* Моска 1950

Игнатьев А. В. *Русско-английские отношения накануне первой мировой войны* 1908—1914 гг. Москва 1962

История дипломатии. издание второе, переработанное и дополненное. Том 2: Дипломатия в новое время 1871—1914. автор тома В. М. Хвостов. Москва 1964

Коковцовъ, графъ В. Н. *Изъ моего прошлаго.* Воспоминания 1903—1919. Париж 1933

Кутаков Л. Н. *Портсмутский мирный договор* (Из истории отношений Японии с Россиеи и СССР 1905—1945 гг). Москва 1961

Нольде, барон Б. Е. *Далекое и близкое.* Исторические очерки. Париж 1930

Патуканис С. К истории англо-русского соглашения 1907 г (*Красний Архив* 69—70 с. 3—)

Похлебкин: *Признание* . . . см. Публикации документов

Похлебкин В. *Балтика и борьба за мир.* Москва 1966

Русская периодическая печать

    1. 1702—1894 гг Москва 1959

    2. 1895—1917 гг Москва 1957

Соловьев Ю. Я. *Воспоминания дипломата 1893—1922*

Тарле Е. В. *Европа в епоху империализма.* Москва-Ленпнград 1927

Шацилло К. Ф. *Развитие вооруженных сил России накануне первой мировой войны.* Военные и военно-морские программы царского правителььтва в 1906—1914 гг (Автореферат диссертации на соискание ученой степени доктора исторических наук) Москва 1968

Шацилло К. Ф. *Русский империализм и развитие флота* (1906—1914 гг) Москва 1968

Хвостов см. *История дипломатии*

Фейгина Л. *Бьоркское соглашение.* Из истории русско-германских отношений. Москва 1928

Новое Время 1906, 1907, 1908

Речь 1908

Слово 1908